THE SHAVETAIL
and
THE ARMY NURSE

The Bride Wore Olive Drab

by
ELI & BERNICE FISHPAW

Eli J. Fishpaw
and
Bernice N. Fishpaw

DeLand, Florida
1998

ISBN 0-615-11580-2

Library of Congress Catalog Card Number 98-92692
Printed by E. O. Painter Printing Company Inc.
DeLeon Springs, Florida, USA

Table of Contents

Dedicated to our Parents

John and Florence Fishpaw
and
Clarence and Elizabeth Newton

Preface

I wanted to be insulted when our daughter told me that our reminiscents of our early life was like studying anthropology. So I looked the word up in the dictionary. The definition is, "the study of the origin and physical, social and cultural development and behavior of humans.".

She is right. It is like a modern anthropology. Looking back on the events that shaped the twentieth century, Eli and I are two ordinary people who lived during the extra ordinary times of the two defining events of that century. They were what is now called the Great Depression and World War Two. As we sorted out the memory of these events and our part in them, we realized that they did indeed have great influence in our social, culture and behavior as manifest today.

The constant need to acquire necessities such as food and heating fuel during the depression causes many people of my cohort to avoid wasting these precious commodities today.

The ridged discipline of a Catholic nun operated nursing school and the United States Army were really only an extension of the strict authority of our parents.

To the older reader, our stories will bring back memories of their own maturing years. To the younger reader, I hope that it may help to explain how their own parents were challenged and shaped by the events of the time. Perhaps it may help them to better understand us older folks.

If not, at least we have had fun remembering the good times and the times that were stressful. To our surprise, the stressful ones are some of the best.

~ 1 ~

Pigtown

Eli:

The house where I was born and grew up was on Ramsey Street which ran through the part of southwest Baltimore called 'Pig Town'. This was because they used to drive pigs from the stockyards down town to the meat packing house on Hanover St. They came right up Ramsey St. Of course, this was great sport for us young, active boys who lived on the route.

We would run with the pigs for several blocks. This was useful as we helped keep any strays from heading up the side streets. Most of us would only run a few blocks when other boys would join the chase. However, my brother, Hoodie, would go all the way to the packing house. Then one day, Hoodie started bringing home a pay check. He had a job that turned into a position with the packing house that would last him his whole life.

We were a fairly large family. I had an older sister, Carrie, and three older brothers, John, Horace Leonard (called Hoodie) and Charlie. I also had two younger sisters, Anna and June. There had been two children who had died as infants. Hoodie had brain fever when he was two. Although he was completely functional, he never developed any real interest in school.

My nickname as a kid was Iggy. One day when we were playing ball, I wasn't paying attention and somebody threw me a ball which hit me in the head. At the time there was a character in the funny paper called Iggy who got hit in the head with the ball and someone had said, "Iggy, keep an eye on me." The guy that had thrown the ball at me yelled, "Iggy, keep an eye on me" and the name stuck.

Eli as a school boy in front of the house at 1818 Ramsey Street in Baltimore, Maryland.

My dad and his brother, Uncle Eli, were painting contractors, a business they had inherited from their father. My father sold out to Uncle Eli and used his money to buy row houses which he rented. It worked well until the economic depression came along and people quit paying their rent. My dad did not have the heart to throw his neighbors out of their homes.

With no money coming in, he was unable to pay the taxes and lost all his property. It was amazing how these same people were able to find rent money after the new owner had removed a few of them.

With his primary source of income gone, he went back to work as a painter for Uncle Eli. Uncle Eli's son-in-law was the foreman but Pop didn't like Harry Arnold so Uncle Eli always personally dealt with Pop.

When I was five, I started kindergarten. The school, PS 98, was only a few blocks from the house. I liked kindergarten where we played a lot. By the time I started first grade I was completely spoiled and resented having to sit down and do lessons. I would do all sorts of things to get out of going to school.

Of all the teachers, I remember Miss Iola best. She seemed to be really old. I thought she must have been at least 70, but she was rough. She had only the best interest of her students at heart. She tried to make us learn. My handwriting was not very good. She would keep me after school and make me write until my writing looked just like the letters that were above the black board. They never did, but at least I could make them look good enough that they could be read.

One time, a teacher sent a note home to my father saying that I was not doing my arithmetic assignments. Pop took over. I had to be in the house an hour ahead of every one else and do my assignment while he sat beside me. If I was doing it wrong he would give me a whack on the head. It didn't take long for me to figure out that it was easier to do it right the first time.

My mother was more subtle but just as effective with her punishment. One day when I had gone to the store across the street, I had hooked a Baby Ruth candy bar to take home to Mom. I knew she liked candy but never bought any for herself. When I gave it to her, she demanded to know how I got it. When I told her, she took me back across the street by the ear and made me give it back and apologize. That was hard to do. The store keeper said, "Aw Florence, keep it. He was just trying to do something nice." She said, "You're just as bad as he is. He's got to learn not to steal." She was right and it was a lesson that I never forgot.

One day Freddie Tarbutton and I were over on Wilkens Avenue throwing little stones. We threw some at a truck and one of them broke the windshield. Of course we ran. I ran home but Tarbutton had to go back to see what was happening. Just as he stuck his head around the corner, a blue arm reached out and grabbed him by the back of his neck. It was Beanbelly, the neighborhood cop.

When I got home, my mother was cutting hair, so she had plopped me down on the stool and was cutting my hair when Beanbelly came to the kitchen door with Freddie. He told her what had happened and wanted to know what she was going to do about it so he could tell Mrs. Tarbutton. "Eli is going to stay in the house for ten days." That was probably the longest ten days of my life. All my gang decided to play right outside our window and always wanted to know why I didn't come out to play.

I discovered that because my name was Eli that I could play hooky from school on Jewish holidays. The teachers would think that I was Jewish and was observing the holidays. Of course I couldn't go home or I would be in big trouble. I would go down to the court house and watch the trials. One day, one of the teachers must have gotten suspicious because the truant officer showed up at home and asked my mother if I was sick. That was the end of that particular trick for skipping school.

Even when I was very young, I was able to contribute to the family finances. Around the corner there was a family by the name of Stillings. They had a gang of kids. One of them, Bernie, was my age and we were good friends. Mr. Stillings was a huckster. He had lost one arm. He had a horse and a wagon and would go to the wholesale market early every morning and buy fruit, vegetables and sometimes crabs or maybe fish on Friday. However, even with all his boys, he preferred to hire the Fishpaw boys. John had worked for him and later so did I.

He would leave the wagon at one end of the block and I would take a couple baskets with little boxes of strawberries or other produce and walk up the middle of the alley calling, "Strawberries, Strawberries, ten cents a box, three for a quarter". Meanwhile he walked up the street chanting his call. The horse would follow without any driver.

He showed me how you could handle crabs without hurting your hands. He would just lay his hand in the basket of crabs and they would grab it. Instead of throwing them off he would just put his hand down in the kettle that the buyer brought out and the crab would let go. Crabs have very sharp claws. If a crab grabbed you, and you tried to shake them off they would cut your hand. Even though I tried many times not to throw them off, I never was able to do it. I don't know of any other person in this world who could do it his way. Maybe it was because he only had one hand which was tough as leather.

I used to be happy when I would wake up in the morning and it was snowing. My brother John had given me his snow shovel and I could go up and down the street where many people would pay me to shovel their sidewalk. I had regular customers who I knew would be up early and would pay me, so I did their walk first and took the money home. Then Carrie and John would have streetcar fare to go to work. They usually walked. Carrie worked for the phone company and went about a mile and John worked at a hat factory about three miles from the house. My mother had a rule that every dollar any of us earned, we would get a quarter back. She never broke this rule, no matter how urgently she might need the money.

I used to like to ride the ice wagon. The ice man would let me deliver smaller chunks of ice while he carried the big chunks. He would pay me ten cents, all in pennies, so that if I lost one, I wouldn't lose the whole dime. And, I could have all the ice I could eat.

In the summer my friends and I would walk down to the river with a chicken neck tied to string and a dip net and catch crabs which many times served as our supper.

There was a curve in the railroad yard not far from the house where the coal cars, heading south, heaped up with the Pennsylvania hard coal, would spill lose coal on the ground. We used to take our coaster wagon with a couple of bushel baskets in it and go down there and pick up coal two or three times a week. We called this wracking coal. What we didn't use in the kitchen stove at home for heating and cooking we could sell for 50 cents a bushel.

We had a gas space heater in the living room. There was an outlet in the floor with a lever to turn the gas off and on. It was connected to the heater with a rubber hose. One day we were horsing around and I tripped over the hose and pulled it off. It was a lucky thing that the fire went out. It scared me and I ran outside. Someone else turned off the gas and re-connected the hose but I was afraid to go back in the house. When I finally had to go home, I was firmly punished as much for running away as for tripping over the fuel line. Very early, we even lit the house with gas. All the street lights were fueled with gas.

Brick fights were just part of our usual activities. More than once I was hit in the head with a brick. I would go home bleeding and my mother would get out the razor and shave off the hair around the wound and clean it with peroxide before putting on the Iodine. Iodine hurts bad and I would holler. She would crack me beside the head and tell me, "It serves you right."

Once we were at Druid Hill park when I got a finger smashed between a boat and the dock. It was open the full length of the finger. We walked all the way home, two and a half miles. Mom took one look at the finger and said, "This is too much for me, we're going to the hospital." Then I had to walk another mile to the Franklin Square Hospital. The doctor said he couldn't sew it up because it was too ragged a wound. They cleaned it up, drew the edges together and wrapped it with something like a cast.

We used to like to catch snakes and take them home. One time we got in real trouble too. We had some poisonous water moccasins that we put in Melvin Dash's back yard in the rain barrel. The lady next door found out about it and called the police. They pulled up in a police car and asked us about our snakes. We had to tell them of course. They quoted ordinance so and so that forbid bringing poisonous snakes into the city and told us we had to get rid of them. The snakes had gotten loose so we had to find them. We found two of them under the garbage can but we never did find the other two. There was a big rat hole under the garbage can and we figured they had gone down that hole and into a spring in the cellar.

Another time we were out catching garter snakes in the woods by the railroad track north of the Montgomery Ward store, which was not too far from our house. I was looking for something to put them in when I saw a new looking gallon can sitting on a little improvised fireplace used by the hobos. It had some clear liquid in it which I thought was probably water so I dumped it out. Just then, one of the hobos came back with some wood to build a fire and saw me dump out his can. He and his friend started chasing us. They were mad as hell and would probably have hurt us if they could have caught us.

We figured out that the can actually had wood alcohol in it and they were getting ready to do something by cooking it to make it fit to drink. It was against the law to make or sell alcohol for drinking, but wood alcohol was used for all sorts of things such as antifreeze for cars and for thinner for shellac, so it was available. However, it was known that drinking wood alcohol would cause a person to go blind. But the hobos knew how to mix it with water and cook it to make it safe.

We even had our own neighborhood hobo. His name was Joe Bates. He was actually the leader of the hobos. Sometimes when the older boys wanted to hop a freight car, they would ask Joe. He would tell them where to catch a ride and where it was going. He was sort of our travel agent. Some of us were even planning to be hobos when we got old enough and he was our trainer.

Pat Nolan lived on the corner of Fulton Ave. and Ramsey St. where pop could go and get a beer which was illegal. There were little businesses all over Baltimore like this.

One year pop bought a bottle of root beer mix and we followed the instructions and had our own little root beer supply ripening in the cellar. We had it in bottles which were capped. One day, I sneaked a bottle out for me and my friends. I must have shook it up because the cap blew off and all the root beer blew straight up. It put a tell tale line right up the front of the house, all the way to the roof. Before long all the bottles in the cellar started blowing their caps whenever anyone touched them. We figured out that there was twice as much yeast as there should have been.

Around the corner there was a real illegal distillery. From the outside it looked just like every other block of row houses in Baltimore with people living in them. But upstairs Jimmy Nolen, Pat's brother, had a very thriving whiskey factory. One day, the revenuers raided it and were throwing the whiskey, which was stored in wood barrels marked Coca Cola, out the second story windows. It ran into the gutter and down the storm sewer. Joe Bates and his gang were all over there scooping up as much as they could before it got away.

Sometimes, after a rain, we would walk over to where the storm water from all southwest Baltimore drained into a stream that lead to Glynn's Falls which was a good sized creek. We would take a dip net to catch the balls that had washed into the storm sewers.

Making and flying kites was one of our favorite activities. We would fly them in the field north of Montgomery Ward. Once we made one with a couple of clothesline props. It must have been five feet high. One windy day we took it over to the field. It was so strong it took three guys to hold on to it. We had to use a rope for the kite string.

One time we had an old football that needed a new bladder so we went over to the Montgomery Ward and asked for a new bladder. They didn't have any at the counter but because the building was the supply center for their whole northeast mail order business, they called upstairs to have a bladder sent down. The package came down in a basket that ran along a cable and was used for moving small bundles around the store. It was all wrapped and the clerk gave it to us for the two bits we had collected. When we got out of the store we opened the package and discovered we had a whole dozen. We tried to take it back but the clerk didn't know how to handle the problem so he told us just to keep them. We put new bladders in every football in the neighborhood.

Once we accidentally broke the front window of one of the neighborhood grocery stores when we were playing ball. We took up a collection and got the 75 cents needed to replace it. We didn't have enough to pay to install it, so we figured we could do it ourselves. We were doing just great, except that it was cut so

7

exact that we couldn't get it all the way in the frame because our fingers were in the way.

Brother Witt got the bright idea that we could use a toilet plunger to hold it. We used the plunger and it was just about in place when the plunger let go. The new window pane was shattered glass on the sidewalk. We tried to borrow another six bits from Barney Goldberg's father so that we could get another piece of glass. He refused and instead said he would give the hardware store a dollar and a half and they would put it in. He could afford it because he was the local bookie and so had enough for such emergencies.

We often played at Carroll Park which was across the street from Montgomery Ward. One day we were playing in a part of the park that was not intended for ball playing. One of the park cops caught us and took our ball away. Charlie said they couldn't do that and we should go to the police station and demand our ball back. We all went to the station which was in the basement of the Carroll Mansion in the park. That was a mistake. They threw us in their detention room. My dad was the Republican ward boss and another guy, who's dad was the local Democrat boss, came down and got us out, but we didn't get our ball back. The fact that we were all so young helped. David Witt (we all called him brother), who was the biggest one in the bunch, was taken home by the police because of his size. They wanted to check out his age. He was actually the youngest kid in the group.

It was the custom in Baltimore at election time to rent the front room of a row house in the center of each precinct to use as a polling place. I can remember when our front room became the polls. We weren't allowed in the front room during the election but would hang out on the side walk and watch the people come to vote. One day a lady drove up in a fancy car and said if I was a Democrat she would give me a quarter. I became an instant Democrat, probably for the only time in my life.

There was a Methodist church just around the corner from our house on Monroe Street. Our family were good members. My dad was even president of the men's bible class. In the winter of 1931 he volunteered to paint the sanctuary at night after working hard all day. It was cold and he was run down physically from working so hard. My mother thought he shouldn't work so hard but he wanted to finish the job. He got pneumonia and was sick at home. He died on the 21st of January.

Financially, it was difficult before, but now life became even more difficult. Uncle Eli offered to send me to the McDonald Military School. I guess he favored me because I shared his name. My mother said that it was up to me. I didn't want to leave home so I said no. Carrie, John and Hoodie were working. Carrie, who was the oldest, paid for board. John and Hoodie helped out when they could. Mom also got a small $35 pension because my father was a partially disabled veteran of the Spanish-American war. All of us did what we could to help out and we kept the family together.

Mom made the best chili sauce in Maryland. It included a bushel of tomatoes, a quarter bushel each of peppers and onions with vinegar and spices. It was a lot like what is called salsa today but it cooked longer. It was cooked down to half the size which took two days. While it was cooking, it put out an aroma that went all over the neighborhood. Everyone would tell Mom how good it smelled and she would give them some. They would always offer to pay for it but she wouldn't take any money. One day she did. All of a sudden, the chili sauce was no longer so popular. Annie even thought we should have a stall at the market and sell chili sauce.

Hoodie would sometimes gather up the little pigs that were born on the trains or the trucks. He had a place at the stock yard where he could keep them and feed them. When they were about a hundred pounds he would have them butchered and bring them home. It was my job to cut up the carcasses. I got real good at making pork chops and cutting out the hams and the spare ribs. We tried making head cheese once, but that didn't work too well.

Navy used to play their home games at the old Baltimore Stadium. Woodcock's dad was a Baltimore police officer and often he would be on duty for the games. We would go to the stadium on game day and he would arrange for us to come through the gate without paying. One day, one of the Pinkerton security guys, who were supposed to keep out the non-paying customers, saw us come in without a ticket and started to chase us. We ran onto the field right in the middle of the game with the Pinkerton men in hot pursuit. They had to hold up the game while the whole stadium was cheering for us. They caught us and threw us out but it wasn't long until we were back in.

Sometimes we would hitch hike to College Park for the University of Maryland games. The rest rooms were built so that they were part of the outside wall. We would pool our money and one guy would buy a ticket. He would go to the men's room and open the window for us. Once we were in, we would walk out as we were buttoning up our pants as though we had every right in the world to be there.

When I was in seventh grade, I started Junior High. It was two buildings downtown at Fayette and Green Streets. Half the kids from Baltimore came here. It was about two and a half miles from the house, and of course we walked. It was called Edgar Allen Poe and was across the street from the cemetery where Edgar Allen Poe was buried.

I didn't like school any better here than I did at 98 but there were lots of things to do that I did like. Basketball was one of my favorite activities. We had a good coach and he taught us how to play the game right. He had a whistle on a rawhide cord which he used whenever we got out of line.

One day I was eating an apple and threw the core at Brother Witt, who ducked just as the coach came around the corner. It hit the coach; justice was instant. Since I didn't seem to know what to do with garbage, I would be responsible for picking up all the trash on the school grounds for the next two weeks. My Pigtown friends joined me in the project. Instead of picking up other peoples garbage, we organized the "Pigtown Patrol" and every time someone threw something down, one of our guys would be on them and make them pick it up. The coach didn't seem to think this was violating his punishment as he never objected to our system.

I may not have been the best behaved kid in the school, but one day when we were in art class, one of my classmates hit an older lady teacher with his fist. I thought that was wrong, so I grabbed him and pushed him down the hallway and across the street to the principal's office. After that, I don't think that kid got into any more trouble. That is called peer pressure now. It sure works.

One day, in algebra class, the teacher was putting problems on the board. Instead of writing the problem down and showing how I worked it, I would work the problem in my head and just put the answer down. She thought that I must be cheating and copying someone elses answers so she sat behind me and watched. When she realized I could actually do the problem in my head, she was so impressed that she thought I should be put in an advanced class. This was discussed with the principal. The other teachers thought this was a terrible idea and voted against it because of my low grades in English, History and Music. I stayed right where I was.

2

Poverty Creek

Bernice:

They were the biggest wheels that I had ever seen. They were three times as high as I was. But there was no time to be scared or awed because our family was being hustled along the platform and loaded onto the train that stood there belching steam.

This is one of my earliest memories. I was a little over three years old. That was the year that my mother and dad, my brother and I went to California to visit my Aunt Cora (my mother's sister) and Uncle Charles in Modesto.

I can remember a lot about that trip. I remember the smell of the coal dust and the red plush seats that prickled in the first train which we took from Milton Junction. That was the village closest to our farm where the through trains stopped. To this day I can remember the conductor of the train walking through the coach calling "Davis Junction". That was in Illinois. We were to change trains there.

There was a scurry as my father gathered up our luggage and my mother guided Kenneth and me off one train and onto another. The second train was sitting cross ways of the track on which we had arrived. It was heading west. Its cow catcher was just a few feet from the south bound track. It was waiting just for us. We had to walk along the platform, right past that enormous locomotive.

This was the train from Chicago to San Francisco. We were to be on that train for several days. I don't remember how many days it was, but it was long enough that it seemed like home before we got off. The seats were like two sofas facing each other.

Each group of seats was called a berth. Our family had tickets for one complete berth.

At night a man called a porter came through the car and changed the berth from seats into two beds. His face and hands were black. I had never seen a black man before. The ceiling had a panel on hinges that let down like a door. It was secured in a horizontal position to make the upper berth or bed. The back cushions from the seats were arranged to fill in the space between the seats to make the lower bed. A thin board was placed between each berth and heavy green curtains were hung between the berths and the aisle to give the passengers privacy. They buttoned up with great big buttons. The curtains and bedding were stored behind the door during the day.

My mother and I slept in the lower berth and my dad and Kenneth had the upper. My mother had always had a fear of heights so there was no way that she was going to climb up there. To get in and out of the upper, the porter brought a ladder. To summon the porter, there was a button like a door bell. There was a net hammock hung on one side of the bed for clothing.

I thought I was being discriminated against because I had to sleep in the lower berth, so one night they permitted me to sleep in the upper with my brother who was seven. I promised to be good but couldn't resist putting my arm down between the inner edge of the mattress and the side of the train where it was seen by my mother and dad. Somehow they thought I was being naughty by doing that and I never got to sleep in the upper berth again.

The big transcontinental trains had dining cars but they were expensive and my frugal mother had packed one suitcase with non-perishable food and we ate in our little space. The porter would bring a table at meal time and attach it to the outer wall. It had a single leg next to the aisle. Then my mother would lay out our meal from the suitcase. I don't remember if we had dishes or not but would guess that we probably had tin plates which were washed in the basin in the rest room.

I remember being in California and going to see the Pacific Ocean at Santa Cruz. I had a sand bucket and a shovel but several shovels kept breaking at the handle so my Uncle Charles bought one of galvanized metal that was strong enough to plow the garden. I had that shovel for years and years. It is probably still around the farm somewhere.

My Aunt Cora thought that I should go down to the edge of the water and put my hand in the ocean. Just as we reached the

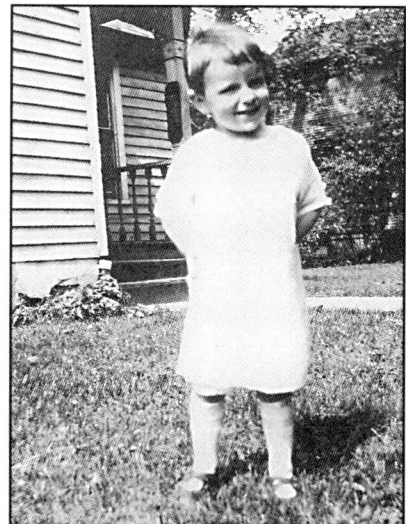

Bernice as a kid.

edge of the water, a big wave came splashing in and scared me. I can still remember running away from my aunt yelling, "dry tan, dry tan". I never did touch the Pacific Ocean until I was almost fifty years old when Eli (my husband) and I drove to California to visit our daughter Mary in San Francisco.

My Uncle Charles had a bicycle with a basket over the back wheel. He put me in the basket and Kenneth sat on the handle bars and I had my first bike ride.

On the return trip we went all the way to Chicago to visit my mother's cousins. They were showing their country cousins the sights of the big city which included an amusement park. That was where the roller coaster bug bit me. I watched my brother and my dad go on the roller coaster but they wouldn't let me go because I was too small. Of course, riding the roller coaster was the very last thing that my mother wanted to do.

I was born and grew up on a dairy farm in Rock County which is in Southern Wisconsin. We were not affluent and times were hard because the country was in an economic depression. Everyone in the family was expected to contribute.

In 1920 it was not common practice for people to go to the hospital to give birth. The doctor came to the home. According to my mother's hand written notes, I was born at 2:50 P.M. on Saturday, September 25, 1920. My weight was 8 pounds with the blanket. Dr. Hull was in attendance. He was what we refer to today as "A Country Doctor".

My dad was there and saw me being born. He said that there was a membrane over my face which the doctor removed. This is actually a part of the amniotic membrane. There are all kinds of superstitions about what this means when it occurs. The one I like the best is the one that says the baby will be blessed with a long and bountiful life.

My full name was Bernice Virginia R. Newton. The R. was just an initial but represented my grandfather Richmond who had been disappointed when my folks had not named my brother Richmond.

I can remember that when I was very small, the whole family slept in the downstairs bedroom. There were double doors between the bedroom and the parlor, a room that was seldom used. The doors remained closed and my crib stood against the doors. Kenneth slept in the trundle bed. It was stored under the big bed during the day and trundled out at night when the folding legs were opened so that it was a foot or so off the floor.

Kenneth was the first one to move upstairs. He had the southeast bedroom. I moved upstairs when I was probably about six. I had the northwest room. There was a collection of cracks on the ceiling which, when the moon was out, I could lay awake and make all sorts of strange pictures with the cracks. One was a stick man with a stove pipe hat. I thought he looked like grandpa Newton who was tall and had very long legs like Lincoln.

I slept in the crib long after I was big enough to get in and out without any help. When they finally got around to moving me to a bed, my mother painted the walls a light shade of pink and then stippled it a darker pink with a sponge, because pink was my favorite color. Then I could really make imaginary pictures.

They put a hot air register in the wall shortly after that but it never worked very well. The problem, there was no cold air return to the furnace. When it started to get cold in the fall, we would put a feather bed over the mattress and instead of sheets to sleep between there was a double wool blanket topped with a comforter or two. Once it got warmed up at night it was very cozy, no matter how cold the weather. I know it got very cold because sometimes the urine in my slop jar would have ice in it in the morning.

I wore Dr. Denton sleepers which were a one piece garment with feet built into the bottom of the legs. It was just too cold to get ready for bed at night or to get dressed in the morning upstairs so I took care of this detail on the hot air register in the dining room. I left my day time clothes on the floor next to the register. Since the furnace was banked and did not go out during the night, the downstairs was relatively warm in the morning and so were my clothes.

I even had my very own kerosene lamp to carry upstairs to bed. It had a little tiny burner but gave off enough light so that I could see where I was going. One year for Christmas I got a flashlight for my very own. It was one of the first smaller flashlights and used two batteries that we know today as 'D' cells. Before that, the flashlight was attached to a battery that was about three inches in diameter and at least nine inches long. These were called dry cells and they didn't last very long so we were cautioned to only use it when absolutely necessary. I often finished reading a story while completely covered up in the bed, using the flashlight.

The kitchens in the farm homes of that period were the family center. Our kitchen did not get heat from the furnace but was heated by the cook stove. It was fueled with wood cut and split from the farm wood lots. Keeping the wood box full was one of my earliest chores. I am sure it was the chore of my brother, my father and probably my grandfather before me. There was a large box in the back kitchen behind the kitchen door and a smaller box next to the stove. The large box was the reserve during the day while the designated wood box filler was at school.

Besides cooking, everyone ate at the kitchen table in the center of the room; it was also used as a laundry. We had a second, unheated kitchen behind the regular kitchen where our laundry was done when the weather was not too cold, but in the winter the benches and the two big galvanized tubs came into the regular kitchen. On wash day it was very crowded.

The Newtons were often leaders in developing new and better ways to take the drudgery out of doing the hundreds of tasks on the farm. We even had a Maytag washing machine. It had a wooden tub and the agitator called the dolly was in the cover.

There were times when it was just too much trouble to move the washing machine into the kitchen. It was noisy and dirty and took up a lot of space. But my mother was no stranger to the wash board. She had a good hand cranked wringer too.

Often I had the honor of turning the wringer crank. For this I was rewarded when she put the tops of the socks between the rollers first and they would puff up like balloons and spray wash water back into the tub. It didn't take much to entertain kids in those days.

The kitchen was also the bathroom. In fact, I used to make fun of the city cousins who referred to the outhouse as the bathroom. Who would want to take a bath out there?

Saturday night was the night of the bath on the farm. Since I was the youngest, I always went first. One wash bench and one wash tub came into the kitchen. The oven door to the cook stove was left open for extra heat and three or four inches of warm water were put in the tub as well as the kid. The part I really hated about the bath was having my hair washed. My mother always seemed to get soap in my eyes and I always cried.

When I was old enough to take my own bath, the activity moved to Sunday morning while the men were milking. We used a smaller oval foot tub and took a sponge bath. That was the only kind of bath that I knew until I went to high school and lived with my Newton grandparents in Milton Junction during the week. That was big city stuff and they had a real bathtub that had legs that looked like lion claws holding a baseball.

Our dining room was for when we had company for dinner. It also doubled as a sewing room and a play room. The dining room table was always stacked high with unread newspapers. The telephone was in the dining room. At first it was attached to the wall next to the east window and was about four feet off the floor. That was the old fashioned phone on the party line. To reach other neighbors on the same line, each had a distinctive ring such as one long and one short or two shorts, etc. To call a neighbor you cranked in their ring. The crank turned a tiny generator.

There were nine parties on our line. If you heard your ring you were supposed to pick up but leave other people's calls alone. It was a standard joke though, about how people listened to each others calls. It was referred to as rubbering. I suppose a reference to when people would stretch their necks to try to overhear what other people were saying. To call out of the neighborhood, it was necessary to ring up the operator in Milton Junction and give her the number of the party you were calling. The numbers were short. Ours was x96 and the grandparent's was 1383.

About 1925, our phone company installed what was referred to as the silent ring. You only got an audible ring for your own calls but it was still on the party line. The only way you could listen in was if you happened to pick up. There were some people, usually the women, who talked and talked and talked.

Sometimes, if you really needed to use the phone, especially the men, who didn't have time for that non-sense, would just flat tell them to get off the line. For people calling in, they could tell the operator if you had a real emergency and she would break in. Sort of the original call waiting.

In the summer, when it was too hot to need the wood stove for heat, we had a two burner kerosene stove. It was a very efficient way to cook. There was a glass tank on one end that was refilled with kerosene from the fifty gallon tank in the cellar. This was filled periodically by the oil man who delivered kerosene and gasoline to the farms with a small tank truck. The man filled five gallon cans from the big tanks on the truck and carried them down the outside cellar steps and poured the kerosene into our tank. We accessed it from a spigot at the bottom. Kerosene was also the fuel used in our lamps. Long before I was a teenager, one of my daily chores was to keep the lamps trimmed and filled and also the tank on the stove.

Our drinking water came from the well which was about a hundred yards from the house. It was near the barn yard where there were large cement water tanks for the cows and horses. Water for the pigs was carried by the men from the tank to the trough in the hog house. Water was pumped by a wind mill.

For household water there was a white granite water bucket that sat on the kitchen cabinet. Everyone used the white granite dipper when they needed a drink. For meals we filled a pitcher that was used at the table. Carrying water from the well was just the right sized chore for the youngest member of the family.

Water for washing, bathing and laundry came from the cistern. It was a large, cement lined egg shaped hole in the ground which was deep enough that it did not freeze in the winter. Rain water came from the roof through a system of galvanized gutters and down spouts. There was a small pitcher pump on a pipe next to the wash stand that was used to draw rain water from the cistern. A galvanized bucket with a somewhat larger dipper sat on the wash stand.

On the back of the wood burning cook stove there was a large tank. It must have held ten or twelve gallons. It was called the reservoir. When the stove was in use the water in the reservoir was always nice and hot. A dipper full of this and a dipper full of cold water was a nice amount in the wash bowl for dirty

17

hands and faces. Three dippers provided enough hot water to wash a meal's worth of dishes. I was expected to be sure the reservoir was full before I left for school in the morning and again in the afternoon when I came home.

We got our first radio on the 17th of March, probably about 1930. I can remember the exact day because every other song was 'My Wild Irish Rose' or 'Mother McCree'.

There were two dials that were twisted to change stations. It was very tricky to get them both lined up just right. It was powered by a twelve volt battery, the same type of battery used in the car. My dad built a shelf for the battery in the cellar under the floor.

We had two batteries, one was hooked to the radio while the other one was out in the milker room being recharged by the gasoline engine that ran the milking machine. A battery would give real clear reception for about a week. The signal was received by the aerial which was a long wire that ran from the roof to the telephone pole, about fifty yards from the house.

Soon after we got the radio, my mother decided that I should learn to embroider. I spent one whole summer laying on my stomach listening to the Cubs baseball games and embroidering a dresser scarf. By the end of the summer the scarf was almost black. Since it must have been before the repeal of the 18th amendment that forbid the manufacture or sale of alcoholic beverage, the advertising was for something called 'Atlas Special Brew'. The announcer made it sound so good. I could never understand why my mother wouldn't buy any. After all, she bought Wheaties and Ovaltine which were advertised on the radio shows that I liked.

Ovaltine brings up a memory too. The Little Orphan Annie show had a contest to see which listener could make the most words from the letters found in Ovaltine. I took the big dictionary and went through it letter by letter. I must have had five hundred words. The prize was a wrist watch. One day a box about six inches square arrived in the mail for me. I was sure that I had won the watch. What a disappointment when it turned out to be an Ovaltine shaker. My mother thought that since I was so fond of Ovaltine, she had sent in the required number of labels to get a free shaker. I was so disappointed that Grandma Newton bought me an Ingersol watch for five dollars.

The local radio station had a children's program called "Uncle Sid's ABC club". ABC stood for Always Be Careful. Kids were encouraged to write letters and to be members. There was always a small studio audience of members and those who had talent would perform. I didn't really have any talent, but my mother was always having me learn cute little poems that she would have me recite at various occasions. The ABC club also would announce birthdays on the air.

The year that I was ten, my mother decided that instead of taking my birthday cake to school, as we usually did, that she would make one of her very special Angel Food cakes and we would have the party on the ABC club program. I was to recite a piece. Because it was the ABC Club, my piece was called, "All Letters Of The Alphabet".

All letters of the alphabet
The righteous way should choose
But two of them especially
Should mind their Ps and Qs.

The 'A's and 'E's and 'O's and 'Y's
Do work that's good and great
But 'U' and 'I' can do the most
To make this old world straight.

After I had spoken my piece and it was time to announce the birthdays, two of the regular girls on the show came in with one of my mother's cakes, all lit up, and I got to blow out the candles on the radio.

My Grandfather Richmond died at our house. Grandma and Grandpa had moved over from their house on the town line road so that my mother could help take care of him. They put a bed in the sitting room. I didn't really understand everything that was going on at the time but I knew that he was dying. They even hired a practical nurse for a few days near the end. His death certificate says that he had pneumonia.

After Grandpa's death, it was decided to sell their little forty acre farm which was a couple miles from where we lived and my Grandmother would move into a small apartment created from two rooms in the big farm house. My mother and dad moved their bedroom upstairs and what had been the downstairs bedroom quickly became her kitchen and the parlor, which was seldom used, became her bedroom.

She had a good three burner kerosene cooking stove and a very efficient free standing kitchen cabinet with a flour bin, a sugar jar and a pull out work surface. The table and chairs completed the set up. We all took over the water carrying chore when the weather was too inclement for her to go to the well.

The standard outhouse of the period were always less than ideal. We had one of the better ones of the period. It had two adult holes and a child's hole. We also had covers on the holes which could be called a luxury as it reduced the fly problem that went with these accommodations. But even the hardiest of souls found the privy unpleasant in the cold Wisconsin winters.

Thus it was that my dad ordered a chemical toilet from Sears that could be used inside if properly vented. It was a bucket with a small amount of water and a disinfectant which sat inside a larger can with a seat and a cover. He installed this next to the chimney where it was connected with a pipe for ventilation. A folding screen shielded it from view. Once a week, my dad would carry out the contents and re-charge the chemicals.

I was not supposed to use this as that would make it fill up too fast and make extra work for my dad. However, my grandmother knew how much I hated the frigid outhouse so whenever she thought no one was looking, she would slip into our side of the house and invite me to use her toilet. That was one of the things that convinced me that she was a saint.

During the summer, Grandma would set up her quilting frame in an unused house behind the big house that we called the tenant house. I spent many happy hours with her as she taught me how to quilt and how to tie comforters. She even designed a quilt that she called the cross word puzzle because she got the idea from a cross word puzzle that she had seen in the paper.

It was a marvelous opportunity for me to get to know this very remarkable person. Her story would make a very readable book of its own. She had led a hard life and had not had an opportunity to have any formal education to speak of as she grew up on a homestead on the prairie in Kansas. She was determined that her daughters, my mother and Aunt Cora, would have an education and both of them graduated from Normal School. But she stayed up on the news of the time by reading the newspaper.

In the summer time we always went barefoot. There was a small creek that ran the full length of the farm across the north pasture which was partly marsh. Our neighbor, John Fanning, often referred to his place as "Poverty Hill". My brother and I thought that had a classy sound so we named our creek "Poverty Creek". Kenneth may have known what poverty meant but I just liked the way it sounded. The aptness of the word would be debatable as the poverty we see today bears no resemblance to my childhood. If we were poor we didn't know it.

One of my many duties in the summer time was to take the cows across the road and down the lane to the pasture after the morning milking. It is a habit of cows that when they start moving, they lift their tails and leave a dotted line of warm, soft manure.

Taking cows to pasture can be dull or it can be rewarding with a little imagination, a quality with which I had been richly endowed. I always enjoyed these little dung splats and made sure that I placed a bare foot in the center of each one. This could be tricky and required some agility if I was to keep up with the herd who were always anxious to get to the fresh grass on the marsh. The reward was the warm squish that oozed up between the toes.

My mother never expressed her feelings about this form of entertainment if she even knew about it. I always suspected that she would not approve so when the wire gap to the pasture was secured, I would wade in the creek for an hour or so, washing away all the evidence.

Our creek was maybe three or four feet at the widest and two feet at the narrowest, just a nice challenge for jumping on days that were cold enough for shoes. At the east end there was a tributary that came from the Bevens woods to join our 'mainstream'. This branch had an added attraction of a fallen willow tree that made a natural bridge.

By following the Bevens branch, I could go up stream to a quite delightful glen where there was always a variety of wild flowers and expanses of cool, spongy moss to lie on and daydream.

Another exciting possibility was a gully where the Bevens family disposed of their trash. Their trash was always much more exciting than our trash. They even threw out some of Lawrence's boys' books which I salvaged and I am sure are still around the farm somewhere. The Newtons never throw anything away.

For the most part, the creek ran slowly and had a rather soft bottom but there was a narrow place where the water could be seen moving over the sand and pebbles. In my imagination this became a fast flowing river. I even built a paddle wheel to capture the power.

It was a crude devise of two notched lath with a two nail axle suspended from a 2 × 2, but I had designed and built it and it went around, propelled by water power and I was proud of it.

When Uncle Charles saw it, he too was impressed. (Uncle Charles and Aunt Cora Brockus had moved to Wisconsin from California when I was about five.) In fact, he made me a real neat water wheel. It had eight blades mounted on an octagon axle and had a tapered flume to be anchored in the creek bed with a broom handle. It even had a pulley and a belt to transfer the generated power. It was real neat and made mine look sick and amateurish. I put it in the creek once and it worked, but it was too good. Too much work had gone into making it to be left in place where the cows might break it. It was hung on a nail in the woodshed. It may still be there. Somehow the mighty river had become just a silly little creek.

One year they were remodeling our barn and there were boards with rusty nails laying around all over the place. My dad was Clerk of the School Board and he and my mother had gone to Clinton to interview a prospective teacher. While they were away I stepped on one of those rusty nails. Aunt Cora was looking after us and she washed it out but the next morning the puncture wound was showing red.

I will never forget laying on the couch on the screened porch with my mother holding me down while my dad cut the wound open with a sharp knife and took out flakes of rust with the tweezers and then poured tincture of iodine on it. Ouch!! I had never had tetanus shots and that was a situation that surely called for one. If they were available at the time, it was not even discussed. I have often believed that I had built my own immunity, even in my tender years, from constant exposure to the farm environment.

My Grandpa and Grandma Newton owned a cottage at The Mounds located at west end of the Lake Koshkonong about ten miles from our farm. It was built on property which belonged to two of Grandma's brothers. It was called the Aunt Hill. It was really quite primitive but was just up the hill from the lake and had a large screened porch. The main room had overhead wires stretched and red percale curtains created sleeping cubicles at night for the miscellaneous cots, couches and beds. Naturally there was no electricity or running water and the outhouse was the standard toilet accommodation.

I was not very old when the Marquart brothers sold the farm and the Mounds. The cottages that the various members of the family had built there, had to be removed. The Newton cottage was not all that sturdy, so there was no thought of moving it. It was torn down and the lumber was hauled to the farm where it provided a supply of boards for years.

But my grandparents loved the lake and bought a cottage which was much better built at Charlie Bluff a few miles east of the original. It too was named the Aunt Hill. As at the Mounds, there was no electricity and no plumbing. There was a flowing well across the street on Uncle Earl's lot and it ran cool water constantly into the wooden spring box which was where we filled our bucket for drinking water and where we stored the perishables in tightly covered fruit jars.

The Aunt Hill was a popular place with all the family. Uncle Earl and Aunt Gertie, grandpa's brother and grandma's sister, had a smaller cottage across the street and Grandma's brother, Uncle Will Marquart and his wife Aunt Rosie had a cottage down the street. Also a nephew, Carr Marquart, who was a teacher in Chicago, had a cottage three doors away where they spent their summers. Both the Newton families and the Marquart families showed up at the lake almost every Sunday during the summer, but it was the Aunt Hill to which everyone came. There was a very large screened porch where the food that every one brought was laid out and enjoyed by all.

Uncle Earl had a launch with an outboard motor and a canvas roof. It was a good sized boat that could hold as many as ten people. Riding up and down the lake on the launch was very popular. Uncle Earl and Aunt Gertie had four sons. The oldest, Harry, was a successful entrepreneur who had developed a machine tool factory in Rockford. He and his wife both drove large, black Cadillacs, a fact that was not lost on the family. One brother, Pearl, worked for Harry and another brother, Jay was the head of the Madison Gas and Electric.

The fourth brother, Thurlow, had encephalitis when he was two and never developed mentally beyond that age. However, even retarded, he was a very remarkable person. He loved mechanical toys and the family provided so many of them. It was always a treat for me to visit Uncle Earl and Aunt Gertie at Fort Atkinson because we got to play with Thurlow's toys.

Every year my dad's cousin Grace would come from Reedsburg for a week visit with Grandma Newton. She had a daughter named Betty Lou who was about my age and I was always invited to spend the week with them at the Aunt Hill. Betty Lou could do all sorts of things that I couldn't do, like stand on her head and cartwheels. She could also swim which I never learned to do until I was in the Army.

Grandpa had a row boat and we became very good at rowing. We even tried fishing with bamboo poles but never caught anything bigger than a blue gill which were very boney when they were cooked. There was a sandy beach and there was one place along the shore where there was some real nice blue clay. We used to enjoy making all sorts of objects from clay. She made dishes. I liked to sculpt figures and faces.

Across the street from the cottage was a store. One year the store built a ramp from the roof with a metal track that ran into the lake. For 25 cents an hour you could rent a board with wheels that coasted down the track and into the water. We always ran back up the steps in order to get our money's worth. If they weren't too busy they would even let us go over time to attract attention and maybe more customers because it was a very noisy thing.

One year the store burned down. I think that Grandma was rather glad that it did, because she had complained from the day they built it that it blocked her view of the lake and the coaster off the roof was an abomination when anyone was trying to talk on the porch.

After the fire, we walked around where the building had been and there were hundreds of nails. In the spirit of thriftiness that was so ingrained into our lives, we picked up two or three big bags of nails to take home. My dad said that was nice, but they were useless. The fire had taken the temper out of them and they were so soft that they could not be driven into anything.

When I started first grade in 1926 our school was known as the Bevens School. I tell everyone that the education I received there compares with anyone else's in my age group no matter how big or fancy their school may have been. I believe it may even have been better than the schools of today.

The rural schools in Wisconsin were operated by individual school districts which were laid out so that no student would be required to walk more than two miles. They usually included

24

four square miles or four sections of land. I only had to walk a half a mile.

Each school district elected its own school board of three members and had taxing authority. They were the clerk, the treasure and a director. They selected, hired and paid the teacher. They were also responsible for the physical upkeep of the grounds and buildings which usually consisted of a one room 'School House', two outhouses and often a small barn for shelter for horses or ponies driven or ridden to school by the teacher or students.

By the time I attended school, all the teacher had cars but several students, usually the boys, had ponies and one large family that lived the farthest from the school would drive a horse with a surrey when the horses were not needed in the field.

The Bevens school was a fairly new building, having been built in 1920 to replace the Old Stone School which had been there since 1840 and was no longer thought to be safe.

My dad had replaced my Grandfather Newton on the school board. Being a graduate of Whitewater Normal School and also an experienced teacher, this was a natural. He designed the new building which had a basement with a furnace and separate coat rooms for boys and girls. It had high windows on the north side which gave good natural light, even on dreary days, but did not run us out with the bright sun. This was quite deluxe compared to most of the one room schools that were just that, one room.

The Old Stone School building was still standing when I first started to school. The windows were gone and the floor had deteriorated, but we still played in it, jumping from one rotten floor joist to another. When I was in third grade it was decided that it really presented a safety hazard so that summer, the school board took some dynamite and blasted it into rubble which was hauled over to the town line and put in a low spot in the road.

The desks were so sturdy that they were moved to the new school. In fact, there are still a few of them in the basement at the farm that my dad salvaged when they closed the school. He had a sentimental attachment to them as he remembered when they were delivered and his father and grandfather attached them to the runners and placed them in the Old Stone School. He always said that he was the first person to sit in the new desks when he wasn't even old enough to go to school.

By the time I went to school those now old desks had taken on personalities of their numerous occupants over the years in the form of initials carved in the wood. Every farm boy carried a jack knife. It was standard equipment for boys, so most of the initials were those of boys, many of them fathers of later students.

I didn't always enjoy the walk to school, especially in the cold rain or blowing snow. My mother would never allow us to miss school, no matter how bad the weather was. Gloves would not keep my hands warm and mittens were not much better. One year my mother dug out an old fur muff. It was great. I could put my books and my lunch in it as well as my hands and they would be toasty warm.

It was unthinkable that girls could wear anything but a dress to school. We had long underwear and long black coarse knit stockings. When we put on a freshly laundered pair of drawers on Sunday morning, the cuffs would fit nice and smooth around the ankles so that pulling up the stockings was not a problem but as the week wore on, the cuffs became stretched and had to be folded to get the stockings over them. This was not easy and usually ended up as a big bunch. We wore over shoes that buckled up but when the snow was deep, snow would fall into them from the top and melt from the body heat which made a wet, cold lump that stayed wet all day. All winter long, I would have a rough, chapped patch on both ankles.

If the wind was blowing, which it did a lot in winter, it would sting my face. I had a fuzzy scarf that I could tie around my face but when I would breath through it, my breath would freeze on the fuzz and be just as uncomfortable as the wind. But I never missed a day until I was in 5th grade and got chicken pox.

In our school the text books, work books, reference books, wall maps and other teaching aids were provided but each student was responsible for paper, note books, crayons, pens and pencils.

The curriculum was dictated by the state and the County Superintendent of Schools monitored the districts to assure that all schools met the minimum standard. Besides the superintendent there were two supervising teachers who visited every one of the 200 some schools two or three times a year.

When a student had completed eight years of elementary school or reached the age of sixteen, they were no longer required to attend school and were considered to be educated.

Our whole school never had more than 30 students at one time and it was usually around 20. Of course, we all lived on the surrounding farms. There was only one teacher and she taught all eight grades. We did assignments at our desks while other grades went to benches at the front of the room to recite their lesson that they were supposed to have learned from their reading and to have new material explained.

There were times when students did not behave well. We were even graded on deportment on our report cards. I always got excellent here. I think I was well enough behaved but some of my peers suggested at times that my parent as clerk of the board could influence that. It was not unusual for the teacher to administer a rap on the knuckles with a pencil or a ruler.

Whispering to other students was a no-no. The only time I was punished at school, I had been trying to help one of the boys who was not very bright. The teacher thought that I was giving him answers which would be cheating. We both had to stand arms length away from the wall with one finger on a single spot for a whole recess. That doesn't sound very difficult or painful but I assure you, I knew that I had been punished.

Of course, I felt very abused. At the same time upper graders were often called upon to help younger or slower students with the education process. That was ok because the teacher assigned us to do that. I think you could call us mentors or tutors. It was a good way to develop our own skills and many of the women who grew up in the one room schools became teachers.

There were some things that the entire school did together. First and second grade had two 30 minute recesses and third through eighth grade had two fifteen minute recesses. When the whole school was on the playground, the older students were expected to look after the younger ones.

We all had an hour off for lunch. We carried our lunch to school, usually in a gallon syrup pail with a tight lid. Later, some of us had regular factory made dinner pails, some even had a thermos bottle for hot soup or cocoa. On nice days we ate outside but ate in the basement or the classroom if the weather was bad.

Twice a year we had a program, at Halloween and at Christmas. We learned and recited poems about the holiday. We put on plays where we had costumes and we sang songs.

Some of the dads would come to school a few weeks before the program and assemble the stage. This was some low wooden horses about two feet high with flooring nailed to it. Then there would be a wire about six feet above the stage that was used for a curtain that could be opened and closed between acts.

The programs were always at night so that the families could come and be the audience. There was no electricity and kerosene lamps didn't put out much light. My folks had two big Coleman gasoline lamps that put out a very bright white light. They were hung over the stage. We always knew that they could not start without the Newtons because we brought the light. When the lights were glowing, even though we thought the audience couldn't see us behind the drawn bed sheet curtains, they could see our shadows and everything we did.

At Halloween there was usually what was known as a box supper. All the ladies decorated a box with colored paper and ribbon. They would pack a nice meal for two in the box. After the program, the boxes would be auctioned off to the man who bid the highest on each box. The winning bidder got to eat his dinner with the lady who had fixed the box. It was supposed to be a secret who had fixed each box but we always believed that was more fiction than fact. And you can bet the men knew which ladies packed the best meal.

Our teachers were always young, unmarried women and the men would bid the teacher's box way up, especially if they knew that her boy friend was there. The girls had separate boxes that the boys bid on. The money was used to buy special equipment for the school such as the phonograph.

At Christmas time we had a Christmas tree and exchanged names for Christmas presents. One of the dads would turn his sheepskin coat inside out so that the fleece showed and would wear his black rubber boots with the mud and manure washed off. The outfit also called for a red stocking cap and a false beard. It was Santa's job to distribute the gifts. We all knew or tried to guess who Santa was. Sometimes it would be one of the hired men that we didn't know or the teacher's boy friend so we couldn't guess who it was.

Softball was the favorite game. We played it every time we had enough people. If we didn't have enough bodies for two teams, we would play work up. There would be two people at bat at a time. When a player made an out they had to go to the outfield and work their way back up the line until they were a batter again.

In many ways that was a good system as every one learned to play every position. With only two batters, stealing second was almost routine. Over the fence was out. That was because we were not supposed to be in the neighbors corn field.

There were many other games and activity that we also played. We had swings and teeter-totters (see-saws) which were popular with the little kids. Even when we were older it was fun to stand up and pump the swings so that we would be way above the top pole. Sometimes we would stand two at a time on the swing facing each other. That way we could really go high. Our swings were home made and went much higher than the store bought kind. The seat was a board and they were hung on one inch hay rope.

Hide and seek, tag, ring around the rosie, streets and alleys, drop the hankie and anti-I-over the school house were also popular. That was where we would have two teams and one team would be on each side of the building. Someone would throw the ball over the roof and if anyone on the team on the other side caught it we would all race around to the other side. The kid with the ball could tag as many people as they could with the ball. Everyone that was tagged became a member of the other team. This could go on for a whole recess.

In winter, snow often provided recreation. We would lay out a big circle in the snow with cross paths. One kid would be the fox and the rest would be the geese. The fox could chase the geese and when he caught one, that kid became the fox. Building snow men was another activity but we never got one to look like the three perfect snow balls portrayed on Christmas cards.

Snow ball fights were an activity I purely despised. The boys, especially my brother, loved to gather up huge handfuls of snow and put it down the girls necks.

The boys used to get a charge out of drowning out gophers. The gophers would have holes all over the playground and they were all interconnected. They would actually carry water all the way from the neighbors well to pour down a gopher hole and try to catch a gopher coming out one of the other holes. The idea was to hit him with a ball bat. Usually the gophers were quicker than the boys and I always cheered for the gopher.

We also tried to jump rope. Some girls were very good at it but I always got tangled up in the rope. Sometimes two girls would swing each end of a long rope and one, two, or even three girls would run into the swinging rope and jump as a cute little rhyme was repeated. Then they would run out and other girls had a turn. Since I always messed up the rope, I was usually the one doing the swinging.

One of the big events of the spring was playday. Every township had a playday where schools competed against each other and the winners progressed to the County playday. Our playday was always held on the grounds of the town hall in Johnstown Center.

There were about ten events for the elementary students and three or four for the men and women. For the very young there was a team of four in the bean bag toss. There was a 100 yard relay race for the first and second grade, too. Softball was the premiere event but there was also volleyball, horseshoes, standing long jump for boys and baseball throw for girls. The two hundred yard relay race was always the last event of the day.

All the families brought food for a big picnic. Each school had their own picnic. Tables were brought out of the town hall and set up in the shade of a tree. All the food was laid out and everyone found a place to sit on the ground to eat it. The older folks would go into the town hall where they could sit on chairs but there were not enough tables so they balanced their plates on their knees or set them on another chair.

I would work for weeks before playday to earn enough cash to be able to go across the road to Freddie Pratt's general store and buy ice cream cones, candy, pop and cracker jacks. I would get a dime if I picked up the sticks in the yard before my mother mowed it with the old push mower and there would usually be a dime for me if I spent an afternoon chopping down weeds that always grew in abundance around the backyard.

A week or two after the township play days, they had the County Playday at the fairgrounds in Janesville. My dad was game chairman for this event and so was always very busy. He had to be sure that people were assigned to have the ball diamonds laid out, the volley ball nets in place and the horseshoe stakes the proper distance apart. Then umpires were recruited and assigned.

On the big day, he had a big score board where he entered the winners on the various tournament trees. Each time a round of an event was finished and a new round ready to start he had a big megaphone that he would announce the teams and which venue they were to use. Even with his big voice it was impossible for him to be heard very far from the scoring area. But everyone knew when they had won and would have someone hang around the scoreboard to get the new information and have their team in the right place at the right time. I was very proud of him.

My mother was no athlete but did enjoy being a score keeper for the Johnstown teams. Winners got blue, red or white ribbons.

All the activities of that little one room school out in the middle of the country have come back to me as useful knowledge that I use every day.

Every Friday afternoon we would put away our books a half hour early and held a student government meeting. One of the primary duties of this meeting was to elect the duty officers for the following week.

All eight grades participated according to their ability. The most coveted duty (chore) was the flag honor guard. There were always two for this duty. We took such care be sure that the flag never touched the floor or the ground. It was such a marvelous thing to be able to dash from a class to retrieve the flag if it should start to rain.

We didn't call it politics, but in many ways it compares to that often maligned activity. It was not unusual for two scholars to get their heads together and work out an agreement such as, "If you nominate me to clean the black boards, I will nominate you to sweep the outhouse." That was to avoid the hated water detail.

Water had to be carried from the nearest farm well, about a quarter of a mile away. In winter this was particularly distasteful as the pails were always filled to the brim to avoid having to return later in the day. A brimming pail of water will always spill on the legs of the bearers. In the winter, this means ice on the leg. Democracy had its limitations and no one had to repeat a duty until everyone else had taken their turn.

At fourteen, farm family members were important contributors to the family's economic success. For many this would be the end of their formal education. Therefore seventh and eighth grades were crucial. To hold the districts responsible, each county gave seventh and eighth grade final examinations every spring.

The examinations were held in a central location in each township and were monitored by the supervising teachers or teachers from other townships. Each exam, in all the various subjects, consisted of ten sections and a perfect score was 100. They were given on the same day all over the county and took two days. The subjects included arthritic, language, geography, history, civics, agriculture and spelling.

During the school year, seventh and eighth grade students kept their note books, assignments and work books which were examined at the end of the year by the supervising teachers. If the note books were satisfactory, the student was awarded up to 20 points in each subject and was permitted to substitute these points for any two part of the final test.

31

If a student failed any of these tests they were required to repeat that grade. All the eighth graders who passed all the tests were eligible to graduate and received a diploma. Those who could not pass were allowed to drop out when they reached the age of sixteen.

The county held a graduation ceremony in the county seat at the high school auditorium in Janesville. We graduated by township and each township had from thirty to fifty graduating. This did not include students from the villages and cities, as their education systems were entirely separate.

The year before I graduated, they had a very elaborate ceremony where each township did a costumed skit from American history. I guess it was an outlandish task, so our graduation ceremony was somewhat understated. There was a speaker I think but I can't remember who or what was said. I do remember that they had a male quartet from the Wisconsin School for the Blind which was in Janesville. They sang "Without a Song" and "Wagon Wheels".

The Bevens school had a large class of six. Our teacher was Irene Jones and she took us to lunch at the Meyers Hotel after the ceremony.

For over sixty years now, I have retained the lessons of that classroom. Every time I lift a gavel to conduct a meeting, I do so with the confidence learned from many years ago. There are no parliamentarians as demanding as a classroom of preteens with their peers.

Starting High School was a whole new adventure. The year before I started, Kenneth had accidently hit a boy with the model 'T' that he drove to school and broke his leg. This had been very costly as we did not have any insurance and had to pay for his care and some damages too. My father and mother were unwilling to let Kenneth drive his senior year and I wasn't old enough for a full license. They were unwilling for me to have even a restricted license.

There was a new family in the neighborhood who had a son that was also a senior. His name was Al Bentz. Somehow, a deal was struck that Al would drive their sedan and that we would pay them enough to cover the insurance and gas. He had two other passengers, Forrest Gerloff and Clara Gallager.

After Kenneth graduated, I stayed with my grandparents in Milton Junction during the week. This was very nice as I didn't have all those chores on the farm and was more or less free to pursue a social life which was mostly walking down to the post office to check the mail and to stop off at the drug store for a cherry coke or a three musketeers candy bar.

On the way home I came past the Methodist parsonage and often stopped to talk to Ruby Nagler for and hour or two. Her dad was the minister. Her brother, Jim, had a thing going with Dorothy Albright and we used to watch them make out on the opposite corner.

Before school started, there was an orientation session which I surely needed. At that meeting we were given an IQ test. Changing rooms and teachers for classes was a new experience. However, I didn't seem to have any problem with it.

My very first class was with a Dr. Rachael Salisbury. She was a Milton Junction native and was a professor of education at the University of Wisconsin in Madison. She had written a work book called "Better Work Habits." She was using our first year English class as a laboratory for her to test teach her creation. It was basically a system for teaching the student how to organize thought and learning. She had selected some very good essays to illustrate different styles of writing. It was probably the most useful class that I ever had and I will use her system for the rest of my life.

Right away I wanted to join the band. A traveling band teacher came around every Thursday and held band practice before school and during the noon break. All the band members were also expected to report to the band room during their study period. Mr. Anhault, the band master, found an old slide trombone and assigned Gwen Crandall to teach me how to play it. I took it home and practiced but had no success at all as I never figured out where to place the slide for the various notes.

Uncles Charles was living in the tenant house at the time and was going door to door selling Watkin products (Vanilla, spices, etc.) in Janesville. He knew how hard I was struggling and was sympathetic. I figured that if I just had a coronet with those three keys, I could learn to play. So he asked every house where he called if they had a cornet. Sure enough, one lady had one and sold it to him for $10.

It was a $10 instrument and the valves stuck, but with lots of spit and evil thoughts, I did learn to play it and eventually was promoted to the regular band. I was a perennial third chair and was lost as often as not. My mother took pity on me and bought me a brand new Holton trumpet one summer and even arranged for me to take lessons.

I enjoyed the lessons which were from a lady named Mrs. Pritchett who lived in Whitewater. She had been Aunt Polly for Uncle Sid's ABC club radio show of my childhood. I think the biggest attraction for me was that I was allowed to take the car by myself for the trip to Whitewater once a week. She even had me give a recital.

When I started my senior year, the mellophone player had graduated and we had a new band master. It was his idea that maybe I would be more useful to the band by playing the melophone. My mother swallowed her disappointment gracefully but expressed her frustration years later when my daughter, Virginia, took up the trumpet. She said, "Well at least someone will get some good out of it."

But all was not lost. I had a friend named Muriel Rasmussen who was quite a talented musician, both with clarinet and piano. There was a much older man (maybe 10 years) who was a student at Milton College but was also the band master there. Muriel had a crush on him. He wanted and needed high school musicians to fill out the college band. I think it was Mrs. Rasmussen's idea to encourage me to tag alone and served as the unofficial chaperone. We got to play for the college football and basketball games and were able to be in the village band during the summer where we played concerts in the park on Saturday nights.

My favorite class was physical education. The coach had three periods of girls and three for boys as well as football and basketball. We had class every day for one hour which included ten minutes to put on our gym suit and another ten minutes to redress for class. Our gym suit was a pair of blue one piece rompers with bloomer legs. It was really great for all kinds of activities which included soft ball, basketball, field hockey, volley ball, folk dancing and tumbling. I was a lousy tumbler. I just didn't have the co-ordination. All four grades were represented in each class.

Every year the coach had all his gym classes put on a "Stunt Show". A heavy curtain was strung the length of the gym and the whole student body of around two hundred was behind this curtain awaiting their event. It included boxing, wrestling, tumbling, and statues for the boys and tumbling, and folk dancing for the girls. I wasn't any good at either. They also had clown acts, so my senior year I volunteered to be a clown to avoid the embarrassment of being a clutzie dancer and forget about tumbling.

My act was to dress up in a swallow tailed coat and a top hat. I wore a pair of my grandfather's size 12 shoes. One of the teachers made me a stage beard and I had an enormous suit case in which I put my trumpet, in its case, and a camp stool. I wandered out on queue, opened my suit case, took out the stool and set down to play.

My song was to be a popular number called La Cucaracha. The only problem was, I only knew the first two lines. So I had arranged for two other clowns to run out after the first two lines and drag me off.

Somehow, either they got the message mixed up or they were pulling a fast one on me because after I played the first two lines, there I was, all alone in the middle of the gym floor stage and had no idea what to do next. I started the song over. Still no clowns. I started getting very upset and started waving my arms for my clowns to rescue me. The crowd roared. Then I settled down on my chair and in desperation, I played the one song I knew, "Yankee Doodle". More roars as I was finally rescued. It was probably funnier than I had planned.

My sophomore English teacher was Virginia Barrass. She had eyes that slightly protruded and a very large bust that she emphasized with tight sweaters. She also was unable to control her classes and for the most part I behaved myself. But one day I baited her with some horrible slang which she felt required to correct. My reply was a sentence that Uncle Charles had taught me. "While eschewing mediocrity of expression through platitudinous phraseology, it behooves one to beware of ponderosity, bearing in mind that pedantry, indicative of the inherent megalomania, defeats its original purpose and succeeds only in obnubilation." The stunt show wasn't my only clown act.

Another memorable teacher was Miss Louise Gardener, the math teacher. She had total control of her classes. She was cross eyed but no one ever dared giggle about it. She preferred boys but if girls were willing to work hard and understand the subject, she would put up with us. I think she actually liked some of us.

Math was my passion in those days. Maybe my Newton name let it go to my head. I did especially well in geometry and trig. Many of the lessons that I learned in geometry live with me today and I found algebra useful during my nursing career. I couldn't tell you the difference between a sine and a cosine now though. I have observed at times that two most important things that I learned high school were how to bisect an angle and how to make a bound buttonhole.

Miss Gardener also coached serious declamation. This was an event where girls memorized a long monologue type dramatic or humorous reading and competed to be selected to be a representative at a district meet. I first tried this as a sophomore with a humorous piece and did not do well. The next year I tried the serious stuff and was just as bad, but did get to interact with a very fine teacher.

As a junior, I learned to type. Miss Ruby Agnew was the typing and short hand teacher. She was a local girl who's family ran the lumber yard. This fact was not lost on the irreverent students, since she had lost a leg in her childhood and wore a prosthesis, which in those days was made of wood.

She was also the faculty advisor for the year book. My friend, Jeanne Townsend was the editor and I was the assistant editor. We had lots of fun writing captions and comments about the various class mates. All were complimentary.

The photos had been made and the plates engraved and returned to Miss Agnew who had me put them in her closet. The day came for the plates to go to the printer but no one remembered where they were. I got a panic call out of Trig class and really felt important when I marched into the typing room and triumphantly removed the missing plates from the back of the closet.

The school principle was Mr. Dorr. He also taught one class which was physics. Physics was not a subject that girls took. However, I wanted to take it very much because I liked science and took as many classes in scientific subjects as were available. Mr. Dorr's classes were famous because he had a reputation for racy jokes. My presence in the class however prevented this and the boys resented my being there.

By my senior year, I had done well enough to be selected for the National Honor Society.

3

Teen Age Foreman

Eli:

When I was fourteen in May of 1934, I got working papers and went to work for my Uncle Eli. I was the painter's apprentice. My first job was to load a truck with little pails of white lead. They were kept in a cellar and I was to take them up several steps. The boss asked me if I thought I could do that. They were so little, I said, "Sure." There were no handles on the pails. I soon found out why. They were heavy as lead and it took two hands just to lift them. I got them all on the truck but I sure knew being a painter's apprentice was going to be hard work. I earned 22 cents an hour.

I had many duties. Every painter had his own brushes and he was supposed to clean them but I was expected to made sure the trays where they were stored had the right amount of linseed oil in them so they wouldn't dry out.

One time we had a contract to paint a new school that was being built. Instead of waiting until the trim was in place we went to the mill where the wood for the trim was being milled. That included the frames for the blackboards, the windows and the doors. The door and window frames were given a coat of primer, front and back, and the blackboard frames were stained with midwax.

Another time, we were going to paint a new bowling alley. It was going to be sprayed with a water paint. I would put the right amount of powder in a fifty gallon barrel and fill it with water. Then I would mix it. When the paint was ready, I put a pump in the barrel and the painter would spray the walls while I pumped with a long handle. As soon as the barrel was empty, I would mix up a new batch while the painter sat down and had a cigarette. As soon as it was mixed, I started pumping again. We painted the whole eight lane Baltimore Athletic Club bowling alley in one day. When the supervisor came around in the evening he was surprised that we were finished and gave the painter hell. "What are you trying to do, kill that boy?"

Times were bad and lots of men were looking for work. Many of them thought that they had experience painting and would apply for a job with Uncle Eli. He had a system to tell if they were actually trained painters. He would tell them to paint a window. Professional painters always paint the wood between the panes first before painting the frame. Because I was just a kid and they wouldn't pay any attention to me, he would send me over to check, to see how the guy was doing. If he painted the frame first he didn't get the job.

By the time I was fifteen I was a big kid. Charlie was working at the Bethlehem Ship yards. Joe Bacotto and I went down and told them we were twenty one and got jobs as chippers. It was our job to use jack hammers to knock off old paint and rust on the hulls of ships that were being overhauled. They were mostly old British World War ships that were being brought back into service. It was hard work and dirty, but it paid well. I was making more money than Carrie and John put together. We wore respirators over our mouth and goggles to protect our eyes but the chips were beginning to get under our skin and my mother wanted me to quit.

It was about time to go back to school anyway. If we quit we would have to give notice and wait a couple weeks to be paid, so we decided we would get fired. The chisel that did the work was held on with a wire which would break after a while. So we broke the wires on purpose. As we were on our way to the tool room for new wire, we were sitting on a stack of steel and waited for the Polish pusher to come looking for us.

Shortly, he arrived and started cussing us out for loafing. He was using mighty bad language and was threatening us. Joe took exception to the way he was talking and challenged him to a fight. That big old rough pusher suddenly became very polite and told us to take the rest of the day off. I gave Joe hell for screwing up the plan. We came back the next day and quit but we had to wait for our pay.

When I was sixteen, John, who was by now one of the foremen at the hat factory, got me a job at M.S. Levy's. Because we made and sold hats, we were expected to wear a hat to work. We would carry our hat until we got near the factory, where we would put it on, walk in the door and hang it up.

I went to work in the braid department. This was where straw braid came in from China. This was what was used to make straw hats. About a hundred women, working at sewing machines, would sew the wet braid to make the hats. My job was to open the crates and sort the bundles of braid so that the braid to be used in a single hat would all be the same size and color. Then I would deliver it to the sewing room.

My boss was Mr. Hines. I was his understudy. He was an 82 year old man and was suffering from a lung disease. He coughed an awful lot. He had set up a small area in the braid room behind a stack of boxes where he could go to lay down. If Mr. Moses, the owner, came around and asked for Mr. Hines, I would tell him I though he might have gone to the machine shop. One day while Mr. Moses was there, Mr. Hines got a coughing spell. When Mr. Moses heard him coughing he said, "Tell him I'll be back in half an hour".

Mr. Hines often told me, "If you have to walk across the street to pick up a million dollars and risk your health, leave it lay." Not long after that, Mr. Hines died. I got my first grown up suit with long pants to go to his funeral. Owen, the other helper, who had been there longer than I, had never been able to get the hang of sorting and grading the braid so they made me the foreman. I was 17.

Sometime, shortly after that, another hat factory merged with Levy's and it became 'Men's Hats Incorporated'. The braid supervisor for this new outfit was training his son to be his replacement. After much discussion, it was actually written into the merger contact that I would be transferred to another department. I was moved to the felt hat division.

My new job was to use brushes to start putting the finish on the felt cones that would eventually be the hats. We were paid by the number of pieces we finished. I actually made more money as a finisher than I did as a foreman. My brother, Charlie, worked in the felt hat division too. He was so good at it that he never turned in all his chits because he reasoned that they would decide to lower the value of the chits if he turned in too many.

There was one of the women who was getting old and could not put out as many hats as she had before. They fired her so that her machine would be available to a faster worker to make more hats. Every one in the factory was mad about this. We all felt that she could have been given a job as an inspector or something. There were no pensions and social security was unheard of.

Everyone was so mad that Charlie and Owen went to the Garment Workers' Union who gave them the material they needed to organize the factory. They signed up 98% of the people in one day. My brother John, who was a foreman, was sure upset about his brothers organizing the union.

Not long after that, Charlie quit to go in the Navy. When he quit he turned in all the chits that he had saved in a shoe box. They didn't want to pay him for them so he threatened to throw all the finished hats out in the street. He finally was paid, but very reluctantly.

One time Hoodie got into a scheme to raise rabbits. He started with a pair and eventually we had a whole bunch of rabbits. The supplier had agreed to buy back all the rabbits we could raise, but when we were ready to sell them, they refused and we were stuck with a bunch of rabbits. Hoodie took them out to the stock yard and had them slaughtered and skinned. When he brought them home, my mother refused to cook them and threw them away. We had all gotten attached to them and it would be like eating someone in the family.

After the rabbits were gone, I bought a pair of racing pigeons. The first pair had two baby pigeons. Then rats got in the coop and killed the mother and the babies, and put a big cut in male's neck. We sewed it up and he lived. I was sick about losing my pigeons, so we built a rat proof coop and we raised several litters. We would race them on Sunday morning.

There were racing pigeon clubs in the neighborhood, but we didn't belong to any of them because we didn't want to spend the money for the dues, transportation and entry fees. We did take our pigeons as far away as Washington and they would come home. Ollie Harrison had a motorcycle and we would take a whole crate of them to Silver Springs and let them go. Sometimes we would take several crates in Woodcocks car. The pigeons would always beat us home, even with Ollie going 90 miles an hour on US 1 on his Harley Davidson.

My best friend, Elsworth Woodcock, bought a used Chevy which we put in his garage. We took it apart and overhauled it. We put in new rings and bearings. With the bearings, there were these little copper half circles. We didn't know what they were for so we threw them away. We thought it had something to do with the shipping. After we got everything back together and tightened up we started it up, it ran great.

We had delivered a load of pigeons to Silver Springs and on the way back it started to make an awful knocking sound. By the time we had it back in the garage, that baby was really hot. We went back to the guy that sold us the parts. He asked how many shims we had used. We didn't know what he was talking about. When he said they were those copper rings, we realized we had thrown them away. We had to do the job all over again.

About this time, Woodcock and I bought a Meade kayak kit. It was fourteen feet long and used a light outboard motor which I had bought at a bargain counter at Montgomery Ward. It was only $15 because it had a dent in the gas tank. The wood parts of the kayak were already cut and we put a frame together. It was covered with canvas, which we treated with airplane dope to shrink the cloth tight over the frame and make it waterproof. It had two seats and a floor and held five people.

We built it in the garage next to our house which Woodcock rented. Charlie, and some of the rest of the gang, help build it. It was quite a social event. When it was finished we put it on the roof of the car and took it out to the Patapsco river near Brooklyn and launched it. It was so light that two people could pick it up and put it on the roof of the car. Coming in to shore we punched a nail hole in the bow that we had to patch. When we all eventually went in the service it hung from the ceiling of the garage at Woodcock's place.

We had three different neighborhood football teams that were called the Ramseys. John played for the Ramsey Collegiates, (there wasn't a college man on the team.) There was another team called the Ramsey A.C.s (for Athletic Club). These were older men, some were up in their thirtys. They were like semi pros. The team that I was on was the 'Ramsey Red Skins'.

Three of our gang were regulars, Charlie, Bernie and me. David Witt was on the team but, big as he was, he tended to be clumsy and didn't play very much. The assistant coach, named Michaels, worked at Men's Hats and he recruited me and Charlie. We brought Bernie along. The team lost its first game before we joined. After we joined they never lost another game, but tied one with Lansdown. Bernie was a printer.

We played other teams from other parts of the city. Some of them were teams sponsored by different companies who provided the equipment. Our team didn't have a sponsor. They would take up a collection at the games which was used to pay the referee. After John quit playing, he often worked football games as a referee and umpired baseball. In those day there was only one official for any one game. I suppose the collection reflected how the spectators felt about the ref.

When I joined the team, I inherited John's pants and helmet. The pants were made of canvas and the helmet was leather. There was no face mask. Our home field was in Carroll park. We would practice one or two nights a week and play on Sunday afternoon.

I played right guard and Bernie Stillings was the left tackle. We played both offense and defense. One time, on the kick off, the ball accidently came to me and I picked it up. The whole other team must have landed on top of me and I knew right then that I never wanted to carry the ball. It was a lot more fun to block and tackle than to be tackled.

By now Barney Goldberg and the Bach brothers were students at Loyola University and were on the basketball team. They were very good, even champions in the catholic conference that included teams like Georgetown, DePaul, and Loyola of Chicago.

When we had been kids together we had nailed a peach basket to the wall of a garage and became very good at the game. Many of the bigger churches also had gymnasiums. Some communities had gyms too. The Polish gym was so small that the out of bounds line was painted on the wall four feet from the floor.

Our little rag-tag team would get games with different church and community teams. We even went out to St. Mary's Industrial School for Boys that was run by the Catholic brothers. The brothers were the officials and we could never win out there. They kept the floor real shiny and our worn out sneakers had us sliding all over, while their guys had fancy basketball shoes.

Loyola had a rule that their players were not supposed to play outside their supervision, but one day four of them got up a game with the Polish/American club. They needed a fifth guy and that guy was me. They were all great shooters. I would get under the basket and get the ball and put it in whenever they missed. I ended up getting most of the points. There was a reporter there. He said he knew these other guys played for Loyola but what college did I play for?

Barney and the Bach brothers were taking horse back riding lessons. One day they wanted me to go with them. The horse that

I rented was supposed to be a gentle old nag. The man running the stable told me just to hang on, that Joe (the horse's name) knew what to do. That animal took off like a race horse. When we came to a log he just jumped right over as I hung on. It wasn't pretty but I stayed on over all sorts of obstacles and got back without any problems. The schooled and experienced riders got to the log and their horses stopped dead and wouldn't jump. They were embarrassed because they had to go around all the obstacles. I felt lucky to get back alive.

One sunny day in winter, we were sitting on the steps of our house when we saw a guy running away from a middle aged cop named Mr. Phelps, who was running a losing race. We said, "Lets get him" and took up the chase. There was a man shoveling his walk who saw what was happening and got in the fugitive's way. When the runner bumped into him and fell down, three of us jumped on the bad guy so he couldn't get up until the cop caught up.

Mr. Phelps asked us where the gun was. If we'd known that he had a gun, we might not have been so brave. The man with the shovel said he saw the guy throw something in the snow bank when he went down. There was a small hole in the snow. When the cop reached into the hole, he pulled out a loaded 38 caliber pistol. The bad guy had just robbed the Coney Island at Wilkens Ave. and Monroe Street.

Another time, someone came running to tell us that Babe Cheney, who was about 25 or so, was being attacked by a rough downtown gang on McHenry St., about two block away from where we were playing basketball. We all took off running and hollering to where they were. Babe had a heavy tow chain that he was whirling around above his head. It was keeping them away but even as big and strong as babe was, he could not have done this for very long. When we came roaring around the corner his attackers didn't realize it was just of bunch of kids and they all took off.

By the end of the 1930s things were pretty good for the Fishpaws. All of us had jobs except June who was still in school. Every night we would listen to the evening news on the radio. Most of the people on Ramsey St. would sit on their front step and enjoy the evening and generally socialize. Many of us would gather on the corner and sing the popular songs we heard on the radio. The neighbors seemed to enjoy this. We would also discuss all sorts of things including the news we had just heard and what it might mean to us. There seemed to always be revolutions going on in South America.

There were things happening in Europe that had an undercurrent of uneasiness about them too. A little guy named Hitler had taken over Germany and seemed to be leading his people in a direction that didn't sound too good. After the World War, a part of the peace treaty put severe restrictions on Germany's right to have a military. Hitler thumbed his nose at the treaty and started building up the German army. They had also agreed not to have an air force but Hitler ignore this agreement too and was building up what was called the Luftwaff.

Italy also had a leader, named Musselini, who was using strong arm methods to run that country. In Germany they called themselves the National Socialist Party or Nazi for short and in Italy it was the Fascist. Italy and Germany had made an agreement with Japan to help each other in case of a war. They were known as the Axis.

In Baltimore, groups of people, whose families were German, were forming clubs called The German American Bund. The barber in our neighborhood was always talking about how great the happenings in Germany were. He really hated the British and called the royal family decayed and immoral as the results of intrafamily marriages.

There was one group that the FBI knew was getting pretty subversive. They met in a beer joint on Fredrick Rd. and had a big picture of Hitler over the bar. Alcoholic beverage had become legal in 1933 so the FBI could not raid the place without some reason. The Klu Klux Klan were recruited to go out there and start a disturbance. One Klansman threw a glass of beer in Hitler's face and all hell broke lose, bringing in the Baltimore police who broke up the fight. The FBI was right behind them and found a large supply of machine guns, rifles and explosives in the cellar which was what they were really looking for.

Many of us felt that things seemed to be headed in the wrong direction. Congress had passed an act to draft able bodied men between 18 and 35 into the military service if needed. Some of the older guys were joining different military reserves or actually going into the service.

It was in September of 1938 that the situation in Europe had reached the point where it seemed necessary to hold a peace conference in Munich, Germany. Hitler was demanding that Germany be allowed to annex the part of Czechoslovakia where the people were mostly German. It was known as Sudetenland. Nevill Chamberlain, the prime minister of Great Briton, was at the conference and lead the movement to allow the annexation in exchange for an agreement that Germany would make no further aggression on its neighbors.

When we heard about all this, we all agreed that we were probably going to have another war and that sooner or later the United States was going to get into it. I thought that if I was going to have to be in the military, I didn't want to be drafted. I wanted to be able to choose what kind of an outfit I was going to be in. Charlie, Billy Holmes, Woodcock and Woodcock's older brother were in the Navy Reserve and attended drill one night a week. Charlie's reasoning was that he wanted to be close to the kitchen.

I remembered seeing the old horse drawn artillery coming down Fulton Avenue every summer on their way to camp. Now I wanted to be one of the guys to shoot those big guns. Joe Gerben was a sergeant in the National Guard outfit out in Pikesville where those guns came from. It was the 110th Field Artillery of the Twenty Ninth National Guard Division. They sent a truck out to southwest Baltimore every Thursday night to pick up their members for drill. One Thursday night, I caught the truck at Baltimore and Monroe street with Joe and rode out to the Armory where I enlisted in the Guard. I was in battery 'A'. It was 22 September, 1938.

The horses were gone by now. In 1936 they had been replaced with Dodge trucks. They were the same kind of trucks used by civilians for all sorts of thing and had no special features for the military. The guns were called French 75's. Also gone were the ammunition wagons, called cassons, and so were the wooden wheels with iron tires that made that great noise on the stone streets of long ago. They had been replaced with high speed carriages using steel disk wheels and regular rubber tires with inner tubes. But it was still the same artillery, left over from the war.

The uniforms too, were the same as had been used during the war. Our fatigues were blue denim and we had fatigue caps with a round crown and a rolled brim. In the winter we wore a felt campaign hat, with red braid for artillery, like you saw in western movies, along with our wool uniform. At first we were issued leather boots that laced up to just below the knees. They were shined with ox blood polish which was dark red, thus the name for the artillery was red legs. Later we were issued brown shoes, ankle high, and we had a legging that was worn over the shoes and covered the bottom of the pants legs. The helmet looked like a wash basin turned upside down on our head.

The 110th had a polo team and the inside of the armory was the polo field. It was a dirt floor covered with bark. It was in the armory where we learned to be soldiers. From the very beginning we would do close order drill. I had asked to be a cannoneer so started right out learning everything about the guns and doing cannoneers' hop.

When I first got to fire the guns it was at service practice. We would go out to the Aberdeen Proving Grounds, north of Baltimore, where there was a firing range. We would fire over the Susquehanna River which was very wide there. The range would be marked off so we did not interfere with any boats that might be there. There were thousands of wild duck in the area but they just ignored us.

My first summer camp was in upper New York near Ogdensburg. It was a big damn maneuver. It included regular army divisions and National Guard divisions from all over the northeast. We didn't begin to have enough equipment and they were using coal trucks marked TANK on the sides and make shift artillery such as logs or stove pipes. Almost everything we had was left over from the World War.

President Roosevelt came to the camp and made his famous speech. "Ah hate waw. Eleanah hates waw. There will be no waw." There wasn't a soldier there that believed him. We knew that we had better get trained fast. It was the summer of 1939.

Even with such high assurance, the country was preparing for the worst. Army camps were being enlarged and new ones were springing up all over the country. One of them was Fort Meade, just south of Baltimore, near the city of Glen Burnie. We were told that as soon as the buildings were ready we would be called to active duty for a year.

Many of the men in our neighborhood were getting good paying jobs building the camp. I knew that my civilian days were numbered so I applied for and got a job as a sheet metal helper. It paid twice what I got at the hat factory.

Miller Heating and Sheet metal had a contract to install the furnaces and heating ducts in the new wooden barracks. The foreman was Mr. Miller's son and he showed Bill Reynolds and me what we were expected to do. The furnaces and the ducts, which had been cut and bent to fit, had been delivered to the building site.

We were to put the furnace in the building, on the concrete slab in the furnace room. Then we were to put the hangers on the ceiling beams and fit the ducts into them. It was something like an erector set. The ducts were held together with something called 'U' slips and 'S' slips. We put these together, but since we were helpers, we were not allowed to use any tools. The sheet metal mechanics would come along later and clinch the slips in place with their hammers and fasten the hangers to the beams.

It wasn't very hard work and the first day we finished our part of the job in about fifty barracks. When the foreman came around to check, he gave us hell. He said that we had done too many, that we should only do six or eight a day because the whole job was cost, plus and they didn't want it finished too soon so they could collect more money.

We were discharged from the National Guard on 1 February, 1941 and were assigned to the Army of the United States on 2 February.

~ 4 ~

The Mercy Years

Bernice:

As long as I can remember I always knew that I would go to high-school and later I would go to college. Kenneth had gone to Milton College for one semester but his greatest interest was to play football. The season was not half over when he dropped a course or two in order to remain eligible and dropped out of school as soon as the season was over. When my class graduated there was a scholarship available to Milton College for a Milton student but it went to Bob DeLand who had a higher grade point average than I did.

I really wanted to study science anyway and wanted most of all to go to the University of Wisconsin at Madison. There was no tuition required of Wisconsin residents then. I could even have had a $100 a year stipend, but even in 1938, that would not cover the cost of books, lab fees, housing and food.

There was also a private college in Milwaukee called Milwaukee Downer whose catalogue was very exciting to me. One of the majors that they offered was in occupational therapy. That was every thing I wanted. All kinds of crafts and science too. My mother studied that catalogue as thoroughly as I had, and then came up with the idea that the program seemed very much like nursing (it really isn't), so she got information from our nearest nursing school, Mercy Hospital in Janesville, for me to study. The cost would be $125 for the first year, $75 the second year and $25 the third year. She felt we could afford this. That is how I came to be a nurse.

One day I skipped school and my dad took me to Janesville to see Sister Cor Marie who was the director of nursing. The interview went well and I was accepted. While we were in Janesville we came upon a radio person who was doing street interviews and he asked me what I was doing in town instead of being in school. This was how I announced to the world that I was going to be a nurse.

The nursing program would last three years including summers but we only had classes from September to June. During the summer we did eight hour shifts in the hospital taking care of patients and developing our skills as nurses. That was why the cost was so reasonable. We literally staffed the hospital.

The first step in this new world was probation. Probation lasted six months. We started with simple tasks and progressed to the more skilled responsibilities. We lived in a dormitory known as the nurses' home. Our class of 22 occupied the entire third floor. Each of us had a room mate. Several of the new class knew each other from school, 4 H or had older sisters or friends already in the school who had set up room mates. I was a total stranger to all and accepted whom ever I was assigned. My room mate was a woman named Beata Felland. She was at least 30 and had a lot more of life's experiences than I did. She was tall, red headed and very fair. My first impression of her was when I saw her spit on her mascara. I didn't even know what mascara was but I thought this was not very sanitary.

We ate our meals in the staff cafeteria in the hospital. There were several RNs on the staff who also ate there at their own special table. The nuns had their own dining room called the refectory and there was a special dining room for the private duty RNs. The food was not the greatest. The scrambled eggs were always cold as was the toast. We were expected to be in the cafeteria no later than 6:30 AM. After breakfast we lined up in the corridor by class, the seniors first and the freshmen last, to march single file up the back steps, which were built around the back elevator, down the hall a short distance to the chapel which was just inside the convent. The convent had been the original Palmer home turned hospital early in the century.

The main building had been built in two stages. The original building was on the north end and was beginning to show its age. Since there were patients along our route to the chapel we were expected to be quiet. Because the chapel was a dedicated

Catholic sanctuary, the custom was that every female was to have her head covered when we entered. The nursing cap filled this requirement but until we received our caps we just placed a handkerchief on our head. We all knelt on the wooden kneeling benches and repeated a short prayer asking for guidance for the day. This routine completed, the real nurses went to their assigned floors and the new students returned to the nurses' home where the class rooms were located.

House rules were very strict. Lights must be out and all students except those on duty were to be in bed by 9PM. This rule was enforced by Sister Cor Marie who had a private room on the second floor of the nurses' home near the door to the hospital. She made bed check every night. The doors were all locked at 9 PM. After our probation, we were allowed to get late leaves once a month when we could stay out until 11 PM. If you had a late leave you went to the front office of the hospital and someone would escort you to the nurses home with the key. I usually just went home so I never had any problems with the arrangement. Some of the students dated. For them it was a problem. The standard procedure was to have the room mate arrange pillows under the covers to appear to be a sleeping student. Getting in was another challenge. Sometimes a daring friend would sneak down the back stairs and unlock the back door. Sometimes a class room window which was on the ground level would be left unlocked. Both methods were hazardous and I don't think Sister was ever fooled. Sometimes, if she found an unlocked window, she would put some piece of furniture, such as the skeleton, under the unlocked window.

The first six weeks was spent mostly in the classroom. We studied such subjects as microbiology, anatomy and physiology, chemistry, and a class called The Mathematics of Drugs and Solutions. Our primary instructor was Sister Mary Matilda. She was from Chicago and spoke with an unmistakable Polish accent. The th sound was her biggest problem. Sister Bernidett (the director of the clinical laboratory) taught microbiology and a young nurse from Mercy in Chicago, Olga Kekut, taught nursing practice. I really enjoyed the anatomy. One of the teaching aids was a model head and torso of the human body with the various organs that could be removed and reassembled. It was like a big 3-D puzzle and made learning exciting and permanent. There was a skeleton too, which helped us to learn the bones. Sister Matilda told us that there were 206 bones in the body and when she was finished they would all be in our brain. I didn't do as well with the muscles but eventually they were all in my brain too.

I had not had the opportunity to study chemistry in high school so found it very difficult but squeaked by. However, I never felt that I learned enough for the information to be of any value in practice.

It was Mathematics of Drugs and Solutions where I really excelled. The problem was, Sister Matilda did not understand algebra so she taught us some very complicated arithmetic to achieve a result. I immediately applied some simple algebra which was much easier. This upset sister no end and she forbid me to use my method. I should have known better, but I argued with her. I felt this built a barrier between us because for the next three years I was never able to do anything to please her.

At the back of the classroom was a mock up of a hospital room and it was here that Miss Kekut taught us nursing art. In the bed was a life size doll called Mrs. Chase. One of the first procedures we learned was the bed bath. After we had practiced on Mrs. Chase, we had to take turns being the patient and give each other a bath and change4849 the bed. When we were learning how to give hypodermic injections we also practiced on each other, using sterile water.

The technique for giving an injection was very crude by todays standard. We would take our two cc syringe and put it in a small canister of cotton balls covered with alcohol. Alcohol was drawn up in the barrel and allowed to soak while we put the needle in a tablespoon of tap water and propped it over the gas burner where it boiled three minutes. Now the syringe was supposed to be sterile so we lifted it out of the alcohol and carefully mated it with the boiled needle. Some of the boiled water was drawn into the syringe and the empty spoon received the tiny pill of whatever narcotic was to be given and dissolved with the water in the syringe. After giving the injection, the needle and syringe got a quick rinse in the alcohol and went back in the nurses pocket. However the line was drawn and we didn't have to give each other enemas or douches.

When we had completed the first six weeks we were ready to go into the hospital and take care of real patients. We were all issued 6 white starched uniforms with long sleeves. The style was buttoned down the front with the placket on the left side. Large pearl buttons were removable which was always a hassle whenever we changed uniforms. First year students wore black stockings and black shoes which we all disliked immensely and complained about, but to no avail. A finger tip length, gray cape was to be worn when going from the nurses' home to the hospital. Our initials were embroidered in the red lining. Somehow mine came with the initials BM. We joked that I had BM (short for bowel movement) on my cape, even before I wore it. As probationers, we were issued the same cap that the rest of the school wore and which eventually, with the addition of a black velvet stripe, became the graduate cap of the Mercy RN. The probie cap had the brim folded down and the peak folded over. They were held in place with bobby pins. I wore my hair very short and people used to wonder how I kept my cap on. I had two stock answers. One was thumb tacks and the other was a vacuum. We were allowed three uniforms a week. The hospital laundry kept us looking white and clean. The sisters were very proud of how professional their students looked. Most other schools were still wearing blue and white stripped dresses with white aprons.

Each of us was also issued a pair of bandage scissors and a small plastic box with a glass syringe and two 24 gauge needles. These, along with several safety pins, were to be in our pocket at all times. We had to provide our own watch with a second hand for counting pulses. I had a $5 pocket Ingersol.

Our first experience with live patients was from 4:00 to 6:00 PM which included serving the evening meal. My first assignment was in pediatrics and my first act was to serve a tray to a young boy. Simple! It was a disaster. I dropped it on the floor. Not only did I have to go to the kitchen and explain what had happened, but I had to clean up the mess which Sister Magdeline, the supervisor, had left for me. I had made my first impression on the hierarchy and I wanted to quit.

Before long we were also released from the classroom to go to the hospital for an hour in the middle of the morning where we started doing nursing care. That included everything from giving the bath, and making the bed to cleaning up the room or the cubical, sweeping the floor and dusting the furniture. At first we were assigned only one patient but it wasn't long until we were taking care of two and even three at a time. Sister Matilda and Miss Kekut kept close watch over us to be sure we were doing it right and Sister in particular was an expert at showing up whenever I was not doing as well as I should have been. It seemed that I was always behind and making all kinds of mistakes trying to catch up.

All the time we were learning new procedures and new insight into disease and treatment. Kekut always accompanied us when we performed any procedure for the first time. How proud we felt when we had successfully inserted a catheter or had good results from an enema. My first enema was on one of my high school class mates, a guy, and we were both pretty embarrassed, but the ingrained professionalism pounded into me by the nuns paid off and we both survived.

I was still a probationer when the Christmas-New Years holiday came around. The classes were suspended and half of the freshmen were given one week off for Christmas or one week for New Years. I drew New Years. Grandpa Newton had been admitted to the hospital for prostate evaluation but had developed the hiccups which became so severe that he became exhausted. I was still in pediatrics and I remember looking out the back window on Christmas day and seeing my dad drive into the ambulance ramp at the back door of the hospital and get a wheel chair for my Grandmother to visit Grandpa. I was somehow very lonesome.

Grandpa had a private duty nurse who worked a twenty hour shift which was the custom then. She was permitted to sleep but had total responsibility for the patient except for her four hours off during the day. I was at home when he passed away. My dad was taking me back to the nurses home to get a good dress to wear to the funeral when we had a car accident. There was not much damage but I hit my head on the windshield and there were some cuts on my forehead which bled enough that when I showed up at Sister Cor Marie's office for permission to go to the nurses home, she decided that I should be admitted. They put on some butterflies and took an x-ray. The next day I was able to go to the funeral. Not a very good way to start 1939.

After six months our probation was over. We were ready to be initiated and receive our real cap. It was the same piece of cloth as the probie cap but now it stood up, proudly displaying the Mercy peak. The class ahead of us held an initiation. We had to wear crazy outfits with green ribbons in our hair, then go on stage and do some crazy act. I had to imitate the tobacco auctioneer. I used the excuse that I didn't have any tobacco and proceeded to auction off my green ribbon. It seemed to satisfy the critics. On the serious side, we all made the Nightingale Pledge and became genuine members of the nursing profession.

With our newly acquired status, class time diminished and duty time increased to eight hours. Now we did a lot more than give baths. We became very expert at shouldering trays and emptying bed pans. We cleaned rooms when patients were discharged and we folded and put away linen. We passed medication and we learned how to chart the patient's progress. I remember one day I saw a brown, wet and yucky looking blob in an emesis basin on the bedside table of a man. I disposed of it in the hopper and conscientiously charted fecal emesis. I found out how carefully our instructors reviewed our charts even though we were reasonably sure that the doctors never read a word we wrote. It was Kekut who saw this note and asked me to explain. When we went into the ward to talk to the man, he was sitting up in bed in no apparent discomfort, smoking a cigar and putting the ashes in the emesis basin. I had charted a cigar butt for a piece of dodo.

With added responsibility came the increased experience of new shifts. The relief shift was from seven to eleven and we were left alone or sometimes with two students to care for as many as thirty patients. I hated relief. The visitors were in the building and the patients were often tired and cranky. After the visitors left we had to settle the patients for the night before the night shift came on and then chart it all. We were allowed to pass routine medication but could not give oral sedative or inject narcotics without calling the supervisor as she had the keys to the narcotic drawer.

When we first started taking night duty, we were assigned one student to a unit. This was not too bad on fourth floor which only had a maximum of 16 patients. It was all private rooms as surgery, x-ray and the lab took up the north end of the floor. But first and second were large units with up to thirty-two patients which included a big eight bed ward on second and an eight bed and two four bed wards on first. We were either too busy or things could be so quiet that it was difficult to stay awake. Sleeping on duty was cause for instant dismissal.

The night supervisor was an RN by the name of Laura Feidler. She seemed ancient to us but she had a baby sometime along the way so she couldn't have been as old as we thought. She always wore Ked tennis shoes which gave a whole new meaning to the word sneakers. We lived in fear of being caught napping. Any time Mrs. Feidler thought a student was struggling to keep awake she would show up with a bag of washed gauze and a square board edged with sharp nails. The little wads of gauze, sponges from surgery that had gone through the laundry, were to be opened up and stretched over the board, held in place by the nails. When the wads had all been stretched. Each 16" square was then folded to create a new 4×4. They were remarkably soft and absorbent and made wonderful dressings. If the student got drowsy enough to let her head drop down on the board, the nails would wake her up.

But Mrs. Feidler had a good heart too. One night when it was very quiet, she learned that I had a case study due which I had not completed. She relieved me for a couple hours so that I could go to the library to finish the assignment. Case studies involved selecting a patient and writing a complete history of their illness, describing the treatment and nursing care that presumably we had given.

About four thirty in the morning we became very busy. We were expected to wake up every patient, give them a bed pan or urinal if needed, (it always was) and a basin of warm water so they would be ready for breakfast by 7 AM. We also were to take the temperature, pulse and respiration of every patient, and give any medication ordered before breakfast. Often many of the Catholic patients wished to receive communion. They were to be washed and the bed tidied up by 6:00 AM when the priest with two nuns would come through the hospital with the Host. All the other doors were to be closed. We were expected to be out of sight when the entourage came through.

Another task was to return all the flowers and plants to the patients' rooms. Every evening they were placed on the floor in the corridor as it was thought to be unhealthy for them to be in the room while the patient was sleeping. This was a truly hectic two or three hours and we often combined the tasks. One morning I sat a tray of thermometer on the dresser of one of the private rooms. While the patient was warming her thermometer, I was slinging what was an unusually large number of plants and vases onto the dresser. Of course, all the thermometers went on the floor and most of them broke. Mrs. Feidler had to open the supply room so that I had enough thermometers to complete my temps. I had wiped out the entire first floor's supply. I had to pay a dollar apiece for every one of them and neither my folks nor the nuns took any pity on me. It took all the money I had saved as a child. All thirty dollars.

This was not as bad as what happened to my room mate. She, in her rush, had rolled a comatose patient over and put a rectal thermometer in place and left the room to do other duties. We were supposed to hold a rectal thermometer whenever it was in place in a patient. Of course, Mrs. Feidler happened to see it with no one around. She removed it and hid it until the hapless student returned. With no sign of the thermometer, either in the patient or in the bed, the student thought that it must have been drawn into the patient and proceeded to use her bare finger to look for it. About this time the supervisor appeared. There was much trouble. I felt the student would be dismissed, but after much agonizing, she was allowed to continue.

It was while I was on night duty that I had an attack of acute appendicitis. I was hospitalized and had an appendectomy. This was my first encounter with scopolomine. That was the pre-op medication and besides making my mouth very dry, it made me a little bit goofy. I wanted to kiss everyone in sight. I had a private room on the same floor where I had been on duty the night before. In my drugged condition I dreamed that I had gone to sleep on duty, so I got up and made rounds. My replacement found me in my split back nighty in the men's ward. They must have all been asleep or it could have created quite a sensation.

In those days, post operative patients were supposed to remain in bed for at least a week. Since my incision was so small and I had no ill effects from my early ambulation, I was allowed to go home in four days but could not return to duty for six weeks. Early ambulation did not become acceptable until the army introduced it during World War II. One night I had a doctor's wife for a patient. When she got out of bed unattended, Mrs. Feidler was so upset she immediately removed the lady's dressing and to my great relief found the incision intact.

The economic depression was beginning to abate and more and more people felt that they could afford to go to the hospital. We were getting so busy that the nuns decided that perhaps another pair of student hands should be added to the assignment. This person became known as the float nurse and was sent to whatever area needed help. It was actually a pretty good assignment as that nurse always had company and shared responsibility.

Obstetrics shared third floor with pediatrics and the new born nursery. Each had a separate nurse. We were not assigned to any duty on OB or New Born Nursery until after we had taken the class in those subjects, which was during the second or Junior year. However, one Sunday morning an OB patient came in ready to deliver at about six o-clock, just when the patients had to be awakened and the babies taken out to be breast fed. So the supervisor sent me up to third to help out.

I was sent to the delivery room to give an enema to a patient who was on the delivery table. By now I was totally comfortable giving enemas and went at it as usual. I had just emptied the can and put the patient on the bed pan when the enema, feces, baby and all, explode right in my face. I had enough presence of mind to grab the baby and holler for help. The Doctor and the extern had been standing just outside the door and came to my rescue with great mirth. That was the first time I had seen a baby born. What I did not know at the time was that this lady was having baby number seven and that the doctor had ordered thytuitrin, a drug to induce labor, because he was going to Madison and wanted to get an early start.

At the start of the second year we became known as Juniors and were able to throw away the despised black shoes and stockings. However, everything good has a responsibility. We now had to keep the new shoes looking white and wash the strings at least once a week. I have to confess that I did not always have the whitest shoes in the class.

The learning curve took a sharp rise this year as we moved into the specialties. I liked obstetrics. It was usually such a happy place and it was a pleasure to take squirming babies to their mothers. However, there were those moments that stand out, not because of their joy but because of their sorrow. One case I vividly recall was a baby born with severe abnormalities. It was my duty to take this child to his mother. I wrapped him very tightly and hoped she wouldn't see the deformed little body. I am sure she probably opened up the blanket as soon as I was out of the room. The baby did not live but a day or two.

It could get very hectic in the new born nursery. Twenty to thirty hungry, screaming babies can get on ones nerves. We did not give soap and water baths but only cleansed the folds with cotton dipped in oil. We washed our hands a great deal and they became very rough and sore. The scourge of the nursery was a fear of the dreaded skin condition called impetigo. We did not have any cases of impetigo during the three months I worked in the nursery.

A newborn baby is usually covered with a cream cheese like material called vernix. We cleaned this off with a cotton ball dipped in oil. One day a baby was born with more vernix than usual but we were very busy with the mother and didn't get around to moving him to the nursery for ten or fifteen minutes. When we did turn our attention to the baby all the vernix had been absorbed. That baby had the best looking skin in the nursery.

The month in the diet kitchen was a popular assignment because we were allowed to eat whatever was available from the big kitchen. Best of all, we had access to the keys to the ice cream freezer which was across the hall from the special diet kitchen behind the back elevator. The kitchens were supervised by the dietician, Miss Mitchell. Mrs. Hoppie was the cook. It was here that special diets were prepared. The most common special diet was for diabetics. Weighing out the portions was one of our duties. We also hand carried the trays up the elevator to the patients. The back elevator was hand operated by a nice older man named Mr. Kauphman.

This was during a time when a great many men were out of work and had taken to the road, presumably looking for work but more likely just wandering. They were referred to as hobos and many of them rode the freight trains. The back door of the hospital was very near the railroad tracks where the trains started to slow down coming into the yards at Janesville. It was not unusual for them to jump off and come to the kitchen door looking for food. The nuns never turned anyone away but there was one hard rule. If they wanted a hand out, they had to come to the front door. Some did, many did not. Whenever someone did show up, the front office would call down to the diet kitchen and the student would put together whatever was available and take it upstairs.

Not nearly as popular was the month in the clinical laboratory. At last, science! Not so! Even though there were test tubes and bunson burners, our primary task was doing urine tests. Each morning after breakfast we reported to the lab where anywhere from ten to thirty bottles of urine awaited us. We learned to test for specific gravity, sugar, color, and albumin and to fill and label a measured amount of urine into glass tubes and spin them in the centrifuge for the professional technician to examine. Our tests finished, we washed the glassware and loaded a basket with clean bottles which we delivered to each unit before reporting to our regular assignment where our assigned patients awaited us.

The most exciting and challenging assignment of all was surgery. Here was the heart and soul of everything we looked forward to. Surgery was on the north end of the hospital on the top floor and had big glass windows for light. Of course, we had electric lights but it was thought that daylight was best for surgery. Being assigned to surgery was like starting all over again. There were two major clinics in Janesville. One was the Pember-Nuzum clinic and the other was the Munn-Farnsworth clinic. There were three main operating rooms, one for each of the clinics and one for the non-clinic surgeons, the most respected being Dr. Ralph Hartman and Dr. Joe Kelly.

The doctors wore scrub suits which started out white but were soon quite brown. The RNs had scrub dresses and Sister wore a gown over her habit with the veil underneath. The students wore their regular uniforms. Now we could roll up our sleeves neatly before donning our uniform in the morning so they would be nice and neat and stay up all day. It was sort of a status symbol to go to the dining room with your sleeves rolled up. The supervisor was Sister Mary Jane Frances and the two RNs were Venida Filter and Betty Yuengst.

We all started at the back table. The back table remained set up and supposedly sterile all morning and as each case was finished, another took its place. This is where the second scrub nurse worked. The reason we were called scrub nurses was because we scrubbed our hands and arms for ten minutes with a brush and liquid green soap. Then rinsed them with alcohol before putting on a sterile muslin gown with long sleeves and sterile rubber gloves.

Now that we were sterile, we took the table cover and other linens from special steel drums. They had two sides with holes in them. While they were in the autoclave (steam sterilizer) the holes were lined up to be open and allow the steam, under pressure, to permeate the contents and kill all bacteria. When the necessary exposure to the steam was finished and the drying period completed the outer side was rotated to make the drum airtight. The drums were on a stand and could be opened or closed with a foot pedal. The idea was to never touch the outside if you were supposed to be sterile.

Counting the gauze sponges with the RN was the most important thing the back table nurse did. This was to be sure that the same number of gauze sponges came out of the patient as went in. It is often very difficult to see a blood soaked sponge in a bloody operating site. At that time there was no way that a sponge left in the patient could be detected with x-ray as there is today. Back tables for multiple cases are history now and certainly their demise was a step forward in sterile technique.

Catgut sutures came in sealed glass tubes which were kept in sterile glass jars filled with bichloride of mercury. When a certain suture was required, the circulating nurse would fish the appropriate tube out of the jar with supposedly sterile transfer forceps and drop it on the back table. The back table nurse would then wrap it in a folded towel and snap open the tube to reach the suture which was in a special solution. It was a real art to get the tube to break cleanly. They were scored to make a clean break but more than one scrub resorted to whacking it with any instrument handy which created a messy towel with tiny slivers of broken glass.

After serving what seemed like forever at the back table, we got to be the first scrub nurse and stand beside the surgeon and hand him instruments and sutures. The externs (student doctors) also scrubbed. It was usually their duty to hold the retractors and all the surgeons had another surgeon who was their assistant. Some doctors had a reputation for being impatient with the nurses and were said to throw instruments at them if they handed them something wrong. Actually, they seldom threw anything, but they could get very sarcastic, so we all tried very diligently not to upset them.

Anesthesia, which is an important part of surgery, was not taught to student nurses. Each of the clinics had an MD who gave their anesthesia but they were not Anesthesiologists. Dr. Frietag, the urologist was the Pember-Nuzum anesthetist and Dr. Richard Farnsworth, an internist, did the honors for Dr. Munn.

They used different gases which were stored in steel cylinders and dispensed through a system of valves, hoses and a rubber face mask. Cyclopropane was just coming into use and was considered to be on the cutting edge of practice. Its popularity was due to the fact that the patient was not as nauseated when they woke up. The draw back was that it was explosive.

Dr. Hartman's office nurse, Mena Arneson, gave anesthesia for him and Dr. Kelly. She gave drip ether. This was probably the simplest and safest anatomically, although it too is volatile. The ether came in half pint cans with a soft metal seal. To administer it, an ordinary safety pin was inserted in this seal and this allowed the liquid ether to drip down the pin onto a very simple mask composed of the shaped screen covered with gauze. The ether vaporized quickly and the patient breathed the vapor. It is not a pleasant odor and many patients would resist it.

When the days surgery cases were finished, the work had just begun. There was always a hamper full of linen from the laundry to be folded. Each piece had a special way to be folded so that when it was put into use as a table cover, as a drape on the patient or as a gown for the surgeon, it practically fell in place. Then the drums were packed in a special order to be sterilized.

In 1940 there were very few ready sterilized, packaged supplies. As student nurses we learned how to cut crinoline and rub in plaster of paris to make cast material. We soaked the tips of applicator sticks in sugar water and rolled them in cotton to make applicators. We made cotton balls from bats of cotton and cut and folded bolts of gauze for sponges.

There were always instruments to be washed. This was done piece by piece by hand with a brush. Instruments were boiled, both before and after use.

The used gloves were washed by hand, turned by tucking the fingers in and flipping the tops to force air into the hand and turn the fingers. After they were washed and rinsed, they were hung on a rack to dry, again requiring a turn. Once dry, each glove was tested for holes by filling them with air and distending each finger one at a time while holding it close to the face to feel any escaping air. The faulty gloves then had to be patched with little patches cut from unusable gloves. Then the gloves were powdered, paired, and put into cloth folders to be sterilized. Good unpatched gloves were for the surgeons. The patched ones were for the scrub nurses. All new gloves were size seven and a half or eight, bought to fit the surgeons. These were much too large for most nurses so we always had to work with floppy gloves.

After the case, the needles had to be examined and if any burrs or hooks were present they were removed with a special stone.

In surgery we even made and sterilized IV and Sub-Q solutions. The glass jars were filled from the still in the basement behind the elevator and a counted number of salt pills were added to make normal saline. If glucose was ordered the cover was removed and sterile 50% glucose was added to make the desired strength. Even the administration sets were assembled in surgery. These were reused until the rubber became too sticky and weak after which the glass and the shut off clamps were put on new tubing. Needles were returned to surgery where we ran a stylus wire through them and rinsed them with ether. If there was a hook, it was removed and the needle was sharpened on the stone before it went into a glass tube which was corked with cotton to be sterilized. Intravenous was not used as frequently as it is today which was a good thing as there was too much room for error and contamination with our home made equipment. The hypodermoclysis was the fluid method of choice which we all hated. It absorbed slowly and was always uncomfortable for the patient.

I believe it was a great mistake when the operating room experience was taken out of the student nursing programs. It was in surgery where aseptic technique was ingrained into our every thought and deed. You can believe that we developed a wholesome respect for supply economy as we were the ones who made the supplies. But the most important lessons learned from surgery was the chance to see the inside of the human body and appreciate all the things that could go wrong. We could appreciate the patients' pain after seeing how much handling of delicate tissue was involved, and we learned why some surgeons' patients always recovered faster than others.

For all the hard work, our three months in the operating room were a welcome interlude from the daily grind of emptying bed pans, giving baths and serving trays. We always had the company of each other and there was a certain amount of banter when the nun was not around.

When we become seniors, we added a black velvet stripe vertically on each end of the brim of our cap. I also got another very unusual privilege. Grandma Newton was still living in her big house in Milton Junction and had a live in housekeeper. She had never learned to drive and she missed being able to get around. My folks arranged with the nuns for me to keep Grandpa's Chrysler behind the laundry at the hospital and I could use it on my day off to visit my grandmother. This was unheard of but I soon learned why they choose to be so open to the idea. They didn't have any car and they were not allowed to drive. The deal was that in exchange for the privilege, I was to drive them wherever they wanted to go. It sure beat emptying bed pans.

That year the Wisconsin Nurses Association was meeting in Fond du Lac and I drove several of the nuns to the convention. They stayed in the St. Agnes Convent and I was given a room for the three days in the nurses home.

The Fond du Lac yacht club had planned an outing for the nurses on Lake Winnebago. I drove the nuns to the club but I sure didn't want to be on the same boat with them. There was one boat where there was a great deal of laughing and the owner was dressed up like an admiral from a comic opera. That was the boat I wanted to be on.

After we were away from the dock I discovered that this was a real party outfit. The Admiral broke out a bottle of whiskey and passed out drinks all around. I didn't want to be stuffy and I wanted to feel all grown up so I took mine and started to drink it. It was awful. I didn't really know what to do with it. I was afraid that the one or two swallows would render me incapable of driving the nuns back from the outing and I was sure that they would smell it on my breath. One of the more mature nurses solved my problem. She had figured it out and simply poured my drink in the lake when the Admiral wasn't looking. If I smelled of booze, the nun never mentioned it and I was steady as a rock driving them back to the convent.

Late in the junior year and early in the senior year we were sent to hospitals in Milwaukee to receive special training in pediatrics and psychiatry as there were not enough of these type of cases to give adequate, comprehensive training in these fields. This was called affiliation. There were other student nurses from most of the eastern part of the state. It was as much a part of the learning experience to meet and live with them as the program itself. My first assignment was at Milwaukee Children's Hospital, on Wisconsin Ave., not far from Marquette University. My room mate was Margaret McLean. She had finished her three months at county and gave me a lot of help learning how to get around Milwaukee and what to expect when I would later go to County. We were the only Mercy nurses there for that three month period.

At Children's, every patient was treated as though they were contagious. All the cribs and bassinets were separated by glass partitions. At the entrance to each cubicle was a cloth gown turned wrong side out and hung in such a manner that a nurse or doctor could don it without touching the outside which was the part that touched the patient, linens and furniture. Before removing this gown we were required to wash our hands and then remove the gown by putting our now clean fingers under the cuff. The gown was then put back on the hook in position for the next time it was to be used. Again the hands were washed and the water turned off with the paper towel. The faucet handle was treated as dirty.

It was winter when I was there and one of our most common conditions was the croup, called laryngotracheobroncitis. A tracheotomy tray was kept in the front office and it was not unusual for the interns to do a trach as the patient came through the door.

63

As student nurses we got a lot of experience taking care of tracheotomy patients.

We were not assigned to surgery but often saw the OR staff when they brought patients back. It was here that I first saw the surgical green linens. It looked so much fresher than the brown stained linen we were used to.

It was also here that I first became aware of negroes. Oh yes, I knew there were people with black skin and kinky hair but I had never really seen or met any of them. About half of the patients at Milwaukee Children's were black. Christmas is always an exciting time around a children's hospital. Santa Claus came and everyone enjoyed the reactions of some of the kids. Cleophus Gibson was a charming little black boy that we had all gotten attached to. When he first saw Santa Claus he started to scream in terror. The good Santa did not force the issue and went on to other children. When we asked Cleophus why he had been so frightened he said it was because Santa had 'cureacrome' all over his face. It took a lot of explaining that the red face was because Santa had to be out in the cold. Of course, Cleo was closer to right than we were.

It was while I was at Children's that I really became aware of the war. It had been going on for two years and we knew about it but it seemed far away. We were not allowed radios in our rooms and we seldom had time or money to go to the movies where newsreels were routinely shown. None of us received a newspaper. Also we were so caught up in the tasks of the day that war was far from our thoughts. However, one of the instructors left Children's to join what was referred to as the Massachusetts Unit. This was an army general hospital being formed to go to England to help the British who were suffering from German bombing. Going to England had always been one of my fantasies and I think I knew that this was what I wanted to do.

The next stop was The Hospital for Mental Diseases at Milwaukee County Hospital which was in Wauwautosa, west of Milwaukee. This was an enormous hospital and had a huge nurses home. The affiliates occupied one complete floor. I had a single room but four other Mercy classmates who had been there for six weeks had a room which they shared.

If Children's had seemed different from Mercy, HMD was a whole new world. We didn't give baths or serve trays. Our duties were varied to say the least. We were supposed to talk to the patients and learn about their condition. The men patients especially enjoyed the student nurses when we joined them playing cards or checkers. Some seemed totally normal, others were so far out they could be frightening. There were six units. Three for men and three for women. Patients were assigned to the unit according to their level of severity. All the windows had bars to prevent patients from escaping and the doors were always locked. Every student had a key, which was stored in a big cabinet, and it had to be turned in at the end of each shift.

The Hospital for Mental Diseases (HMD) was separate from the Milwaukee County general hospital and was about a mile down the hill from the nurses home. Of course we walked down and back every day. They were very strict about everyone being in the building and in bed on time. They were also strict about nurses wandering around the grounds by themselves at night. This meant that when the evening shift was completed, we always went as a group back up the hill.

One of the duties of the evening shift was to roll cigarettes out of Bull Durham tobacco for the use of the patients who could not afford commercial cigarettes. Because smoking was not allowed at the nurses home, the smokers always wanted to stop in a dark area behind some lilac bushes where we couldn't be seen from the top. Naturally, if a non-smoker went on ahead, she would be very unpopular because the matron at the home would know the group was tardy. There was a smoking room at Children's but I couldn't afford cigarettes so never used it. Now I was in a situation where not smoking was definitely a deviation and the cigarettes were so easy to hook. However, Bull Durham is not a mild tobacco. I think I did more pretending than smoking.

We also did a block of time in the various treatment areas. Hydrotherapy was one area. Here they had about a dozen deep bath tubs where patients who were severely agitated would be brought and confined in a tub of warm water in a hammock with a canvas cover. Only their head was out. It was amazing how quickly this subdued the most violent patients. There were some very strong women, called attendants, who were experts at wrestling unruly patients into the tubs. Our duties consisted of monitoring the temperature of the water and not letting it get too cold.

We could also help take patients out of the tub and return them to their ward. Another method of subduing unruly patients was called the pack. Screaming, tormented women would be brought into the pack room and a long narrow sheet, which were always ready in a tub of ice water, would be wound around their body in such a way that no skin areas would touch. Quickly they became quiet. Most would go to sleep. Some times I though that some would fake an episode in order to go to hydro, because the tub was relaxing as were the packs. With the advent of tranquilizers such as thorazine, these forms of treatment have thankfully become obsolete.

Shock treatment was another assignment. Insulin shock was popular. The patient would be given an excessive dose of regular insulin and allowed to go into shock. Each student was assigned to monitor one patient. When the specified period was up, a stomach tube was passed and orange juice was introduced to reverse the shock. It was certainly a graphic way to become familiar and learn to recognize insulin shock.

Metrozole was another barbaric treatment. Here a resident doctor would inject an IV dose of metrozole which would induce an instant and violent convulsion. It was so violent that every joint had to be held to prevent injury. I always tried to get a knee because there I could use my weight in a downward thrust. I don't know how effective these treatments were but they too have been replaced with other protocols.

It was while I was at County that I came home for the funeral of my Grandmother Newton. I had loved her dearly, but knew that at 83 she was at last free from the arthritis that had tormented her for so long. I had never known her without a cane. She was at our house on the farm where my mother took care of her. My Grandma Richmond was also bed ridden and terminal. Aunt Cora had taken a leave of absence from her job at the Rock County Asylum to take care of her. She lived until September. About the last thing she did was have my dad buy me a camera for my graduation.

Back in Janesville, we were now assigned living space in the 'penthouse'. This was two bedrooms with four beds each on the fourth floor of the nurses home. There was a bathroom in the middle. The nice part about this was that sister didn't like to climb all the way up there to check on us, so if we maintained reasonable conduct we had a little more freedom.

Our special training complete, full energy was now directed toward preparing for state boards. To be a registered nurse, we were required to pass examinations in many different areas. We had review books of questions and answers that we studied together in groups, in preparation for the climax of our three years of training.

The actual test was taken at the capitol building in Madison. It took three days. Most of us stayed at a hotel except the girls whose homes were in Madison. My room mate for the three days was Phyllis Newman. There were fifteen separate tests, six the first day, 5 the second day and 4 on the third day. I was most apprehensive about chemistry but passed. We sat in the legislative chambers. I sat in the senate. The capitol was fairly new at the time and was very attractive. We had to wait several weeks before we received our grades and be allowed to wear our pins which were the symbol of the Registered Nurse.

Our graduation ceremony was held on the back lawn of the nurses' home and was a solemn occasion. We had new white uniforms, entirely different from our student uniform, and we wore the black stripe on our cap horizontally which denoted a graduate Mercy Nurse. We also wore our Mercy pin for the first time, but couldn't wear it again until we had been notified that we had passed state boards. Our diplomas were on parchment in a blue suede cover and were very elegant. All the families were on hand to celebrate with us. For many, it was as much their success as it was ours. Most of them had made a sacrifice to allow us this opportunity for an advanced education.

It was time to leave the nurses' home to make room for the new class. Many of us had time to make up before we could keep our diploma. Mary Jane Uphoff and I had the most time, about six weeks apiece, because we had missed time for our operations. We found an apartment on the second floor of an older home about a block from the hospital which we rented. Calhoun, Cheplac, Newman, I think Procknow and maybe Veling also had time to make up. Uppie and I took the bed while anyone else who needed a place to stay could sleep on the couch, the floor or anywhere they could find. We were at the apartment when I had my 21st birthday. Sister Cor Marie sent over a bottle of wine for us to celebrate. I was the youngest member of the class.

Life as a student nurse was not all work. We managed to get in some good times too. Every year we had a Christmas party in the big living room. I always volunteered to clean up afterward and could salvage enough wrapping paper to wrap any Christmas presents that I had been able to procure. I remember at one party while everyone was doing party things, I happened to look in the fireplace which had no fire and there was Kekut, dressed up like Santa Claus, curled up in a ball waiting for her cue. She must have been extremely uncomfortable. One year, Kekut and I played a duet, she on the violin and I on the trumpet.

Across the street, in the next block there was an ice cream store called the Swiss Maid. We were not allowed off campus in our uniform, nor were we supposed to be out and about before 3 PM. However, some of the students had become hooked on cigarettes and would take off their caps and put on a coat and duck over to the Swiss Maid for a quick smoke and a soda. I never did because I was too stingy to buy the soda.

I also remember one occasion where our class produced a play. I played the part of a college boy. I think I may have stolen the show because I had a pipe. Because it was a play, I actually smoked it to everyone's delight because smoking was not allowed in the nurses home. Since I didn't really know how to smoke I had to constantly keep lighting the damn thing, just like real pipe smokers.

We even had a dance once. It was supposed to be a barn dance and we had bales of hay sitting around. Some of the students had dates but the nuns had insisted that we invite our parents which certainly made the whole affair rather subdued. A nurse in the class ahead of us named Violet Polyach had a date and they did the jitterbug. This was the first time I had seen that dance.

Peg Johns lived about a mile or so from the hospital and she would ask us to her place quite often. This was always a treat as her mother made the best brownies. One time there was a Ford Trimotor airplane at the airport which was on Milton Ave. and US 14 just around the corner from their house. They were selling rides for a dollar a head. Peg's dad took some of us over and bought us a ride. That was my first time in the air. He was production manager at the Parker Pen. When we graduated, he gave each one of us a Parker pen and pencil set with our names on it.

Fifty some years have passed since I first went to Mercy Hospital to become a nurse. I realize that we were privileged to be in the first wave of a new era of health care. It was during our first year that the sulfa drugs were introduced. The first one was called sulfanilamide. This drug was the first specific for the dreaded streptococcus. One of our classmates developed peritonitis and everyone thought she was going to die but she was given sulfanilamide and recovered. It certainly had some adverse effects. For one thing the patients would become extremely nauseated. We learned to crush the tablets and mix the powder with applesauce. This seemed to work.

Bernice Newton, RN, September, 1941.

Another dreaded disease bit the dirt that year. Sulfapyridine was specific for pneumonia. We were taught how to make mustard plasters and use pneumonia jackets with camphorated oil. These treatments quickly became obsolete because of sulfapyridine.

The use of cold to treat cancer was in its infancy. Dr. Koch had a patient with a colostomy and an inoperable colorectal cancer. He did an experiment which the students did not take part in but which was of great interest. The patient was given paraldihyde through a naso-gastric tube which put him to sleep. Then his body temperature was reduced to about 90 degrees f. with ice bags and remained there for four days before being warmed up and he was allowed to awaken. The man eventually died, but the tumor had been reduced to about half the original size.

Promine was another experimental drug. Dr. Koch had stock in Park-Davis and was using it for just about everything. Other, better drugs have been developed but promine is still the drug of choice for Hanson's Disease (leprosy).

Nursing practice has changed along with medicine but what we learned from 1938 to 1941 made a wonderful foundation for everything that has developed since then.

5

PFC to Shavetail

Eli:

We spent the first week on active duty bivouacked in the armory at Pikesville getting ready to move to Ft. Meade. My first assignment was walking guard at the officers' club. It was bitter cold and the old World War overcoats might have looked warm but they were like funnels to bring the cold air straight up a man's legs to his body. Guard duty was two hours. After about the first hour, an old master sergeant, who was the regular army advisor to our battalion, came out to see how I was doing.

He was wise in the ways of the service. He told me that I needed a cup of hot coffee. I was not really a coffee drinker and I knew that it was against army regulations to drink anything while walking my post. I told him no, but he brought me a cup anyway. I didn't really want to drink it, but the temperature was seven below and it sure smelled good. Down it went. It was mighty strong coffee and it did the trick because it sure warmed me up from my toes to my ears. That was because he had slipped a shot of bourbon from the club into it.

When we moved out to the post, the weather had warmed up and it was raining. The place was one big sea of mud. There was a nice black top street in front of our barracks but there was no way for water to run from the high side of the road to the low side, so it ran over the street and was ankle deep all around our barracks and getting deeper. It was apparent that something had to be done and done soon.

What was needed, was a way for the water to cross the street. The battalion commander was shown the problem and even though it meant closing the street, which he didn't have the authority to do, he ordered us to break up the black top and dig a ditch that would send all that water away from our barracks. We made some barriers to close the street and started digging on the low side.

Every outfit has at least one man who is stronger than anyone else. Our man was a stevedore named Gephardt from the Baltimore docks and he could really make the dirt fly. When we were about three feet from the edge of the high side, we all got out of the ditch and just poked our shovels at the dirt from the top. It only took two or three pokes and the water broke through with a mighty gush and finished the job. In the next couple days the post engineers installed a culvert and reopened the street.

They were still building a fire station across the street. Since I had been working on these very buildings less than a month before, I was right at home. I told the Lieutenant about the cost plus thing and suggested that we could probably get some lumber to fix up our area from across the street. Since I knew the men over there, I was sent out to arrange for the lumber. No paper work was involved and we just took what we needed with their permission. We got enough 2×6 planks to make walkways three or four planks wide for our whole area. That sure helped control the mud problem.

There were no shelves in the supply room and some fire station 1×12 boards were being put to use to build some. I stuck my head in the door to watch how they were doing it and couldn't believe how messed up they seemed to be. The idea was to cut notches in the board to let it fit between the studs. No one seemed to be able to get it right. I asked if I could try. I took the board and held it up to the wall and just made some marks with my thumb nail and then cut the notches. It fit perfectly.

When the Lieutenant saw this he informed me that I was now the battery carpenter. There was no such position as a battery carpenter in the table of organization but there was a slot for an artillery mechanic so that became my assignment. I was probably more qualified for that job than I was as a carpenter anyway. It was even a promotion.

Our original pay was $21 a month. By the time we went on active duty I was a PFC (private first class) and now I was something called a First and Third Specialist, Artillery Mechanic. I had one chevron and four rockers. My pay was increased to $52 a month. That is a couple dollars more than a corporal but less than a sergeant.

We were still using the old World War French 75s when we went on active duty. That spring we went to Indiantown Gap in Pennsylvania for service practice. The first week end up there, three of us decided to climb the mountain near the motor pool. We discussed the possibility of what we would do if we ran into a bear. We all agreed that we would just not move and stare him down. Sure enough, when we got close to the top of the mountain, a bear appeared right in front of us. Without further ado, we all three turned around and ran as fast as we could down the mountain, bouncing off trees and rocks, back to the motor pool.

We had a big discussion at the motor pool on why we didn't stare him down and which one of us ran first. Truth was, we all ran at once. We never saw the bear again but every time we told the story that bear got bigger and bigger. He was probably as scared of us as we were of him.

One day, when we got a fire mission, one of our rounds landed right at the foot of the observation tower where the general and his staff were observing. Something was awfully wrong. We were ordered to cease fire and find out what the problem was. I was the one who discovered that the sight had not been seated completely so the piece had not been properly lined up and was way off target.

Right there, I was promoted to corporal, who is the man in charge of the sight. In those days enlisted promotions could be made and rank could be taken away, right on the spot. It was a reduction in pay but that put me in the chain of command and in line for promotion through the ranks.

It was at Fort Meade that we were issued the first 105 mm Howitzers. This was the latest thing in weaponry and we got some of the first to be issued to the troops. As the artillery mechanics, Porter and I studied it from end to end and top to bottom. The field manual had not arrived but using just good sense, we took it apart and put it back together. We knew every bolt and screw, what they did and where they went.

In a few weeks, post ordinance set up an artillery section using mainly drafted men. Porter and I spent about two weeks teaching them everything about the 105 that we knew. In a couple months we had to take our gun over to ordinance for repair. They needed to take the tube off and level the gun to remove the locking ring. I stopped them because they needed 2 × 4 as a block in the equilibrator spring to lock it so that when the center of gravity was changed, the tube wouldn't fall out on the ground.

The tech sergeant, who we had just trained, said we didn't need the block. His Lt. backed him up and told him to just push the tube back. After the tube was about a foot and a half out of battery (in position to fire), it went flying back and the breach landed on the ground, just like I told them it would.

To lose a 105 during our intensive training was considered inexcusable by all the brass and it had to be reported all the way to Washington. The locking threads were badly stripped and the whole tube had to go back to the factory. During the course of its absences, there were many reams of paper of investigation as to the cause, but at least our unit was clean.

One weekend, Charlie and Woodcock were in Baltimore and, with Witt and Bernie, they came down to visit me. Charlie and Woodcock had on their navy uniforms. Witt and Stillings were still civilians. We had just gotten one of the very first jeeps (short for General Purpose Vehicle-GP). I took them all for a ride around the field behind the motor pool where there were lots of hills and bumps to show it off. This bunch of sailors sure enjoyed the jeep ride.

I asked them to come on down to the mess hall. Because most of the outfit would be in Baltimore, there would be plenty of food. Sunday night was always cold cut night. When I asked the mess sergeant if my buddies from the navy could eat with us, he said sure, and even offered to fix them all steaks. They refused because that variety of cold cuts looked so good. I took the steak.

Charlie had joined the navy to be near the kitchen but had discovered that the consolidated mess at Norfolk Naval Training Center was very stingy with the food. He said that when he went through the chow line he would stick his tray way over the steam table so that he wouldn't be seen as he grabbed an extra potato and stuck it in his pocket.

His first sea duty was delivering old American destroyers to the British. He was later assigned to the Cruiser, Quincy. Many of the Baltimore navy reserve guys were on the Quincey. They were on patrol in the Pacific. Charlie didn't like the Quincey. He was convinced that the officers didn't know what they were doing, so he decided to get transferred. He could be ornery, but knew just how far he could go before he got into real trouble. He got his transfer. Woodcock stayed with the ship. He was in the number one gun turret when a Japanese torpedo hit the number one powder magazine and the ship was lost.

Corporal Eli Fishpaw. December 2, 1941. The bandage was not a fake. He had been hit with an ax on maneuvers. The weapon is a 45 caliber Tommy gun.

Charlie moved up the ranks of Petty Officer fast. He could read a manual and know everything in it in a matter of a few hours. He could pass the tests, used by the navy for promotions, with ease. Before long he was a Chief Bosun's mate. That is like a first sergeant in the army. He could have been an officer but his low opinion of officers prevented him from even trying.

In the fall of 1941 we went on Carolina maneuvers. Maneuvers are always rough. They were two months of intensive field training and we would be glad when they were over. Our year was soon to be up and we would go back to being civilians on the first of February.

While we were on the way back to Ft. Meade on a Sunday morning early in December, people were out on the streets, all through North Carolina and past Richmond, VA, waving to us. Some even threw candy and fruit into the trucks. In several towns the high school band was out on the corner playing patriotic songs. I remarked to the guys in back of the truck that the way people were acting you would think there was a real war going on instead of just maneuvers.

When we pitched camp for the night at Camp AP Hill, north of Richmond, we discovered that we indeed had a real war. The Japanese had bombed Pearl Harbor in Hawaii. No one had to tell us that we were not going to be discharged. It was December 7.

The Christmas of 1941, the MPs from Ft. Meade were given leaves and my section was assigned to MP duty in the communities around the camp. That included Glenn Burnie, Odenton, Laurel and Jessup where the state police barracks were located. I was in charge of the detail and moved around the communities in a vehicle called a carryall which had seating capacity for 8 or 10 men. I would use it to post one man in each place where soldiers would be gathered. It was also a paddy wagon to pick up and transport any soldiers that misbehaved or were too drunk to make it back to camp on their own. It was another bitter cold winter.

I got a call that there was going to be a fight at a tavern in Odenton, the nearest town to the camp. My MP had called the guard on the gate, which was where I was located when not making rounds or answering calls. I told him that I would meet him outside the joint. When I got there, he told me that there were two groups of GIs in the tavern that were about to get in a fight. The manager had told the waitresses to pick up all the bottles but that both sides refused to let them have them.

I told him to stay outside for a while until my driver, who was a real big guy, and I went in to assess the situation. We sat down at the lunch counter and ordered coffee. The whole place quieted down when they saw us two big guys with our night sticks and our 45s and the big MP arm band. After a few minutes, I instructed the manager to tell his girls to pick up the bottles and not one man refused.

After that, men started to drift out and before long the place was almost empty. There was one man who had passed out and had his head on the table. We woke him up and checked his ID. I told him to get into the carryall and we took him back to his company. He was sure that we were going to arrest him or at least turn him over to his first sergeant. But when we got to his barracks, I let him out in front and told him to get a shower and go to bed. He thanked us as we drove off.

One night the 44th Infantry Division was moving from Fort Dix, New Jersey to Camp A.P. Hill in Virginia, just south of the Maryland border. They were to bivouac at Meade. They were so fouled up that the convoys were getting lost. We called the highway patrol to guide them to Ft. Meade and we spent a lot of time chasing them down and heading them to the bivouac area. By 2300 we managed to get them fairly well into the proper place. There were rumors the next day that some of them had frozen to death but this was denied by their officers.

Not long after that, our 29th Infantry Division was also moved to Camp A.P. Hill which is near Fredricksburg, VA. There was nothing there but pine trees and open fields. Historically it is known as the location where President Lincoln's assassin, John Wilkes Booth was captured. We set up a tent camp with pyramidal tents for the troops and canvas kitchen flies, which were canvas roofs but no sides, where the field stoves were. We ate out of our mess kits, standing up or any place we could find to sit down. The officers had a mess tent where there were one or two field tables and some chairs. In my mind, I would look at those officers and wished that I could have a table where I could sit down and have an orderly to serve me. About this time they introduced a separate tent for the Sergeants, but no orderly.

It was so close to Baltimore that everyone who could get a pass, went home on the week ends. The senior NCOs (Non Commissioned Officers), who were not on duty, would usually be gone week ends and didn't get back to camp until just before reveille on Monday morning.

One week end, the men in my section thought it would be funny to take all the NCOs duffel bags and hang them off the center pole of their tent. Come Monday morning, about 10 minutes before reveille, they arrived to find their bags, with the clothing they needed to wear, hanging from the center pole of their pyramidal. One guy shinnied up the tent to the top of the pole and threw the bags down as the bugle sounded. Of course, they were all late for formation.

All the men in the battery thought it was very funny. Since they were my section, the BC (battery commander) held me responsible. The punishment was that my gun section would dig all latrines for the battery for 30 days on their own time.

Matty Mathis of Cumberland, Maryland found a field manual on latrines. One section was on how to create a fly proof latrine. We all hated flies in the latrines, which were a big problem. We decided we would build ours just like the manual described. It involved soaking burlap in old crankcase oil and allowing it to hang into the pit about 2 or 3 feet. The latrine itself had a box, with five holes cut in it, that set over the pit. Sure enough, the set up worked as the saturated burlap kept the flies away.

When the division medic came around to inspect latrines he was so impressed by the lack of flies that he went back to division headquarters and told them all about it. The division commander thought that was a great idea and ordered every company commander and first sergeant in the division to come see our fly proof latrine and ordered that all latrines would be built just like it.

Because I was the corporal, I had the detail of explaining how it worked to every one that came around. Many of them were very unhappy about such a lowly assignment as looking at a latrine and my popularity wasn't too great. Even the rest of 'A' battery resented the attention we were getting.

Our battery commander was so pleased with the positive publicity that he took us off the detail. That was the last latrine we had to dig. Our section was in the dog house with the rest of the men, but we came out smelling more like roses than latrines. This proved the old theory, that when you get a job you don't like, doing it the very best you can will be the fastest way to get rid of it. That worked on everything, including KP when I had to scrub the pots and pans or peel potatoes.

The draft was in full swing and we has received several draftees from Cumberland, MD. These were real outdoor types and they knew everything about nature. One man had a raccoon that he had caught. He kept it on a leash behind the tent. We had a large cardboard box, probably toilet paper had come in it, and it was in our tent next to the center pole.

Capt. Raymond McIntosh III was the battery commander. One day he and the 1st Sgt. were inspecting tents while we were in the gun park training. He asked what was in the box. The 1st. Sgt. didn't know except he thought it was personal possessions of the men. The captain decided to look in and when he did, he saw a dozen or so harmless black snakes that our men had capture. He took one look and went screaming out of the tent. From that day on he was known as 'Screamin' Reemin'. It seems he had a real fear of snakes. The name followed him through out his military career. He even got to be a full Colonel, maybe higher.

It was spring of 1942 when the whole battalion traveled by convoy to Camp Edwards near Cape Cod, in Massachusetts for the Field Artillery battalion tests. We set up base camp with pup tents, a pyramidal tent for supplies and the kitchen fly. The latrine fly was just a canvas screen around the box.

We practiced two or three weeks getting ready for the tests. About the fourth week we started taking the tests. Just before battalion test #3, which is mainly survey and night firing, we were treated to a special supper of New England clams. After we were back on the guns, firing the test in the dark, more than half of the men got sicker than dogs. Right away, we suspected the clams and were sure that we had food poisoning.

We started sending men to the hospital at Camp Edwards. The soldiers that were left continued to fire even though they were sick. I was corporal of the first section and my number one man, was Agnew. We were both sick. The section was down to about four men. When we got fire missions we would get up, set off the data, load the shell and fire on command. Then we would run over to the side and throw up.

The battery commander sent orders down for Agnew and me to go to the hospital but we stayed and fired until the next to last problem before we left. Instead of going to the hospital we went back to the base camp where the only thing standing was the supply tent. We tried to get some sleep in the tent, hoping we would feel better by morning. There were at least ten other guys including, the Lt. exec, who had the same idea. In those days, usually when you went to the hospital, you were kept there three or four days. We were due to go back to A.P. Hill in a couple days and didn't want to miss going home.

The next morning when the battery rolled in, Agnew and I went to the motor park, feeling much better. We told the two men who hadn't been sick to get some sleep and we would clean up the truck and the gun. As we were cleaning the gun, the battery commander, Captain Bottom came along. The first thing he said was, "How come you are not in the hospital?" I told him my story, which was no excuse for disobeying his order.

Because we had had a few hours sleep, I had given the rest of the section off. He said, "You are now Sergeant Fishpaw." I knew then that we must have passed the test.

Later we learned that the battalion supply sergeant had gotten a special deal on a barrel of clams. In those days, it was standard procedure for the battalion mess section to buy food on the local market. But this time he got a bad deal. Someone stuck him with a barrel of contaminated clams that made the whole battalion sick, right in the middle of our battalion tests. I will always have mixed feelings about Cape Cod and I never touch clams.

There was a shortage of junior officers, so some of the sergeants were designated as Third Lieutenants. We didn't get a bar but we wore a red, white and blue braid on our left shoulder and were given the same responsibilities and were supposed to be saluted, the same as the officers.

My first night as OD (officer of the day), what could have been a serious incident occurred. I had just posted the guard when I heard a gunshot. When I investigated, I discovered that one of the men had been cleaning one of the old Enfield rifles that had accidentally discharged. The round had gone through a whole row of pyramidal tents. I went to each one of the tents to check for injuries but nobody had been hit. It had landed harmlessly in the ground after making holes in four or five tents. My heart was in my mouth before I looked in each one of those tents. I was sure relieved that nobody was hurt.

Once, everyone in the battery got crabs (pubic lice). To find out where they came from, the medics had an inspection where everyone fell in, wearing only their rain coat, and shoes. When they got to one of the new draftees, he was covered from head to foot with the crabs. They were even in his eyebrows.

Those are miserable things to have. The medic gave us all blue ointment but it didn't help much. We had to shave off all our body hair to get rid of them. When it grew back in, it itched like hell. The guy's sergeant and his corporal gave him a shower with GI soap and scrub brushes. He was nice and clean but he went AWOL (absent without leave). Nobody even tried to get him back.

It was just before graduation at West Point and a bunch of cadets were assigned to the battery as Third Lieutenants for two weeks of field training in the artillery before graduation. Several of them started asking me a lot of questions about the guns. I hadn't wanted to go home as long as I might still have the lice so I gave them a couple days of informal classes in cannoneers' hop, firing battery and maintenance of the howitzers and vehicles. By the end of the weekend, they were all thoroughly indoctrinated in the subjects. They were so impressed, that Monday morning they went to the Captain and the Colonel and told them that they thought I should go to OCS (Officers' Candidate School).

I was called in, first by the First Sergeant and then by the Battery Commander who told me to apply for OCS. I didn't want to do it for two reasons; I was only going to be in the army for the war and I didn't feel that I was qualified. A day later, the battalion commander saw me on the street and wanted to know why I hadn't sent in my application for OCS. I said that I didn't think I could make it. He said that he didn't think so either, but gave me a direct order, just to get these guys off his back.

I applied for Ordinance, Field Artillery and Infantry. I was accepted for Field Artillery first and assigned to Ft. Sill, OK.

At Fort Sill we lived in tar paper huts, twelve men to a hut. There were twelve weeks in the course and each week, each one of us would be assigned to each of the twelve duties of a junior officer.

I did fairly well in the classes that dealt with the firing battery. Sometimes, I knew the subject better than the instructor. One day, the subject was the recoil mechanism. Since I had been an artillery mechanic when the 29th had received the first 105 mm Howitzers, I knew the subject well.

The instructor thought I was not paying attention. He said, "Mr. Fishpaw, you look like you are bored. Maybe you should come up and teach the class." Everyone thought that I was on the way back to the 29th. I took the pointer and said, "First we need to go back to the history of the hydropneumatic, recoil system. It was designed by the French in 1898 and adopted by the US in World War I. Our Army used the French 75 mm. artillery during that war."

"The first fifteen 105 mm howitzers made by the US in 1941 did not have the respirator that the Lt. was describing. They found that after firing one or two rounds, the gun would not return completely to battery so would not fire. That is why this respirator was designed." I then proceeded to teach the class the entire working of the recoil mechanism. I got a high grade on that class.

The cadets who had caused me to be at OCS were now 2nd. Lieutenants. They were at Ft. Sill for their special training in artillery which was the same as the candidates were receiving but without the harassment. When they found out I was in camp, they started coming to my hut to get help with their assignments. This caused big problems because 2nd. Lieutenants were something like God walking through and really disrupted the study time with every one yelling, "ATTENTION". I was told to meet these guys somewhere else.

I was doing OK until we got to gunnery. This involved a lot of higher mathematics that I was not familiar with and I was completely lost. I went to my Tac (tactical) Officer and asked him if I could drop out. I didn't want to be thrown out. He looked at my record and said that I was leading the class so far and that I should stay. He suggested that I give it two weeks and if I still didn't understand the material they would throw me out. I stayed and sure enough it all came together before the two weeks were up.

Most of my gigs were when I was hut commander. When we would fall in (line up in formation) we were in platoons in alphabetical order and were never in front of our own hut. Just about everyone smoked cigarettes back then. We would all be standing around where we were to fall in. At the last minute, everyone would put out their cigarette, tear the paper off the butt, dump the tobacco on the ground and roll the paper in a little ball and drop it where ever he was. This is called policing the butts and is standard military practice everywhere except OCS. The tac officers knew this and would look in the gravel in front of the huts and gig the hut commander for poor police of the area because of the little balls of cigarette paper and tobacco.

Another time I got gigged because one of my shirts in the middle of the stack had a button unbuttoned. I think the tac officer had unbuttoned it when I wasn't looking, just to catch me.

I had seldom taken a pass to go into town. It was very close to graduation and I had ordered my pinks and greens (dress uniform) from Hart, Shaffner, Marx in Lawton. The family back in Baltimore had taken up a collection so that I would have enough money to pay for them. I needed to get a pass to pick them up, but had too many gigs. I really needed to get into town, so I went anyway. I was lucky and didn't get caught.

I thought I had really had it on the day before graduation. I saluted a lieutenant with my pipe in my mouth. As soon as I did it I realized what I had done and yanked it out and put it in my pocket. He yelled "Mister" and bawled me out but didn't report me.

We wore our khaki shirts for graduation. The tailor shop would cut off the shirt tail to make the epaulets needed for an officers shirt. That was why new second lieutenants were called shavetails.

Dick Fuchs' (another OCS student from 'A' Battery) mother and sister drove out to Oklahoma for graduation and to pick us up. As soon as graduation was over, we headed for Baltimore. We drove all night, we were so glad to get out of Fort Sill. The speed limit during the war was 35 miles per hour. Dick and I took turns driving. One time, when I was driving, the highway patrol pulled 15 or 20 cars off the highway for speeding.

As they came down the line, they recognized us as soldiers because of our uniform. They wanted to know why we were going so fast. I told him we had just gotten out of OCS and were headed home to Baltimore and that we were putting as many miles, as fast as we could, between us and Ft. Sill. He said, "You guys are excused", and away we went. All I had was a military driver's license which is not recognized for use with civilian cars in many states. I was glad he had not asked to see my license.

Officer Candidates were called 90 day wonders. Even though it was not supposed to be a compliment, it was a good name for us, as we wondered how the hell we ever got through it.

A brand new shavetail, 2nd Lt. Eli Fishpaw with brother Charlie and Bernie Stillings. 1942.

~ 6 ~

Big City Country Girl

Bernice:

Some of the classmates were given jobs at Mercy Hospital after graduation but I was not one of them. Some of the girls went to Madison and acquired jobs at Wisconsin General which was the hospital affiliated with the University of Wisconsin. I was not one of them. I didn't really know where I was going or what I was going to do. I knew for sure that I did not want to do private duty.

My Grandmother Newton had been a school teacher and both my mother and father had been teachers. The family had been somewhat disappointed when I had rejected the idea of teaching. However, I had discovered while I was a student that I really felt good when I could help the newer students as they struggled to learn many of the lessons that I had struggled with. I was also a great admirer of Olga Kekut, our nursing arts instructor. She had graduated from Mercy in Chicago from a four year program which included a BS degree from Saint Francis Xavior's, a women's college run by the Sister of Mercy in Chicago.

We had received a diploma and had passed state boards which gave us the title of Registered Nurse, but we did not have a degree which was required to teach. I felt that I wanted a degree and that I would find fulfillment as a nursing arts instructor. After conferring with Sister Cor Marie, she suggested that I could attend St. Xavior's and earn the necessary credits while working as a staff nurse at Mercy Hospital in Chicago. This sounded like a good idea so that was the route that I decided to follow. I was hired, sight unseen, upon her recommendation.

I therefore took the train to Chicago where a job was waiting for me. My first project was to enroll at St. Xavior's which was on Cottage Grove Ave., about ten blocks from the hospital which was at 26th and Prairie. The back door of the hospital was on Cottage Grove which was a diagonal street running south east. There was a street car route that went right past the college. I only signed on for one class. It was genetics. In this class we would breed fruit flies with different colored eyes. By mating a red eyed male with a brown eyed female we were supposed to get seven red eyed off-springs to one brown eyed offspring. This was to prove that brown eyes was a recessive characteristic. If a large enough number were so tested, we would prove Mendall's law of inheritance. The fruit flies were anesthetized and we inspected them with a magnifying glass to determine their sex and eye characteristics.

Meanwhile, I was assigned to second floor west. I requested and was given the job of night nurse to help me be available to attend class and study during the day. I received $70. a month plus a shared room in the nurses' home and a meal ticket for 90 meals a month in the hospital cafeteria. How nice it was to have money of my own. We were paid every two weeks with cash in a brown envelope. Sister Delores was the nun in charge of RNs.

The nurses' home was large and had the same rules as we had known in Janesville except that now, I was an RN and didn't have to observe any of them. Chicago was a big city and the door was always locked but to gain entrance all we had to do was ring the bell and identify ourselves to the woman in charge of the home. A buzzer would sound and the lock would open. If we came in after nine PM when there was no one on duty at the desk, we needed to go to the emergency room at the hospital and the security man would accompany us with the key through a labyrinth of tunnels to the nurses' home.

Mercy was the oldest hospital in Chicago. The original hospital had been destroyed in the Chicago fire. The original stone cross from that building was still there. The facility had grown by increments over the years. There were at least three major build-ings. Each faced a different street with a grass compound in the center. I think it was supposed to be a 500 bed facility.

Second floor west was in the newest building and was made up of private rooms and private suites except at the end of the south side where there was an eight bed ward for men. The suites were expensive by the standard of the day, from $35 to $50 a day and were mainly occupied by the elite catholics of Chicago and the physician of the staff or their family's. The very rich would have around the clock private duty nurses, some even had two at a time.

Needless to say, these rooms were often vacant. Therefore, the priests of the diocese, including the Bishop, would have these rooms when they were hospitalized. The mother house of the Mercy order was in Chicago so when the lowliest of nuns become ill she would be cared for on two west so as not to take up space that was more likely to be rented by the paying public. Private rooms without an attached bath cost as much as $15 a day.

One of the pioneer surgeons at the turn of the century had been John B. Murphy who had practiced at Mercy. He was legendary for his stature in intestinal surgery. He was not living when I went there to work but his spirit stalked the halls through the history, often repeated by the nuns who had known him. There was an amphitheater deep in the bowels of the hospital where JB had done surgery while eager students observed from the tiered seats above. Nobody did surgery there any more and it was mostly just a curiosity. During the presidential campaign in 1912 the former president, Theodore Roosevelt, was running as the progressive party candidate. When he was shot in Milwaukee, John B. had spirited him out of that city and taken him to Mercy in Chicago where he recovered. He had been a patient in suite 212.

Now that I was on my own and making money, I missed my classmates and I was very homesick. Chicago was so different from Janesville. I tried to adjust by going to the movies and shopping in the big department stores such as Marshall Fields or Carson, Pierre, Scott. Some of the downtown movie houses had large stages and the big named bands would be included in the double features. Ozzie Nelson played there with the female vocalist, Harriet Hilliard. They always had a news reel with the movie but the war seen on a movie screen did not have much impact. It was just another movie. I learned to ride the street cars and the elevated. I even took the train out to Des Plaines where Betty Yuengst, the RN from surgery in Janesville, was living but it was a different world and we had nothing in common.

I became captivated with the railroad stations, especially the Union Station and would go down there just to watch the trains come in and to get a hot fudge sundae. They made the best sundaes in Chicago. My mother's friend Marie Applegate who had been superintendent of schools in Rock County was living in

Evanston and working on advance studies at Northwestern University. She had me come out to her apartment and took me to dinner at Robin Hood's barn.

The biggest surprise though was Sister Prudentia. She had been the superintendent of the hospital in Janesville and had seemed very stern to all the students. She never smiled and any time we saw her coming we would duck into the nearest doorway so we didn't have to face her. Sometimes there would be three or four students in the little closets where the hoppers for disposing of the vilest of waste were located.

She had left Janesville sometime before we graduated and to my surprise was the receptionist at the front door of Mercy in Chicago. She was Sister Information. She directed visitors to the patients' room and fielded incoming questions from a large desk equipped with two telephone. This was before they had developed buttons on telephones. She would answer an incoming call on one phone and then use the second phone to get the answer from whatever department was concerned. It says something for the atmosphere of the times because she actually was not very busy and I think was probably bored. I would go over to her office and we would sit and chat for hours about everything imaginable and we became good friends.

She thought that I should go to church and took the Chicago phone book and found a Methodist Church which she thought was in the right location for me. I went a few times but no one ever spoke to me or even noticed that I was there.

I thought that maybe I should get out of the nurses' home which was primarily for students. In its prime years, the hospital had been surrounded by fine homes. The area was known as the Gold Coast. During World War One the city had been inundated with a lower element of society who had taken over the area and it had become a slum. The rich home owners had moved to the suburbs but the hospital had remained in its original location. Some people had even given their fine homes to the church to use for nurses' residences. One of these was at 2716 South Prairie Ave., about a block from the hospital. About ten or twelve RNs lived there. When I learned of a vacancy I moved in and became more adjusted as I was now living with people who were more my peers.

It was an interesting building. There was a grand staircase in the front and also a staircase in the back for the servants. Every room had a pull cord which would cause a number to be displayed in the kitchen for the maid to answer the call. We would pull the cord but of course no maid would answer our calls. In the parlor was a player piano with rolls of paper with punched rectangular holes. We could put a roll in place and then pump the pedals and the piano would play as long as we kept pumping. The plumbing was unique to the 1890s. The toilet tank was near the ceiling and the flush was accomplished by gravity.

The house next door had been taken over by the federal government and was being used as a school for women to learn the profession of housekeepers for the affluent. It was part of the PWA (Public Works Administration). It was said that Eleanor Roosevelt had personally sponsored the project and often visited there, but I never actually saw her.

There were other young nurses from out of the city with whom I made friends. The Chicago White Sox used Mercy for their injured players and many times there would be tickets for us. I enjoyed Comiskey Park. We even tried Wrigley Field because I had been a big Cub fan when I was a kid but I didn't get the same feeling as we experienced at Comiskey. Of course, the seats we had to pay for weren't as good either.

There were two big dance pavilions in Chicago. One was the Aragon Ball Room on the north side the other was the Trianon Ball Room on the south side. The big named bands such as Billy Jurgens and Lawrence Welk played there. Anyone could go and often a group of nurses would go on a Saturday night. Unless you had a date, which I did not, we would dance with each other. I was still as awkward as ever and never really learned how to dance.

Work was OK. I remember one night a man in the ward had lit a cigarette and the match had caught the paper in the waste basket on fire. The quickest thing I could find to douse the fire was a urinal with urine in it. The fire was put out quickly but the smoke and odor was very unpleasant. All the elevators were the open kind with the stair steps winding around them. The ward was next to the elevator shaft which acted like a chimney that carried the smoke and the odor all over the south wing of the building. I had a lot of explaining to do and had to make out a red bordered report.

The pride and joy of the nuns was the million volt x-ray. It was in a separate building. At the time there were only two of these in the country and people would come from all over to be treated. Most of them were quite wealthy and usually terminal. Many of them were patients on two west. Some would have trouble breathing and would be in oxygen tents. One lady could not lay down and we had the oxygen tent rigged over the chair.

There were times when the smog would be so bad in Chicago that only the patients in the oxygen tents escaped the discomfort but there was no way that any of us would have wanted to change places.

Chicago's famous gangsters would sometimes be hospitalized at Mercy. I think that many of them were Catholic. We could always tell when there was a gangster in the house because there would be body guards sitting around all the entrances and there would be two in the hall outside the room. They always had a retinue of special RNs to take care of them. The nuns spent a great deal of energy praying for their soul.

There was a brothel in one of the mansions across the street. It was a good location because chauffeured limousines were often parked outside the hospital and would never arouse suspicion. It was raided one time and provided some extra entertainment for the country girl from Wisconsin looking out the window and seeing rich men running with their clothing in their arms and jumping into the limousines.

One Sunday morning in December, I was very tired so went straight home from work and went directly to bed. I slept clear through the day until it was time to go to work at 11 PM. I took report without incident and had hardly settled down when I got a bell. It was a young girl who was frantic. She wanted to know if the Japanese were coming. I could hear a siren outside but there were always sirens in Chicago. I reassured her that there were no Japanese but her sense of urgency prompted me to call the supervisor and find out what was going on. She told me that the Japanese had bombed Pearl Harbor. I had to ask where Pearl Harbor was.

Suddenly the eyes of the fruit fly became very unimportant. However, I had paid my money to study genetics and I was going to get my moneys worth so I completed the course and took my credit but did not sign up for any more college. I knew I was going to try to go in the army, but I felt that I was not really prepared professionally.

Mercy offered a four months post graduate course in Operating Room Procedure. They provided a shared room, meals and $10 a month stipend.

We had six RNs in the class. There were two nurses from the coal country around Johnstown, PA and a young nurse from South Carolina. Two young Mercy nuns completed the group.

Just as it had been in training, it was a way of getting inexpensive help for the hospital. However they did have classes and we become much more involved in the theory and technique of asepsis. Since the same nun ran Chicago's surgery as had run the one in Janesville, there wasn't a whole lot of difference in the actual practice. What was different and exciting was the much greater exposure to a wider variety of conditions and procedures.

We were assigned call duty with a staff RN for surgery coming up during the night, which was frequent. On the night we were on call we stayed in a semiprivate room in the hospital just a floor below the OR.

I was particularly fascinated with brain surgery and wrote a long and detailed letter to my mother. She was so captivated by it that she took it to her club meeting to read to her friends. It was so graphic that some of them got nauseated and had to leave the room.

Besides the Operating Room course, a course in anesthesia for nurses was also offered and they had two students learning this new specialty.

Some research was also being done at Mercy. One surgeon was using cotton thread for internal sutures and ligatures. He had done animal research at Loyola University. We took ordinary cotton thread from the notions counter, cut it in thirty inch lengths and wound it on little pieces of cardboard which were wrapped and sterilized. We used size 40, 50 and 60. It was much easier to handle than catgut and did not react with the tissues as catgut often did. It would eventually be absorb but that took years. However there was minimal tissue reaction. On the negative side, it was hard to see once it touched blood.

Another surgeon, a urologist, was experimenting with something called ribbon gut. It was rather thin and about a quarter inch wide. He used this for prolapsed kidneys by lacing it around the outside of the kidney, using it to suspend the kidney in the normal position. After 20 some years had passed and I was again involved in surgery, cotton suture was a standard and came in prepared packages and nobody had ever even heard of ribbon gut.

Mary Jane Uphoff had enrolled in a post graduate course in obstetrics at Michael Reese Hospital which was less than three blocks from Mercy. I seldom visited her because the territory between the two hospitals was a no mans land of crime.

When we completed our course we were given a certificate and a small silver pin of the Mercy emblem.

The procedure for nurses to join the Army Nurse Corp was by way of the Red Cross Nursing Service. I joined the Red Cross in June but deferred active duty until September when I had completed my OR course.

~ 7 ~

Come See My Howitzers

Eli:

My first assignment as a commissioned officer was at Fort Jackson, South Carolina with the new 100th Infantry Division that had not yet been activated. We were billeted in new, tar paper huts. The cadre, which was the nucleus of the new division came from the 76th Infantry Division at Fort Meade. These were Regular Army and National Guard officers and the men around which the new division would be built. It would be filled out with reserve officers, newly commissioned lieutenant from the different officers candidate schools, and with enlisted recruits and draftees.

We were in camp, getting acquainted with our duties and each other for a couple months before the division was formally activated with a ceremony and a parade on December 15, 1942.

My first hut mate was Bob Richards. He was a tall man with a great sense of humor. He was actually a professional actor, a skill which we utilized to the fullest. We started right off being assigned different classes to teach. The first class that I was assigned was military courtesy. I recruited Richards and as I would describe the origin of different customs, he would act them out, such as the hand salute started when the knights shaded their eyes as they passed in review so that they could see the queen, who would stand with her back to the sun.

I even got to do a little acting myself. The class was to be a simulated court martial. I was the prisoner and was supposed to have stolen a watch. I was dressed as a private and they even had an armed guard. I actually felt guilty as hell. After all the evidence had been presented, I was given an option of making a sworn statement or an unsworn statement.

I made an unsworn statement. I said that the watch had been planted in my foot locker because this other guy had a grudge against me. I said that he was a trouble maker and that I was always trying to get him to quiet down. I told how everybody knew the lock on my foot locker was broken, so that would be easy to do. I said my dad had a jewelry store in Baltimore and I could have any watch I wanted. I almost cried, really. I felt so upset that someone would do that to me.

Well, the court was so moved that they acquitted me. The Colonel in charge of the class was really ticked off. That wasn't the way the case was to have ended but, it was a great example of how military justice was not supposed to work.

Bernice:

My first assignment was at the Station Hospital, Fort Wayne in Detroit, Michigan. Fort Wayne was an enormous ordinance depot, but the military garrison was very small. Most of the workers were civilians. The hospital was almost Rinky Dink, with only six nurses and two doctors. It was more of a dispensary with beds. Our patients came from several small detachments stationed around Detroit.

I was given the rank of 2nd Lieutenant in the Army Nurse Corp. At that time this was known as relative rank. We had all the privileges of commissioned officers except the pay. I received $75. a month, which was $5.00 more than I was making at Mercy Hospital in Chicago. I was also issued all my uniforms instead of getting a uniform allowance, as the men did. I did received a mess allowance.

The duty uniform was a white dress with a white organdy cap. We were issued six blue seersucker fatigue dresses, but I never wore mine. There was also a very nice, warm, navy blue sweater. I wore it a great deal with my white dress, as the hospital was not too well heated. A real nice knee length, wool, navy blue cape with a maroon lining completed the duty layout.

The class 'A' uniform for the nurses, to be worn in public when off duty, was navy blue with maroon piping. It was a hold over from the blue uniform of the Union Army, I think. It included a jacket with a built in belt at the waist and a powder blue skirt. We were also issued a navy blue, knee length wool overcoat. It was such a good coat that I wore mine for years after

I was out of the army. Our cap was a navy blue overseas cap with the black and gold piping that designated an officer.

A second Lieutenant rated a gold bar. This was worn on the overseas cap and on the shoulders of the class 'A' uniform. We also wore the Second Lieutenant's gold bar on the right tip of the collar of our duty uniform with the insignia of the nurse corp on the left. It was the caduceus, that signified the medical corp, with an 'N' on it for the Nurse Corp. The caduceus was also worn on both lapels of the class 'A' uniform under the US. They were not issued, but we were permitted to purchase and wear a navy blue off duty dress, and also a light tan, two piece uniform. I had both of these as they were much more attractive than the government issue, civil war blues. The first time I wore my class 'A' uniform off the post, I was so excited to be wearing the uniform of my country that I completely forgot to attach my brass.

I had selected Fort Wayne in Detroit because it had specified on the orders that the assignment was for operating room. What a surprise when I got there and discovered that there was only one surgeon and nobody to do anesthesia. The O.R. was primitive and the only surgery we did was an occasional hernia or appendix. The surgeon would give a spinal anesthesia.

The post itself was an historic relic of the war of 1812, complete with star shaped ramparts, an empty moat, cannons pointed at Canada and all the trappings. The enlisted men's barrack was the ancient brick buildings of the Fort.

The nurses' quarters was the last house on a row of about 20 officers' quarters. There were about six nurses for the station hospital. A major, who was a professor of nursing at Wayne University, was organizing a general hospital unit. The most military thing about the place was the bugle calls. They were played on the PA system for every occasion. It was kinda neat to lay in bed and hear tattoo followed by taps every night. Every good army person gets goose bumps when everything on the post stops for retreat in the evening, when the flag is lowered.

In front of officers' row was a beautiful parade grounds, but with only a minimum garrison of soldiers, they never had any parades or reviews. Beyond the parade grounds were acres and acres of motor pools, filled with every conceivable type of military vehicle, from jeeps and command cars to heavy tank, all made in the Detroit area.

Social life was non-existent. Once I was outfitted in my class 'A' Navy Blue uniform, I was able to ride the street cars and buses without paying a fare. I also got theater tickets free or at a discount and really enjoyed that. I learned to bowl and I took swimming lessons at the YWCA.

I put in for a transfer for overseas duty soon after I arrived. My orders finally arrived in March and I was sent to Fort Jackson, SC for training in the 222nd Station Hospital. When I boarded the train, I found myself among about fifteen army Nurses from Custer General Hospital of Battle Creek, also bound for the same unit.

We had a short lay over in Washington, DC. I will never forget my first look at our nation's capitol, gleaming white in the morning sun, as I saw it from the front of Union Station. I think I was even more impressed by the street cars that did not have any overhead wires but ran from a third rail buried in the street between the regular rails.

Eli:

I was assigned to battery 'B' of the 374th Field Artillery. This was a battery of four 105 mm Howitzer that I knew so well. The battalion commander was Lt. Colonel Claude Liles from Texas. Other Second Lieutenants from our OCS class in 'B' Battery were Piper, Synan, McGuire, and Hensen. The First Sergeant was Lester Frew, who came with the cadre from the 76 Division.

We had an assortment of enlisted men assigned to us. Many of them were from out of the way places where they had never learned to read or write. It was one of the duties of the sergeants to read their mail to them and to write their letters. Some of the sergeants, who had been teachers, decided it would be a lot less trouble just to teach these men to do their own reading and writing, so they organized a class. It wasn't long before the illiterates not only became literate but many of them became outstanding soldiers and were promoted to positions of responsibility and leadership.

When we received our first assignments in the battery, I was the battery executive officer. The battery executive officer's primary duties were to oversee the firing battery and was also second in command. Most of the troops are directly under him. I was assisted by Staff Sergeant Meyer Segal, the chief of firing battery. His knowledge of artillery was as good as mine, and a pleasant and unexpected asset to me. I never expected to get someone with his experience and expertise in the job.

In a few weeks we were assigned our first recruits. Most were straight from being civilians. There was one who had a couple years experience as an infantry soldier in the regular army in Panama. His name was Burgess and we used him to help train the recruits in the manual of arms and how to use a rifle. He was also good at teaching dismounted drill.

One day, during a class describing how to distinguish the ranks of various army people, I noticed that he was very nervous and couldn't sit still. I gave the class a ten minute break so I could talk to him. I asked him what his problem was. His answer surprised me. He said, "Lieutenant, I just feel like breaking all the windows in this place." Then he told me that he had been using drugs while he was in Panama. He had been two or three weeks without them and it was driving him crazy.

I turned the class over to Sergeant Segal and took my best rifleman to the medics across the street. I briefed the medics on the problem and they said they would take care of him. After I went back to the class, he got tired of waiting and hit the corporal in the face, raising a knot the size of a silver dollar. Then he started tearing up the aid station, throwing furniture and causing total confusion. Five or six medics held him down while they sent to the hospital for a straight jacket.

He was put in a padded room for his own protection. They were going to rehabilitate him. They did whatever medics do for such cases and after thirty days he was returned to duty for a trial period.

In a few days, as I was the OD (officer of the day), I was standing in the guard house at about 0200 when a private on guard called for the Corporal of the Guard. We went to see what the problem was. Burgess was walking up the road, moaning and groaning. There must have been thirty dogs following him and they were all howling and barking. We took him back to the guard house and called the medics.

For no reason at all, he hit the corporal right smack in the middle of the forehead, just as he had the medic. He said he intended to bust up the guard house. The guards subdued him until the corpsmen from the hospital arrived with the straight jacket. He was removed under guard to the hospital.

This was the hardest thing for me. This man was the best soldier I had, but the drugs wouldn't let him go. In a week or two he was returned to the battery for separation from the service. He was given a general discharge for a condition that existed prior to entering the service. We were given a voucher for $64. for a new suit, and clothing. We bought him a railroad ticket back to his home. Before he left, he said good bye to everyone and thanked us all for being his friends. That was the last we ever heard of him.

Richards was quite a joker. One day, after I had been up all night as the OD, I had gone to the hut and was in bed. He thought it would be a great joke to throw a tear gas grenade into the hut. When it landed, I tried to pick it up and throw it back out, but it started sputtering so I dropped it and ran out to someone elses hut. The joke was on Richards. He had gassed his own hut. When he realized what he had done, he had to borrow a gas mask and go in to open the windows and let the gas out.

Gas was in all our clothes and bedding. It was weeks before we could get dressed without crying. Not long after that, Richards and I were going into town to buy a dog. We took a cab and the driver said he couldn't understand it because all of a sudden tears were rolling down his face. We knew why but we didn't tell him.

Another time, a new officer was assigned to our hut. Lt. Wicham, one of our friends, was the Division Artillery Commander's aide and he told us that the new man was a relative of some big shot. Neither Richards nor I wanted this guy in our hut. We thought he might get us in trouble with higher headquarters, so we staged a fight between us. Richards was good at that. We scuffled for a while and landed right on his cot as Richards came down with his bayonet, not six inches from the man's head. He decided we were both nuts and left in a hurry. He found a new hut to sleep in and even got a transfer out of the battalion.

New units and new styles of warfare were being developed and everyone was being encouraged to volunteer for different things. The idea of soldiers jumping into combat with parachutes was one of these activities. That sounded interesting to me so I volunteered for the first airborne artillery to be formed and signed up Richards too. Neither one of us were selected. Later I volunteered both of us for another overseas assignment. He got selected but the Divarty Commander, General Buechler, pulled me off the list. He didn't want me to go because I was doing a good job teaching firing battery for his Division Artillery officers' school.

The trigger pull on our new carbines was too strong. I knew that if we filed the sear pin just a little, they would be much easier to fire. That would make them more accurate. I filed off all the sear pins in the battery. The next time we went out to fire, I was in charge of the pit where the targets were being pulled. When 'B' battery started their slow fire practice, instead of single shots, it sounded like machine gun fire. I knew without being told that I had filed off too much.

Everyone in the battalion knew what had happened except the 'Ole Man'. However, he sent word to relieve me in the pit and get me to fix the problem. It took some time, but by re-working the sear pins, the artillery mechanic and I got them all so that they fired with just the right amount of pull. When we finished our test, we had the best scores in the battalion. The 'Ole Man' was bragging to the staff, "I knew he could do it."

After duty hours, some of the officers said they had dates with some nurses and wanted me to go with them. I had been playing touch football and had aggravated an old football injury to my right knee. I told them OK, but it would have to be someone who wouldn't expect me to dance. I didn't mention that I never had learned to dance. We met the nurses at the day room of their quarters and went to the officers' club of the number two hospital.

The nurse, who was my date, was named Bernice. She was a farm girl from Wisconsin. She seemed to be very interesting in hearing about the artillery. We spent the entire evening talking about the howitzers and how they operate. By the time we parted that night I had asked her to come down to the gun park to see my howitzers. I never expected her to do that, but the next afternoon I looked up and here was a nurse about a half a block away, headed for the gun park.

There was no way that I was going to allow this woman in my gun park. I ordered the battery to 'March Order' the guns (close them up) and take the rest of the day off. I jumped in my jeep and rode over to where she was. It was the same nurse from the night before. I asked her if she wanted a ride in a jeep. When she accepted, somehow the jeep went in the direction of the hospital. The men had figured out the situation and were much slower than usual closing up, even with the prospects of some extra time off. They were hanging around to see what would happen.

Bernice:

At Fort Jackson we were really turned into Army Officers. The first six weeks we were taught how to drill. When a group are in formation and doing close order drill, it brings them together better than any other experience I have ever had. We also learned military law, military procedure, and survival.

This included gas mask drill which I hated. We were issued gas masks and taught how to use them. The gas chamber was a squad tent in which tear gas was released. We had to enter before we were allowed to don the mask so that we could experience the gas and appreciate the protection we received from the mask. Some people got sick and threw up, but I held my breath so I didn't have that happen to me.

We also were issued field equipment and learned how to put up pup tents, make bed rolls and prepare meals and clean our mess gear in the field. One little glitch was our fatigue suits which were one piece coveralls and did not have any accommodation for people who sit down to relieve themselves. This presented an interesting problem when using a straddle trench. Fortunately, it was summer time and hot.

It was during the training phase that I met Eli. The 100th Infantry Division was newly activated and training just down the road. One day, word was spread around the quarters that there was a 2nd. Lt. artillery officer who needed a date, but had hurt his knee playing football and was unable to dance. Since I had never learned to dance, this seemed like a good opportunity. When we were introduced, I misunderstood the name. I thought they said Eli Fishball. I really thought someone was putting me on.

Our quarters were across the street from the number two station hospital and we had the privilege of the use of the hospital officers' club. It was air condition, which was not generally available, so it was a good place to spend an evening. Since we were not dancing, and I didn't really care to drink very much, we spent most of the evening talking. What did we talk about? Eli talked about his howitzers. As a kid on the farm I had tagged along with my dad a lot and had learned all about machinery, so I was actually interested. Before the evening was over, he had invited me to come to the gun park and see the howitzers.

I don't think he actually expected me to do that because the next day, when I was walking down the road toward the 374th Field Artillery area where they were training, he saw me coming and quickly gave the order to close up the guns and knock off for the day. He hopped in a jeep and came to where I was. He asked me if I would like a ride in the jeep. Strangely enough, we ended up back at the nurses' quarters.

Eli:

Col. Liles used to give me a hard time. Every time my name was on the list for promotion to 1st Lieutenant he would pull it off for some silly reason. It got to be a standing joke. He would brag to the staff that Fishpaw did his best work when he was mad. Kramer, the warrant officer, would tell me that Liles would brag that I was the best officer he ever had. I went along with the joke and would pout, just to make him happy. It didn't matter to me. I was getting 1st. Lieutenant pay anyway because of my time in service and I had no intention of staying in the army when the war was over.

Some of the senior officers got a kick out of harassing the shavetails. We got together and decided to form a Second Lieutenants Club to support the guys who were being harassed. They elected me president. Any time there was a problem with the young officers, the Colonel would call me in.

One time, several of the 2nd. Lieutenants had been restricted to the area. It was Saturday night. Since we couldn't leave the area, a bunch of the nurses came over to our little club in our own area. We were having a good party. The Colonel was wondering why all the young officers were not at the post officers' club. Quite naturally, they had preferred to be where the nurses were.

Later in the evening, the old man showed up at our party. He was a party man and got right into the swing of things. He was telling a story about one of the NCOs who had gone home to get married. The man had been given a ten day furlough, but Liles had called him back to duty on the fifth day. The man had to return to camp only a couple hours after the ceremony.

Bernice was there that night. She said, "Colonel, I think that was mean." There was total silence. You could have heard a pin drop. The next morning he pulled my promotion again. He said I talked too much, and I hadn't said a damn word. I think it was as much because I was the leader of the second lieutenants as because of any statements made by my date.

The battalion was shaping up pretty well from the ragtag group of men that we had started with. Due to the intensive physical training, the fat got leaner and the lean got heavier and we all got stronger and better co-ordinated. After the basic training, we had moved on to more advanced section training. Team work and co-operation was essential. After several service practices and small unit maneuvers, we had become a cohesive unit. Morale was excellent. Disciple was paying off as our men had high appreciation for each other. The Esprit de Corp for such a young unit was outstanding.

About this time, our battery commander, Captain Palmer was transferred and Walter Henson, our reconnaissance officer, who was a First Lieutenant, became the BC. He was about 29 and had a large family. I was still the exec. When we took our battery tests, we received an outstanding evaluation. The battalion tests also went well with excellent results which proved the thoroughness of the training. We were ready for the winter maneuvers to be held in Tennessee.

Major Green, the battalion S-3 (operations and training officer) owned a V-12 seven passenger Lincoln. He also had a smaller Pontiac. The Lincoln used an awful lot of gas. Gas was rationed and a family had what was known as an 'A' ticket which allowed the owner to buy three gallons of gas a week. He loved that car and didn't want to take it to a used car lot, so he offered it to any of the officers who wanted it for $45. Richards, Lt. Synan and I each threw in $15 dollars and we had ourselves a real nice car.

We called it the prime mover, which is what we call the trucks that tow the guns. It was supposed to hold seven adults but there were many times that we would pack in as many as twelve officers and nurses to go off post or out to Heiss's Pond for an evening of swimming or partying. When we would be in the field for a week or more, I would leave it with Bernice at the hospital. The nurses would shake down their patients for their ration coupons that they could not use before they expired.

Bernice:

After we had finished our training, the Doctors and the enlisted men of the 222nd went to AP Hill, Virginia and set up a tent hospital but the nurses were left at Fort Jackson and were attached to Station Hospital #2. I worked the operating room some, but all nurses had to take their turn at night duty. One nurse would usually be responsible for six wards. Enlisted medics did most of the work.

About this time, Eli and two of his friends had acquired a big old car. When the men were on field problems during the week, they would leave the car with me. Gasoline was a problem because their 'A' sticker only allowed three gallons a week which didn't go very far in twelve cylinders.

It was too hot in South Carolina during the day to even think of sleeping. I would tell the other night nurses at supper that if they would get some gas coupons from their patients, I would take them out to Heiss's Pond. If a man was in the hospital, he wouldn't be needing gasoline.

Heiss's was designated as a 100th Division Officers' area but if they were out in the field, they wouldn't be using it and it would be a shame to let it go to waste. It was in the piney woods and was spring fed. The water was deep and cool. It was much nicer than Legion Lake that was designated for us and was rain fed, hot and dirty. We could lay around in the shade which was much nicer than trying to sleep in a hot and noisy nurses' quarters.

I was glad that I had learned to swim in Detroit. We would swim out to the raft and go diving. One day, we decided to try skinny dipping. That was even better, so free feeling. What we didn't realize was that the Division CP (command post) was on a hill just above the lake. What a treat that must have been for the men up there with their high powered binoculars.

By the end of the summer, Eli and I, or any way I, had decided we should get married. The division was scheduled to go on maneuvers in December and we were rather in limbo as the 222nd had left A.P. Hill and was heading to the Pacific.

One Saturday in November we drove to Camden in the next county and purchased a marriage license. We could have been married there, but I thought it would be nice to get married by a chaplain. We went back to Columbia, but on the way to the post, we had to pass the University of South Carolina football stadium where there was a game in progress. We decided to wait until the next week and went to the game instead.

We even planned to get a little fancy, invite the 374th officers and the 222nd nurses. I even rented a small apartment off the post.

Eli:

Bernice and I had become good friends. She wanted to get married. I wasn't too sure. We were both obligated to the army. One weekend, we drove to Camden where there was a Justice of the Peace who did weekend marriages. We got the license but Bernice wanted to go back to the post and be married by the Chaplain.

As soon as our intentions became public, everyone wanted to get into the act. The battery were going to form an arch with the howitzers at the entrance to the chapel and elevate the guns as the bride and groom came out. Even the Red Cross offered to decorate the chapel. It didn't happen.

I was in the gun park, giving gun drill when I received word that I had a phone call. It was Bernice calling from her quarters. When I returned the call she told me that they had been alerted for movement and everybody was restricted. She said she had just had four shots and was feeling dizzy. I said, "Don't do a thing, I'll be right there." I had never known her to drink much of anything and I figured four shots would probably kill her.

I jumped in my jeep and motored up the hill to the hospital. When I got there, I went to the day room where she was rolling her bed roll. I had expected her to be passed out. I asked what she was doing, and about the four shots. She said, "I had typhoid and tetanus in the right arm and cholera and diphtheria in the left arm." They thought that they were heading for the Pacific to be with their unit. Instead they went to Camp Forrest near Tullahoma, Tennessee.

A few week ends after they left, we were riding around South Carolina with the prime mover when we were pulled over by the sheriff in Camden. I didn't have any idea of what we had done, but we followed the police car to the station. The sheriff asked us if we wanted to sell our car. It seems that he was looking for a big vehicle to use for his riot squad. No new cars were being made and when he saw ours it was the answer to his problem. He offered me $75 for it. Since I was the only one of the original owners left, I accepted on the spot.

On the eighth of November, the 100th Division followed the nurses to Tennessee for winter maneuvers in the mountains between Nashville and Chattanooga. By December 15th, we were in position, ready to start a major maneuver. It was exactly one year from the date of activation. It was raining continually. Before long the rain turned to ice and sleet.

I was promoted to First Lieutenant just before maneuvers. The new Division Artillery Commander, Brigadier General Murphy had lost patience with Col. Liles and gave him an order to either promote me or transfer me. Then he told the 'Ole Man' that he would not approve a transfer. My friend, Piper was Murphy's aide and kept me informed.

~ 8 ~

The Bride Wore Olive Drab

Eli:

There were eight problems to the maneuver. Each problem lasted a week. We maneuvered against other divisions. On some problems we were the enemy and on others we were the friendly forces. After each problem, many of the officers and men would be allowed to go to near by cities for the week end. Most went to Nashville but I headed for Tullahoma. The weather was bad. We would do anything for a shower and a warm bed.

One week end, I was the battalion duty officer and the senior officer with the battalion, which made me the battalion commander. All the married officers and the ranking bachelors had gone to Nashville. While they were gone, we got orders to move to a new position about 200 miles away, to be ready to start the next maneuver at 0700, Monday morning.

We had no idea where to find the rest of the officers. If there was a list of where they were staying, we couldn't find it. Each battery had a 2nd. Lt. in charge. Before we left the position on Sunday, I left a detail from Headquarters battery and one man from each of the other batteries with maps of our new location and some ten in one rations for food. They were to stay at the old position until all the officers and NCOs had showed up and were briefed. Most of the officers had their own military vehicle in Nashville, which was legal, so they had transportation to the new position.

When we were moving the battalion to the new position, it started to rain which turned to sleet, which froze on the road. I was in the lead with the big Dodge command car, which spun out and ended up in the ditch. I stood beside the road and signaled all the vehicles to keep moving and not stop as they would have ended up in the ditch with me.

Everyone of them made the trip safely. They had all been trained on how to drive on ice and seeing the leader in the ditch alerted them to icy condition of the road ahead. When the whole battalion was past, we put the dodge in four wheel drive and were back on the road. I was happy that a 1st. Lt. and five shavetails, with some outstanding NCOs, had moved two hundred miles, under extreme conditions without any accidents. I thought we performed better without the senior officers.

On Monday morning the battalion was in position to jump off at 0700 and were well into the problem when the colonel showed up. We had already advanced about thirty miles. He greeted me with, "Do you know what the hell is going on?" It was obvious that he was very upset. After the first shock, he was really pleased that his junior officers and NCOs had moved the outfit without any mishaps. To my knowledge, no one at higher headquarters even knew that the weekenders were not with the outfit when the problem started.

Bernice:

Camp Forrest was located near the city of Tullahoma in Tennessee about half way between Nashville and Chattanooga. In 1943 it was an all wood barrack post, so familiar at all the military posts that had mushroomed with the coming of the war. The thirty 222nd Station Hospital nurses were assigned here to become the nucleus of the 216th General Hospital which was being organized. Our Chief Nurse, Hazel Dill, was to be the Chief Nurse of the new unit.

We were billetted in the nurses quarters of the Camp Forrest Station Hospital and would be assigned to duty in their hospital. Most of the nurses were in one of the separated barracks some distance from the hospital. Because I was to work in the Operating Room, I was in Building #1 which was closest to the hospital. All the female O.R. staff were in this building including the nurse anesthetists.

The barracks, although they were very plain, were quite comfortable. Most of the rooms included two metal, flat spring, army cots with about a two inch mattress. The walls were unfinished wall board with the two by four studs open. This made convenient shelves for things such as tooth brushes and soap boxes.

There was a rod for hanging up clothing. We each had a foot locker which is a small trunk that sat at the foot of the bed where we kept our underwear and personal belongings.

Each building had a latrine, but unlike enlisted barracks, the toilets were in cubicles, as were the showers, although the wash basins were in the open. There was steam heat which was nice because it was November when we arrived and it was getting rather cold. There was also a day room with floor lamps and a couple metal framed leather sofas and some comfortable chairs where we were allowed to have male guests.

Being an O.R. nurse had an advantage because each of us had a single room and also could have a chair and a small table. The down side of the arrangement was that I sort of lost contact with the rest of the women I had gotten used to during our training period at Fort Jackson. But I quickly became friends with the people that lived in our building. I met one of these ladies, Polly Rothermel, years later when we moved to DeLand. By then we both had different names. She knew mine, but I had never heard her new name.

The primary function of the Station Hospital was to support the medical needs of the troops on Tennessee Winter Maneuvers which were going on all over north central Tennessee from Tulla-homa to Nashville. We had all sorts of cases from pneumonia and contagious diseases to severe trauma and burns.

Burns were especially common because the troops in the field were fed from mobile field kitchens which were large canvas enclosed trucks where the food was prepared on gasoline stoves, often while the truck was moving on the road. It was not unusual for containers of hot food to splash with the bumps or to fall off and burn the cook. This area of the state is mountainous and snow and ice were a common occurrence. We had a great many road accidents as a result of this lethal combinations.

Of course there were also the usual surgical requirements of any group of people as large as four army divisions; appendecto-mies, hernia repairs or gall bladder and stomach problems. The war had arrived right on the heels of what we called the depression. Because many of the soldiers came into the army with existing sur-gical problems they had not been able to afford to have fixed, we also did a good business in corrective surgery to make them ready for the rigors of combat for which they were being prepared.

Another activity, that most people would not realize but which was very important, was a thriving obstetric business.

Many of the soldiers' wives and families had come to Tullahoma to be with their husbands on week ends between problems and many of them came due during this period. At that time OB was not included at Station Hospitals but was done on a space available basis. Deliveries were done in the operating room. It made for a lively night activity to say the least. It also had one big advantage over most of the smaller hospitals of the time, in that if we had a surgical emergency during a delivery, there wasn't the usual hassle of moving a patient from one department to another.

Camp Forrest was our first encounter with the enemy. On a military post it is very common to hear groups of soldiers marching along the streets with their sergeants calling cadence. The first day we were there I heard the same chant but instead of the familiar hut, hope, hip, four it was ein, zwie, dry, fere. These were German prisoners of war. They were billeted in a compound on the post and were being marched to their various work details. They too had medical and surgical needs which were treated at a small infirmary inside the compound. There was a small operating room and frequently a surgical team would go over there to do surgery.

I was certain that it was my destiny to marry Eli when the 100th Division was assigned to Tennessee maneuvers shortly after our arrival at Camp Forest. This made it possible for us to see each other on week ends between problems. Eli has always insisted that he came to see me just to get a warm hotel room but it might be pointed out that there were probably better rooms and more activities directed toward military men in Nashville than in Tullahoma.

In December he finally agreed that we would get married but since the court houses were closed during the week ends that I would have to get the license. He had the battalion surgeon give him a letter certifying that he was free of venereal disease while I had the appropriate tests done on post and took the bus to Manchester which was the county seat to get a marriage license. However, the clerk would not issue this important document because she could not accept the letter.

It was well known that Georgia did not require a certificate of health to issue the license. Rossville, GA was a small town just over the state line from Chattanooga. It had a reputation as a weekend wedding site. With this knowledge, we decided to get married on the weekend of January 1, 1944 which was on a Saturday.

Usually on Sundays and holidays everyone was given a half day off. However the people who took call on New Year's eve could have the entire next day off so I volunteered to take call that night. It turned out to be an unusually busy night. The weather was at its worst with a sleet storm on the mountains. That night we had five jeep accidents, most of them serious, where the officer was killed and the driver critically injured. This was very stressful for me as I believed that Eli was on the road traveling to Tullahoma.

Just to add to the mix we had several deliveries that night too, so that I had absolutely no sleep. The place was still jumping at 7 A.M. and I had not heard from my fiance. I continued to work until about 10 A.M. when I gave up and went to the barracks and went to bed thinking that I had been stood up.

Eli:

Bernice was going to be free for the whole New Year's week end and it looked like a good time for us to get married. On Friday night before New Years Eve, I put in for an overnight pass. Col. Lyles denied it. On Saturday, Major Coleman, the battalion exec, stopped by early in the morning and told me to go ahead and take the pass. It was probably a good thing that I had stayed in camp because Bernice told me that she had been up all night taking care of accident victims from the icy roads.

Bernice:

About noon I was awakened and told that I had a phone call. It was Eli. He had not been able to leave the battalion the night before because all the other officers had departed and he was the only one left. I caught the shuttle bus into town and met him at the King Hotel. He had done all the driving he wanted for that day so we took a bus to Chattanooga.

It was a very busy travel day in Tennessee and the bus company had put on an extra bus which was old and tired. The driver was the mechanic, which I found somewhat reassuring. We left Tullahoma about 1300 heading into the storm and the slippery mountains which got higher and the roads narrower as we approached Chattanooga. The ancient bus would shift into low and when I thought it was about to stall it would go into a lower gear and chug on. It seemed to have an endless number of low gears.

After getting to the top of each tortuous mountain going down became much more exciting as the bus preferred to do it sideways. It was 2000 by the time we arrived in Chattanooga. With no idea of what to do next, but we found a taxi driver with an old fashioned wooden leg who knew all about Rossville and "Marryin' Sam". He drove us out to that city's hall and he accompanied us upstairs where the mayor/J.P. was doing a thriving business. When it was our turn, our driver served as our witness. The ceremony, though short, was not totally meaning-less as "His Honor" read and we repeated the traditional vows. Eli tipped the driver $20.

Years later while Eli was at the auto races at Daytona Beach, the fan sitting next to him was from Rossville and said Mayor Bowman was interested in how many of his war time marriages had worked out. He gave us his name and we sent him a letter.

Returning to Chattanooga, we had had enough of mountain roads, so decided to take the train back to Tullahoma. We had a steak dinner with some wine in a restaurant at the station, before catching the north bound around midnight. It was packed. The coach we boarded was jam packed with sailors returning to Great Lakes near Chicago from furloughs. There were sleeping sailors in the seats, sleeping sailors on the floor, even sleeping sailors in the overhead racks. The only place we could find to stand was on the platform between the cars. Even this was crowded. There must have been six or seven people who had just come aboard. One was an older lady. There was a duffle bag sit-ting on the floor so she was given the bag to sit on.

While I was cold and tired after having worked 27 hours and all the stress of the day, I was too numb to care. Only when we went through a tunnel did we notice the inconvenience as we were showered with coal smoke.

Back in Tullahoma, we retired to the King Hotel where Eli had rented a room on the fourth floor. As we were climbing up the stairs, I met an officer who was dating one of the nurses from the 222nd. I was embarrassed to be caught in a sleazy hotel at four in the morning and wasted no time announcing that we were married and even flashed our new certificate to prove it.

But there were chores to be done before we could fall into the bed. It was raining and the ceiling was dripping water. This was corrected when we found an old fashioned chamber pot in the closet. There was a real bath room too and Eli wanted to wash his underwear and fatigues, which we did in the bath tub, stomping them primitive style with our feet and then spreading them on the radiator to dry.

Eli:

Next morning, when we went to breakfast at the King hotel, I discovered that my jeep was missing. We were right across the street from the MP station. I called the MPs and reported that my jeep had been stolen. They told me that happened every night and very seldom any of them were recovered. It seems there was a thriving black market selling jeeps to farmers who used them for tractors. I got dressed and went to look for it myself. When I stepped out of the hotel door, I looked to the right and saw a jeep parked in front of the theater a half a mile away with a wire bracket that sure looked like mine.

It was pouring rain and even though I was wearing my pinks and greens, I kept my eye on it until I reached it. It was my jeep alright. I was so glad to see it that I jumped into it before I realized that it was full of water. When I turned the switch on, it popped right off. There were drain holes that were clogged up with mud. I took a stick and opened the holes as I thanked my lucky stars that somebody had just taken it for a joy ride. I had no idea how I was going to explain to the Colonel how I lost a jeep. Between the two of us we didn't have the $787 dollars it would cost to replace it.

Bernice:

I did not need to report for duty until noon and Eli had to be back at the battery for duty the next morning. The captain we had met on the stairs had a civilian car which he wanted to leave with his girl friend at the camp and he also needed a ride back to the maneuver. That worked out well. I drove his car back to the post and Eli gave him a lift back to the field. This was the first time I had driven a car with the gear shift on the steering column.

The maneuvers were finished in the middle of January and the 100th Division moved to Fort Bragg near Fayetteville, NC. As soon as they had settled in, Eli was able to take leave and so was I, so it was time to meet each other's families.

First we went to Wisconsin. My mother had been pretty disappointed about not being able to throw me a big wedding or even be present when I was married but she made up for it by having a big reception at the farm and invited everyone that had ever known me. She even had made a wedding cake but the ornament with a bride and groom in military uniform didn't arrive on time which was another disappointment.

I think she was reasonably satisfied with Eli and felt that he would be a stabilizing influence on me. However, I don't think either one of them ever really understood each other.

Eli:

The Tennessee maneuvers were highly successful. The conditions that we endured and the problems we had with the weather and the mud turned out to be almost prophetic of the situation we would encounter in combat less than a year later.

Prior to the maneuver, I had put in my application for a leave for ten days after the maneuver was over. I had fifty days of leave time accrued, so had plenty of time coming. From Tennessee we were making a permanent change of station to Fort Bragg near Fayetteville, North Carolina.

As we left the maneuver area, we had stopped for the noon meal when the Colonel came up to me and said, "I see you have put in for a ten day emergency leave." He asked me what the emergency was. I said, "I don't have an emergency. I'm just asking for an ordinary leave." He came back with, "There is no such thing as an ordinary leave. Permission denied," and drove off. When we arrived at Fort Bragg, the battery commander, Captain Henson, told me that my leave had been approved.

Bernice's new outfit was scheduled to go overseas in late February and they were all being encouraged to take leaves before they were alerted. I met her in Chicago at one of the railroad stations. Rooms were not easy to find in that busy city, but I had been told that the Palmer House usually held back a few rooms for people in uniform. Sure enough, we were able to get a coveted room in that exclusive hotel.

Together we took the train to Janesville, Wisconsin where we were met by her father and mother. Her mother had a big reception and had invited a hell of a lot of people. Things seemed to be bogged down in the kitchen and I went out and helped them get organized. Sort of an assembly line set up. The ladies thought that was great.

We had tried to get airline reservations but couldn't, so from Wisconsin, we took the train to Baltimore to introduce Bernice to my family. We stayed in my old room at 1818 Ramsey St. With so much distance to travel, we did not have a lot of time to ourselves before we each went our separate way. I went back to Fort Bragg and she went back to Camp Forrest. We didn't see each other again until over a year later.

Bernice:

From Wisconsin we went to Baltimore to meet the Fishpaws. They had already put a new service flag in the window with the fourth star for the new in-law to go along with Eli, his brother Charlie and his sister Anna's husband John Downey. His brother John hadn't joined the Seabees at that time. Every family who had members on active duty had a service flag in their window. This was a white background with a wide red border and a blue star for each member in the service. A gold star indicated that a member of this family had been killed in action.

It was first time that I had seen Baltimore and was surprised by the rows and rows of brick houses painted red with white stripes to simulate the mortar underneath and all with white steps. There were three bedrooms upstairs. The room for the boys with two double beds had been the one in the middle. To reach the back room where the girls slept you had to go through it. June and Carrie were still living at home. Anna was married and lived about a mile away, not far from Johnnie's family. Their mother had the front room. We slept in the bed that had been Eli's when he was growing up.

His sister Anna had two children, Linda and Billy. Linda must have been about two. When she arrived at the house the morning after our arrival she ran upstairs to see Uncle Eli and was surprised to find him in bed with a woman.

Eli's older brother, John, with his wife Catherine and daughter Florence lived a short distance away and we spent one night with them. John and Catherine both worked and Florence went to school so we were free to sleep as late as we wanted to in the morning. All too soon our time together was over. Duty called. I went back to Camp Forrest and he headed for Fort Bragg.

~ *9* ~

It's Off to War I Go

Bernice:

During the time that I was making all these major decisions in my personal life, the 216th General Hospital was taking shape. The commanding officer was a full colonel named Harry Hammell. He was a physician and a career army officer, so he developed his unit more along military protocols than most of the new units where commanders came from civilian life. We had formations and reviews which I found invigorating and helped to bind the group together.

There were to be 100 nurses. Many of the Camp Forrest nurses joined us as well as many of their enlisted personnel. More were brought in from all over. I had been the Second Lieutenant nurse with the longest time in grade in the 222nd, but with the new transfers, I was way down the list. Col. Hammell even brought in his niece, who was a Captain, to be the surgery supervisor. She in turn brought nurses that she knew with more rank than I had so I was bumped out of the O.R.

We were issued the additional equipment that we would need for going overseas. The class 'A' navy blue uniform of the nurse corp which had been standard issue from the beginning of the corp finally was replaced with the Olive Drab. This did away with a lot of the confusion about which service we were in. It had been authorized but not issued while we were still at Ft. Jackson. Most of us had purchased at least one set of 'greens' for dress wear.

Now we were issued two more sets, along with new two piece fatigues to replace the one piece coveralls, ankle high field shoes, leggings, and 6 brown and white vertical striped seer-sucker wrap around dresses to be used in the hospital. White starched uniforms were not practical for the new phase which we were so eagerly entering. We still had our gas masks, the steel helmet and helmet liners, canteen, pistol belt, mess kit, muzzette bag, our shelter halves and our bed rolls from the 222nd.

There was great excitement when our orders came in February to proceed to Camp Kilmer in New Jersey. The shot records were reviewed and more shots were administered. Everyone who wore glasses was issued two pairs of the Government Issue style. There were about six nurses from building #1 who were going.

We used the day room to lay out our bed rolls to be packed. Beside the shelter halves and the blankets, we put everything that we expected to need in the bed roll, including our extra olive drab snuggies (long underwear), seersucker uniforms, capes, raincoat, the whole load. We were certainly not traveling light. I was the one who ended up being the chief roll packer. I got all our building's rolls nice and tight and they all held up for the complete journey. A lot of others fell apart and were a mess.

On 17 February, we took a troop train to Camp Kilmer, New Jersey and arrived on the 19th. It was another cantonment camp of wooden buildings but this one was different. Each barrack was randomly painted at least three different colors such as pink, brown and green, intended to make it look like a residential area if there was overflying enemy aircraft. There had never been any that I know of. I don't know who they thought they were fooling as the place was alive with military vehicles of every description.

We were assigned to a single barracks with 100 cots designed for enlisted personnel. The cots were arranged with the head of every other bed at the wall with the bed in between having the head by the center aisle. This was to avoid breathing in each others face while we were sleeping. The latrines were communal, with six commodes on one wall facing six commodes on the opposite wall. Most of us found this total lack of privacy embarrassing but nature did not respect our embarrassment and we learned to accomplish what was necessary.

The trough at the end was of no use to us and we used it to store the toilet paper. There were no hired civilian housekeepers here and we took our turn at the duties of keeping the facility clean. We referred to the assignment as the 'latrine queen'.

Now there was a whole new set of training to go through. We were given lectures on how to abandon ship, including climbing down cargo nets from ten foot high walls into life boats floating in little cement tanks of icy water. We learned about the equipment in the life boats and were told that the utility bucket was not to be used for urine. If you were out in the middle of the ocean in a life boat you were supposed go do your elimination over the side. I was convinced that rule had been made by a man.

We were also shown how to make a life preserver by tying knots in you pants legs and filling them with air. We didn't have to practice this. There was even a dummy railroad coach which was used to teach us how to get on and off the train. Each of us had a number and we were expected to board by the numbers.

When the training was completed there was a delay in our departure so we had an opportunity to go into New York City. This was my first experience in New York. It seemed so different from Chicago and Detroit. For one thing, there was the subway. What a dungeon. But it sure made it easy to get around.

With my friend, Genivieve Middleton, we climbed the Statue of Liberty and looked out over the city from Miss Liberty's crown. We went to the top of the Empire State Building and we toured Radio City. It was here that I first saw television which was very new. If it was actually broadcasting, I am not sure, but they had a receiver in one room and the cameras in another. Genie and I took turns standing in front of the camera while the other one watched in the next room.

We went to the Music City and saw the Rockettes and also had tickets for a Broadway show. The one we saw was called 'Harriet' and starred Helen Hayes in the title role. It was about Harriet Beecher Stowe and her experiences as she wrote UNCLE TOM'S CABIN. We even went to watch a radio show being broadcast. We saw the popular comedy called ABBY's IRISH ROSE.

We departed from Camp Kilmer on 13 March. We put on our steel helmet, which felt like it weighed a ton, our gas mask slung over our shoulder and our muzzette bag on our back. Now that we were thoroughly uncomfortable, we boarded a real train by the numbers and in less than half an hour were in the city of Hoboken where we detrained by the numbers and boarded a ferry boat. We stood on the deck as there were no benches. Most of us took off our helmets and our muzzette bag and dropped them on the deck in front of us.

The ride across the harbor was not long. As we approached the docks in the Hudson River we looked up at the stern of the biggest ship I had ever seen. It said QUEEN ELIZABETH. A band played 'Lady be Good' and we put on the steel pot and the muzzette bag and marched, route step, up the gangplank and across the pier where the IL DE FRANCE awaited us. The Queen had been damaged on the inbound voyage and was not our ship.

Even though it was after midnight, several Red Cross women were there with a huge pot of hot coffee and fresh doughnuts. Never had anything tasted so good, even though I had never learned to like coffee. One of the Red Cross ladies said that the women usually didn't come down at night for troop ship sailings but tried to be there when nurses were on the passenger list as we were all Red Cross too.

The IL DE FRANCE was a converted luxury liner that had been confiscated by the British when France fell to the Nazis in 1940. It had been converted to a troop ship and was operated by the British Merchant Marine and was carrying U.S. troops as a part of the lend lease program where we provided armaments and munitions and they provided support services. We were originally scheduled to sail on the QUEEN ELIZABETH which was considered to be the top of the line but she had ran into a storm coming in and the entire schedule was pushed back while she underwent repairs.

We boarded on 'B' deck, up a covered gang way and through a hatch with steel doors in the side of the ship. As we passed through this part of the ship, we could see the space where the troops were quartered. They were double pipe and canvas racks from the floor to the ceiling with narrow aisles about two feet wide. There must have been at least five levels. They slept head to foot and each man's pack shared his bed. Packed would be the only adjective that you could use to describe the arrangement.

We were on 'A' deck. Each of our compartments held about twenty nurses and our bunks were only two high. They were arranged in double rows which necessitated head to foot sleeping. I was the first one into the second compartment and since there had been no training on how to fill a compartment, I got to pick what I hoped would be the best bunk. We were in the very front of the ship. There were port holes which reduced any claustrophobia factor. I selected an upper bunk as far away from the head (navy for latrine) as possible and next to a port hole. There was a six hole head between each two compartments which turned out to be not nearly enough.

It was about 0200 by the time we had gone aboard and gotten settled down. We were tired from the day's excitement and physical activity. Most of us were soon asleep or at least glad to lay flat and let the others sleep. By the time the bell rang for first seating at breakfast we were awakened to find that we were under way. No port hole was required to know that we were at sea. The ship was audibly creaking.

Our supervisors arrived with meal tickets and instructions. There would be two meals a day. We would be second seating. We would carry our life jacket and helmet at all times. We were told that we were traveling without a naval escort and changed course every seven minutes. At 29 knots, we could out run any enemy submarines, but flotsam from the ship would leave a trail that could be followed. There would be absolutely nothing thrown overboard. No cigarette butts, no candy wrappers, no throwing up over the railing. That was why we were required to carry the helmet.

The ship was moving along quite smoothly and we dressed and went to breakfast. The officers' mess was on the promenade deck and had been the tourist class dining room in the heyday of the "Ildee". We now got our first experience with lend lease food. The main ingredient seemed to be kippered herring and boiled beans. I learned to drink hot tea which was necessary to wash the food down. One thing for sure, the British know how to make good tea.

By 0900 we were allowed out on the open deck. The open promenade deck was above 'A' deck and went all the way around the outside of the ship. It was reserved for enlisted personnel. Above this deck was the boat deck where the life boats hung in their davits and above it was the sun deck. The sun deck was reserved for the officers. Although it was far less crowded than the promenade deck and had chairs, the wind was biting cold. The North Atlantic can be very windy in March.

We could tell when we had passed the continental shelf when the creaking acquired a whole new and ominous voice. The deck began to rock and yaw. The bow went up and the stern went down. Then the bow went down and the stern went up. Walking became a challenge. Most of us including myself had never been in the open sea and became nauseated. I tried to not throw up because there was no place in the head to do so. Besides the stench was unreal. I grabbed my life jacket and my helmet and headed for the open deck. At least the wind would blow away the smell.

116

We had to pass through the open promenade and boat decks to get to the sun deck. In doing so, I discovered that the middle of the ship was much less unstable and there was nobody on the boat deck. I found a cubby hole in the sun and out of the wind and adopted this place for the trip. The tourist lounge had been converted to the officers' club where books, cards, backgammon, checkers and all sorts of recreation equipment was supplied. However, I was freshly married and had no interest in the social life. I visited only long enough to check out some books. My companions for the trip were Perry Mason and Della Street.

Throughout the trip we did not see any other ships except one night the Stockholm which belonged to Sweden, so was neutral, passed us going west. She was a hospital ship and was carrying sick and wounded, Americans I suppose. She was lit up with flood lights which clearly revealed the white ship with big red crosses visible for miles.

My service records shows that we arrived in the United Kingdom on 22 Mar 1944. After nine days at sea we had adjusted to the constant creaking and motion. Early in the morning a buzz went through the grapevine that we were approaching land. This was confirmed when we were told to pack our muzzette bags and fill our canteens with water. It seemed forever from the time we first sighted a thin black line along the starboard horizon and when we could make out the beautiful shore of Scotland. Greenock, on the River Clyde, flanked by the mountains, will always rate with me as the most beautiful harbor in the world.

With our pot on our head, our gas mask slung from our shoulder, our canteen on our hip and our muzzette bag on our backs, we descended, by the numbers, to the promenade deck and stepped through a gate in the rail onto a steel set of steps about thirty feet long that rested on the deck of a small boat called a harbor tender. Still standing, we were quickly whisked to the quay and solid land. It was such a strange sensation as we still felt the movement of the ship.

A train sat on the siding beside the wharf. It looked just like the trains you see in the movies, with doors the full length of each coach. We boarded the train by the numbers and discovered why there were so many doors. There was no center aisle to the train. Each door represented a compartment large enough for eight people. There was even a tiny latrine for each compartment.

We were each given three boxes of 'K' ration; supper, breakfast and lunch. 'K' ration is supposed to be a complete and balanced meal. Each meal was different but in many ways, they were all alike. There was a can containing the entree which might be scrambled eggs or beef stew. Of course they were unheated.

There was a can of dessert such as pudding or fruit cocktail and there would be cookies or crackers. One especially interesting wafer was supposed to be loaded with vitamins and tasted just like alfalfa hay. A small package of instant coffee, useless without hot water, and powdered milk completed the meal. There was always two cigarettes, a tiny match book and two squares of toilet paper. There was also the neatest little can opener. I still have one of them.

How excited we were as we rumbled south through the midlands of England. The first sight of quaint thatched roofed cottages brought oohs and aahs. As night arrived we pulled the shades down. We turned out the lights before we peeked out because blackout was the rule. We thoroughly expected to hear German planes and to be bombed but we never were.

The next morning we detrained at a place called Tidworth. We were on the Salsbury plain where the United States was building up an invasion force to cross the English Channel and liberate western Europe. It was a chilly day when we mounted up in the rear of several two and a half ton trucks for a long ride to an industrial and railroad center called Swindon, about two hundred miles. It was a bumpy ride and we spent most of the time singing to relieve the boredom. We would be here for a couple of weeks, billeted in English homes while our hospital was being made ready for us.

Every standing home had been surveyed and if there were two people living there and they had two bedrooms, they were required to house one service person. Genivieve drew an older couple who shared a bed so she had a bedroom and a bed of her own.

I drew an older man and his middle aged maiden daughter who each had a separate room, so my resting place was a canvas cot in the bathroom. I didn't have a mattress and only two blankets. I made up the bed by putting a blanket on the bottom with half of it hanging over one side and the other blanket with half hanging over the other side. They were folded over the top so that I had as much thickness below as above. It was entered from the head. My trench coat went on top. My hostess gave me an earthenware jug of hot water every night to put below my feet. I was cold.

Most of the homes were heated with coal fireplaces. Of course, coal was scarce. My host and hostess were very gracious and always asked me to join them in the kitchen where they kept a low fire burning and a teakettle for tea was always hot. We didn't eat with our families but occasionally I would accept their invitation to have tea with them.

Tea is an institution in England. It is actually a separate meal served at 4 P.M. A simple tea would usually be bread and butter with maybe some jam on it. The bread was cut very thin. At first I couldn't understand how they could spread butter on such a thin slice of bread, then I saw my hostess cut the whole loaf of bread in the middle and spread the butter and jam on the open face before she sliced the bread. Even this must have taken some practice. She always held the loaf against her breast and brought the knife toward her.

For our regular meals we went to a central place where a field kitchen served hot American food three times a day. It tasted great after two a day aboard the ship. We ate from our mess kit, which we cleaned and sterilized after the meal by washing and rinsing them in three 30 gallon galvanized cans of boiling water.

Two or three nights the air raid siren sounded. My hostess was an air raid warden whose job it was to put on her helmet and patrol a certain area to be sure that no lights were showing and to report any suspicious activity. She told me that if I wanted to, I could get under the stairs which was supposed to be the safest place in case a bomb hit the house. I never heard any bombs but did hear the Luftwaffer planes. They sounded different from the British and American planes which we heard all the time. Once I was in my bed, I was unwilling to get out unless all hell was breaking lose.

Our new hospital was located on the western edge of the Salsbury Plain between the villages of Warminster and Fromm. It was on the estate of the Marquis of Bath known as Longleek. It was about a mile from the manor, which was out of sight. The buildings were in the game preserve and deer roamed freely in our area. Sheep were also herded in and out to keep our grass mowed; very picturesque but somewhat of a sanitary problem.

We were quartered in brick buildings known as huts. There were eight nurses to a hut. The windows had heavy drapes for black out use and the door was concealed from the outside and also had a curtain to keep light from escaping. Heat was provided with a very primitive stove which was little more than a large can with a clay lining. There was a door at the bottom and a lid and a stove pipe at the top. There was no grate. The fuel was coke, which makes a nice warm fire but is almost impossible to start and no kindling was provided.

Tending the stove was the responsibility of the tenants of each hut. Unlike many of the city girls, I had built many a fire in the kitchen stove on the farm so had some knowledge of how to do it. The first thing was to bang up enough of the coke into powder and mix it with used Stars and Stripes, the newspaper of the Army. When we got the kindling going we added smaller chunk and eventually the big chunks.

I quickly decided that what I needed was a hammer so I wrote home and requested one. Because of the heavy demands of the war, anything that we wanted from home had to be requested by us. Uncle Charles sent me a hammer with my new initials on it. It sure beat banging two pieces of coke together. I still have it and use it. I didn't really mind starting the fire but it didn't take long to discover that if I didn't build one there wouldn't be a fire.

The weather in England was never really cold, it was just never really warm either. The water pipes in the quickly built army camps ran along the top of the ground and even the permanent buildings had the plumping running up the outside walls. We had been issued olive drab two piece wool underwear called snuggies. I wore them all summer. The lining of our trench coat was designed to double as a bath robe. We wore our high top field shoes with wool socks as the floors were also cold. It wasn't unpleasant though and made for great bicycling.

When I quit building fires every day, we found other ways to keep warm. That was by spending our time in the hut in the bed. We made our cots up in the envelope style. I would crawl in from the top, remove my cloths and put on my pajamas under the covers. When morning came, I would put the day time clothing under the covers to get them warm and then dress, still under the covers. We all got pretty adept at this exercise. Those seersucker dresses worked well because they didn't show wrinkles, being just one big, all over wrinkle.

The latrine was a separate building in the center of the nurses' area. It had private cubicles and showers but no hot water. The same style stove was there also. However, no one was assigned to tend the stove so it was seldom lit. We all got in the habit of filling our helmet with water and taking it to our hut and heating it on the stove when we wanted a bath. Daily bathing was quickly abandoned by even the most fastidious nurses. Most of us learned to put corn meal in our hair and then brush it out. It beat trying to shampoo in a helmet.

We quickly learned that lend lease toilet paper was harsh and not very effective. Eli was still at Fort Bragg and we wrote each other every day. He asked me right off what he could send me and right away I said I could really use some descent toilet paper. His reply was that he couldn't go to the post office with a letter saying his wife wanted toilet paper. My mother also wanted to send me something so I asked her for the paper. She was more than happy to provide me with this important amenity. She probably even read my letters to her club.

I think the capacity of the hospital was supposed to be 500 beds. Each ward was a separate building just as it had been in the states. Wood was scarce so all buildings were made with cheap brick. The floors were made of a black material similar to black top roads, with a smooth surface called pitch mastic. They were quite soft and easy to work on. One problem was that they showed dirt badly and the Colonel, being military, wanted them to shine at all times. Maybe that was good. It gave our patient's something unpleasant to do which made them anxious to get back to their outfits. The wards were heated with the same tin cans as our huts. There were three in each ward.

Because I had been bumped from the O.R., Captain Dill, our original chief nurse, wanted to make it up to me. She assigned me to ward #1 which was designated as the 'Shock Ward'. It was the building right next to surgery. The army was developing the concept of the recovery room and the intensive care unit. We would get the post anesthesia patient which we transferred out as soon as they were awake if there was no potential for complications. The serious ones we kept.

We had four nurses, more than any other ward. Two for day shift, and one each for evening and night and we only had the one ward. Most of the other night nurses supervised two, three or up to six wards. We rotated shifts. We also had four corpsmen. The nurses' duty was to be constantly alert to the condition of the patients and to administer medication or do required treatments. The corpsmen did most of the actual care. In the other wards, patients who were able were assigned the housekeeping duties including shining the floors and keeping the stoves working.

It was not the O.R. but the job was challenging and I really didn't mind it. It gave me an opportunity to stay on the cutting edge of advances going on at the time. One of the big ones was the introduction of penicillin. This was a new antibiotic that had just been developed. I believe that we may have given the first dose administered in the European theater. We had a master sergeant who had a perforated ulcer and had peritonitis.

The new medicine came as a powder which was mixed with saline and given intramuscularly. It was bright yellow and must have stung severely from the reaction of the men who received it. However, it was a genuine wonder drug. Many casualties came home that would have otherwise died from infection if we had not had it. A system was devised where one nurse would mix up a bottle of powder with 50 cc of saline. With a 50 cc syringe and a pan full of sterile needles, she would visit every bed with a yellow tag. She was known as the bumble bee.

To begin with, most of our patients were trauma cases received during the training activity that was on going as the troops practiced for the planned invasion. One incident I recalled vividly was an artillery accident where a 155mm howitzer had a breech explosion and hot shrapnel injured four of the gun crew. One man was holding a powder bag that had blown up and he lost both hands. He was understandable very depressed.

About this time Joe Louis, the world champion heavy weight boxer, was visiting the troops and came through the hospital to visit the patients. He was a staff sergeant and was traveling with a Sgt. 1st Class who was his sparing partner. They put on exhibition bouts, which the patients and the corpsmen all appreciated. He didn't seem too articulate and seemed to have trouble talking to the patients. His partner communicated better than he did.

The air raid siren for the area was on the roof of our headquarters building. German air raids occurred only at night so when that big siren went off it could be quit a shock if you were asleep. The rule was that when the siren went off, every one was supposed to get up, dress, put on their helmet and report to their assigned work area. The patients were told that if we had a raid, they were supposed to seek shelter under their bed.

One night the siren sounded and the staff all came on duty. We couldn't hear any bombs and maybe there were German planes overhead and maybe there weren't. Having nothing to do but be there, a couple of the day nurses decided they would go down to the back door of the ward and look out to see what was going on. In the dark, they forgot about the stove in the middle of the aisle and one of the girls fell over one, sending stove parts and ashes in all directions, making a terrible noise. When we turned on the lights to see what was going on, all our patients were under the beds. Who could blame them?

It was the calm before the storm. Our census was not high and we had an opportunity to get acquainted with our staff and to learn the routine of the ETO (European Theater of Operation) which the higher headquarters was trying to standardize. The purpose of this was to make it so that every nurse could go into any ward in the whole theater and be immediately functional. The idea was a good one though many of us did not understand the need for it and it suppressed initiative.

We were getting acquainted with our host country. Bicycles were a primary means of transportation. Before long, most of us had acquired a bike and when not on duty would ride into Warminster or Fromm or around the area. You could even take your bike on the train. One week end Genie and I went back to Swindon, just to visit our former hosts. We often rode around Longleek. In the carriage house of the manor, there was a very elegant carriage which the Marquis used for formal occasions such as the coronation of King George the VI.

Col. Hammell thought we should take advantage of our opportunity to see what today we would call the attractions. He had the staff arrange for trips to the Roman Baths in the city of Bath. We also went to Stonehenge. I was rather unimpressed at the time. It looked like a bunch of rocks out in the middle of a field. I could see rocks in the middle of the pasture at home.

Something I did enjoy was riding into town for tea. The tea rooms would serve a variety of goodies with the tea which we enjoyed because the food we were getting at the mess hall was less than great. Powdered eggs, potatoes and milk have their limitations.

Lend lease was a part of everything we did. I always said half the farmers in England must have paid their taxes with cabbage. Australia was a part of Great Briton and they kept the Kingdom well supplied with sheep. I had never eaten sheep before and I developed a thorough dislike for it. Another little quirk of the army mess was lemon crystals. They were required to use what seemed like a large amount of them because they contained vitamin C. There is only so much lemonade you can drink. The cooks mixed lemon crystals with everything they could think off. We could taste them in the vegetables and in the dessert. They even encouraged us to take packages back to the hut to use for hair rinse.

Although I wrote Eli every day, about the middle of May, I started getting letters from him asking why I had quit writing. At about this time, the U.S. had developed a shuttle run of bombing, where our planes would fly from Briton to Russia, who was our ally at the time. They would refuel and reload for the return trip.

To service the mission, a hospital had been sent to Russia and Eli deducted that since he wasn't getting any mail that I must be in Russia. Either that or that I had found a new male interest. No matter how many letters I wrote denying either situation, he never got them because all mail had been held up to prevent security leaks. It was a good idea but of course the German army knew we were coming and were ready for us.

All day and all night we could hear the constant drone of airplanes doing their runs to the continent, bombing the industries and communication of the Nazi war machine in preparation for the invasion to come.

I was on night duty on the morning of June 6th. About 0200 I stepped outside to get some fresh air. In England in June it was already daylight and as I looked up at the sky I saw that all the airplanes were marked with black and white stripes around the wings and the fuselages. I didn't need to turn on the radio to know that the invasion of the continent had started. The planes had all been striped overnight to provide new identifying markings to reduce the confusion that such a large undertaking could create.

It was only a few days when I received a letter from Eli, who was still at Fort Bragg, telling me that he had been delivered a whole bag full of letters on the 6th and had spent a couple hours reading them as he listened to accounts of the invasion on the radio.

~ 10 ~

Meanwhile, Back in the States

Eli:

There had been an airborne division stationed in the area that the 100th took over. They had been moved out to another nearby camp. Many of their people had girl friends in Fayetteville and when they came back to visit them, they discovered that the 100th had not only taken over their barracks but had also taken over a lot of their girl friends.

In the center of town there was a large bar a half block long known as the Town Pump. The first week end, a fight broke out. The Fayetteville fire department used fire hoses to help the MPs and police break up the riot. The next week end every unit had to furnish one officer and one big NCO with MP arm bands, night sticks and 45s to help patrol Fayetteville on Saturday nights. It was a quiet night and the airborne didn't come back. After that, there were not any major problems.

Not long after we were settled in at Fort Bragg, our units were all hit hard by requirements to send officers and men for replacements to the units fighting in North Africa. To take their places, we received men from many sources, such as the air corp, anti-aircraft artillery and service oriented units such as the quartermaster.

The most conspicuous group were hundreds of young men who had been in a special program where their assignment had been to go to various colleges. They were called ASTP (Army Special Training Program). They were like raw recruits, but all of them were bright young men and shaped up into soldiers in a short period of time. To say that they were less than thrilled to be in the 100th Infantry Division would be an understatement.

Most of the married officers found rooms and apartments around Fayetteville for their wives. Since my wife was already overseas, I offered to take their 'Officer of the Day' and 'Duty Officer' assignments so they could have time with their families. My offer was eagerly accepted by most of them. I spent most of my week ends on the post and became the expert on that part of military life.

Bernice and I were writing each other every day. Because of the limited amount of shipping space, a service person overseas had to request something before it could be mailed, and the post office wanted to see the letter with the request. I asked Bernice what she needed and her answer was toilet paper. There was no way that I was going to show the post office a letter from my wife requesting toilet paper.

Even though I was now married, I ended up as the defacto leader of the unaccompanied officers. It became a standing joke that I was the father figure of this group. As officers came and were sent out, they started hanging blue stars on my door, just like the service flags that all the folks at home displayed. I must have had six or eight stars in our service flag when the Chief of Staff at Divarty spotted it. "What are those for?" "Those are for all the Lieutenants who have gone overseas from the 374th Field Artillery." He told me that it was unauthorized and to get rid of it.

On another occasion, this Colonel came to the battery to see a demonstration of a new method I had discovered for bore sighting. He didn't believe that my method would work. After I had showed it to him, and he had tried it himself, he had to admit that it worked and was a lot less complicated than the book method. I said it was sure a damn site better than the old method. He chewed me out good, on the side, for using profanity in front of the men. I had that coming. In those days, officers were referred to as gentlemen and were not supposed to swear, not even an occasional damn.

One night, a Captain came into the officers' quarters drunk, and was smashing up the place. He actually shoved his fist through the cardboard wall. The Lts. subdued him and put him to bed. The next morning, I was ordered to the Colonel's office and informed that he wanted the Lieutenant who had done the damage in the quarters.

I recommend that he have an officers' formation and request the guilty party to report to him personally after the formation. Within the hour, the Captain, who was a battery commander, reported and confessed the whole incident. He was married and his wife had been gone for the weekend so he stayed on the post and had gotten drunk.

On Sundays we would go to chapel in the morning and play softball, touch football or volleyball in the afternoon before going to the Center Grill, a civilian run restaurant on the post. Quite often, the Division Commander, Major General Burress, would join us. He enjoyed listening to the young officers. They had good steak and hamburgers but the beer was lousy. One day we took our own beer and keep it under the table. When the proprietor saw this, he asked us if we thought he was running a free area for picnic baskets. After that he made sure the beer was a little colder.

The allied armies were massing in England to invade the continent across the English Channel. I thought that Bernice must be in England although I wasn't sure. She was not allowed to give me that information. However, she mentioned that she had bought a bicycle and that she was visiting castles.

There was much speculation as to when the invasion would take place. The battalion motor officer bet me a hundred dollars that it would be on the Fourth of July. I took him up on the bet because, all of a sudden, I had not received any mail from my new wife. Something must be up. On the 6th of June, the radio broke the news that the invasion was under way.

I went to collect my bet. He took me to the quarters and started looking for a paycheck. He had so much money, he never bothered to cash them, but hid them around his room. He finally found one and cashed it to pay me my a hundred bucks. The whole battalion knocked off that afternoon so that we could listen to reports on the radio from the front. About four days later, I got a whole stack of mail.

During that summer, all our guns and vehicles were sent to the port to be prepared to go overseas. We continued our training with some old, much used howitzer from the Fort Bragg Artillery Training Center.

These guns were so used and abused that we never knew what to expect. One day, during service practice, I report that one gun was stuck out of battery. The old man said he would call post ordinance but I asked him to wait until I had a chance to see what was wrong. Sgt. Segal already knew what was wrong. They had been removing oil from the recoil mechanism and the extractor had been left on the cradle. Next time the gun fired it rolled into the cradle and jammed between the recoil mechanism and the cradle. It was stuck tight.

We ran a cable anchored with a 4 × 4 through the tube and hitched it to the winch of one of the trucks. Even with all that power it wouldn't budge. Segal and I decided that the only way we could get it loose was to remove all the oil from the recoil mechanism. That worked. Then we had to refill it. We had the screw fillers from the other guns and the whole gun crew took turns pumping oil for four or five minutes. It was hard work. When I reported that the gun was ready to fire, the old man said, "I knew you could do it."

To get practice using the howitzers for direct fire, we went to Myrtle Beach, South Carolina. I was on the advance detail to lay out the camp. We designated areas for the different batteries as well as locating the kitchens on the top and being sure that the latrines were on a lower level. We were to be on land that belonged to the government which included a very large airstrip.

There wasn't much at Myrtle Beach then, just one hotel and a lot of older homes that had been converted to rooms for tourists. They did have a small amusement park with a merry-go-round, a Ferris wheel and a bowling alley. Prior to the arrival of the troops, a couple officers discovered that we could rent a house with ten bedrooms for $75 a week. We decided to rent it and then rent rooms to the other officers at $10 a piece.

That included bed and supplies such as ice, soft drinks and beer which we bought at the PX. When they arrived, we had about fifteen customers. When the week was up we even had money left over so we returned $3.74 to each of our guests. This sure beat sleeping out in pup tents. Of course, the duty officers had to stay with the troops. Most of the married officers and the NCOs had their wives in town and it was like a working vacation.

One night, two of the officers brought some women into the kitchen. They got to laughing and talking pretty loud. There was no air conditioning, so all the windows were open. About 2300 the sheriff turned up at the door and wanted to see the person in charge. I got out of bed and listened to what he had to say, which was pretty direct. He said that if we didn't get quiet, he would put us all in the lock up. It seems that his house was next door.

He had made his point. We got quiet real fast. There would have been big trouble if the Ole Man had to get us all out of jail.

The Coast Guard used a motor launch to tow the targets, which were made of wood 2×6 skids, about twelve feet long. The cable was about a half mile long. The target was made of burlap, attached to a wooden frame about ten feet high, which we were to shoot at. They would pull these targets at about 20 knots. This would be similar to the size and speed of vehicles such as an enemy tank that we might encounter in combat.

They were off shore about 1600 yards. A lot of our men had been hunters in civilian life so they understood how to lead the target. I had measured the targets when they were sitting at the docks. With this information I was able to determine the exact time of flight and the gunner could adjust and fire the piece so that we usually hit the burlap on the first round. We used a delayed fuse so that the shell would go through the cloth before it exploded in the water behind the target.

Col. Lyles was the umpire on this problem and was observing and calling out hits or misses. Routinely he would call out "OVER". That meant a miss. I had the same high powered scope as he did and I could see that we were actually hitting the target every time.

We were about out of ammunition, so I quietly told the battery to change to fuse quick, which would go off on first contact. When I did this, the first round blew the target off the skids. Then I told them to fire at the skids which they did, and even though they were right on the surface, they were able to hit them and blow them out of the water. 'B' Battery had more direct hits than the rest of division artillery combined.

Our work was over, our ammunition gone and our target destroyed, so we knocked off the battery and we all went swimming. The Coast Guard added another half mile of cable so they were a mile from the target. They swore that shell fragments had reached their boat. The Ole Man had a grand old time bragging about his 'B' battery's accuracy around battalion headquarters. He said they were the best firing battery in the whole army. He didn't mention that to me, I learned it from his staff.

At last the time had come to put into use all this training and preparation. When we were packing up all our battery equipment, preparing to ship out, supply had dumped a whole truck load of excelsior at the battery to use for packing. I remembered Bernice's comments about the sad condition of European toilet paper, so told the men to pack everything with rolls of TP instead of the messy excelsior. They even drove around the post and gathered up paper from other supply rooms who were trying to get rid of it.

In September, we pulled out of Fort Bragg and moved to Camp Kilmer, near New Brunswick, New Jersey. This was known as the Port of Embarkation. We had to be sure that every single soldier was qualified to go overseas. There was a big chart on the wall with the names of the whole battery on it and squares to be checked off. As each requirement was completed the square was checked off. This included things like shots, wills, insurance as well as marksmanship, etc. When the deadline arrived, all the squares were filled. Many of the men were nervous. I reassured them that they were well trained and would do a great job in combat.

Before we left Kilmer, we each had a chance to take the train to New York City for a day. I got there in the afternoon and as I was walking around, I discovered that I was at Jack Dempsey's bar. I went in and ordered a drink.

Before long a huge hulk of a man came in and announced that he was paying for all drinks for men in uniform. He had a much smaller guy with him. In the course of conversation, I learned that he was Buddy Baer, the brother of Max Baer, once the heavy weight boxing champion. Buddy was in the merchant marine.

We had a few drinks when he suddenly staggered and fell backward. I was able to break his fall. The little guy, who was probably his manager took over. I decided it was time to get back to camp. I fell asleep on the train and would have missed my stop if the conductor hadn't woke me up. It would have been hard to explain if I had missed the boat and turned up in Baltimore.

A few days later, we boarded a train where we were taken to the ferry slip in Hoboken, NJ. We rode the ferry, standing up, across New York harbor to where our boat was waiting.

~ 11 ~

A Storm at Sea and a New Destination

Eli:

We sailed on the George Washington. This was an old World War One ship that had been confiscated from the Germans. It had been used to haul troops then too. After the war, four of those old troop ships had been placed in mothballs (storage) in the Patuxent river.

When we were civilians we often went down there to crab. We had often discussed these ships and wondered what it would be like to be on one of them. I had even wished that we could board her and see what it was like to stand on the bridge. It was operated by the Merchant Marines but the Captain was a Navy Captain who had come out of retirement to command the ship.

Elements of Battery 'B' were assigned to temporary duty with the navy to provide the armed guard for the trip. I was the officer in charge of the army element of the detail. My duty station was on the ship's bridge.

When we left New York we thought we were headed for England. Our advanced detail had gone there to arrange for our arrival. I was the only 100th officer on the bridge when we cleared the New York light and the sealed orders were opened. The Captain dramatically proclaimed, "Gentlemen, we are going to the French Riviera". The destination had been changed to southern France.

The officers of the armed guard consisted of three navy officers and myself. There was one Chief Petty Officer and about twenty six men from my battery and about the same number of navy enlisted men who were a permanent part of the ship's crew. Machine gun turrets were all around the ship. There was even a five inch cannon on the stern. Because we were artillery trained we had no problem adapting to this assignment. It was a good deal for us because we got to eat with the navy and got three meals a day while the rest of the troops only got two.

I didn't have the privilege of navy sleeping quarters and I shared a very small cabin with three other Lieutenant from the battery. I always wore my parka with big pockets when I went to lunch in the Navy officers' mess and the mess orderly from the merchant marine would fill my pockets up with sandwiches and other goodies unheard of in the troop mess for me to take back to my cabin mates.

We were traveling in a convoy of perhaps 16 or 17 ships. The entire 100th Division, including all our equipment, was in that convoy as well as the 103rd Infantry Division, and the advanced elements of the 14th Armored Division. The navy had seven destroyers and destroyer escorts around the perimeter of the convoy for protection from submarines. Every ship had machine guns to fight off enemy aircraft. The Washington could probably go 18 knots but we could only travel as fast as the slowest ship which was about 10 knots.

Several days after we were out we hit a storm. In the middle of the storm, in the middle of the night, one of my men saw something straight ahead that looked like the broad sides of another ship and called out, "Ship dead ahead". The helmsman reversed the twin screws and slowed our ship enough that we just missed the other ship.

The Washington had lost the control of the rudder making it impossible to steer. This had happened before. One navy guy said it happened every time the weather got bad. We had to drop out of the convoy and the rudder was rigged with a block and tackle on each side. These were manned by merchant marines and they steered the ship. A destroyer escort was left behind to guard us to ride out the storm. While the repairs were being made, it was a good time to get in a little anti air craft practice shooting at balloons. We fired the five inch cannon as well as all the other weapons, mainly the 50 cal machine guns and the twin Bofors (French). Being a faster ship, we were able to catch up with the rest of the convoy before we reached our destination.

Spain was neutral but was not friendly to the Allies. Therefore, when we entered the Mediterranean we went all the way to the African coast. When we cleared the Straights of Gibraltar we stayed just off the African coast until we headed north up the Italian boot and circled west to Marseilles and the Riviera.

Bernice:

We did not immediately receive casualties from the invasion. The wounded were returned to England on the same ships that carried them to the beaches as they returned to pick up more soldiers and supplies. They were unloaded at South Hampton from where they were taken by ambulance to several hospitals on the coast where they were evaluated and sorted by the nature and severity of their injury. From there they were dispatched by hospital train to the specialties and general hospitals in the midlands. Our first train arrived about the 9th. We became very busy.

Early in July I was reassigned to the operating room. I thought it was because they were busy and needed extra help. I was delighted to be back where I most wanted to work. I was soon disillusioned. On the 15th, I was told that I was being transferred to the 106th General Hospital, near Wimborne Minister near the southern coast.

It seems that several new general hospitals had been activated, trained and sent to England but had no assigned nurses. The plan was to reduce the table of organization to 75 nurses for a general hospital and to draw the ones they needed from the hospitals already in place. The 216th had to send an O.R. nurse so they had drawn me in long enough for them to fill their quota without sacrificing the clique. Of course, I was glad to be back where I thought I belonged.

The new hospital was commanded by a Lt. Col. Miller, a doctor who had no military background. The whole atmosphere was much different. I never felt we achieved the cohesiveness of the 216th. The war had moved onto the continent and our mission now became one of getting the wounded back to the war or back to the USA.

Harriet Blair was another nurse from the 216th who was assigned to the 106th. We ended up in the same corner of the new hut and we became good friends. The nurses' huts at the new hospital were twice as big and held 16 nurses. These women had come from several different outfits and were as diverse a group as you would ever meet. None of them were anymore interested in building a fire in the two little stoves than the nurses at the last station had been. But I had learned my lesson and only built a fire when absolutely necessary.

All the British people seemed very friendly and the best way to meet them was to get on our bicycles and get out of the areas frequented by Americans. On one occasion we were in a village where men were bowling on the green. It was a field about twenty yards square with a crown in the middle. The grass was as short and even as a golf green.

They would roll a small white ball across the surface from the four corners and from the four mid points of the perimeter. Each player would then bowl a ball about the size of a cantaloupe, which looked like it had been squashed. It was weighted so that it would not roll in a straight line except when it rolled up and over the crown, when it went amazingly straight.

Each man bowled four balls. The point of the game was to score by getting the ball closest to the white marker. The game was over when they had bowled from all eight positions. I was amazed that they had a game going at each position at the same time, but the balls never hit another ball, while there might be six or seven rolling at the same time. They explained the game to us but never offered to let us try it.

One day we were riding our bikes out in the country and met a very nice English lady who was a widow. She was running a chicken farm. The government controlled all the agriculture and told everyone what they could raise and where to sell it. Her assignment was to raise laying hens to produce fertile eggs for the hatchery. She was not even allowed to eat them herself.

I enjoyed talking to her and she seemed to enjoy my company too. The farm girl enjoyed being on the farm again, if only for an hour or two. In fact, I got in the habit of riding out quite often. One day she had a treat for me. She had discovered that she had a hen that habitually laid double yolk eggs.

Since a double yolked egg is not suitable for hatching, it was perfectly legal for her to eat them. Fresh eggs were something that our mess hall was not able to serve and the powdered kind were not very appetizing. I carefully took my prize egg back to the hut and built myself a fire so that I could boil my fresh egg in my helmet. Of course as long as I had a good fire and a helmet full of hot water, I took a bath too.

Bournemouth is a resort city on the English channel about ten miles south of Wimborne Minister. It had a very nice beach which had been totally covered with rolls of barbed wire and iron stakes protruded from the shallow bottom, precautions taken when the invasion of England by the Germans seemed imminent. They had an opera house there and the London Opera company would come out and present operas. I had never seen an opera before. I saw Rigoletto and Labohme. Both were sung in English.

I never rode the bike to Bournemouth as there was a bus that ran regularly and was very inexpensive. The many hotels had become rest centers for British and American service people. Betty Anderson, the sister of my good high school friend, Doris, was a physical therapist stationed in the midlands. She came down one weekend and stayed in one of these accommodations. We enjoyed a good visit.

There were also housing facilities especially for the female troops in London. We took the train to Waterloo station. It was about two hours. The apartment we stayed in was probably a very high class town house. There were hints of grandeur, but the furniture was straight Government Issue, British style. Most impressive was the pink marble bath room.

London was much different than New York. A great deal of the city lay in ruin as a result of the German bombing. The area around St. Paul's cathedral was especially hard hit. However, the fastidious brits had cleaned away most of the rubble as quickly as it was created, so the area looked like all basements.

The subway was our primary means of getting around. It was a great contrast from New York. The stations were beautifully tiled with mosaics on the walls and the trains were clean and modern. The thing that impressed me the most was the rows and rows of wire racks used by the Londoners for sleeping during air raids. The air raids had mostly stopped by late 1944, but many people's homes were gone and they had no other place to sleep.

We did the usual tourist things like going to Westminster Abbey and parliament. We visited the Tower of London but the crown jewels were not there as they had been removed for safe keeping.

We saw Buckingham Palace but the guards were real soldiers carrying real weapons and no foolishness about bearskin hats or red coated sentries, looking straight ahead. Big Ben was bonging out the time every fifteen minutes and London was going about its business. We didn't get to see the king, except in the wax museum where the royal family held the central exhibit. Our own Franklin Roosevelt sat in the front of the display of American presidents.

We had a chance to do some shopping. I bought a set of antique silver candle holders and some pictures for the home I would some day be furnishing. There were two etchings, one of London bridge and one of Parliament, and two water colors of the lake region.

Eli:

We arrived about dusk and prepared to debark. As this activity was getting under way, we got an air raid alert. Sure enough, there was a German plane, way high in the sky. This was the first time I had ever seen or heard of a jet.

Baker Battery had already started climbing down the cargo net into an LCI (landing craft infantry) when the alert sounded. My detail of guards were the last of the battery to go down and were still on the deck. They all headed for their stations as ordered.

The battalion executive officer saw one of them run in the opposite direction of the landing operation and thought he had gotten chicken. When he grabbed him, the sergeant explained that he had to get to his station and kept on running in that direction. The Major became angry and confronted me as I was reporting to my station on the bridge. I assured him that the man was acting on orders and was correct as we were in the navy until our feet touched the ground.

By now, the three navy officers had put on their class 'A' uniforms and gone ashore with the mail boat, which was the first vessel to leave the ship. This made me the officer in charge of the armed guard. The chief petty officer was still there.

The plane was, no doubt, gathering intelligence for the Germans. It was much too high to reach with any of our guns so there was no point in shooting. As soon as the alarm was sounded a smoke outfit laid down smoke which obscured the harbor and all the activity. When the 'all clear' sounded we finished loading our LCI and took off for the shore. When we arrived, the ramp that made the front of the craft wouldn't drop. We had to climb up to the top, about 10 feet, and jump off onto the beach in the dark. That was fun with a 60 pound pack on your back.

Once ashore, we left our packs piled up at a designated site, fell in, in a column of two, and headed for our staging area. Captain Henson was leading and I was bringing up the rear. The battery clerk was right ahead of me with his typewriter on his back. As we were about to go through the gate of the harbor, I saw two more guys with a couple boxes of 'C' rations on their backs. This didn't look quite right to me.

As we went through the gate, I told the guard that these guys didn't belong to me. They right away recognized them as Frenchmen they had seen before. They were stealing stuff and trying to move out, unnoticed, with the troops. The guards grabbed them and were glad that I had called them to their attention.

Our route took us through the city of Marseilles and up a twelve mile hill. By now we were traveling light with just our helmet, gas mask, carbine and pistol belts with our canteen, ammo, rain coat and first aid kit. We were all a little nervous and didn't quite trust the local people.

The city had just been taken by the 45th Division only a week or so before. Every time a door would opened, we would bring our carbine around and be ready to fire. These were French Moroccan troops. They would come out of the bars with sabres and machetes hanging from their belts and really looked fierce. It was a good thing that none of them bothered us, or they would have been dead.

When we got to the staging area at the top of the hill, it was a real mud hole. Someone turned on the radio that belonged to the day room. Popular American music was playing. Then we heard a woman making an announcement. "Welcome 100th Infantry Show Division. We have 20 divisions just waiting to welcome you." We knew that this must be the well known Axis Sally that we had heard about back in the states. The Air corp were known to keep Sally supplied with the latest record. We enjoyed the music but her statement about twenty divisions waiting for us took the joy out of it.

Our packs would be up in the morning. We posted a guard and everyone got comfortable in the mud, wrapped up in our rain coat. In the morning our equipment started arriving. General Burress came around with General Devers, the 6th Corp commander and General Patch, the 7th Army Commander.

When they saw us unpacking, the first thing that caught their attention was all that toilet paper we had used for packing back at Fort Bragg. They wasted no time instructing their aides to confiscate some of it for their own personal use. They had experienced the same lend lease paper that Bernice had told me about. General Murphy, the Divarty Commander told Col. Liles that we had more than we needed and to re-allocated a lot of it to the other battalions.

Our first staging area was near Dijon, the mustard town. As we drove into Dijon, sitting there in a Jeep was Lt. Synan from Ft. Jackson. It was sure great to see him. He was an aerial observer for the 45th Division. He gave me a lot of good information. Our first assignment was to relieve the 45th who had been through the invasion of Italy at Anzio and the invasion of Southern France. Synan said that they had heard we were coming about two weeks ago and that since then, their guys wouldn't even lean forward in their fox hole. They went into reserve.

We heard our first sound of real war when an American 155mm battery in the area opened up on a fire mission. Everyone hit the dirt, since we didn't know if they were going out or coming in. I was under a jeep. Captain Hensen started running. We never knew where he ran to. He didn't come back for an hour. The men had scratched out some half hearted fox holes, but after this, the dirt started to fly. It is amazing how much dirt a man can move when he wants to.

Bernice:

In the fall, I learned that the 100th Division was scheduled to come to Europe. All such troop movements were supposed to be secret but secrets were not well kept. By now the Atlantic harbors of France were in full operation, so I held no hope that they would come to England. However, Cherbourg was just a short hop from South Hampton and a great deal of channel traffic moved between the two ports.

I even had what I thought was a shipping number of the 100th and in my head I thought that maybe I could catch a ride and be on the quay to meet Eli. However, I got chicken and didn't try that. It turned out to be a good decision because instead of Cherbourg, they went to Marseille on the Mediterranean.

The 100th arrived in Europe sometime in October and before long we started getting casualties from them. The grapevine kept me informed of when 100th soldiers were in the hospital and I would try to visit them and get a fix on what was going on with the division. They were in the 7th Army under General Patch and were engaged with the enemy in an area of Europe known as Alsace-Lorraine.

$\sim$ 12 $\sim$

They Said It Couldn't Be Done

Eli:

We were now a part of the Seventh Army under General Patch. Our mission was to advance through southern France to Alsace Lorraine, across the Vosges Mountains and eventually into Germany. This involved confronting the fortified Maginot line, now held by the German army.

This heavily bunkered line had been built to protect France from the Germans but had been ineffective as the Germans had simply gone around it through Belgium. At the eastern end of the line lay the ancient fortress city of Bitche. For centuries, it had never been taken by any enemy army. Now it was our mission to take it. Some said it couldn't be done.

In about the first or second position that we occupied an anti-aircraft platoon was assigned to us for extra protection. After we were in position on the farm we had occupied and fired a few missions, I got word that the ack ack section was sending over a side of fresh pork. I questioned where it came from. They had butchered two hogs from the farm to get fresh meat. My first reaction was to refuse to take the meat because it had been taken from a French family. I gave them orders that if they ever did that again they would be court martialed.

After being in combat a couple weeks, I realized that was a stupid statement. These guys had been in combat since Anzio. Despite all the supplies, there were times when a soldier needs to live off the land.

I went down and told them so and to forget about what I had told them, just use a little discretion. Every week or two after that, fresh pork would show up at meals which the men all enjoyed. Also we found that every French house had a cellar full of old potatoes and turnips. The potatoes especially were a great substitute for the government issue powdered potatoes.

A World War Two infantry division was made up of three infantry regiments. They were each divided into three battalions. To furnish the foot soldiers with fire power, there were four artillery battalions. In the 100th, the 374th, 375th and 925th artillery battalions each had three firing batteries of four 105 millimeter howitzers for direct support and the 373rd had three batteries of 155s.

The idea was for each of the 105 battalions to work closely with each of the regiments. The 155s were for general support. They were heavier, put out a larger round that could travel farther and were used wherever the situation called for extra fire power.

To get the best use of the artillery, there was an artillery officer with a radio operator and a recorder from each battery assigned to accompany each of the infantry battalions. It was their job to work with the infantry company commanders to determine where artillery was needed and to radio the necessary information to the battery which was usually two or three miles behind the line.

They were called FOs (forward observers). Once a shell had been fired, the observer could radio back information to fire direction, who would tell the guns the adjustments to make in range and deflection to get the best use of the firepower. When we first went into combat, each battery had one forward observer for each infantry battalion. Since the infantry had three rifle companies each, it soon became apparent that to be effective, more forward observers were going to be needed.

Lt. Nick Devereux was our original FO. We made our detail sergeant, Peter Moynihan and Sgt. Herbert Lutz FOs. They lived and traveled with the 397th, second battalion. Since the job called for an officer, it was decided that Moynihan who had been doing the job the longest, should be given a battle field commission. The firing battery had settled into the business and was running smoothly. I volunteered to relieve Moynihan at the front so that he could go back to Division Headquarters to get his commission and have a short orientation on how to be an officer.

When I arrived at his position he was with 'F' company. He said that the second battalion was to be in reserve for a few days and that everything was quiet. He and his party had dug a nice big fox hole which they had covered with logs and had pine boughs in the bottom to sleep on. It was very plush as fox holes go.

The jeep that brought me up was hardly out of sight when I got word that all FOs and company commanders were to report to the battalion commander. Higher headquarters had discovered that they had only taken the nose of the hill which they had reported that they had taken. They were ordered to finish the job and take the rest of the hill where the Germans were still entrenched and DO IT NOW!!

It was no surprise to me that they hadn't taken hill 508 because coming in, I was headed up the road to that hill when an infantry machine gun outposts halted us. I told the guard that I was suppose to report to hill 508. His remark was, "The battalion is in reserve about 1500 yards back. If you're going up there, you better learn to speak German." I thanked him very much and we turned the jeep around and got to hell out of there.

At the meeting I was changed from Co. 'F' to Co. 'G' because 'G' Company was going to lead the attack. Because I was the ranking observer, I volunteered to go with the lead company.

We immediately moved out to our jump off point where I had been stopped just a short time before. As we approached the jump off point, we started getting small arms fire from the enemy. The Lieutenant platoon leader and I were trying to see where the enemy fire was coming from. I adjusted a few rounds into a thick woods in front of us and announced that I was firing a preparation of 'battalion two rounds' (24).

After they had landed we were still getting enemy fire so the infantry company commander said, "Bring them in closer." I told him I would drop the minimum of 50 yards but it was possible that a round might catch one of the tall trees we were under and could cause friendly casualties. He said, "Fire them anyway."

When I gave the order to fire, the lieutenant and I were the only ones standing up because we needed to see where the shells landed. As soon as the rounds started coming in, one caught the same tree that we were under and shrapnel rained on our heads. A piece hit him in the left shoulder and knocked him flatter than a pancake. He was less than a foot and a half from me. I swear it went over my shoulder.

I went down on my knees to give him first aid and we called for the medic. I found he had a three inch piece of shrapnel imbedded in his shoulder just below the bone. I apologized to him because I knew it was one of our own rounds. He said, "Don't worry about me, this is a state side wound, I feel sorry for you because you are going to have to stay here." As the medic approached we got orders to jump off.

When I had relieved Moynihan, who was by now a battle smart veteran, he advised me to stay right behind the lead platoon. That was the exact position I had when the fragment hit the platoon leader. Once we jumped off we didn't get any enemy fire and we were moving fast.

My two men, Corporal James Bailey and the radio operator were carrying the sixty pound radio and the battery pack as well as a full pioneer kit which included a 'D' handle shovel, a pick and an ax. They wanted to stay back with the heavy weapons platoon who were burdened with mortars and machine guns and couldn't move as fast as the riflemen. I gave them hell. I said "Moynihan said to stay with the lead platoon and that's just what we're going to do. We'll take turns carrying the radio".

Three fourths of the way up the mountain we heard intense firing of enemy burp guns to our rear. We had continued to the top of the hill when we got word that the heavy weapons platoon had been wiped out to the man. Their platoon leader, who was trying to make connections with the rest of the company, was the only survivor. The rifles were moving too fast. This was the same platoon that the FOs had wanted to be with.

It was dark when we took the hill and I learned that we were completely surrounded by the enemy. I ordered close defensive fires to the front and on both sides of our position but not to the rear where the heavy weapons platoon lay dead in a shallow dip.

We had a serious decision to make. We decided that if the infantry surrendered that we would try to make our way back to the main line of resistance. Bailey and I even flipped a coin to see which one of us would eat the pre-arranged code. We were all a little scared, but none of us wanted to show it. We dug in, in two man fox holes.

One person would sleep and one would be awake and on watch for two hours and then we would change. The company commander wanted me to sleep in his CP which was under a big rock. I had declined because I needed to be where I could get observation in case we needed more defensive fire. The infantry only had inadequate entrenching tools so when our holes were dug, the shovel and ax made the rounds of the platoons.

In the morning, just before daylight I could hear men talking to each other in German. They must have come in and dug in right in the middle of our platoon during the night. I'm not sure to this day that they didn't use our shovel.

About twenty feet to my right, a nineteen year old infantry soldier told the Germans, in their language, to get out of the hole or he would shoot them. A minute or two went by. They shut up but didn't move, so he fired a single round into their slit trench. They all dropped their burp guns and stood up. He took the entire squad prisoners.

About then the Lt. who had just lost all his heavy weapons platoon arrived and wanted to kill them all. An infantry sergeant and I restrained him and took his weapon away. It was about this time that I learned that the company commander had cracked up during the night. When I was told that he had been evacuated about two o-clock that morning, I knew that we could probably get back to the rest of the battalion if we went through the dip where the dead weapons platoon were. In a couple hours the prisoners were sent back to the battalion headquarters and we were relieved by another platoon.

The battalion continued our march in the mud and rain across the high ground north of Roan L'Etape which was a major road junction for supplying the German army. We continued east with very little resistance.

After about ten days of marching during the daytime on those muddy secondary roads and sleeping in the small towns, usually on the driveways, a new FO party came out to relieve us and told me that I was to report immediately to Col. Liles.

As we were leaving the area, the lieutenant who had been hit in the shoulder arrived back for duty. He gave me hell because I hadn't completed the job of getting him back to the states. I waved good-bye as I headed back to the relative safety of the artillery.

It seemed that while I was away there were some errors made by the firing battery. Liles had not realized that I had volunteered to be an FO until the problems started happening. Before we confronted the Ole Man, we took a detour by the shower unit and got a shower and some clean cloths.

When I reported, he immediately said, "Don't open your mouth, I'm giving you a direct order to never volunteer for any job that takes you away from the firing battery." I tried to tell him that I had no plans to volunteer ever again. I had found out in the first five minutes that I had made a mistake. He wouldn't let me say a damn word. Finally I saluted and went out the door of the house where he had his CP (command post).

Corporal Bailey had shown so much courage, aptitude and leadership ability during our time with the infantry that I recommended that he be made an FO and put in for a battle field commission.

I realized from my own experience that it was important to give the FO parties a break from time to time. We made up enough FO parties so that at least one at a time could be back resting with the firing battery. Lt. Devereux would never come back as he preferred to stay with the infantry but would send his men back.

He was a small man with a high pitched voice and he was determined to show his father, who had been a Major General in World War I and who had married a French nurse, that he had what it took to get the job done.

When a party would come back from the infantry, we would put them up in a house and assign the medic to stay with them when he was not needed in the battery. Our medic, Kraus, had found a concertina and would entertain them with music.

I usually kept some wine that the French gave us along the way for just such occasions. We let them have that too. Sgt. Shim, the ammunition sergeant, was put in charge of the wine from the time we hit the Rhone valley. He was in charge of rationing it out to the gun sections when they were off duty.

Since we often fired around the clock, we tried to give half of each section time off to rest or do whatever they wanted to which was usually sleep. Of course if we were extremely busy or changing position, everybody was on duty. There were quite a few men that didn't drink, period. We would try to be sure that coffee was always available.

One day I heard the accordion playing. I saw Kraus leading the FO party and they were all singing. One man was walking beside Kraus with a five gallon bottle of wine on his shoulder. They were headed for a 155 artillery battalion that was behind us. Sgt. Segal and I spotted them and quickly moved over to see what was going on. They told us that they appreciated the cannoneers and the accurate fire they put out, so they wanted to share the wine with them.

144

The FOs knew better than anyone the value of accurate and fast artillery. When we told them they were going to the wrong outfit, we turned them around toward 'B' Battery. I agreed to allow a small amount to any of the guys that wanted some. Business was slow that day. Sergeants Segal and Shim made sure that nobody got more than a half a canteen cup. After Kraus played a few tunes and the wine was half gone, they went back to the house, singing all the way.

The toughest and most important job by far in the field artillery is that of the forward observer and his party. He must live like an infantryman, face all the elements with little shelter, must carry a heavy radio on his back, a full pioneer set and keep up with the riflemen. One day in January or February, while we were in reserve, all the radio operator specialist and one of the corporals told the first sergeant that they wanted to turn in their stripes. As in the past, when a man turned in his stripes, I always accepted them.

However, the next time a party went out, they were all assigned to their same job, only now they were privates. Of course, they screamed. They had taken a bust so that they wouldn't have to go out. But it didn't work. I said, "I took your stripes but I didn't say that your duties would be any different." They were unhappy but they had to perform their duties and did, just as well as they always had. After they went out I told the first sergeant not to even report the incident and they got their stripes back the next time they came in.

One day, while we were going into a new position there was an American B-25 overhead going around in circles. With each circle he got a little lower. Sometimes he was over our territory and sometimes he was over enemy territory.

We thought he was lost, so we made an arrow from ammunition boxes pointed toward England. Before long we realized that his controls were not working. We tried to signal for the crew to jump out over our territory, which they did. The pilot was the last one out and landed in a big snow drift at least ten feet deep. His parachute had opened less than 200 feet from the ground.

When I got to him, only his fingers were sticking out of the snow but he was alive and uninjured. He was shook up to say the least. He told me that they were on what was called the ball bearing run. They were trying to knock out all the ball bearing plants which would make it impossible for the Germans to make the machines of war. Everything needed bearings. After the war it was learned that Germany was actually getting their bearings from Sweden which was supposed to be neutral.

He was on his way back to England when his controls stuck. That caused them to go in a continuous circle. They had circled until they ran out of fuel hoping they could get the thing to straighten out. I drove him over the aid station.

This was another time the fox holes suddenly got deeper. We knew that when the plane crashed, it could be in our area. It finally did crash in friendly territory in a wooded area just a few hundred yards from our position. That was the only place any where around that there weren't any of our troops. Normally, any wooded area was top priority for troops to hide. No doubt about it, the man upstairs was with us that day and took care of the men on the plane and the men on the ground. As soon as the plane hit the ground, all the digging came to a halt.

One day while we were occupying a position on some farm land, a man on a bicycle rode by our area. That night we were shelled with German artillery. Most of it fell behind the battery. There were no injuries and no material losses. The following night we were shelled again.

This time the shells fell a hundred to two hundred yards short of the battery. The next morning we received a call from the infantry headquarters that they had picked up a man on a bicycle who had been adjusting the fire on us. Any artilleryman knows that after you get overs and shorts, the next barrage is going to be right on target. We needed to get our butts out of there in a hurry.

Everyone knew where to go to the alternate position. As I was supervising the departure, one gun section seemed extremely slow moving out. When they finally came by where I was waiting for them, I stopped them and asked the sergeant, "What in the hell made you so slow moving." He said they took a little more time than they thought to get the truck loaded.

I told him to get moving, fast. I jumped in my jeep and followed them up the road. I noticed a GI raincoat was covering something in the middle near the tail gate. Next thing I knew I saw the coat fly off and there was a 600 pound, live steer swinging his tail. I had to laugh.

It seems that they had captured it about a week before and were waiting for the weather to turn cold to butcher him so the battery could have some fresh beef. It took a little extra time to fit their prize into the two and a half ton truck along with all the ammunition, equipment and ten cannoneers.

After a couple days in the next position, early in the morning, I saw a commotion going on near that gun sections. Sgt. Segal and I went down to see what was going on. They were all upset because someone had stolen their steer during the night. They could see a unit behind us had a steer tied to the trail of one of their guns. They knew it was their steer and were going to take it back, by force if necessary. I told them no.

Then a young private asked me, "Sir, can I say something"? "Go ahead". "I was on guard from two to four with the section and it was getting real cold. I knew that they would butcher him in the morning. I had gotten real attached to him, so I turned him lose. That was how he got over to the other outfit. They didn't steal him." For an hour or two we had to look out for his safety. Everyone went back to normal duty and the other unit had fresh steak for a few days.

One day we had just pulled into a position in mud up to our knees. It was pouring down rain and windy. Most of the vehicles with the guns and the kitchen had to be pulled into position by our M-5 tractor used for towing 155s and 8" howitzer. Without the tractor we would have been unable to get the guns in position at all.

About the time the guns were ready to fire, we were putting up a pyramidal tent to use for our fire direction center. When the tent was about half way up we got a fire mission. A strong wind, coupled with the rain, blew the tent down on top of us. While we were under this wet tent trying to get the fire mission through, the battalion S-3 called up and wanted to know why we were so slow. I said, "Maybe it is because we don't have a steam heated room like battalion fire direction. Rounds are on the way".

On 13 December we established our position in a field between Bining and Rohrbach. This was the first fortifications that we encountered in the Maginot line. I had taken over a small concrete box about seven feet square for my fire direction center and living space which I shared with the recorder and the medic. It was about eight feet high with about four feet below the ground. There were two small openings about two feet long and four inches high facing east about eye level.

There was a small German stove with a pipe that served as a chimney. It was pretty crowded, what with the charts needed for plotting fire missions. But it was warmer than being out in the snow and safer than being in a tent. It was located between two of the larger forts of the Maginot line. The guns had been dug in and the bunkers for the men were sheltered with logs. They had stoves in the bunkers to keep warm.

We had liberated a portable German gasoline powered electric generator which was small and easy to take with us. The wire section would run an electric wire to each bunker so they even had electric lights. It was believed that my shelter had been used by the Germans for storing sensitive fusses and dynamite that they didn't want stored in the bigger forts. I had complete communications directly with the guns and with higher headquarters and battalion fire direction center.

One day I saw a flight of four American fighter-bomber planes dropping bombs on our own battalion headquarters which was in the back of a building in Bining, France. Fortunately, at least for our battalion, it hit the other end of the building where there was a medical collecting station. Nobody was hurt from battalion but all the wounded in the collecting station were killed. I did not know that at the time but when I saw the plane coming back for another run on battalion headquarters, I ordered my men to shoot. I didn't care if they were Americans, they were killing our people and I ordered my antiaircraft section and our machine guns to open fire.

I reported to battalion headquarters that we had fired on that flight of planes. At the time there was an order out that nobody was to shoot at American planes, even if they attack us. Col. Liles told me he would need to call an immediate report to the division commander. He said, "Now you've really done it. There is no way you can get out of this one." I told him that if they bombed us again I would certainly fire again. "To hell with higher headquarters". When General Burress heard about it, he said he would have done the same thing and told Liles to forget it.

One day, early in the morning, just about dawn I got an air raid warning that planes were approaching from the rear, heading north toward the German lines. We sounded the alarm to the battery and I ran out in my long johns to man fire direction's fifty caliber machine gun that was mounted on a tripod for antiaircraft defense.

I looked to the south and saw a single enemy aircraft coming in, flying close to the ground. He was headed right smack for my position. It appeared that a little smoke was coming out of the plane and that he was trying to get back to the German lines about 3000 yards north of us. As he got within my range, I pressed the trigger and only one round went off. I quick spun around and fired another one as he was going away.

I had failed to check to see if the gun was set on automatic. The other guns in the battery did not fire because they would have been firing right at me and they figured I had him cold and couldn't miss. He was still smoking when he went over the hill and over the German line. There were many other people behind us that reported that they had shot this plane down but I assure you, he got back to his own lines. The whole battery got a good laugh at the battery exec in his underwear, who had failed to check his weapon. The laugh did as much good for morale as hitting the plane would have done.

One day, I was told that I could not requisition any TNT blocks because they would be needed for setting up defensive lines to our rear. That was to be prepared to blow up bridges, roads, trees or anything to slow up the enemy if we need to make a rapid withdrawal. The preparation was being done by 'B' Company of the 325th Engineers. We knew that because it was so cold, we would need TNT to break the frozen crust of the ground so that we could dig in our guns and personnel bunkers if we moved. At this time, the feelings were that we would eventually have to drop back to the Eisenhauer defensive line twenty miles to the rear.

When I told Sgt. Segal he said, "Let me call a friend over at the engineers." When he called, their supply sergeant said they had plenty of TNT and it was not necessary to cut off the supply. "Come on over with your jeep. We'll have a cup of coffee and you can have a whole jeep load." We took my brand new jeep and a bottle of whiskey to express our thanks for his assistance. We went to his supply point and they loaded up the jeep with cases of TNT. We even had a couple cases piled up on the hood.

We thanked him and headed back to the position which took us through Bining. On the main street of Bining in the snow storm, who do we meet but Col. Liles coming the other way. He signaled for us to stop and he came screaming up to us, "I thought I told you not to requisition any more TNT."

I told him we hadn't requisitioned it, that a friend had given it to us because they had more than they needed. "I'll tell you what I'm going to do. If you deliver those two cases on the hood to Headquarters Battery, I won't make an issue of it." We thanked him, delivered the TNT, and returned to our battery.

149

When we were moving, we often encountered road blocks. They could be anything from trees to old vehicles to banks of dirt. We had to be very careful as they would often have explosive booby traps. One day Colonel Liles was in Bining and saw a little French girl playing in a trash pile when she was blown up by a grenade. It upset him terribly. He picked her up and took her to her mother. He said he was so sorry and her response was "C'est le Guerre" (that's war).

Bernice:

Winter was beginning to take over and a major problem was developing with feet. The condition was called trench foot. Trenches were a WWI phenomenon but the fox holes of 1944 were every bit as cold and damp and muddy as any trench. The problem was manifest in a vascular problem where the feet became swollen, red and itching. If not taken care of they would actually become black and gangrenous.

Various procedures were established to help prevent the problem. Clean dry socks became as important as food and every man was ordered to change socks. If the clean socks did not arrive, each man was supposed to remove his boots, take off his socks, massage his feet and put the sock on the other foot. What this did was release the pressure of the boot and improve the circulation.

Something else happened. The soldiers discovered that if they got trench foot they would be sent to the hospital and would not have to be exposed to enemy fire and the generally miserable existence of a combat soldier. It was a court martial offense to develop trench foot.

There were specialty hospitals with the general hospital designation but ours was not one of them. Most of our surgical patients were men with imbedded shrapnel and various fractures.

It was discovered that the corpsmen made very good sterile assistants and more and more the RNs became overseers. This was the origin of the surgical technicians. It had a profound and long range effect on hospital staffing patterns. Eventual even nursing education changed because the operating room experience was eliminated from the curriculum.

Some corpsmen even learned to start IVs and administer sodium pentathal, the anesthesia of choice for our type of work.

We didn't require relaxation and there were not as many respiratory and systemic risks of the more sophisticated gases. Of course, it didn't explode or burn like ether.

The back table technique was very useful for our type of surgery. There would be four gurneys used as tables parked like spokes of a wheel with the sterile supply table in the center. Each tech would have his Mayo stand and the tech in the center would keep him supplied with sutures, sponges, etc.

Getting the men back to duty was our constant mission. It was not always appreciated by our patients. One man in particular was having an unusually hard time learning to walk after a leg injury. He simply could not seem to be able to bear weight, even with a crutch. One day he was on the treatment table in the orthopedic clinic when an ancient oak tree outside the clinic gave up and fell through the roof.

The place was total chaos. After the dust had settled, they started to assess the damage and account for everyone who was in the room. They realized that the full trunk of the tree had landed on that table and had broken it completely in half. When they started looking for the patient, he was no where to be found. They finally discovered him four wards up and moving fast. The next day he was on his way back to the front.

An interesting side light of the event was that the British government charged the USA for the loss of the tree because all trees were the property of the crown and our men had cut it up to get it off our clinic without permission. No big deal. I doubt if the lend lease book ever did balance.

A French general named Charles DeGaul had organized an army of French Freedom Fighters which included troops from many of the French colonies such as Morocco and Algeria. Many of these men were Arabs. The French army had been disband during the German occupation so there were no support organization for their troops. But troops are troops and the US provided them with ammunition and support, including the medical service.

The French casualties were evacuated through our regular evacuation channels and thus it was that we became the host of several Moroccan soldiers who spoke no English. We also had French soldiers. The communication problem was solved when one of our corpsmen, who spoke french, would tell the French soldier who spoke Arab who would then tell the Arabs. Their reply was the reverse procedure. Needless to say there wasn't a whole lot of communicating but the GIs found a simpler way with gesture.

One of the little details of housekeeping that plagued the staff was cutting the grass. There were no lawn mowers. The only tools provided for this job were old fashioned sickles like the one on the Soviet flag. Most of the Americans had never even seen one of these. They thought it was great sport to get the Arabs to cut the grass. The Arabs didn't seem to mind. They even seemed to enjoy the activity.

The allies were moving steadily and surely east. The First Army under General Hodges was working the northern sector through France, Belgium, and Luxembourg. Early in December, the German army made a heavy attack in the area known as the Ardennes in Belgium. The 106th Division that had been at Fort Jackson with us, had just come on line in that sector. It was an unusually young group of men which I am sure Nazi intelligence knew. They were unable to hold the line.

This became known as the Battle of the Bulge. In fact, the 101st airborne division was surrounded for a time at a place called Bastogne. Our beds filled up fast and everybody became quite grim. Many of our nurses had husbands and fiances in the area.

It could have been demoralizing with Christmas coming on. We went all out to make the holidays as cheerful as possible for the patients. A ward decorating contest was organized. It was the patients and the corpsmen who really got in the spirit. Christmas trees were issued to each ward but some of them were rather scroungy. More than one soldier visited the top of King George's trees with a saw. I don't believe the forester noticed, or maybe he just ignored it in the spirit of the season.

It was a real challenge for the patients. They made all types of improvised tree ornaments from paper chains, the ever popular popcorn garlands, icicles from foil cigarette packages, even broken thermometers. But the ward that won the prize were the guys who made balloons from condoms and painted them with poster paint to look like real ornaments. Not only did they have the most unique tree, which actually looked good, but there was a patient who was an artist and he had painted all the windows with Christmas scenes.

During the week before Christmas they had made their ward off limits to everyone except their own people. When it came time for the judging, all the black out drapes were closed. There was a patient stationed at each drape. When the judges arrived at the ward, the drapes flew open as they enter and the group burst forth into 'We Wish You A Merry Christmas'.

On Christmas Eve all the hospital personnel formed into groups and went from ward to ward singing carols. At midnight the Catholic Chaplain said mass and visited all the bed bound Catholic patients with communion.

Christmas morning, the protestant Chaplain presided over a full house. There was electricity in the air. You could feel the presence of God as every soul was praying. For many, this may have been a new experience but it was very real. Dinner with all the trimmings was almost an anticlimax.

The rules on packages had been relaxed for Christmas. One afternoon I was huddling over the stove when I noticed a loaf of bread in the ash can. The strange thing was that the bottom had duct tape on it, so I checked to see why. Inside the bread was a pint bottle of brandy. I showed it to the girls in the hut and one girl claimed it, but she sure didn't offer to share it with any of the rest of us. I will never forget the Christmas of '44.

Eli:

For Christmas, Bernice sent me a complete bible which was just the right size to fit in my field jacket pocket. When the men found out that I had it, they often borrowed it. It was very popular when the shells were flying around our heads. The popularity of that bible closely matched the intensity of the war. When things were dull the men seemed to worry more. It was during this time that it was heavily used but it would always come back to me for safe keeping.

Our Christmas dinner was complete with all the trimmings in comparison to the food right after that. The battle of the bulge was given priority on all the supplies including ammunition and gasoline. Our class 'A' rations were not delivered and all that we received was 'C' rations and canned SPAM.

That was OK for a few days, but before long the men started getting sick of it. In fact they actually got physically sick and would throw up after the first bite. I had a meeting with them and told them that it was all in their head. The cooks used all kinds of imagination to disguise it. Sometimes it would be ground up like hamburger. They would mix it with pancake batter for spamcakes, or mix it with catchup and rice for Spamish rice. Before long, nothing worked.

153

I had a meeting with the whole battery and tried to convince them that it was all in their head, like being seasick, where one man gets sick and makes everyone else sick. The following meal was lunch. I was at a small table and the men were scattered around in the area of the kitchen.

The first bite I took, I got sick. I had to run through the men to get out of the area because I was going to throw up. I got behind the barn and it was just like being seasick. For a few minutes I really felt like hell. When I went back to the battery, slowly walking back to the table, some of the men called out, "Its all in the head, Lieutenant, its all in the head." I told them it was all their fault cause they put it in my head.

Fortunately, we had discovered a German army warehouse near Bining that was loaded with wine and cases of lard. Potatoes were plentiful. Every cellar was well stocked with old potatoes. They also had turnips and potatoes stored in mounds in the field. The cooks took that lard and the potatoes and made french fries. The men really liked this and it saved us from starvation. The quartermaster made and delivered fresh bread that came in large round loaves with a thick hard crust. An occasional deer was shot during this time, which also improved our meals. The regular class 'A' rations were restored in the middle of January.

Our winter offensive had bogged down. This area was the center piece of the Maginot line south and west of the city of Bitche. In this city there was an ancient citadel that had been built in the twelfth century. It was a massive walled in area with a moat and stone walls fifty feet thick. It was designed to be a self contained fortress on the top of the highest ground around and went five or six stories under the ground.

For centuries, wars and battles had been fought over this territory but the city and the fortress had never been taken by force. Even when Hitler's forces over ran France, the 'Country of Bitche' held out. It had been ceded to the Germans after much negotiation between the Germans and the puppet Vichy government of a conquered France. The French army was ordered to withdraw to the French controlled area.

There had always been a dispute about which country owned the Alsace-Lorraine provinces and all through history it changed hands many times. In 1918, after the first World War, it was determined to belong to France. In 1939 when the French withdrew from the area, it was immediately annexed once again by the Third Reich and was regarded by Germany as part of their country.

The 100th Division had actually penetrated the outer limits of the city in late December when the better publicized 'Bulge' developed in the area to the north.

Because it was necessary to reinforce the First Army where the Germans had broken through, the Third Army had moved to the left and the Seventh Army pulled back to hold the ground where the Third had moved out. The 44th Infantry Division which was on our left moved to the left six or seven thousand yards. This left our entire left flank exposed. Two light tanks had been sent over to partially cover the gap. They were located between the 3rd. battalion of the 397th and our battery who had the responsibility of covering the gap with direct artillery fire if that became necessary.

On New Years Eve I gave the gun sections permission for volunteers to fire four rounds by each gun to celebrate the new year. Every cannoneer could dedicate his round to anyone or anything he wanted to. At midnight the selected target was a ware house in enemy territory known to be used by the Germans for troops. The rounds were no sooner on the way than we received an urgent request for Nan-Baker (normal barrage). This is a pre-established target between the infantry and the enemy, prepared every night for the purpose of protecting the infantry if an attack should occur during the night.

At 2359 on 31 December 1944, that is exactly what happened. The Germans had launched their last offensive thrust of the western front. Years later we learned that this was operation Nordwind (north wind) which Herr Hitler had personally planned and supervised. It was the last major offensive of the German army.

We fired continuously the rest of the night and into the morning. About noon, the battery commander, Capt. Henson came to me and said that there was a gap of five or six thousand yards on the left flank that had left the 100th exposed by the withdrawal of the 44th Division. We already knew that. He said that the Germans were expected to break through at any time and when they did they would come over the hill on our left front with tiger tanks. These were their biggest and best tactical weapon. They had a reputation as being very good maneuvering in deep snow.

He said we had been given permission to pull back ten miles by battalion headquarters. In uncharacteristic army protocol, he also said the decision was up to me. It was my feeling that as long as the infantry was in position, we should stay to fire their missions. At Myrtle Beach during training, 'B' Battery had an outstanding reputation for direct fire accuracy. We had actually made more direct hits on moving targets during training than the rest of division artillery combined.

I elected to confer with the chiefs of section. They all agreed that we should stay. "Let them come." They didn't want to give up their well prepared bunkers and parapets for the crews and guns and have to start all over again in a new position in the hard, frozen ground. The snow and blizzard like conditions were really bad. It was the coldest winter that they ever had before or since in that region. During a lull we even ran a jeep back and forth below the ridge while the gunners practiced aiming and adjusting the guns.

During the second night we were firing almost continuously with a wide range of fire missions. The Chief of Firing Battery came to me and said they were running low on ammunition. When they had been unable to locate the ammunition section for more, he had discovered that not only was the ammo section gone but so was the Battery Commander. The entire CP including the kitchen, wire section and survey were also gone.

About 0200, First Sergeant Lester Frew showed up to let me know that the rest of the battery was about ten miles to the rear along with the rest of the battalion. I was shocked and disturbed to learn that they had left the firing battery without support and had not even told me. I gave him a direct order that we were to have hot food and ammunition in the position before dawn. The ammo and 'K' rations with one stove arrived as directed.

When ammunition again ran short the following night, we tried to contact Service Battery for re-supply and were told that it would be two to three days before we could expect any as they were moving. Fortunately, there was a battery of French armored 105s a few hundred yards away who seemed to have a good supply of ammo, and hadn't fired a round all night. They had all retired to their buttoned up vehicles for the night and did not even have a guard out.

An unauthorized transfer of ammunition was made, which kept the battery firing. I didn't understand how we could have fired so many rounds until the French Captain came over the next morning to complain that we had stolen his ammunition. I showed him the empty boxes and pointed out that every one of them was marked US Army. There was not a French box in the lot.

My inability to speak French and his inability to speak English was a blessing. He left shaking his head, going back along the well worn path in the snow from his ammo dump to

156

our position. It was obvious that we had re-supplied our battery from their dump. Shortly after that, they march ordered and returned to the French position on the right flank of the 100th.

The German army had inflicted heavy casualties on the 397th Infantry at a village called Rimling just north of us. We had an FO party, headed by a newly assigned officer, Lt. Preston Chamblis, in Rimling with the infantry. They were in an old house on the second floor, along with one squad of riflemen, left to protect them while they directed fire to cover a successful withdrawal of the 2nd Bn. of the 397th.

There were two Tiger Tanks sitting in front of the house. Chamblis had directed fire for about two days when they ran out of small arms ammunition. This was because of a lot of German soldiers coming up the stairs looking for loot. The only way to avoid being killed was to shoot them. The noise of our artillery fire prevented the Germans outside from realizing there was gunfire inside the house. Our guys would push the bodies out the window into the alley in the back yard where the other Germans couldn't see them. Their bodies were soon covered by deep snow.

Later in the third day, the rest of the battery had returned to the gun position. Captain Henson was back with the battery and was told of the FOs situation. He gave them an option of surrendering or trying to make their way back to the American line. The lieutenant decided to surrender his party and gave the infantry sergeant the same option. The sergeant decided that they would try to make their way back to their company. They were all killed except one PFC. He came to us and explained what had taken place.

After the FOs had surrendered, the Germans made them stand in the street when the American planes were overhead strafing with 50 caliber machine guns. This caused the lieutenant to be wounded in the knee. German medics in the POW camp took good care of him. They were eventually liberated by US troops and back in the states before VE (Victory in Europe) Day.

About this time, Captain Henson decided to deliver a box of hand grenades to our other FOs who were with the infantry. They were in reserve and were occupying one of those massive forts 500 yards to our front. Somehow, a grenade went off, causing him to lose part of a hand.

When he was evacuated, as the Battery Exec, I took temporary command of the battery. My first act was to order Sgt. Segal to go into the town and get fresh water to wash the mess kits and lumber to build tables inside the fort where the battery CP and the kitchen were. I wanted the men to have better protection while they ate. Before this they were only allowed to get their chow and would have stay out in the open to eat it. Fifteen or twenty men had diarrhea.

The next day, Col. Liles came to the position and made me the battery commander. He said that he had made a mistake by not making me the CO back at Jackson, but he thought that I was too young and carefree. He arranged for Lt. Jackson from 'A' Btry to be our new exec. At that time, Jackson was an FO and Liles thought he was going to marry his niece and wanted to get him in a safer place. The following day, the Colonel also became a casualty when he turned himself in for battle fatigue. He had been unable to keep any food down since the German offensive had begun.

After about nine days, the German offensive had been halted and most of the fighting consisted of both sides firing artillery at each other. This was what we called harassing fires and interdiction. Every night just about supper time they would harass us with incoming artillery. The firing battery was dug in, in an open field and my little shelter was in the middle. The kitchen was about 500 yards behind us in a concrete fort.

It was my policy to not eat until after all the men had been fed. It would be just about dark when the recording clerk or the medic and I would start up the hill to eat. That was when the rounds would start coming in. They never all came in at once. As a round would come in, we would hit the snow. The men on the guns would be watching us and found it very amusing as we stumbled up the hill.

I finally thought that I had found a better way to get to supper. We would take the jeep and go along a farm trail to the west and turn south to a chateau and left again to get to the fort. It was two and a half miles but I thought it was much safer as no rounds had ever landed on the roads.

One day, while returning to the fire direction center, we had just parked the jeep when the rounds started coming in again. The driver wanted to put the camouflage net over the jeep but I told him to forget it and get in the hut. That was a good decision because the next round went right through the space between the windshield and the seat and landed about twenty yards on the other side. Again we thanked the guy upstairs as the net would have caused the round to go off right where we were.

Shortly after that we moved up from Bining/Rohrbach to a farm house in the forest near the village of Petit Rederchen. It was occupied by a French family. We referred to it as Annie's place. Annie's husband was a soldier in the German army and was not home. We took over the front room for our command post while they remained in the rest of the house. The men made themselves comfortable in the other buildings, including the barn.

Although the German army had abandoned their offensive, there was still intermittent shelling going on by both sides. The weather was miserable and neither side had much desire to fight, so the line remained static for several weeks. When we left, Annie gave me a china angel.

During this lull, our warrant officer, Kramer the battalion personnel officer, decided that he would pay us a visit to bring the battalion payroll and spend the night at the front. He figured he was doing us a favor, because then we wouldn't have to drive to Division headquarters in the rear. Of course, I really would have preferred to go to the rear where I could get a shower and hot food in a French Cafe, just like Paris.

He had been told that the battery officers would probably try to freak him out by pretending that the place was being shelled. Well sure enough, he hadn't been in the CP more than ten minutes when we heard incoming shells and they were landing close by. The walls of the house were stone and so gave fairly good protection from anything except a direct hit. We would be safe below the level of the windows. All of us hit the floor while Kramer said, "Yeah, sure, well you can't get me to fall for that". I grabbed him and dragged him down.

When the shelling stopped, I took him to the door and we looked out. Sure enough, there were three brand new shell holes right in the front yard. I said, "Do you remember seeing those when you came in?" He turned white and called to his driver. "We're getting out of here right now." They would probably have been safer with us in the house, because they had to drive blacked out for about ten miles so as not to draw fire from the enemy.

During this period it was important to keep the men busy. Yes, we fired several missions, but had times when nothing much was happening. To keep them from thinking about the danger that we might be in, I had them stay busy cleaning the guns and equipment and generally keeping the place policed up.

It was during this time that General Murphy, Divarty commander, was out visiting the troops and came by Annie's Place to see Baker Battery. He was highly impressed by the condition of the guns and equipment and the appearance and spirit of the men. While in my CP, he saw the picture of Bernice in her uniform on my desk. He asked a lot of questions about where she was etc. He said that in a couple weeks there was to be some R&R (rest and rehabilitation) opportunities to England for the Division and that I would be given one of them.

While we were at Annie's place, a Frenchman came walking up the road. We had a check point at our perimeter and our guard stopped the man. He was wearing a brand new pair of shoe packs. These were a scarce item and were for combat troops only. The corporal of the guard brought him into my CP. I checked the boots and they were definitely government issue.

The corporal handed me the pass the man was using. It said that he was a military government officer with the 397th Infantry and it was signed by none other than Ulysses Grant. I figured this must be a phony pass so we made him take off the shoe packs and gave him an old pair of combat boots. It was fifty years later that I learned that there really was a Ulysses Grant in the 397th and he was actually an infantry captain. It didn't matter. No one was allowed to give away the critical shoe packs.

During this period we were pulled out of line and moved to Sarre Union for a week of maintenance and recreation. Only a few men remained at Annie's place to keep our place there. The officers' quarters was the coat room in the theater and the men were across the street in fairly good buildings. We were out of range of the enemy artillery and everyone enjoyed this.

We laid on a dance with a school of Polish girls, which until they had retreated, had been run by the Germans. They were studying to be secretaries for the Germans. We borrowed a dance band from the French. It ran from 1800 to 2000, when the girls were escorted back to the school. There was no hanky panky that I was aware of. The chaperones that came with them were very strict. The men all enjoyed it anyway and so did the girls. That was on Friday and on Saturday we went back to Annie's and prepared for the big attack on the French Citadel city of Bitche.

Bernice:

About this time, a high wire fence was erected around a vacant area across the road that ran in front of the nurses' huts. Tents sprang up and we were surprised to learn that we were now hosts to German prisoners of war. They wore black wool pants and shirts which were dyed army ODs. On the front of one pant leg was a big white P and a W on the other. The P and the W were repeated on the seat.

These men were to perform work details for the hospital. Before long they were all over the place, doing various duties. Nobody seemed to worry about guarding them. The compound gate stood open during the day. There were two that I remember especially.

One was an old man. He must have been a farmer. He had the duty of cutting the grass. He used the scythe like an expert. A lawn mower could not have cut grass any closer or more evenly. The other one was just a boy, maybe fifteen. He was assigned to the nurses' mess. It was amusing. He would fold a towel over his arm and wait on us as if we were in a fancy restaurant. No cup was ever empty. He wore his PWs as if it were a tuxedo.

About the same time we also came in contact with another group of POWs. The United States Army had liberated a German prisoner of war camp containing British soldiers who were captured during the evacuation of the continent at Dunkirk. They were sent to us through the normal evacuation channel. Two wards were vacated of patients for them.

I had never seen such emaciated people. They looked like skeletons covered with sallow skin. They had been so starved that they could not tolerate any food. They were given chicken broth a spoonful at a time with a small rest between swallows. But not one of them ever complained. They were all so happy just to be in England. We only had them two or three days until the British army arranged for their transfer.

Even though the war was going badly for the Germans, they came up with two last weapons that they hoped would save them from total defeat. The first one was called the buzz bomb. It was a pilotless aircraft which was actually a large bomb. It would fly until it ran out of gas. They were targeted for London, where it would fall and explode. In their usual manner, the Londers accepted this new menace and went about their business, only diving for shelter when the motor cut off.

This was followed shortly afterward by what was known as the V-2. The V-2 was a rocket which was faster than sound. It landed and went off before anyone knew it had arrived. This was very scary. However, the Royal Air Force discovered the launch site in Holland which the Germans were using and destroyed it, ending this threat.

Eli was able to write frequently but couldn't say much about where he was or how he was doing. Our letters were mostly about what we would do after the war was over. On New Year's eve our first wedding anniversary, I wondered where he was and what was going on there.

Eli:

We received a call from special service to arrange for the Red Cross women to visit the battery for a day and give out doughnuts and talk with the men. We made the coffee and they brought the doughnuts. I had twisted my bad knee so had stayed in the CP and was resting on a cot. Also, I didn't want the men to think I was being a big shot with the girls. But when two of the women brought me coffee and doughnuts, I thanked them and decided to go out with the rest of the battery.

When I went outside I saw one of our more colorful PFCs named St. Peter down in the fox hole. When I asked him what he was doing in the hole He said, "I hear airplanes strafing, Get in the hole Lieutenant. By Jesus they're coming, get in the hole." I told him that we had not received any warning of aircraft in the area, and to come with me to where the Red Cross was and get some doughnuts. He said, "Hell no, I'm not getting out of this hole."

I moved over to the doughnuts. With my first doughnut in my hand, I heard planes coming. All the men reacted instantly and jumped in the holes. Two of the girls followed them into the holes but two girls just stood out in the open, admiring the beautiful way the planes were flying.

As each plane reached our position they would do a roll over and went straight up in the air. They were P 51s. I grabbed one of the girls and pulled her into a trench beside a barn. I told her that even though they were American planes, they were shooting real bullets and had already strafed some of our troops. It was only seconds before the planes disappeared and everything returned to normal. The women were ecstatic. They had experienced the real thing.

A few days later, our medic recommended that the battalion surgeon check St. Peter and he was immediately evacuated for battle fatigue. He was the oldest and had been the strongest man in the battery since its beginning. Now he couldn't lift thirty pounds. He was a French Canadian lumberjack who had joined the army so that he could be an American citizen when he received an honorable discharge. He even brought his own double edged lumberjack ax. When ever we needed trees cleared to get a field of fire, he could do it in less time than any ten other guys.

He was a great story teller, especially when there was terrible weather conditions in the field. One of his favorite stories was when they were taking logs down the river, if you fell in the ice cold water, you should never change your wet cloths until they dry on your body or you would get pneumonia.

His solution for a bad cold, or anything else, was to find a spring where deer drank and drink a cup of water where the deer had left their droppings. The men loved him because it made our hardships seem like nothing. No matter whatever bad happened he had a story that was even worse, and he had always come out OK. That way we would laugh at our hardships.

St. Peter had been with the battery from the early days at Fort Jackson and was always a great morale builder. Another one of his quirks was that any time we had a formal inspection in ranks, he would start to laugh whenever the inspecting officer would stop if front of him. When I asked him why he did that, he told me that where he came from, when they took a pig to market they would tie a rope around one of the legs. When buyers would come by, they would look the pig over. "Anytime an officer stops in front of me, looking me over, I can't help but think of that pig and I can't help laughing."

I would always personally brief every officer who came to inspect our battery that it would be better if they would skip St. Peter and explain to them why. Of course this only insured that everyone of them would stop and talk to him. He always laughed but no one ever gigged him or the battery.

Early during our training, a corporal took four men including St. Peter to carry some heavy two by sixes. When they got to the pile, the men started fussing about who had to carry the biggest piece. He told the corporal, "By Jesus, we don't need these guys". He picked up the whole pile by himself. When I saw what was going on, I stopped the detail and asked the corporal how come one man was carrying all the lumber. He told me that St. Peter said, "If they were going to fight about it, he would just take the whole pile." When I asked the private if that was right he said, "By Jesus, that's right, sir." That was my first contact with a very special soldier named St. Peter.

Shortly after St. Peter left, we were given word that we would attack Bitche on 15 March. The weather had changed, it was getting warm, snow was melting fast and it was a real wet spring. We were glad to see the snow go away, although one gun section got flooded out in the middle of the night and they had to move to a better position. The only spot we could put them in was right behind a cherry tree.

In order for this section to have a field of fire, I authorized the chief of section to cut the tree down. Without St. Peter, it took a lot longer too. It broke the heart of the family living there. C'est Le Guerre. It is important to note here that the local people were allowed to submit a claim and they were re-imburse for every bit of damage done by the United States Army in the war ravaged areas. In this case, the cost of that tree would be paid for out of the lend lease funds through the French government.

When the rest and rehabilitation allotment for one officer and eight enlisted men arrived at battalion headquarters, Major Allport was the new battalion commander. I had hardly even seen him since he arrived in the battalion, and he didn't know anything about the fact that my wife was in England. When he received the allotment, he issued a directive that anyone interested in going to England should submit their name.

Even though the married officers all knew that Bernice was in England, most of them put in for the trip. These were the ones that I had taken OD for so many times back at Fort Bragg. This really ticked off the bachelor and none of them put in. I didn't put in either. They held a drawing and Captain McGwire won.

The next day, I got a call from Lt. Piper, General Murphy's aid, congratulating me on my trip to England. "You got it wrong, McGwire got that trip." "How come?" When I told him the story he said, "The General isn't going to like that." I guess the General called Allport personally and asked him how come Fishpaw wasn't going to England. His reply was, "I can't spare him." The General was angry. "No man is indispensable. Cut orders for Fishpaw to go." McGwire never did forgive me for taking his leave to England. I saw him forty years later and he was still sore.

On March 16th, the 398th Infantry entered the city of Bitche as the German army moved out. There was only scattered resistance. The whole city of Bitche turned out to welcome them. Although it was a great occasion for the people of Bitche, the Century men had been warned not to let their guard down, as there might be many German sympathizers in the city.

Our battery went into position at Waldhausen on the 17th. Another division had started taking over our positions as our division was alerted to get ready to make a fast motorized trip across the Rhein River. The new division took over the responsibility of their own artillery fire and we were put on stand by, but the guns stayed in position, ready to fire as a back up in case the Germans came back. All our FOs were ordered to returned to the battery. I had put my CP on the top of a hill overlooking the battery area and we dug in.

About that time, the service battery supply truck arrived with the long overdue liquor ration. The officers' rations had been paid for by the individual officer each month but this was the first delivery in over three months. Some of the officers who had ordered the booze were no longer in the battery and a couple of our young battlefield commissioned second lieutenants didn't drink. I immediately had the ration put in a fox hole to protect it and I called all the Chiefs of Sections to come get a bottle for each section.

They were happy to get it, as enlisted men did not have the luxury of ordering the hard stuff but were allowed two cans of free beer a week. About that time, the FOs started arriving. They took one look at the CP sitting on top of the hill and thought that we should move to a bombed out house not too far away which had a vaulted cellar still in tact.

It was the first time since we entered combat that the complete battery was all together. I OKed the move and the liquor was transferred to the cellar. Major Greene, the battalion S-3 said he would join us with a couple of the other staff officers. They brought their own bottles. Lt. Jackson volunteered to be in charge during this social gathering. The first sergeant and the maintenance sergeant also moved into the old house.

Maj. Abers, the new battalion exec. thought we should bring the prime movers and all the vehicles, including the kitchen into position to be ready to move in the morning. He wanted the stoves to be in the truck so that we could save time when we were ready to roll. I said that was not necessary as we could roll within fifteen minutes of getting the order, but a battery commander can not tell a new battalion exec anything, so the trucks were in the battery position, out in the open and exposed.

They had a going away party for me in the cellar. Major Green, had been with the battalion from the time we were activated. The junior officers were disappointed that he had not been made battalion commander or at least the exec. We all thought he would have been the best choice.

The Germans had shelled us heavily that night and in the morning there were shrapnel holes in all our trucks. Some fragments had even gone through the kitchen truck, right through the ovens on the stoves. We also lost two sights and two truck batteries.

One round had landed in the fox hole where we had first stashed the liquor and another round had landed in the hole where I would have been sleeping. The FOs suggestion to move, probably saved my life and more important, to at least a few of the officers, the liquor survived. We estimated that we had taken about 80 to 90 rounds. It was a clear reminder that the war was not over.

~ 13 ~

Rested, Rehabilitated, Reproduced

Eli:

I hitched a ride with the courier to Division headquarters in Rheems where our group of two officers and thirty five enlisted men were assembled and put on a train to the reple depple (army language for replacement depot) in Paris. Here we exchanged our battle worn uniforms for fresh class 'A's. When I opened my valpack, I discovered that there were condoms and pro kits in all my pockets. While we were partying, the non-comms had thought they would play a trick on me. Condoms were one thing I had no need for on that trip.

We took another train to Cherbourg and caught a ship which took us to South Hampton in southern England. I was made the officer in charge of security, responsible for the conduct of the troops on the ship. I immediately requested the airborne troops to be the MPs for the short trip. It was not because I thought they were so tough but because if they were on duty they would have to stay out of trouble. It was a peaceful crossing.

The Red Cross provided me with the phone # and location of the 106th General Hospital when I got to South Hampton. This worked out very well for me because it was only a short distance to the resort town of Bournemouth, just ten miles south of Wimborn Minster where Bernice was stationed.

Bernice:

One day in late March, while I was at lunch in the mess hall, I was told that I had a phone call. This was pretty unusual so when I took it I was surprised to hear Eli's voice which I didn't recognize at first. He had been given two weeks of R and R and was in South Hampton. I arranged for him to meet me at the Red Cross in Bournemouth and quickly arranged for a leave.

It just happened to be the Easter week end. The war was winding down in Europe and this was the first holiday that the English people were given the freedom to travel as they had been restricted for years in order to keep the trains available for the war effort.

In keeping with the spirit, the US had restricted travel for all the American service people stationed on the Island. Eli could use the train because he was on special orders but I could not. It didn't matter. Bournemouth was as good a place as any for us to spend some much appreciated time together. (29 March to 4 April).

On such short notice we had difficulty finding a hotel room. We must have gotten the last room in Bournemouth. It was in a little, out of the way hotel. The room had a wash basin but the bath and toilet were shared by all the guests and were reached from the hall. Out the window we had a marvelous view of an air shaft. Breakfast, tea and dinner were provided. Eli was not too thrilled with the food and refused to even try tea. I was too happy to care.

Eli:

I called Bernice, who did not know that I was coming. She was able to make a quick arrangement for a leave. The first thing we did was get a room at a hotel. After being in combat for six months, this was a great luxury to have a warm bed and hot water. The food was a part of the hotel fare and wasn't bad but there wasn't much of it.

We didn't go to tea at first which was a mistake as that was when they served the best food. We would supplement the food by going to the Red Cross and getting Spam sandwiches which I had sworn only a few months before that I would never touch again as long as I lived.

I never did figure out their money system. I was trying to buy a newspaper from an elderly English gentleman. I picked up the paper and asked him how much he needed. He said something which I couldn't understand at all. After I had him repeat it two or three times, I finally just held out my hand with the change in it and he took out what he needed. I laughed to myself. Here I was in England and they didn't even speak English. The girl who was managing the hotel spoke perfect American. She probably had a yank for a boyfriend.

I went to the local pub to get some beer and they only had a limited amount so everyone had to queue up. They opened at five. If you got there early, you might get two drinks but if you came later, you got none.

There was a couple Canadian officers in the line and they asked me what the 100th patch on my shoulder stood for. I told them it was for the 100th Infantry Division. They said they didn't know that any of the colonies had a hundred divisions. I told him we were not one of the colonies but we were Briton's best friend. "That is better than being just another colony". I managed to get two drinks. Beer was served at room temperature but was good anyway.

Sometime during this vacation I planted the seed of our next generation. It was a happy reunion with Bernice. This was more like a honeymoon than when we had done all that visiting right after we were married. It was all too soon that I had to return to the front lines.

When we returned to Paris and went to the train station, the train to Strasburg was so overloaded that men were clinging to the sides. I was told that we could hang on like everybody else. A couple of First Sergeants were with our group and they had the men all lined up and accounted for but I refused to let them ride this way. These guys had been through a war and it would be stupid to risk their lives by falling off an overcrowded train.

I went to the Red Cross and arranged for sleeping accommodations for all thirty five men. Most of us were very close to broke by now so this free lodging was welcome. It was another day before we went back to the front which made them all happy. I rented a room in a hotel, not far from the railroad station, for the night.

The next day, I was walking around that part of Paris while waiting for it to be time to board the train and went into a bistro. I had a twenty dollar bill left and ordered a drink. While the bartender was getting my drink, a Frenchman beside me offered to buy my English money. I refused to sell it to him as I wanted it

Lieutenants Eli and Bernice on the English Channel beach at Bournemouth, England. April, 1945.

for a souvenir. When the bar tender came back with my drink, he gave me change in French money for only ten dollars. I told him I had given him a twenty. He denied it and the money changer beside me backed him up, saying that I had only given him $10. For the first time on the trip I started to get mean. I told the bar tender that if I didn't get my correct change that he was cheating me out of, I was going to bust up his place.

About this time, the two big First Sergeants walked by outside and saw the argument. They came in to see if I needed any help. I told them that these guys were trying to cheat me out of ten bucks and the jerk beside me was giving me a hard time. They told me that all of our thirty five men were in the block and one volunteered to go get them. As soon as he went out the door, the bar tender suddenly realized he had made a mistake and paid me my ten dollars in American money. We called off the troops and I bought both the sergeants a drink.

That afternoon we arrived early enough at the railroad station to get seats for everyone and headed for Strasburg. When we arrived at Strasburg we discovered that there was no arrangement for our transportation back to our units. I told the men that we would have to hitch hike back. Most of the supply trucks were headed for the front.

A GI walked by me and saw my 100th patch. He told me that his smoke outfit was headed for the 100th Division area to smoke a river. I climbed up on the back of the two and a half ton truck and sat on a fifty five gallon drum of fuel for generating smoke along with two others from our group. As I was getting on the truck, I saw the markings on their bumper that showed that they were the 100th Smoke Generating Co. No relation to the 100th Infantry Division. They dropped us off near our units at the division area near Heilbronn, which was on the Neckar River in Germany.

The big effort at Heilbronn was to get some bridges built to get the heavy equipment across the river. The first seven bridges had been blown up by enemy artillery as soon as the first vehicles were in the middle of the bridge.

The smoke outfit's purpose was to lay down smoke for a two mile stretch so that the Germans couldn't see where the new bridges were and we would have a chance of them lasting long enough to get the heavy stuff across. The foot soldiers had already gone across in small boats. They had met unusually strong resistance. The mayor of Heilbronn was an SS Lt. General and chose to make a last stand. German soldiers even dressed as women and waved at the Americans to get them close and off guard when they would shoot them.

When I found the battery, it was in an open field on the west side of the river where the Germans surely had direct observation from the other side. There was a castle on a hill which made an observation point that allowed them to hit the bridges. They were so accurate that they could even hit the telephone lines where they came out of the river.

I immediately asked Lt. Devereaux, who had taken over in my absence, why the battery was so exposed. He said that intelligence had told them that the Germans were running out of ammo and would use it only to disrupt communications such as road, bridges, even wire lines, and wouldn't fire at anything else. This was hard for me to believe but was correct. They could have blown the battery to hell if they had wanted to.

Devereaux had developed yellow jaundice while I was gone but had refused to be evacuated until I got back. He looked more like a Chinaman than an French American. I immediately ordered him to turn in and he was sent to the hospital over his strong protest.

Two days later, I was notified that the first bridge would be completed. They wanted one motorized unit to cross it at 0600 the next day under the cover of smoke. 'B' Battery were the lucky ones. Did my recent R&R in any way influence Battalion headquarters decision? We loaded out early and proceeded to the bridge crossing. I told Sgt. Frew to dispatch one vehicle at a time on the bridge. The speed limit was 10 miles an hour.

I would cross first in my jeep and wait for them a half mile down the road. I had no problem crossing and the entire battery crossed without being shelled. The bridge stayed in tact because of the smoke. Most of the drivers obeyed the speed limit until they reached about the middle of the bridge where they put the gas to the floor and came flying off the other end. They had witnessed too many bridges blown up with a vehicle in the middle to waste any time on the bridge.

My orders were to turn south, parallel to the river, and stop five or six miles down the road and go into position. By now most of the trucks had lost their mufflers and sounded like heavy tanks. They were making such a racket that the white flags started popping out the windows in the small towns as we moved through.

The firing battery came first and the kitchen came last. After I selected our position and was waiting for the battery to occupy them, I sent the wire section to gather fresh eggs from the chicken coops. As I was standing by my jeep, a woman approached and asked permission, in English, to speak to me.

She told me that there were German soldiers in the town and they wanted to surrender. There were two squares in this town. I told her to have the officer order his men to put all their weapons in the square to the right of the road and have his men line up on the left of the road and then report to me. She went back to the houses and before long, the German soldiers came out and followed my orders completely.

The Lieutenant approached me carrying his pistol by the butt between his thumb and his index finger and offered it to me. I took it by the barrel and he saluted. It was a 38 chrome plated lugar.

They were a whole platoon of riflemen. I informed him that when the kitchen arrived, I would see that his men were fed. When we needed to leave, I told him what to do. I had the lieutenant march his men north up the road behind a white flag. One of the infantry units would get them to the POW compound. They all put their white handkerchiefs around their arms and marched north. The windows all displayed white flags after seeing their army march away.

We pulled out heading south toward Stuttgart. The first stop we made, we moved into a German youth center. We went into firing position to wait for any call from the infantry who were just ahead of us. About 2100 one of our guards reported an enemy squad making their way up the hill toward his machine gun position. The Sgt. of the Guard and I went immediately to see what was happening. We could make out six or seven men crawling up the hill on their hands and knees toward the youth center which they probably thought was in German hands.

I instructed the Sergeant to have them fire one round from the 50 Cal machine gun when they got within fifty yards. When the shot was fired all the German's stood up. In the dark we could see by their silhouette that they all had their hands over their head. They were told in German to move forward slowly to our position and to keep their hands up.

When they arrived, we checked them and took their weapons away. To my surprise, they were all German artillery officers, forward observers who were trying to make their way back home. We gave them some rations and some water and put them in the latrine of the school where we could lock them up.

I told them we would take care of their disposition in the morning after breakfast. During the night we received orders to pull out as soon as it was daylight and to continue south. We were to support an infantry battalion that was about a mile ahead of us. Having no one to turn our prisoners over to, we took them with us. The only place for them to ride was standing on the lower shields of the howitzers, hanging onto the top shield.

Before we were more than a couple miles down the road we were ambushed by a German infantry squad from the deep woods along the road. Without orders, the convoy stopped and all our men jumped off the trucks and went into the woods after them. They exchanged a few rounds but were never able to capture anybody. I looked back at the convoy and discovered that there were our prisoners, still on the guns, but not a one of my own soldiers.

I told Frew to blow the whistle and get the men back in the battery. The prisoners could have escaped but none of them even attempted to. After continuing a mile further south, we saw a unit of supply trucks who took our prisoners. They agreed to drop them off at the POW compound in the rear.

We proceeded south at night and went into position just north of the Autobahn that ran from Stuttgart to Augsberg along the Neckar river. Early the next morning, just as the sun was coming up we saw two big tanks slowly climbing the hill on the other side of the river. In the haze we could not make sure if they were German. The battery got ready to fire on them but I told them to hold off until I had positive identification.

We tried to radio our FOs, who were with the infantry in that area, but couldn't get any answer. We had no communication with the infantry. We elected, because of the doubt, to leave the tanks go. In about a half hour the FO checked in and told us they had traveled all night by foot and everyone had gone to sleep. They confirmed that the two tanks were German tigers that went over the hill. We all felt that the war was about to end and that maybe it was better not to engage them. We hadn't lost a man and the tanks going over the hill were probably heading home.

The next day we turned west on secondary roads and moved into the outskirts of Stuttgart. All fighting stopped and we got word to clean up and get ready to enter Stuttgart by parade, even though we would be combat ready. The city was to surrendered to the 100th Division. After we were cleaned up and were moving toward the city we saw signs that said, "You are entering Stuttgart courtesy of the Second French Army." We were ordered to stop everything and not go into the city.

While we had been getting ready for a parade, the French had left their designated zone at Tubingen and had occupied the city. The bad part of that was not only that they had defied the Supreme commander's orders as to where they should go, but their troops, many of them Moroccans, were raping and looting. The French Africans were even cutting off fingers to steal jewelry. The women had taken refuge in all the Catholic Churches which was the only place where the French would not touch them.

During all this excitement, Kramer called to tell me that my orders had arrived promoting me to Captain. The date was 1 May, 1945. About this time First Sergeant Frew left us to become a Warrant Officer in the 397th Infantry Regiment and I made Frank Stringline, the motor Sergeant, the first Sergeant.

We were given orders to go to the nearest assembly area and await further orders. We took over a whole block in an eastern suburb of Stuttgart to house our battery. I immediately ordered all civilians to clear the area. I gave them about thirty minutes to take as much personal things as they wanted. They were also told that we would probably only be there one or two weeks and that they would get their homes back.

I was in a house that I had picked to be my CP when there was a commotion in the front yard. A woman claimed that she was an American Citizen and that she was not going to leave that house. She said that the Germans wanted her to live with them because we would not throw an American out. She told me that when she lived in Stuttgart that her neighborhood had been bombed by the American Air Corp, but her house was the only one that had not been hit.

It was just a coincident but the Germans thought that somehow she had not been bombed because she was American. I asked her if she was such a good American, what was she doing here. "She said, Hauptman, were you ever in love?" I said, "I might know something about it." I asked what her husband did. He was an engineer at the Messerschmidt airplane factory in Stuttgart and that she had met and married him when they were both students at Columbia University in New York City.

I told Sgt. Stringline to remove her from the property. He picked her up and gently set her over a three foot fence onto the sidewalk. She was still being very verbal as she walked up the street. About this time, as we were moving into the houses, one of my men came to me with pictures of that woman that showed that she had been a leader in the Nazi Youth Movement in East Stuttgart. We ended up with stacks of pictures and clippings of her and her Nazi activities.

About this time some of the men came to me and told me that Frau Rommell, the wife of the great German Field Marshall who had gained fame from the North African Exposition, lived in middle of that block. General Rommell had recently been reported dead from English strafing while going to duty on the Western Front. The next morning I paid a call on Frau Rommell to express my sympathy at the death of her husband because even though he was an enemy, he had the respect of soldiers all over the world.

She spoke English well. She asked if I knew how he was killed. When I said that I had heard that he had been killed by English strafing, she said, "Hauptman, don't believe any of the reasons that have been put out. He was killed by SS officers by orders of Hitler." It was alleged that he had been the leader of an attempt to overthrow der Führer and end the war.

I gave orders to my men that Mrs. Rommell would be allowed to stay in her home and was to be protected from everyone including Germans, French and Americans and not to be molested in any way. I gave her permission to receive guests if she would let us know in advance.

175

The German telephone system was in tact and she could contact anyone she wished by phone. If she had to leave the area, we would send her in one of our jeeps with two soldiers, but she was by no means a prisoner. She only took advantage of this one time, to go to the grocery store. There were no problems. Stuttgart had been the last city in Germany to join the Hitler movement.

In the mean time, new orders came in to get ready to take Stuttgart from the French, by force if necessary. We were told that if we saw any French troops raping or stealing, to open fire. I immediately went on reconnaissance to locate gun positions along the route we were to take to support the 397th Infantry Regiment.

Eisenhauer had cut the French off all lend-lease supplies as we were getting ready to fight a new war, against the them. We were within an hour or two of actually jumping off when we got word to drop back about twenty miles and occupy some areas while awaiting further orders. After about twenty days the political pressure and losing their logistic support of the lend lease program, they decided to peacefully move to Tubingen which had been their designated area in the first place.

After the city was firmly in control by the 100th Infantry Division, we started getting USO shows that included many well known actors and actresses. Among them was Bob Hope and Larry Adler, the harmonica king. They arrived at the outpost in a big old Mercedes touring car. The guard made a routine signal for them to stop to check identification.

There were clearly marked signs in several languages including English that all vehicles and pedestrians would be stopped. However, Bob Hope was in charge of the vehicle and told the driver to ignore the guard and they drove on through. The guard immediately turned and emptied his carbine in the rear of the Mercedes. They stopped. Larry Adler thought that he had been shot. There were several bullets lodged in his overcoat after passing through the trunk and its contents in the back. None had penetrated his skin.

They were very hostile toward the guard and threatened to file a complaint. The Commander of the guard stood by his man and gave him a commendation for performing his duty as instructed. That was the last anyone heard about the incident.

~ 14 ~

Going Home

Bernice:

By late April I thought that I might be pregnant but V.E. (Victory in Europe) confirmed it. Of course there was the obligatory celebration and I went to the officers' club to join in the festivities. However, I took one swallow of orange juice and gin and headed straight for the latrine. That was the first sign of morning sickness and it wasn't even morning. After that I enjoyed a general state of nausea for about seven months.

On the morning of May 8 King George VI was scheduled to make a radio announcement of the end of the war. Everyone knew that the monarch stuttered and the entire country held their breath as he made the historic proclamation. It was said that only his wife, Queen Elizabeth, could help him control this problem with her moral support. She did a good job because he didn't miss a syllable. I was in the dentist chair having my two remaining wisdom teeth pulled and I listened with the dental clinic staff.

In 1945, if a female member of the service became pregnant she was automatically relieved of active duty and processed for discharge. We were not in fact discharged, we were put on inactive status. If for any reason the pregnancy did not end with a live baby, we were subject to be recalled to active duty. We were given a 'Certificate of Service' which was not the same as an Honorable Discharge. I never did receive a discharge so I suppose that I am still an inactive member of the Army Nurse Corp but since I had a healthy child, I was never called upon to serve.

Pregnancy was such a common occurrence in the ETO that they actually had a special hospital to process those who were in that condition. We were assigned to temporary duty and so were not treated as hospital patients. It was the 10th Station Hospital outside Manchester, which is in the west near the Irish sea. I took a train to London where I changed to another train for Manchester. In fact I even had to change stations. The train from Bournemouth arrived at Waterloo on the south side of London and the north bound left from the Eustice St. station on the north side.

The Chief nurse, Captain Hoekstra assigned another nurse to accompany me and I surely did appreciate it. There were also two nurses from the 104th General Hospital making the same journey and we traveled together. We had a wild ride through London in the back of a three quarter ton army truck which was carrying laundry so we had a nice soft place to relax.

At the Eustice St. Station we were confronted with another problem. The train was full. The English people were at last free to travel after so many years of being deprived of every thing and they were taking full advantage of the opportunity. However, we were able to find room in the baggage car. There were several duffle bags laying around so we were able to get quite comfortable for the six hour journey. I still had my canteen which came in handy.

The 10th Station Hospital occupied permanent buildings which before the war had been a tuberculosis sanitarium. It was located on a golf course. They had a very large nurses' home which made it ideal for the billeting of pregnant personnel. We were even able to have a private room. It was just as plain of furnishings as all the other barracks I had been in for the past three years with one exception, each private room had a tiny fireplace. It was spring and I was in no mood to build a fire. Besides, there was a very large and comfortable living room with sofas and chairs where the women on temporary duty spent most of their time. There was an enormous fire place in this room and someone else built the fire but we were free to stoke it as we saw fit.

There was a large assortment of people in the group. There was everyone from enlisted women, Women's Army Corp officers to Red Cross and Special Service staff and of course Nurses. Many of the girls were totally ignorant of what maternity involved while the nurses were totally knowledgeable and more than willing to fill them in. We probably told them more than they wanted to know.

We were about half and half married and unmarried. Most of the ones who had husbands or fiances near where they were stationed had put off reporting their condition until the last chance to get out. There was a rule that nobody could leave after the seventh month. I was very early in my term, and was repeatedly bumped to the bottom of the list to make room for new arrivals. Nobody wanted to have their child in England as that would make them British subjects.

One day I was sorta bragging about what I had accomplished on a seven day leave. One girls said she had only had a three day pass, but the winner was the one who made it on a one hour AWOL (absent without leave).

The first step in the processing was to have a urine test for pregnancy. There were some people saying they were pregnant just so they could get back to the US. There must have been a problem with this group borrowing pregnant urine because when the specimen was collected a nurse or a WAC stood there and watched.

While I was at the 10th I was promoted to 1st Lieutenant.

I finally got on a shipping list to stay and took the train to the port of Bristol. Here an American hospital ship named the BLANCH SIGMOND awaited us. It was of the style known as liberty ships, that had been fitted out as a hospital. Blanche Sigmond was a nurse who had been killed in Italy.

Again we had the forward cabin on 'A' deck and again I was able to get an upper bunk by a port hole. The first meal aboard the ship was shear heaven. We had whole baked potatoes, beef steak, fresh fruit, everything we hadn't seen for a year and a half. The joy didn't last long. I had hardly reach the outside deck when the sea and the old nausea hit me. I didn't have a helmet but the rail and the sea was now available.

It seemed the voyage took forever. We left Bristol on 15 June by the southern route. Liberty ships were a far cry from the sleek luxury liners like the IL DeFRANCE. Eight knots was the top speed. One morning we could see some land on the horizon. We were told that these were the Azores.

By noon we passed close enough that we could see vehicles on shore. By the time we turned in for the night, the islands were still visible off the stern.

We arrived in Charleston, SC harbor on the morning of the 3rd of July. It wasn't the Statue of Liberty, but the Cooper River Bridge was every bit as welcome a sight. We were to be separated from service at Stark General Hospital. If we did not show we were allowed to walk off the ship. I was only three months and looked very sharp in my class 'A' uniform.

The women who showed were removed on stretchers as it was believed that so many pregnant female soldiers made the army look bad. The men who carried the stretchers were certainly taken back when they arrived in the ward and their burden hopped off. I don't think they appreciated it.

I was able to get a flight on Eastern Airlines to Milwaukee. It was one of the original DC-3s, a two motor passenger plane. There were two seats on one side of the aisle and one seat on the opposite side. When the plane was on the ground, the nose was higher than the tail where you boarded and you had to walk up hill to your seat.

In Milwaukee, I took a bus to Milton. It traveled on state road 59 which went about two miles from home. I had intended to ride into Milton and call to have someone come get me, but on an impulse, I asked to be let off at Bullock's corner and walked home. I was still in uniform and when I got off the bus, all the passengers gave me a big cheer. Nobody gets off out in the country unless they live there. My mother was sure surprised to see me walk up on the porch. She had put a news item in the paper about Eli's visit. She said she figured something like that would happen and she was making sure that nobody got any strange ideas.

~ 15 ~

Peace Was Not Peaceful

Eli:

Each unit was assigned an area to take over and maintain law and order until military government could be established and later returned to the local governments. We were assigned a small city called Alfdorf and the farms around it. The land was controlled by a German Baron Von Fraunstein. There were two large walled castles. The Baron lived in one of them and his son lived in the other, which was right across the street.

I selected the son's castle and all its out buildings for 'B' Btry. I had the son, who was also a Baron, and his wife, move to the house of the farm manager across the street. She was late in her pregnancy. The son had been an officer in the German army but was home and in civilian clothes when we arrived.

To my surprise, the whole family spoke perfect English. I explained to him why he had to move. He understood and said he would co-operate in all ways. I advised them that they could get any possessions at any time during the day light hours. He asked permission to continue to make cheese every Thursday in his castle, which I granted. After the first Thursday, the cheese stunk up the castle so bad that I knew I had made a mistake.

We were lucky to have a good place, even with the odor, for the battery. I slipped over to visit 'C' Battery and have a chat with Captain Langhorne "Scagg" Meems. I discovered that they were set up in pup tents because there was no suitable buildings for them to occupy. It was a farming area and all the houses were in one end, with the barn and the farm animals in the other. It was so unsanitary that he felt it was unfit for his men.

I told him that I had a second castle over in Alfdorf that I could take over and he could house his battery in our area. He agreed to that and I moved the old baron, who was a full Colonel in the German army, out and 'C' Battery moved in.

There was a gate in the wall behind my castle that connected the two castles. One night Meems called and said they were cooking up some hamburger and he was bringing some over for me. With a little wine, we were having a social get together in my room. He appreciated our helping him out but, he complained that our strict enforcement of occupation rules and regulations by our men on patrol, was heckling his men. I informed him that the same rules applied to my men as well as his and would continue to be enforced. During this period we were not allowed to fraternize with the Germans. Even the Germans did not like it but it was the rule.

After a couple hours, he went back to his castle. In a few minutes he called me on the field phone. He said, "While I was walking down your path, I had a hard time finding a place to put my feet on the ground without stepping on your men's backs with frauleins under them." Knowing Skagg and how he exaggerated, I thought he may have seen one or two. I sent the First Sergeant out to check. He reported that there was nobody there but he thought he heard a lot of movement as he approached the area.

I changed the policy on fraternizing to "Fraternizing would only be done in public." Within a week the same policy was adopted by the whole command. We opened up a German beer hall across the street for 'B' Battery personnel, where they could mix with the local people. We named it Gasthaus zur Harmonie. Our guards would check it about once an hour. There were no more problems.

In a few days the whole command was ordered to search every building in their occupation areas. The search was to concentrate on picking up war criminals and weapons of all kinds. We were also to make sure that all German veterans had proper discharge papers. All civilians were required to have valid identification on their person at all times. The search was to start before dawn on a designated day, all over Germany. It was kept secret up to this point. At 0300 I met with the Bergermeister (mayor) and he had the town crier announce that the search of all buildings was underway and to stay in their homes.

About 0400 we set up a CP in The Bergermeister's office and used interpreters which he furnished. My interpreter was an attractive woman who was smart as a whip. She had lived in the Brooklyn for twelve years before the war. She had a German soldier husband who had not yet been released, as he was a POW. I told her during this search that we were trying to find the real Nazis. She told me that everybody in the town was a Nazi supporter so we would need to pick up the whole town. Anyone that said otherwise was a liar. I thanked her for the truth and we went ahead with the search.

As we interrogate people in the homes, those without proper discharge papers and IDs were brought to the Rathaus (city hall) for transportation to Welzheim, about 25 kilometers west of Alfdorf. The local German government officials would check their IDs and discharges, verify the records, and make corrections if necessary. They would issue discharges for those who didn't have the necessary papers if they had some form of record of their service. Then they were put back in the truck and returned to their homes.

While making this check, a corporal reported back to me that there was a brand new Mercedes Benz, covered with hay in the barn across the street from our castle where the Baron was staying. I told them to ignore the fact that it was there. We had already taken their castle. If we picked up the car, it would just go to some big shot at higher headquarters. "Just let the young Baron keep it right where it was."

A couple days later, the young Baron came to me and told me that his wife was in labor. He said she needed to go to the hospital in Welzheim and asked me if we could have her taken there in one of our jeeps.

I told him that we were not allowed to drive civilians in our vehicles but I had a better idea. I told the First Sergeant to give the baron five gallon of gas. "You can move the hay off that Mercedes in your barn and drive her yourself." I gave him a pass on a paper napkin allowing him to go to and from Welzheim for as long as his wife was in the hospital, but not to deviated from that route. It was unofficial as hell, but it got him through every check point with no one questioning it. All the check points were maned by soldiers from the 374th Field Artillery and knew me by name.

Forty five years later, Bernice and I were in Alfdorf and visited the Baroness. The Baron had passed away by then. She said that when he came back and told her what the arrangement was, she told him they couldn't do that because the car didn't belong to them. They were hiding it for a big industrialist in Stuttgart. He told her, "The Hauptman is in command of the area and he ordered me to take it." Of course, I had no idea that it wasn't his car.

Alfdorf was just north of the city of Lorch. There had been a large encampment of Soviet prisoners of war between Alfdorf and Lorch. These men were not the living skeletons as so many of liberated prisoners were. They had been providing agricultural labor to the Third Reich. They were part of the Army of The Republic of Georgia. The Georgians had surrendered their entire army to the Germans early in the war, hoping to be given a sector to fight the Soviet army, even using their own munitions. But instead, they had been consigned to labor by Hitler himself. Many of them had resented this.

Originally, my sector boundary went right through this encampment. This would have been an unworkable situation, so, at my suggestion, the boundary was moved to the edge of the camp and an infantry company inherited the entire camp. Although the camp was not my responsibility, these men managed to make problems for us. There was a gasthaus in the woods, not far from Alfdorf. An informer from the camp told us that the Georgians were going to raid it one morning.

Hearing about this, I sent Lt. Bailey and Corp. Bielski, who spoke Russian, out to investigate. After failing to raise Bailey on the radio, I drove out to check the situation. I met the corporal, armed only with a carbine, marching four or five hundred Georgians back to their camp. I asked him to inquire as to who the highest ranking member of the group, and have him report to me.

A major came forward and, after checking his identification, I told him that he was responsible, and to take the entire group back to camp and tell them to stay out of my area. I told him if he failed to carry out my instructions, I would come into the camp and arrest him. He complied. In the meantime, Lt. Bailey was giving first aid to some people who had been roughed up at the gasthaus.

Less than a week later, I had gone fishing with Bailey, First Sergeant Stringline and Supply Sergeant Urell. When we returned to the castle, there was a commotion near the gate. A German woman on a bicycle was there asking for help. Her husband, a German soldier, was just returning from the war and had been shot by the Georgians just as he approached his home. We drove out to check.

184

When we reached the house there, were several excited Germans milling around. The man had what appeared to me to be a minor wound but we called the battalion surgeon. He was laying in the bed and was in a great deal of pain. I checked him. There was a small bullet hole in his right side. I didn't think it was too serious but the Battalion Surgeon discovered that the bullet was lodged in the base of his spine.

The family told us that there had been seven men and each one had a pistol. They had left in two cars and a motorcycle. We left Sgt. Urell at the house and followed the tracks of the vehicles on the dirt road. When we came to a fork in the road, it was not possible to tell for certain which way they had gone, but the motorcycle left a distinctive track, which we followed.

We soon realized that the road led right to the spot where we had been fishing that afternoon and we knew it was a dead end. By now it was dark so I told Sgt. Stringline, who was driving, to turn the lights out and drive fast to the top of the hill. When we saw their vehicle he was to switch on the bright lights to blind them. We soon found their vehicles in the field with an armed guard, whom we disarmed. I left Sgt. Stringline to guard the vehicle and the prisoner.

We were right beside the trout creek. Since we had just been there that afternoon, we knew there were two foot bridges with two houses on the other side, about a half mile apart. We crossed the first foot bridge to the first house. The German family living there came out and told us that the Georgians had been there and had beat them up, molested the women and stole their wine. The renegades had left to raid their friend's house half a mile down the creek. They confirmed that there were six of them. They said that the men had been drinking and each one had a pistol.

I instructed Lt. Bailey to go back over the bridge and go down the path beside the creek and I would meet him when we reached the second house. This would cut off any escape over the second bridge. I took the parallel trail along the creek until I reach the house. As I approached, I could see a man outside the house and there were lights on inside. He held something in his hand that appeared to be a gun. I identified myself as 'American-ish Officer' and to drop the gun. Instead, he raised his arm as if to shoot and I fired three rounds with my 45 at his feet before he dropped his weapon. When Lt. Bailey heard the shots, he came running right through the creek calling, "Hauptman, Hauptman."

I reassured Bailey that I was okay and told him I had the prisoner and his weapon. The lights in the house by now had been turned off. The Lieutenant, who spoke German, searched my assailant and threatened him, with his 45 to the man's chin. He told him to tell his friends that everything was okay and to come on out.

As each man staggered out, about thirty seconds apart, with a bottle of wine in his hand and a pistol in his belt, I disarmed them and Bailey took the wine bottles until all five were our prisoners. We marched them back to the cars. The first sergeant rode in the first car with a carbine and the lieutenant rode on the back of the motorcycle. Every time they came to a hill he had to hop off and push it to get it up the hill. I brought up the rear in the jeep.

When we returned to the house, the German woman identified the prisoners and pointed out the man who had shot her husband. The husband had been transported by our medical jeep, accompanied by our battalion surgeon, to the German civilian hospital in Welzheim. He later died about 0230. The baroness delivered her baby in the same hospital about two hours later.

We took the prisoners back to our castle and put them in the ancient dungeon. The next morning they were turned over to Division Artillery Headquarters and later to military government. There was a preliminary hearing held in their camp, made up of half United States and half Soviet officers, with the president being a Russian full colonel. The interpreter was a good-looking Russian girl.

It was conducted the same as a regular court, but was actually only a fact-finding hearing, so gave no verdict. The prisoners and all the evidence were forwarded to the Four Powers Tribunal in Berlin for final disposition and sentencing. The most disturbing thing to the hearing officers was that the weapon I had taken away from the guard, had been fired at an American officer three times, and had misfired three times. It was determined that it was also the same gun used to shoot the German.

The third incident was far more serious and could have had much greater international repercussions. We got word from our informer that the whole camp was planning to raid the gasthaus. A Brigadier General from higher headquarters came to Alfdorf for a briefing and told me to use any means necessary to maintain order, including the Howitzers.

Again, Lt. Bailey was dispatched with a squad of men to the gasthaus. He was instructed to position our four 50 caliber machine guns to cover all four sides of the house, which he did, from the second floor windows. The Germans helped build platforms for the guns with four-by-fours. They were ready and waiting. As soon as it was dark, about 2000, Georgians were seen at the edge of the clearing surrounding the gasthaus. They were yelling that they were armed and were going to take over the place.

Lt. Bailey contacted me by radio and informed me of the situation. I told him to tell them to disburse and go back to camp, and to give them 30 seconds to move or he would open fire. When they failed to obey instructions, I told him on the radio to fire all four machine guns and spray the tops of the trees for about 20 seconds, then pause. If they kept coming to lower the fire. I asked him to hold his mike open so that I could hear.

After the 20 second burst, the lieutenant came back on the radio and said, "They're all running back toward the camp". The next morning our informer returned from inside the camp. He told us that when the mob had returned to camp, they said that we had fired artillery on them. The machine guns had cut off the tops of the trees which fell on their heads, and had caused a panic, sending them all back to their camp.

I think because they knew we were an artillery outfit, they had really thought that we had used the Howitzers. We would have too, we were at the castle, loaded and ready to roll. Instead, I canceled the alert and told everyone to go to bed. The group at the gasthaus remained there the rest of the night.

Law and order had been maintained without anyone being hurt. We continued our occupation duty which included collecting two truck loads of sides of beef every Friday from the German villages to feed the former prisoners at the camp. We would keep a side or two for our own mess.

One night, I was in bed when the first sergeant came to me to tell me that they had picked up a man wearing the uniform of a US Staff Sergeant who was riding around in a Mercedes touring car with a good looking blond after curfew. When he was stopped, he started talking and his accent sounded so heavily German that the guard did not believe that the man was an American Non Com. Even though he had complete ID, he was not authorized to be out after curfew.

The story the man told me was that he was with Criminal Investigation and was tracking down valuable contraband stolen from the French. It was believed to be hidden in Alfdorf. It was musical instruments worth over $10,000,000. I authorized my men to let him go but I told him to be sure to get a pass to be out after curfew.

A couple nights later, the First Sergeant came and told me the same sergeant was back again and he still didn't have a pass to be out. A different guard still would not believe that this man was not a German. He again requested to speak to me so I went out and talked to him. The first thing he said was, "Captain, your area must be the best patrolled area in Germany. I have been here only twice and was caught both times. I know now where the instruments are. They are hidden in the school." He asked me to furnish some men to help him raid the place.

I gave him a corporal and four men who helped him carry out the raid. They started in the cellar and went to the roof. The instruments were in the attic. We left two men to guard the treasure and the sergeant told me he would have the French in to inventory the find and remove it within twenty four hours. In the spirit of co-operation he said that if we wanted any of the instruments for a battery band, to help ourselves. I told him that we would guard them but we would not touch them.

I did not pay any attention to his name at the time but years later, there was an American/German Jew who became an important national figure who looked and sounded just like that Staff Sergeant with the CID who had been caught by my guards. His name was Henry Kissinger.

While we were at Alfdorf, Lt. Deveraux rejoined us. He had gone AWOL from the hospital because he was told that he would be discharged to the 'repel depel' the next day. He wanted to come back to 'B' Btry and the best way to be sure of that, was to put on his clothes and go out the window. When the First Sergeant wanted to know what to put on the morning report because he didn't have any written orders, I told him to just say, "Hospital to duty," and let Kramer worry about it.

It was not long until the local officials were organized and ready to take over the control of their own towns and the US Army were being assigned to now vacant German barracks known as Kaserns. The 374th Field Artillery Bn. was assigned to the Panzer Kasern at Bobingen. Before we moved we spent a week having service practice at the Altes Lager Military Reservation.

I went ahead of the battalion to inspect our new quarters. I found the buildings weren't bad, but the furnishings left a lot to be desired. The beds were wooden frames with burlap sacks filled with straw for mattresses. I told my advanced detail to throw all the furniture and bedding out the windows and pile them up in the middle of the parade grounds where we burned them because they were infested with lice and vermin.

When we started the fire, it sounded like the war had started all over again. Apparently the German soldiers had hidden small arms ammunition in their mattresses. When the fire hit them they started going off. Once again, the battle wise 'B' Battery GIs hit the ground. After 15 or 20 minutes, the last rounds went off and we concentrated in cleaning the building. By nightfall we moved in with our bed rolls on the floor.

The next day I started checking the towns in my new occupation area for furniture. I went to the Bergermeister and got the list of the biggest Nazis in town. I had a body guard who had a flare for the dramatic. He would enter the room ahead of me with his carbine drawn and click his heels. While he stood at attention, I would enter the room like a real big shot. The Germans understood and probably appreciated this. They expected the man in charge to act like he was in charge.

"We'll be taking two or three pieces of furniture from each of your residence for our men, but we will give them receipts for every item and it will all be returned eventually." Most houses had one or two sets of twin beds. We would take two or three items from each house and when the truck was full we would take them back to the Kasern. We kept this up for about a day until we had enough for each man to have a bed with all the bedding. Each room would have a radio, a table, some chairs and a rug.

When the war ended, Lt. Jackson and seven men had been put on TDY (temporary duty) to the Dachau Concentration Camp, to help supervise cleaning up that horrible situation and to help with the recovery of the survivors. They required the local citizens of Dachau to do the manual labor of cleaning the camp.

Conditions there were unspeakable, but the living quarters of the SS troops, who had run the camp, were luxurious. They had run out ahead of the American troops and left their fine houses and apartments vacant. Lt. Jackson called and told me that if we wanted the SS furniture for the officers quarters, to send a couple trucks down. We immediately dispatched three prime movers with an NCO and removed as much of the furniture as we needed.

The battery officers took over one end of a barracks. These were all permanent buildings constructed of stone. There was an interior bomb wall about every fifty feet. Before the furniture arrived, we decided to expand our end of the building to make a large living room next to our bed rooms. We hired a German mason to make a double door opening in one of these walls. Never did I know when I told him to do it, that the wall was concrete six feet thick with a half inch thick steel plate in the middle.

He grumbled about it and tried to explain to me what was there but I didn't listen. So he brought in extra men. By the end of the day the job was completed. We paid them for their efforts with German marks that we had found in a foot locker along the way. We used this money to pay Germans for lots of things. We thought that it was basically worthless and were often very generous. However, about a month later, the US announced that they were backing the German currency.

As the furniture came in, the rugs were first. Some of them were as much as three inches thick. There was a big, expensive stereo/radio for the living room. Our beds were about three quarter size and the bedding was luxurious, with silk sheets and down comforters.

When Maj. Allport, the battalion commander, saw our living room, his first remark was that this should have been the officers' club. He questioned my requisitioning furniture from the poor Germans. He held a meeting of all the officers of the battalion the next day. He started off by telling them that Fishpaw had been taking the furniture they saw around them from the Germans and he did not feel that this was right.

I made a statement that the reason we were over here living in fox holes and being shot at and killed, was because of the Germans. I felt that the whole battalion should live in the best quarters with the best furniture that we could find.

I told them that the furniture they were sitting on had come from the SS housing at Dachau, which had been abandoned. The elite SS were known to be the most radical and brutal of all the enemy troops. "My enlisted men are all sleeping in beds and have radios and rugs in their rooms and I think the whole battalion should have the same." The Major came back with the comment, "We don't even have an officers' club." I asked him what he was sleeping on and he said a canvas cot. I told him, "Tomorrow I would equip an officers' club in the middle of the barracks and I will get you a real bed."

190

He wanted to say his final piece. He wanted the officers to vote on my method of procurement of furniture. "Will everybody who is against this type of operation raise your hand?" Out of the thirty some officers there, not a hand went up. Then he said, "You all must be for it," and every hand shot up. He turned to me and said, "Equip the officers' club and I'll take the bed."

I went to Weil im Schonbuch, which was the principle town in my new area, where there were several beer halls. I picked the biggest one. It was a large room that held probably a hundred small tables, with red checkered table cloths, and a couple hundred chairs. At each end there were identical bars. I told the owner that we wanted about half his tables and chairs and that we would take one of the bars.

He was told that he would receive a receipt for everything we took, and everything we took would be returned when we went home. I counted out fifty tables with table cloths and over a hundred chairs plus one complete bar. Both the Germans and the GIs loaded a couple trucks.

As we were about finished, the bar tender asked me if we needed a bar tender. He spoke perfect English. He said that he had been a POW in England where he had run an officers' club for the British army. I told him we would take him. He ran real quick and got his meager belongings. He climbed up on the bar in the first truck. As we drove through town he was waving at everybody and they waved back like he was some kind of a hero. The bar fit our room perfectly. He was still there, doing a hell of a job, running his bar, when I left in August. He was really good.

I got word that there was an American airman buried in the town grave yard. He had parachuted onto a farm where women were working in the field. They had attacked him with their spading forks that they were using to dig turnips.

When I checked it out, I found a white wooden cross with the helmet and the dog tags. There was the biggest pile of flowers that I had ever seen over and around his grave. I reported it to graves registration. The town people were afraid that there would be an investigation, but that did not happen.

Now that the war for us was over, the Division arranged for R&R trips for the men who had not had any real opportunities to relax for months. The 325th Engineers were given the task of setting up a suitable itinerary which took the division through the most beautiful parts of the European alps. It included Bavaria, the southern state of Germany, and the Tyrol in Austria and northern Italy.

The first group to take the trip from the battery were lead by Lt. Pete Moynahan. After they returned, on the second trip for the battery, I went along with about twenty men. We had one jeep and two three quarter ton trucks with a trailer behind each to carry our luggage and plenty of ten in one rations. (that meant a box of rations contained enough food for ten people). There was always toilet paper, matches and cigarettes.

Each day, I would tell the Sgt. in charge of each truck where we would meet that night at 1900. The first meal we ate on the road we pulled into a small church and asked them if they would cook our meal for us. They were glad to do it and we gave them the left overs, plus the cigarettes and some candy bars. We found that more or less, this was the way we would have our meals for the trip. At times we would also be guests of other military outfits along the way.

One of our principle stops for sightseeing was the concentration camp of Dachau, which was just west Munich. We traveled on the storied Autobahns which Hitler had built as a military highway. The camp was still the home of many liberated prisoners who were recovering from their long ordeal. They were dying at the rate of 200 a week.

When these tours were being set up, General Eisenhauer requested that all tours should include a visit to at least one of these death camps along the way. He reasoned that we should all have the opportunity to witness, first hand, the atrocities committed upon millions of Nazi political prisoners. He said that in twenty or thirty years, there would be people saying that it never happened. He wanted to be sure that every American in the theater saw it with their own eyes.

Elements of the 100th Infantry Division were involved in the actual liberation of the camp at Dachau. When they entered the site there were five or six freight cars sitting on the track. When they opened the doors, dead bodies fell out. Everyone in the cars was dead. They had been so crowded that they couldn't even fall down to die. The stench was unbelievable as they had been there at least a week, in the early summer, before our soldiers had arrived. The Division furnished officers and men to supervise the clean up of the area. Two US army hospitals had moved right into the camp and worked around the clock to treat these victims of this horror who were still alive.

While we were there we saw the ovens and the showers rigged with gas where hundreds of thousands of unfortunate people were singled out for extermination. Many of these were Jews, but there were also many others involved. These were people who disagreed with the Nazi rulers and along the way, lots of local Nazis, no doubt, took the opportunity to get ride of people they just didn't like. After witnessing this sad state of affairs, we were happy to be on our way to pleasanter activities.

Our next stop was at the resort of Herren Cheimsee south of Munich. This was the location of one of the mad Bavarian King Ludwig's fabled castles. This one was patterned after the French palace of Versailles but was never completed.

I took my jeep as the advanced detail and left about two hours ahead to make arrangements for our housing at night and supper. I looked over the hotels and picked the one I liked the best. Even though they were not open for business, they agreed to let us use it for a couple days. They volunteered to cook our food and everything.

As my group arrived, they thought for sure that I was going to sleep them by the side of the lake. They were so surprised to have me lead them into this high class hotel with a beautiful beach. Each man had his own private room with feather beds and we ate in the main dining room with table cloths and personal service at every table.

The real German beer was the best part of the entire experience. We spent the next three nights there. The men could go anywhere they wanted to.

They went to Berchesgaden which was the well known mountain retreat of Herr Hitler himself. His mansion had been dynamited because the allied command did not want it to become a shrine to the fallen despot.

While we were there, General 'Hap' Arnold, the Aircorp Commander, arrived in his high class Mercedes touring car. He was talking with a group of us about the fact that the planners for the future said the next war would be fought with unmanned airplanes. He thought that was a big joke and that it would never happen. Most of us agreed.

Another beautiful lake that we visited was the Koenig See near Berchesgaden. After leaving the lake, we visited Salzberg in Austria and were given a tour of the storied salt mines.

After Austria we started back to Bobingen stopping on the way to eat and sleep. All in all, it was a wonderful trip. None of us will ever forget Dachau. We all wished that such inhumanity had never happened and hoped and prayed that it will never happen again.

Back at the Panzer Kasern, Maj. Allport had decided that my battery officers day room was pretty nice. One night he borrowed it to have a party with the battalion commanders from the 397th Infantry that we had supported during combat. I told the battery officers that the Ole Man was having a party and to stay out of the living room.

Between the living room and the bedrooms there was a large bathroom with a bath tub and showers. One of the officers had already filled the tub and was planning to take a bath. I asked him to delay the bath until after the party because the guests might need to use the latrine.

Most of our officers went to their own rooms. One was still out. A little while later, Lt. Moynahan came home and I told him about the party and asked him to stay out of there, but he needed go to the toilet. No doubt, he had enjoyed more than a few beers.

After he was in there a few minutes, I heard him talking to Lt. Col. Wisdom, who was the battalion CO of the second battalion that he had supported most of the war. From what I could hear, the Colonel was praising Moynahan for being a great observer and Moynahan was praising the Colonel and his battalion for being such a great outfit. All of a sudden, I heard a loud splash. I popped out of bed and rushed into the bathroom and saw Col. Wisdom getting out of the bathtub in his class 'A' uniform, soaking wet.

Major Allport arrived as Moynahan was apologizing to Col. Wisdom. I told the Colonel that I would court martial the lieutenant for assaulting a senior officer, but Wisdom said, "No, he did such a fine job for my battalion that we'll let him get away with this one." I sent Moynahan to his room.

When I asked him, "Why did you do that?" He said, "I was talking to him when I saw he was at the foot of the tub and that with just a little shove he would fall in, so I did." The next day, Lt. Moynahan and I had a long talk and I cut him off all booze, except for two beers a day. He wrote an apology to Col. Wisdom and to Maj. Allport.

The 216th General Hospital, which was Bernice's first outfit in England, had moved into Bobingen about the time the war ended. The battalion was setting up a dinner dance for the officers and the nurses at our new officers' club. I told them that I didn't plan to attend. When the nurses heard that, they said they wouldn't be there either unless Fishpaw came. They wanted to find out about Bernice. Reluctantly I agreed to be there.

Moynahan had been picked to be in charge of the bar and promised that he would not touch a drop. Everything went well. When the party was over, he came to me and said, "I am doing great Hauptman, I haven't had a drink. As soon as we inventory the bar, I'll be right over."

In about three hours, he came in and went to bed. The next morning I received a report from the military government officer that Lt. Moynahan and the officers' club corporal had been in a fracas with a German Gasthaus owner in town in the middle of the night. On investigating, I learned that Moynahan and the corporal had left the club with a bottle of champagne and were going to town to have a drink.

All the gasthauses were closed, so they banged on the door of one. The owner had come out of the back door and came around front. He was threatening them with a pick handle. Moynahan yelled for the corporal to hit the German over the head with the champagne bottle, which he did. They got control of the pick handle and left. The German had bruises on his right side where one of the men had kicked him while he was on the ground. I immediately informed my boy that this time he had gone too far and he would have to be court martialled.

The military government captain was wanting quick action and he said he was sending a complete report up through channels. I asked him if he had a girl friend in Weil im Schonbach and he said he did. I told him that Moynahan had such a good war record, I did not want to crucify him for his mistake when he mistreated a German who might have been shooting at him less than two months before. "His direction of artillery had probably contributed to the death of hundreds of them while supporting our infantry".

That didn't matter, the captain said he was going to send the report through. I said that I would wait for the report before I took any action. I had been told by the first sergeant that the captain's girl friend was a big operator in the black market. I sent a sergeant and some men down to her house with a two and half ton truck. They were to raid the house and to load up everything that said US ARMY. They came back with a copy of her ID and a truck load of army supplies and equipment.

The next day, battalion called requesting a second lieutenant to be transferred to Mannheim prison, This was the main stockade for the United States Army, where the really bad cases were incarcerated. I told them it would be Lt. Pete Moynahan. We received written orders that afternoon to be effective the next day. I told Moynahan immediately that he was being transferred for his own good. He didn't want to go but had no choice.

Sgt. Bernard Humphreys, one of the FO sergeants, was assigned to drive him to Mannheim. He loaded into the jeep and said good bye to all his friends and to me and they took off. When the sergeant returned, he immediately reported to the First Sergeant, and me, that Moynahan had cried the whole trip. But the biggest shock was that Lt. Col. Wisdom, the officer he had pushed in the bathtub, was now the prison officer and Moynahan was to be his assistant.

About another day went by when a Brigadier General from division headquarters came by with a stack of paper in his hand concerning one of my officers. He had the complete investigation on Moynahan and wanted to know what I was going to do about it. I informed him that the officer had been transferred to USAREUR (United States Army, Europe) military stockade in Mannheim.

He said that General Burress would want those orders cancelled. I told him of the man's record as an outstanding FO during combat and that he had a battlefield commission. "He is now the assistant prison officer for the same officer (Lt. Col. Wisdom) who commanded the battalion that he supported through out the war."

After more chatter and small talk he said he wanted to talk it over with General Burress. Because of all the various headquarters that were involved, he thought that General Burress would not want to publicize the incident throughout USAEUR. He said that he would let me know the outcome. He took the entire file back with him. I hoped that he would recommend that the case be dropped as I had no way of proceeding without that report. The next day he informed me that General Burress agreed with me and said the case would be dropped.

By now, the German soldiers were back in their communities and the long task of restoring their economy was beginning. The German public officials were being given more responsibility for local affairs. One of the first orders of business was to return control of hunting and fishing to the Jaegermeisters (game wardens).

These men were experts in the field and were highly respected in their community. They controlled all wild life on all land, no matter who owned it. They knew every deer in their area and during hard times or rough weather, they made sure that all the animals were fed. They put out salt spools which were available for the wild life to lick.

When any Americans wanted to hunt in our part of the Black Forest, we would arranged for them to have one of our German Jaegermeisters co-ordinate their hunt. Our area was popular with many of the officers and enlisted men from the units that did not have hunting available. Many came from higher head-quarters including, General Burress.

The Jaegermeister would designate where the deer would be, where the hunter should be and describe the deer that could be shot. Only the older deer were to be shot to assure a continuing supply of game, leaving the healthy does and best bucks to reproduce.

Any deer that had only one horn was a killer. They would kill the healthy deer by using that horn like a spear. Any deformed animals were also legal to take. The breed of deer in our area were called Hersche. They were a large animal. Some weighed as much as five to six hundred pounds and had large racks of ant-lers with as many as ten or twelve points, depending on their age.

Our own unit would have men go hunting every time we needed a new supply of fresh meat. Because the army was trying to get rid of all those 'C' and 'K' rations, the fresh meat was more than welcome by all. I never heard of anyone being injured while hunting. That was because of the careful control of the Jeager-meisters.

It was important for the local industries to get back to mak-ing products for civilian use. To everybodies delight, one of the factories in our area that had been making artillery fuses for the Germany army had been the primary makers of the Marklin toy electric trains before the war. When they started making their trains again, all the Americans wanted a set to send home to their families.

They were different from the Lionel trains that we had grown up with. They were about half the size and had a narrower track. Of course, the style was a miniature of the trains in use in Europe. The box cars were much smaller than those in America. There was not enough for everyone at first, so each month there would be a lottery to see who could buy a set. We must have kept them in business for a year or so until their own economy could justify buying toy trains.

Another local business in our area that converted to civilian products was Wagner Aluminum who made cookware. I thought this was a good thing to send to Bernice to help us get started on our new home that we hoped to have some time soon. We still have several of those pieces that we use today.

The Breweries were the first industries to completely recover because most of them had never really gone out of business, war or no war.

Captain Eli Fishpaw receives the Bronze Star from Maj. Gen. Withers Buress, Commanding General of the 100th Infantry Division. 30 July, 1945.

~ 16 ~

Becoming a Family

Eli:

After the first World War, there had been a great deal of dissension as to the way they had selected which troops went home first. To prevent this problem, the War Department came up with an elaborate point system where points were assigned to each officer and man according to his time in the theater, his time in combat, any injuries sustained, time spent as prisoner of war, and decorations awarded. Because the 100th had been one of the later units to go into combat, many of our soldiers were low on the needed points to go home, me among them.

It was late July when I heard a report that they were forming the 15th Army in Texas to be made up of all experienced combat troops from Europe. Its mission was to take part in the impending invasion of the island of Japan. The plan was to start with volunteers. Because I didn't have enough points to rotate at the time, I volunteered to go to Japan by way of Texas. We had heard a rumor from the Germans that the US had a secret weapon that would probably end the war. This was only a rumor. When I volunteered, I was gambling on that secret weapon to end the war before I got there.

When I was saying good-bye to everybody, about half of them thought that I was crazy to volunteer. Lt. Devereaux took over command of the battery and I headed for Bremerhaven. I shipped home with units from the 7th Armored Division. We hit terrible weather. Our smaller ship jumped around a lot more than the Washington.

We were in the middle of the Atlantic Ocean, heading for New York when we got a report on the radio that an Atomic Bomb had been dropped on the Japanese city of Hiroshima. I have never seen so many happy soldiers as when we heard that report. We all felt it would bring a fast end to the war. To this day I give Harry Truman credit for making that important decision. In my opinion, that bomb saved up to two million American lives plus a few hundred thousand Japanese.

THANK GOD AND HARRY TRUMAN

It was late August when we approached the New York Harbor. We were met by a tug boat with a New York lady vocalist. She was on the boat with an American flag behind her. We were greeted with an array of patriotic songs on a PA system coming from the tug boat. The first song we heard was "It Will Be A Hallelujah Day When The Boys Come Home To Stay." Some of the other songs included "Sentimental Journey", "The Victory Polka," "Roll Out the Barrel", and lead up to the "Star Spangled Banner". Everyone stood at attention and saluted as we passed the Statue Of Liberty. We gave her a big cheer as the tug departed and we sailed a short distance up the Hudson River.

It was only a short time after that we were unloading our own baggage. The stevedores were on strike. Four other officers and I had the detail of unloading the baggage for all the other officers. Most of the officers and the enlisted men were assigned to unloading the whole boat. I can tell you, none of us liked that very much. It was a good thing that we didn't have any live ammunition for the weapons that every man was carrying. You can be sure that we booed the pickets.

WELCOME HOME!!!

We departed the docks by bus to a nearby reception center where I had my first real stateside meal since leaving the country in October of 1944. We could eat all we wanted of steak, fresh milk, fresh eggs, french fries and fresh fruit. It was a happy moment to see all that wonderful fresh food and helped us forget the pickets at the dock.

In less than two days we were all rolling by train, plane and bus to the area where we had first entered the service. There we were given forty five days of rest and rehabilitation. I went to

Fort Meade near Baltimore first. At this time, we didn't have our next assignments. We were told that we would not go to Texas to join the Fifteenth Army bound for Japan. We would receive our orders by telegram at our home of record.

Several days after arriving home in Baltimore, I received orders to report to Commanding Officer, Fort Bragg, Field Artillery Replacement Training Center, (FARTC) North Carolina when my rest and rehabilitation was up.

I was happy to see my Mother at 1818 Ramsey St. and my sisters, Carrie and June. Anna was only a few blocks away on Washington Blvd. Johnnie had not come home yet from the Pacific, but my brother John, who had been in the Seabees, was home with his wife Catherine and his daughter Florence on Brunswick street. As soon as his terminal leave was up, he would go back to work at the hat factory as the boss of the box department.

Charlie was a Chief Petty Officer and was stationed at Astoria, Washington after spending many months on sea duty in the Pacific. Mom's health was beginning to slip and she required supervision which was furnished mostly by Carrie and June. Hoodie was now a foreman at Corkan Hill meat packing factory, getting live stock from the stock yard to the packing house.

I visited with a lot of the old neighbors. Ramsey St. hadn't changed much. It was good to be home.

I only stayed in Baltimore until I got my orders. Before long I left on the train for Wisconsin where Bernice was staying with her folks on the farm in Johnstown.

My father-in-law lent us the 1932 Chrysler Sedan that had been her grandfather's. It was a great help for us to get around.

While on the farm I offered to help out on different odd jobs. When her mother said that she hadn't had time to pick the popcorn, not knowing what I was getting into, I volunteered to do it. She said there were only three row which sounded like a very small plot to me. To my surprise, when I went out there, the rows must have been at least a quarter of a mile long and the stalks were mostly laying on the ground.

Popcorn has a short stalk to start with and a storm had knocked most of it down. As I started to pick and husk the stuff, I regretted opening my mouth. It wasn't my mouth that was hurting, it was my back. Bernice felt sorry for me. Even though she was seven months pregnant, she sat down on the ground between the rows and picked enough to keep me from quitting.

Of course, she had picked pop corn all her life and had the knack. We must have got at least a third to a half of wagon full.

Bernice:

I was quite comfortable at home with my parents. When I got word that Eli was coming home, we all knew that it would be a lot better if we could have some place of our own where we could be together by ourselves.

My dad's cousin, Grace Mepham, worked and lived at the Rock County Asylum but rented a small apartment in Milton to use when she had time off. It was my dad's idea for us to sub-let the little apartment and he arranged it with Grace, who was quite agreeable. Her daughter, Betty Lou, was in the service as a WAC. Everyone wanted to show their appreciation for the people who were coming home from the war. It was in a large house on Main Street. The bedroom was upstairs with a small kitchen and living room downstairs. It had a separate entrance and worked out very well for us.

Eli:

The Chrysler had all retread tires on it as new tires were unheard of during the war. It could go seventy miles an hour but probably never had. One day, we had been to visit her Aunt Cora and Uncle Charles in Elkhorn. We were only going sixty when the tread peeled off one of the front tires and flew right over the roof. When we stopped, the tire had not blown but we were riding on the cords. Luckily, there was a spare bolted to the rear of the body and I changed it.

Come November, it was time for me to report for duty at Fort Bragg. After I signed in, I reported to the Commanding Officer of the FARTC. He took my records and said for me to come back in about an hour. My assignment would be based on my experience as shown in the records. When I reported back to him, he informed me that I would be an instructor in the officers school. All classes, pertained to artillery subjects that every artillery officer should know.

I also had a class of NCO retreads. These are soldiers with no artillery training, who had been successful in other branches. Because the army was cutting back, a lot of their jobs had been eliminated. These NCOs were quick to pick up the artillery sub-

202

jects and turned out to be fine artillery NCOs. The same goes for the officers.

Bernice:

I had gotten established with Dr. Frechette, the obstetrician in Janesville, whom I had known as student nurse. He had a flat rate of $100 per uncomplicated pregnancy, including delivery, pre and postpartum care and a six week check up.

I got busy preparing for a new baby. My mother was up on the latest in baby stuff as Kenneth's son Dan had been born a year earlier. She liked their bathinett so much that she bought one for me. It proved to be very useful. For getting started, I bought a large basket with a hood. It had fold up legs on wheels.

I got very busy making baby clothes and even created six seersucker bedspreads for the basket. I embroidered them with cute little pictures of kittens. My proudest accomplishment was the pink bunting I made from a blanket remnant.

I was due the first of January. The heating problem in my old bedroom had not really been solved, so we put the roll-away bed in the dining room which was never as cold because it was supplied with heat from the furnace.

Late in December, the radio was announcing an impending blizzard. I was a little apprehensive about this, so when I was at the doctor's office, we discussed having me check in ahead of time and he would induce labor. It proved to be a good decision. I checked in on the 28th of December and on the morning of the 29th they started giving me pitocin to start my labor. I was up walking around and acting generally frisky until the pit hit me. It wasn't long until there was a big gush of water on the floor. I was very quickly put in the bed to stay.

By noon they moved me to the labor room. Up until now I had managed not to do any yelling, which so often came with women in labor. They gave me some scopolomine and from then on, I had no memory of anything. If I was yelling, I didn't know it. I surely didn't want to.

When I was ready to deliver, I was moved to the delivery room and woke up enough to be aware of where I was and what was going on. When they put me on the delivery table, they put my wrists in the cuffs that were secured to the rail at the side of the table. This made me real apprehensive. I just didn't want my hands restrained. Because I was familiar with that table, I reached my hand under the rail and released the thumb screw that held the cuff in place.

My hand came out and was flying around with the cuff and the steel bar that held it to the table. It must have been a dangerous situation. At least three people jumped on me from three different directions. The bar was put back where it belonged and this time it was tightened down so it couldn't come loose. I spent the rest of the labor between pains unsuccessfully trying to loosen it up again.

By now I was in the second stage of labor and being told to push which I was doing as best I could. Someone put the ether mask over my mouth and nose and started to drip some ether. Now normally, I don't care for the smell of ether, but at that moment it smelled so good I was pushing my face up into the mask to get as much as I could.

It never did put me out but just took the edge of the pains. I kept thinking that I wanted to go out before they did the episiotomy, but I heard the doctor ask for the scissors and actually felt him make the cut. Instead of pain, I experience great relief as the pressure was released and the baby was delivered. It was about 2:25 PM.

I had called Eli the night before and he was on his way to Wisconsin. He arrived later that evening. My dad met him and got him settled in a room at the railroad hotel near the depot.

He had not had to do the expectant father routine in the hospital waiting room and was happy to learn that he was papa to a health baby girl. We named her Bernice Virginia N. Fishpaw. The name was not identical to mine as the N. was just an initial for Newton to replace the R. in my name which stood for Richmond, my mother's maiden name. We would call her Ginny.

Eli:

On the 27th of December, Bernice called to tell me that she was checking into the hospital the next afternoon. I immediately got approval for an emergency leave to Janesville, Wisconsin.

I called Pope Air Force Base, which was attached to Fort Bragg. They told me that a C-47 was going to fly out for Chicago the next day and that I could get a ride. I left early in the morning in the C-47, loaded with cargo. There was room for about ten passengers. We were briefed that we would be heading into a snowstorm and that we might not make it all the way to Chicago but we had clearance to Cleveland, Ohio.

After taking off, they notified us that we definitely would be landing in Cleveland. As soon as we landed, they gave me a schedule for the trains and advised me to go to Chicago and change trains there for Janesville. I arrived around 1600 on the 29th. My father-in-law met me at the railroad station and told me that the baby had arrived that afternoon around 2:00 PM. and that the mother and baby were doing well.

He had made arrangements for me to stay at the Railroad Hotel. It was only a few rooms over a tavern near the railroad station. It was only about a half mile from the hospital but it was all uphill. He apologized for putting me over the beer joint. I didn't tell him, but I couldn't have wished for a more conveniently place to stay.

The storm was bad and he wanted to get home before it got dark. After getting cleaned up, I headed for the hospital on foot. The wind was blowing in gusts of up to at least forty miles an hour and there was a layer of ice under the snow. When the wind hit me, I would stand still and it was like I was skiing until I would hit a rough spot and I would end up on the seat of my pants. That happened at least three times in the short distance up the hill to the hospital.

Visiting hours were 2 to 4 in the afternoon and 7 to 8 in the evening. I went in the front door and asked to see Bernice. Because this was the hospital where she had taken her training, everyone knew her and they were expecting me. They said that it wouldn't be necessary for me to observe the visiting schedule and that I could use the back door, which was closer to my hotel. I could just come any time that I wanted to. I appreciated that. We had not had nearly enough time together since we had gotten married.

The first time I saw my baby she was asleep in the nursery behind the glass window. There must have been five or six babies in there and they were all red faced and looked alike but the nurse pointed out the one that was mine.

On New Years Eve, after making my visit to the hospital, I returned to my room at the hotel. They were having a New Year's party down stairs in the tavern. It was kinda noisy and I couldn't sleep, so I went down and joined them. Many of them asked me questions about my wife and the baby. Many of them knew the Newton family. I did enjoy the friendliness of this group of people. They were interested not only about the baby but about my war stories and what I had been doing at that time last year on New Year's Eve.

By the first of January, the storm was over and the roads had been plowed so that my in laws could come in from the farm. My mother-in-law had brought a three tiered cake with a bride and groom in an army uniform to celebrate our second wedding anniversary. The hospital staff happily helped eat the cake.

Bernice was not allowed out of bed for two weeks so I had to return to Ft. Bragg before she was allowed to go home. By being three days ahead of schedule, Ginny was now an income tax deduction, which just about covered the cost of her birth.

I took the train back to Fayetteville, North Carolina and resumed my duties as an artillery instructor. The staff was glad to have me back as they had to pull my classes while I was away.

Bernice:

In 1945 it was the practice for new mothers to stay in bed for two weeks. Babies were passed out routinely every four hours to nurse and to get to know their mothers. No visitors were allowed to be in the room during this time. They were expected to admire the new-borns through the glass window in the nursery.

When my two weeks were up, I went back to the farm.

Eli:

One day, when I was setting up for my class, a Captain stuck his head in the door and yelled, "Where in the hell is this damn officers' class." I recognized the voice of Bob Richards, one of my best friends from Fort Jackson when we were 2nd Lieutenants. I had volunteered both of us to go to Africa as replacements. I had been taken off the list but Richards had been left on. I hadn't seen him for a couple years.

The first thing he said was, "Shifty, you damn near got me killed." He wore the arm patch of the second Infantry Division. We bounced around the class room, making like we were fighting, tipping over a few chairs and what not. I said, "Lets go across the street and get a cup of coffee." He said he wasn't going to worry about his class. We jumped in my jeep and rode out the main road. We stopped in a restaurant and had coffee and doughnuts. I dropped him off where his class was in session when we returned to the post.

Every night at 1600 we would have a staff conference with the Colonel, to discuss the day's activities and plan for the next day. The first thing that came up that day was from a Major. He said that he had a Captain that had missed two classes and should be thrown out of the school. I spoke up and asked if his name was Richards. He said "Yes". I told him "It was my fault, we hadn't seen each other for three years, he was one of the finest officers that I had ever known. When he put his head in my class asking for directions we were both happy to see each other. I asked him out for coffee and to find out where all he'd been." I requested that the Major withdraw his complaint. If the Colonel would approve, I would appreciate it. The request was approved and that was the last of it. I never saw Richards again.

I was reassigned to the 46 FA Bn., 5th Infantry Division at Camp Campbell, KY to report on 20 February, 1946. Camp Campbell was about sixteen miles south of Hopkinsville on the Tennessee border. My first assignment there was battery commander of 'B' Btry. The whole army was in a state of transition. The entire division was a collection of drafted soldiers, waiting to have enough points to be discharged, and men who had been released from the army stockades. They were being given a final opportunity to serve six months of trouble free duty so that they would not be given a dishonorable discharge.

My driver was one of these. He had been convicted of man slaughter for losing his temper and running over another soldier in the motor pool. He proved to be a good driver.

At least two thirds of the men who were assigned to my battery had never had any experience in the artillery. They were from all branches of the service, including the Air Corp. I was notified by the Battalion Commander, that we had to have the battery able to function as soon as possible. No battery in the Division Artillery at the time was qualified to even fire live ammunition.

I had two weeks to get the battery ready to fire service practice for all the artillery officers of the division. To my surprise, the men from all the other services picked up the artillery very fast. In less than two weeks, we had a fine functioning artillery battery and were ready.

One morning, while I was getting a haircut, I was talking to the barber about trying to find a place to live. Anyone who was in the service at that time knows what a hard job that was. The owner of the barber shop overheard me. He asked me if we would like to live in the second floor of his home. He said it was set up as an apartment and had a separate entrance with a small kitchen and a bath room.

Bernice:

By the middle of February, Eli had been reassigned to Camp Campbell, KY. I took my baby, got on a train and headed for Kentucky. Eli had rented an upstairs apartment in Hopkinsville. This was our first real home together. There was a kitchen, a living room and a bath room. In the living room was a sofa that became the bed at night. In the kitchen there was a small eating table with 4 chairs, a work table and a free standing cabinet with dishes and cooking utensils. There was an electric stove, but no sink.

This was not insurmountable for the farm girl. I had carried water a lot farther than that. Washing dishes in a dish pan was the only way I knew how to do that chore anyway. Dishes and other wedding gifts came from Wisconsin. In the hall at the head of the steps was an old fashioned ice box. Three days a week I would put a card in the window to tell the iceman how much ice I needed. A 25 pound block of ice cost 25 cents.

The walls had wall paper, which was rather drab, so we got permission from the owner to re-paper the apartment. We put newspaper on the floor to use for a paste table. We were a lot more nimble then than we are now. It made the place look nice and fresh. When he saw how nice it looked, the landlord insisted on paying us $7.00 for each room which covered the cost of the paper.

We bought a used crib, which we put in the kitchen and I was in business. I did the laundry in the bath tub and had the use of the clothes line in the back yard.

Eli:

Bernice arrived with the baby and we were a complete family at last.

We really needed a car. Cars were as hard to come by as apartments. New cars were just starting to roll off the converted production lines in Detroit. We were able to find a used, 1946, two door Ford V-8 with over 60,000 miles on it. It was dirty and had not been well taken care of. We had both been buying war bonds, so we had a large enough supply of money that we were able to pay cash. We cleaned it up and it ran well for several years.

With a car, I was able to get in a car pool. One morning, when I picked up Capt. Smythers and Capt. Heard, who were in my car pool, they said, "Man you made the headlines this morning." They had the newspaper telling about one of my soldiers who had robbed seven people that week end. The headline read, AWOL SOLDIER STRIKES AGAIN.

It was a man that I had tried to have confined for another crime just a few days before he went AWOL. My request had been overruled by higher headquarters. I had been required to keep him in the battery until the Court Martial, but he had gone over the hill again. One of the biggest problems the commanders at the troop level have, has always been the lack of support of the staff officers in the higher headquarters, especially the JAG (Judge Advocate General) section who are the lawyers of the army. They always supported the criminal and not the commanders.

All sorts of weird things were happening in the country at this time. Everyone had been so united during the war. Now, selfish interests boiled up all over. This included an impending strike by the railroad employees. The railroads were so vital to the return to a peace time economy. President Harry Truman threatened to use troops if necessary to keep them operating.

The 5th Division was alerted to take over and operate the railroads if necessary. The 46th FA had been designated to run one of the Chicago passenger terminals. The outfit had been screened to find out how many of the soldiers had railroad experience. It turned out that there were a surprisingly large number of them. We were actually at the airfield, ready to load the planes when the strike was finally called off. We were sure glad to return to our normal duties.

In April, the division was sent to Chicago for a victory parade on Army day. President Truman was going to be there and it was a very big event. The complete division traveled by convoy. There were surprisingly few problems.

We had practiced convoy driving by traveling around the Camp. One day, as we went by the rifle range, Headquarters Battery, who were just ahead of me, went down the range road instead of staying on the main road. There was a road marker from another battalion, standing at the intersection. He thought this was one of his units and had turned them into the range by mistake.

My battery was within sight of them so I immediately turned down the range road to turn them around. My First Sergeant was given orders to continue to lead 'B' Btry. on the correct route by following the strip map.

When I caught up to Headquarters, they had already realized their mistake and had turned around to get back to the main route. As soon as I saw that they had turned around, I turned around too. I was just ahead of them, trying to catch up with my own battery.

That was when I met the Division Artillery Commander who was sitting beside the road observing the convoys. He stopped me. I was trying to explain to him what had happened but he wouldn't listen. He was blaming me for letting 'MY' battery go the wrong way. I tried to tell him that it was not my battery and that my battery was up the road and that I was just trying to help a fellow officer. He didn't believe me and I was just making him madder. I asked permission to return to my own battery. He said, "OK". I gave him a sharp salute and departed, glad to be out of his sight.

At the critique of the convoy exercise, the General gave this horrible example of how Captain Eli I. Fishpaw of 'B' Btry, 46th FA had lead his whole unit into the rifle range, despite having the strip map that we were supposed to follow. His remarks could not have been farther from the truth but he was too hard headed to listen out on the road.

I went to the battalion commander and requested permission to see the General. The Headquarters Battery Commander, Capt. West, also wanted to see the General to explain what had actually happened. He didn't want Fishpaw or 'B' Btry to be blamed for any part of the mix up. The Ole Man refused both requests. He gave us direct orders not to talk to the General and to get to hell out of his office.

Just prior to leaving for Chicago we were policing up the vehicles so they would look nice for the president. All the vehicles were left over from the war and none of the tires matched. One of the Sergeants said he knew how to make all rubber look the same. He bought some Bulldog Stove Black and before long all our tires looked like they were brand new.

When the other batteries saw how good our tires looked, they all went out to buy Bulldog Stove Black. When Division Artillery saw our rejuvenated tires, they ordered the rest of Divarty to make their tires look like ours. Before long, all the stove black in southwest Kentucky and northwest Tennessee had been sold out. The other outfits probably would have gladly killed us if they could have. The men and officers in each battery paid for the stuff from their own pockets.

When we arrived in Chicago, the division ordered all units to make their rubber look like the Artillery. That started another run in Chicago on Bulldog Stove Black. Their stores ran out too. No one could understand why the army wanted all that Bulldog Stove Black. But we did look good rolling down the road.

The division was billeted in a huge hanger at a bomber factory on the west side near what is now O'Hare airport. When we arrived in Chicago, there was a shortage of hoses to wash the vehicles and get them ready for the parade. In one end of the building, where the officers were billeted, I found a nice fire hose near a window.

I had the battery bring the vehicle over and we put the hose out the window. I turned the water on and in a few minutes, all the fire trucks and police in the area were pulling up to where we were washing the trucks. When I had turned on the water, the fire alarm had gone off in the fire station and they were all there. I admitted it was my fault.

I hadn't realized that the hoses were tied into the alarm system. The firemen were just glad it was a false alarm. We served the them coffee. I kept them standing around talking until we could get our last vehicle washed. A lot of them had been soldiers and understood the situation. They parted with a smile and we never heard any more about it.

Chicago is only about a hundred miles from the farm in Wisconsin. I thought this would be a good opportunity to visit Bernice's family. The weekend before the parade, my driver and I took my jeep and drove up to see them. They were glad to see us. They were especially interested in the army jeep. I took her father for an off road ride. We drove across some of the fields and through the woods.

We came to a ditch where I was showing off how the vehicle in four wheel drive could go right through that ditch with no problem at all. But, when I crossed the ditch on an angle, we got hung up. One front wheel and one back wheel were hanging off the ground.

The wheels were turning fine but we were going nowhere, because they had no contact with the ground. Mr. Newton took the shovel and dug out under the front right wheel until both front wheels were on the ground. When we got back in the jeep, it pulled right out. It was a good example of how we often had to solve problems in the army. I am sure the Newtons got a big kick out of my demonstration, especially the botched crossing of the ditch.

We had a meal at the Newtons at noon, but on our way back to Chicago we stopped in Lake Geneva for supper. Because the jeeps did not have a key, it was common practice for the driver to remove the rotor from the distributor to disable the vehicle. After we had supper and returned to the jeep, the driver was putting the rotor back in place when it cracked right down the middle.

Because it was Sunday, there were no garages or repair places open. We spotted a civilian jeep in front of a dealership across the street. We went over, but couldn't find anyone around. Because we had to get back to Chicago, I told the driver to take the rotor. I wrote a note to the dealer, explaining why I had taken the rotor and left it with a dollar bill in the mailbox. In those days a rotor cost eighty cents, but it was worth a lot more than that to me right then.

One night, before the parade, Mike, the warrant officer, woke me up about 0300. He was in his underwear and said he needed $10 to pay for his taxi cab. This was a little strange to say the least as Mike always carried a huge wad of money. He owned half of the land where Fort Bragg is.

Mike had met an attractive young lady in a Chicago bar who had invited him to her hotel room. He had removed his pants and his shirt when there was a knock at the door and the woman said, "That's my husband and he's drunk. If he finds you here he'll kill both of us." She pushed him out the window onto the fire escape and shut the window.

Mike realized he had been set up, but it was a cold night and he was outside in his longjohns. He must have sobered up quickly. He went down the fire escape and stood between two buildings trying to hail a cab. Every time one slowed down they would see this guy in his underwear and take off. Finally he saw a couple of the GIs from the battalion. They were able to get a cab and convince the driver that the man was a warrant officer and the cabbie agreed to drive him back to the bomber plant.

Cabs were not allowed past the outpost but when the problem was explained to the guard, the OD (Officer of the Day) was called. He made an exception and volunteered to ride to the hanger, so Mike could get the cash to pay the taxi.

The story doesn't end there. The next morning there was a call on the field phone which I answered. It was Chief of Staff at Division Headquarters with the bad news that Mike Cunningham's pants with his wallet, had been found in the Chicago river. They were concerned that he might be dead. I told them that couldn't be. He was asleep not ten feet from me. "Tell him he has a direct order to report to the Commanding General immediately to explain why his pants were in the Chicago river."

Mike had a problem. "How are you going to explain this one?" Mike had a plan. "I'll tell them that I took a pair of pants to the cleaner to be pressed and when I picked them up, I changed in a cab and forgot to take my wallet out of the pair I had been wearing. When the cab drove off, my pants and the wallet were still in the cab. They must have taken the money and thrown the pants with the wallet in the river."

I never thought it would work but the General bought the whole story. I'm sure the General was glad he didn't have to investigate some sleazy activity.

When we were lined up in position and were making final preparation, wiping off dust and getting ready to move out for the parade, we heard a loud noise coming down the street that sounded just like an incoming artillery shell or a rocket. In our nice clean uniforms, all the combat veterans automatically hit the sidewalks. There was one screaming noise after another.

When we looked up, there were about four jet airplanes that were buzzing the column. We all looked at each other. We got up, brushed our selves off and laughed. It was probably the first time most of the men had ever seen or heard a jet. I had seen one in Marsaille harbor in October '44 but it was way up in the sky so the sound was not nearly as frightening. It was a good thing they buzzed us while we were still waiting for the word to go. Later they buzzed us as we were going by the reviewing stand and it didn't phase us.

A lot of the people were not friendly and many of them heckled us, especially the officers. We were moving about two or three miles an hour during the parade, when a heckler, who was out in front of a policeman, was yelling profanity at the officers. Headquarter Btry. Commander, Capt. West, six foot, four from Texas got fed up. He stepped out of his jeep and knock the guy cold, right next to the police officer. The policeman completely ignored it. At least that was one spectator that found out that combat troops could still fight.

The next day, the division returned to Camp Campbell, by motor convoy with no major problems. After we got back to Campbell, the Colonel called me in to inform me that he was putting me in charge of the battalion baseball team in addition to my other duties. The team had lost their first game in the post league. He told me that if they could win the league, he would personally buy them all steak dinners.

When I returned to the battery with this news, I found out that my First Sergeant had managed other baseball teams. I more or less turned everything over to him. The next game, we got behind in about the seventh inning. The manager took out the pitcher and brought in the center fielder to pitch. He was also our best batter, hitting over 500 average. He shut the opponents out for the last three innings and hit a home run with two men aboard to win the game in the ninth inning.

I knew then that I had the right manager. They continued to win the next eight games, mainly due to the efforts of that one pitcher/center fielder.

With great pleasure, I headed up to the Colonel's office. He hadn't shown the least interest in the team the whole time, but I wanted to report to him that we had won the league and give him the trophy.

I asked him when he was planning to have the steak dinner. "You think I'm going to buy steaks for that bunch of Jocks?" I reminded him that he had promised the team. All along I felt that he would probably back out when the time came. I took up a collection from the battalion officers. We collected enough to have the dinner at the NCO club. The Commanding Officer did not attend, but I sure enjoyed it.

The army was being drawn down to peace time strength. There was a substantial number of reserve officers who wanted to make the military a career. To do this, the Pentagon (Army Headquarters) set up a program which included background checks, military record check, education, both military and civilian, and a written test.

Those that were approved in these categories would be given a chance to spend six months on active duty, performing the responsibilities of the rank for which they applied for. After six months, they would be rated by their immediate commanders and the information would be sent to career management section of their branch at the Pentagon. In a couple months they would be notified of the results. Those that succeeded were integrated into the regular army.

My battery executive officer, Capt. Allen Dingwall was one of the candidates. Many years later, he was again my executive officer in Germany when I was a battalion commander. I did not apply for the integration at the time. I wasn't interested in being a career officers.

Bernice:

That spring Eli had a lot of leave time coming so we decided to take the train to Baltimore so that his family could meet the new baby. Eli's brother, John, with his wife Catherine and their daughter Florence, lived a short distance away and we spent a few nights with them. John and Catherine both worked and Florence went to school, so we were free to sleep as late in the morning as Ginny would let us. All of a sudden, Eli jumped out of bed and dashed out of the room with his pants in his hands. He had heard the huckster out in the street calling, "Hard Crabs". He bought about five dozen I think. It was the first time that I had ever seen crabs.

Eli started rummaging around in Catherine's kitchen and came up with what he needed, vinegar and spice, and proceeded to steam all those crabs, then stacked them up on a newspaper in the middle of the kitchen table. I figured my new sister-in-law was going to want to kill him for making such a mess in her kitchen, but when they came home, they were thrilled to find all those bright red crabs. They didn't look all that inviting to me, but I knew that I was going to have to try to eat them if I was going to be a Fishpaw. They showed me how to break off the back of the shell and what to throw away and what to eat. I was glad that I could overcome my reluctance, because the meat was the sweetest I had ever tasted.

The lady down stairs had a baby buggy that she no longer needed, so she sold it to me for five dollars. It was wonderful. I could put Ginny in it and go all over. Hopkinsville was not very big at the time, but had good sidewalks.

I would go to the grocery store and use the buggy as a shopping cart. Grocery stores were just starting to let the customers walk around the store and pick up what they wanted and then go to a cash register to be checked out. They had wire baskets on wheels to collect your order, but they were flimsy. No one would even think of putting a baby or child in one. I could get a weeks supply of groceries for less than ten dollars and wheel them home in the carriage with the baby.

When the time came for Ginny to have her shots, we visited the public health clinic where I became a good friend of the nurse. Her name was Mrs. Good. She didn't have any children of her own and would fuss over the babies that came to the clinic.

215

There were other military families in our neighborhood. A major's wife who lived next door asked me to join her with a couple friends to play bridge. I knew nothing about the game but they taught me how it was played. We would play two or three afternoons a week while Ginny slept in her buggy, or laid on the floor and did baby things which everyone seemed to enjoy. If she cried, I could feed her and never miss a trick, although someone else would have to deal for me when I was thus occupied. I was an adequate bridge player but not real good.

Hopkinsville had a baseball team in the class 'D' KITTY LEAGUE (Kentucky, Illinois & Tennessee). We would listen to the games on the radio and once in a while, we would get to go to a game in the evening. I could leave the baby downstairs with the landlady. The team was called the HOPTOWN HOPPERS and it was a lot of fun going to a game.

They sold soft drinks in bottles which made a wonderful racket when you thumped them on the wooden stands. Everyone would thump in unison to get the home team fired up when they needed a rally. It worked too. They had to quit selling bottled drinks all over baseball though, as unruly fan would sometimes throw the bottles at the umpires or at the opposing players.

Probably the big event of our brief stay at Camp Campbell was when the Fifth Division went to Chicago for the Army Day parade. President Truman was there. While the men were gone, one of the other battery commander's wife stayed with me which worked out very well as she did not have a car.

Eli:

In early August, I received orders to report to the Ohio Military District at Ft. Hayes, in Columbus, OH for assignment as Recruiting and Induction Officer at Cleveland Ohio. Our battalion had been given a quota of one Captain to fill the job. I was not high on the Colonels list, so I was the honored one. I have to admit, I was glad to get away from him.

We had two days to report in, which was pretty short notice. The next day, we moved out of our little apartment. Army transportation was to pick up our possessions for shipment to Cleveland. We had expected them early in the morning but when they did not show, I called them up. They said to just go ahead. They would take care of everything. We set everything out in the front yard. I wasn't sure we would ever see our stuff again, but we had to hit the road.

As we were arriving in Cleveland, we saw what looked like thousands of tents and campers along the road and in the fields. We had heard that housing was short all over the country but this was pretty frightening. When we started looking for a place to live, we learned just how short living accommodations were. We were able to find a hotel room for one night. The Jehovah's Witnesses were having a World Wide Convention in Cleveland that week, which was the cause of all the tents, but there was indeed a housing shortage as well.

The next day we started hunting. We saw a brand new apartment complex which looked promising. When I made inquiry, they were all rented, but they needed a manager, which included an apartment in the basement. I could have it if I would be the manager. This was out of the question as I had a full time job with the army.

By late afternoon, we had been totally unsuccessful, when we drove past a sales lot where they were selling house trailers. Almost in desperation, we went in. They had one brand new trailer that they could sell us for $2,000. We bought it on the spot. It was completely furnished. The management knew where different trailer parks were located. They made some calls and found us a spot in a suburb of Cleveland called Brook Park. It was not far from the bomber plant at the airport where the Induction Center was located.

They delivered it to the park and we moved in. It was a good solution to our immediate problem of finding a place to live. It was eight feet wide, twenty five feet long, had three rooms and was completely furnished. It could be hooked up to a garden hose for water for the kitchen sink. The water from the sink ran out through another hose into a hole in the ground. There was a place to plug in an extension cord for electricity. There was a gasoline stove and a space heater with a chimney that burned kerosene. But there was no toilet or bathroom. For this, we had to go to a building in the center of the park that had toilets and showers with hot water as well as coin operated washing machines.

In about three weeks our household goods arrived. It was all there except a ten pound bag of sugar and a yankee drill that Bernice's Uncle Charles had given her. There was no room for the crib so we gave it away. We had improvised a bed for Ginny by putting the gate leg table next to the sofa in the living room. The bathinett was stored under the trailer when it was not being used.

Bernice:

I bought some sheets and a couple pillows and we moved in. I hoped that I would have some dishes and cookware coming from Kentucky, so I didn't want to buy any of these. For the first week we kept house with a can opener and two spoons. The empty bean cans became water glasses.

Our goods finally arrived from Hopkinsville. Going to the community latrine was certainly no great problem for us. We had both been in the army. I did purchase a slop jar, which was a great improvement at night. It was not unusual to see the other residents carrying their slop jars to the latrine every morning to be emptied.

This was the summer of 1946. The world was returning to normal. One important event, that had been a part of Cleveland, was the air races. They were held out at the airport where Eli worked, so of course, we went. I suppose they were exciting but I don't remember. What I do remember was when it was over. We got into one of the biggest traffic jams I have ever experienced. It was total grid lock. We just turned off the motor and everyone stood around socializing in 90 degree heat.

Another big event that year was the establishing of the All American Football Conference. The Cleveland Rams had moved to Los Angeles so the city was ripe for a new league and a new team. They had just built a big new stadium on Lake Erie. We were both football fans, so we hired a baby sitter and went into the city to see the first game of the new league between the MIAMI SEAHAWKS and the CLEVELAND BROWNS.

They had not expected very many people to turn out, but when we got there, it was packed. On the north side of the stadium, where our seats were, there was only one turnstile open and the line was very slow. As it got closer to game time, the people in the back began to crowd. Before long we were really jammed up. It could have gotten ugly, but someone opened the big exit gate and the crowd spilled in. We didn't get to see the opening kick off but we did see the first game, which Cleveland won. We went to several games and saw the great players of the time, such as Otto Graham, Lou Groza, Marion Motley and Lou Sabin. They were coached by Paul Brown. That was where they got their name.

After the war, there were several benefits made available to the veterans. We were given $300 separation pay. I had spent mine on a fur coat while I was in Wisconsin. We also had an educational benefit as part of the GI Bill of Rights. There was an airport for small aircraft right next to the trailer park that had a flight school. My idea was that I could learn to fly and we would go to Alaska where I would be a bush pilot. They could take GI students so I enrolled in flight training. One of the neighbors in the trailer park watched the baby in the afternoon when I would walk over to the airport and take my flying lesson.

I did fairly well. The planes were Piper Cubs, a very basic little aircraft with fabric over wood frames and a wooden propeller. To start them, you grabbed the top of the propeller and pulled it down. I was able to solo in six hours and I was able to land on my first try as a solo. I can remember very well that day. We were practicing take offs and landings. After several successful landings my instructor hopped out and said, "Take her around." I didn't have time to worry about it. When I landed he was standing out in the field right where he had gotten out. I never got to get my license because I had not completed the course when it was time to leave Cleveland.

Eli:

The Commander of the North Ohio Induction Station was due to leave in the near future and I was assigned as his assistant and would take over when he departed.

It was soon obvious to me that discipline was fairly poor. When I went by the room where they were taking blood for testing from the volunteers and draftees, I saw one of the privates with a blown up instructional syringe, making a big joke out of scaring the new recruits with it.

I stood there and watched them draw blood with proper equipment from a few of the men. One man passed out and they made no attempt to catch him. They just let him fall on the floor. Then they all laughed. I told them to quit operations. I wanted to see these four enlisted men outside. For the first time in my army career, I wanted to knock the hell out of all four of them because that was what they would understand. If they had talked back to me, I believe that I would have.

I reported them to the commander who said, "They were just having fun." I told him that I wasn't going to put up with that sort of behavior anywhere. I wanted to start my own program to get the personnel straightened out, but I had to have his permission. He asked what I wanted to do. I said we would start with dismounted drill and calisthenics every morning at 0800, followed by an hour of military courtesy. Every Saturday morning, we would have a full inspection of the Induction Center and the military personnel.

The commander was not at all in favor of any of this but he did not interfere. He was leaving anyway. The personnel had been there for almost all of WWII. It was a really great assignment for them. They were in TDY (Temporary Duty) status, so received per diem pay and lived off post because there were no living accommodations for troops.

Not long after the Commander left, some of the enlisted men filed a complaint with the IG (Inspector General) about the new CO. I received a call from the 82nd Airborne telling me they were sending a Captain over for a few days TDY to investigate the complaints. One morning, when I went out to supervise training, he was waiting for me. I took him to my office. It was right in the center of the induction station with glass windows on all four sides where I could see everything.

He told me he wanted to talk with the men who had filed the complaints and with anyone else who wanted to complain. I cancelled training and had the First Sergeant announce that anyone who wanted to complain should go to the Commander's office at 0900. I would be in the cafeteria having coffee. That way nobody could say that I was spying on them.

About 0915, the inspector came into the cafeteria and told me that some men had been there at 0900. When the first man who came in had failed to report properly and had sat on the desk, he was ordered to remove himself from the desk or he would be knocked off of it. He was ordered to go back to the 1st. Sergeant and learn how to report to an officer.

The guys waiting outside could hear every word that was said and they had scattered like a covey of quail. The man who was told to learn how to report, never came back. The Captain said, "I sat there for five minutes and when no-body showed up I figured that nobody had any complaints so, I decided to have coffee with you and get an early start back to Ft. Bragg". Case closed.

At that moment I could feel the whole outfit change from a route order bunch of bums to a well trained outfit, able to do the job. After about two weeks I cancelled the military courtesy classes, but kept the dismounted drill and physical training.

The principle man who was leading the dissidents was the one who was working in the blood room and had made no attempt to catch the inductee who fainted. I transferred him to the motor pool to be a driver. He actually ended up being my driver. As my driver, he did a good job and I never had any problems with him.

After I thought every thing was straightened out, I learned that the civilians had filed a complaint. During this period of time there were lots of high school graduates enlisting to take advantage of the GI Bill of Rights that included three years of college for a year and a half of active service. Sometimes we were inducting whole classes of high school kids. For a while, more than a hundred a day had to be processed. The twenty minutes break in the middle of the morning and the afternoon was ignored a few times so that we could get the inductees sworn in and on the train to their new assignments by 1830.

The civilians were mostly women typist. They were supposed to come to work at 0800, but most of them had been arriving around 0900 or 0930 which was when the preliminaries were finished and their work would begin. I also studied their time cards and discovered that many of them took as long as two hour breaks when business was slow.

So I made a ruling. All civilians would be given two twenty minute breaks, but that everyone would clock in at 0800 and be at their work station and they would not leave until 1600. I held a briefing and explained the new policy that their complaints had brought about. There would be no more work during the twenty minute breaks and that everyone would clock in and out according to their contract.

After about three days, three of the women asked the First Sergeant for permission to speak to me. Their leader apologized for their complaint and told me that it had been withdrawn. I told them that I would still keep their twenty minute breaks clear and we would relax the clocking routine when we were not busy.

We had both army doctors and civilian doctors who did our physical examinations of the new recruits. Most of the doctors did a good job. I really had a problem though with the psychiatrists. There were two civilians and two Army Captains. I did not have any problems with the civilian doctors but the two Army Doctors were rejecting the recruits who really wanted to be in the service. Those who absolutely did not want to be in the army they would also reject. It was the men who were undecided or couldn't make up their minds that they accepted.

Upon talking with the two officers, I felt that they were mentally unbalanced themselves and yet they were judging who should or shouldn't be in the army. I felt the induction station was inducting more problem type soldiers and turning down the kind of men that would make the best soldiers. I sent them to the Army Hospital for observation. They never returned to the induction center.

Another event, involving the medical examination part of my responsibility, involved the player/manager of the Cleveland Indians baseball team, Lou Beaudreau. I read in the headlines of the Cleveland Plain Dealer (newspaper) that many of the people of Cleveland felt he was a draft dodger because he was repeatedly turned down for physical reasons. That was known as being 4F, which meant unable to perform military duties. The public just couldn't believe this, because he was one of the best second baseman in the Major leagues. After much publicity, higher headquarters gave me an order to call him in for re-examination.

The stated reason he had been turned down was that his ankles were too weak to be in the military. I picked three orthopedic doctors at random from the telephone book to re-examine him. I also invited the newspaper reporters and Cleveland Indians representatives to attend the examination. The draft board sent him over again and we went through a complete examination of his legs and ankles.

Each of the three doctors examined him separately. They rejected him too. The problem was that he had very thin ankles. You could see every bone in his ankles and upper foot. Without heavy taping from the instep to the knee for support they would surely give way on a two mile hike.

When he played baseball he was always taped. The problem that kept him out of the army was probably the asset that made him such a good second baseman. After the results of this examination appeared in the papers and on the radio, the public got off his case and he continued to be one of the all time stars of the Cleveland Indians. Case Closed.

One of our responsibilities was transferring the new inductees from the downtown recruiting station to the Induction Center at the airport and from the airport to the railroad station. We had an old WWII type semi trailer bus. It was an ordinary 18 wheeler modified to carry troops.

One morning, when I entered the office, I was told that the bus had jackknife on the Lakeshore Drive during morning rush hour and had five of the six lanes blocked. There were no passengers but three or four of my army personnel were aboard. No one had been hurt.

I jumped in my sedan and went to the scene of the accident. The men were hooking up the rig, with a streetcar tow chain that they had borrowed from the transit company, to a one and a half ton army truck to tow it back to the airport. There was very little damage except it wouldn't run.

I talked to the corporal in charge about getting a civilian tow truck but he assured me that they could handle it ok on the secondary streets. After we had gone about a mile on the side streets, we were approaching a traffic light. There was a city garbage truck just ahead of our little convoy. We were all traveling about 30 miles an hour when the light changed to yellow. The garbage truck locked his brakes.

My ton and a half stopped about a foot behind him but the eighteen wheeler's brakes didn't work. He pulled out to the left to avoid hitting the smaller truck. When the chain grew tight, it pulled all three vehicles together. The airbrakes won't work unless the motor is running. If the driver had left the vehicle in gear there would have been enough pressure to operate the brakes, but we didn't know that until the damage was done.

We pulled the whole set up back to the induction center at about fifteen miles and hour. The garbage truck was only scratched a little but my bus was so badly damaged that higher headquarters refused to repair it. It should have been salvaged years ago. We turned it in to the salvage yard at Fort Hayes behind a civilian tow truck the next day. We were issued a regular bus to take its place.

It was late in 1946 when I was offered the opportunity to extend my category 3 status as a Captain. It would require that I go over seas again. I decided that maybe we ought to try civilian life and get our family settled down. I was discharged at Fort Hayes and transferred to the US Army Active Reserve, Maryland Military District effective 1 January, 1947.

~ 17 ~

A Civilian Again

Eli:

After a short visit with the Newtons in Wisconsin we took our trailer and headed for Baltimore. We took turns driving. Most of the roads were still two lane but the big cross country highways had wide shoulders. It was a good thing too. Bernice was driving as we were in Ohio heading east on US 40 when a big truck came over the crest of a hill on our side of the road. Her only choice was to hit the shoulder, which can be a little scary at 60 miles and hour.

We had another close call as we were winding our way down a long curving stretch about five miles long, leading out of Ohio into Wheeling, West Virginia. I was driving this time and was

Our home on wheels, parked at the farm in Wisconsin and ready to roll for Baltimore. October, 1946.

using the electric brakes on the trailer to help hold us back on the steep hill. I shifted to a lower gear. After about two miles, the electric brakes did not hold. I could slow it down with the car brakes and I dropped into first gear so that I was able to control the rig until we were safely at the bottom of the hill.

I pulled onto the shoulder where I had a chance to check the cable to the trailer and it was still connected. We took a few minutes to let both sets of brakes cool off and to get ourselves cooled down a little too. I carefully crossed the bridge and tried the electric brakes again. To my relief, I found they worked perfectly. We had learned not to over rely on the electric brakes.

Bernice:

We found a place to park the trailer in Catonsville, west of Baltimore, on Edmondson Ave. It was behind a small family run filling station. It was a small park, able to hold thirteen trailers. There was one water faucet on a pipe in the middle of the park. Running water meant running out to the faucet with a bucket. The toilet for our use was also the one for the filling station. It had an outside door. We had the first space. Our gray water ran down a ditch behind the trailer.

The location was pretty good as the streetcar ran up the middle of the street. Of course, Eli needed the car to drive over to the east side every day. If I wanted to leave the park, I could use the street car. They were quite large and modern. The seats had springs with fixed backs and all faced forward. They ran out to the center of Catonsville where the tracks made a circle for the return trip.

The same line also ran out to Ellicott City, in Howard county. There was no place to turn around out there, so all their cars were the old fashion kind. When they reached the end of the line the motor-man moved to the other end of the car moving the seat backs as he went so the seats faced the other direction. Both styles went into downtown Baltimore and it didn't matter which kind of car it was. I took which ever kind came along. I actually preferred the older version because I thought they had more character. I must not have been alone as this is the style which is now replicated and mounted on bus chassis seen around tourist attractions all over the country.

Eli's sisters, Carrie and June both worked. Carrie was a supervisor for telephone company. They lived with their mother on Ramsey Street, where Eli grew up. Their mother's health was failing and I never really got to know her very well. His sister, Anna, lived on Washington Blvd. which was about a mile from the home place. When I got lonesome, I would pack up Ginny and take the street car to visit Anna who had two small children, Linda and Billy, and was usually home. Across the alley on the next street was where her husband, Johnnie Downey's mother lived. Her mother was bed ridden and confined to the back bedroom. His mother was really tied down. I used to enjoy going over there to visit while Ginny played with Billy and Linda.

One day Eli brought home a trunk full of old fashion lath he had picked up where a house was being torn down. That was what was used in older houses for interior walls to hold the plaster. I bought a saw and a miter box and sawed them all in half with points on the top. When painted white, they made a very decent looking picket fence for our front yard and a place for Ginny to play. I also made a skirt for the trailer, to give it a permanent look and to keep the baby from escaping underneath.

On Friday mornings, Eli turned in the collections for the week and then had Saturday off. This was when I had the car and could go to Catonsville and do the laundry while I did my grocery shopping. Laundramats were something new and very useful as new washing machines were at a premium then. I didn't have room for one anyway. One day there was a new sewing machine store having a grand opening next to the laundramat. New sewing machines, like everything else, were in short supply because all manufacturing had been devoted to making war equipment for the last five years. I checked out the new store and discovered they had a brand new portable singer sewing machine. It was expensive at $75 dollars, but I bought it anyway and cut down on the groceries to make the down payment. Later, when I told my mother about the machine, she paid the full amount of it for a belated wedding gift. I still have it and use it. I don't sew much anymore but do find it handy for mending.

One day, while I was at the store, Eli had laid down with the baby on the bed between him and the wall to listen to the radio. Of course he went to sleep. Ginny was not trained and had a number two accident. When I got home I found a wet sheet hanging on the fence and one very disgruntled husband.

Oranges used to be shipped in wooden crates that could be obtained from the grocery store when they were empty. The next week I picked up an orange crate. With my trusty saw, I created a small chair with a hole in the seat and training began.

Ginny could be very petulant at times. On day she was not having her way about something and was crying. I decided to just let her cry and not give in. It was warm, so the door was open. Mrs. Kennedy, the lady who owned the park and ran the filling station, thought I must be abusing my child. When it was time to pay the rent she told me if I couldn't keep my child quite she would need to ask for my space. I got on the streetcar and went over to Annie's where I could use the phone and called around until I found a park that had a space available.

When Eli came home, I told him about the episode and he agreed that it was time to move. The next day, while Eli was at work, I jacked up the trailer and put the left wheel back on. It had been removed to level the floor because the lot was uneven. Rather than tow the rig ourselves, we hired a tow truck. We followed the truck as we headed for our new park out in Anne Arundel county. We hadn't gone two miles when we noticed that the left wheel on the trailer was wobbling. We tooted our horn with persistence and the tow truck stopped. They jacked up the trailer and tightened up the lugs.

The new park was in Riviera Beach at a private recreation park owned by a man named Heintzman. It was on Rock Creek, which was wider than a lot of rivers at that point. He had a beach with bath houses and charged admission. To the south of the public park, there was also a good sized trailer park and several cottages. The cottages were rented to permanent tenants because of the housing shortage.

It was nice to be in the bigger park and especially to have a full service bath house for the park, with showers, latrines and a pay telephone. There was an electric meter and a spigot for each space. There was even a place where we could let the gray water from the kitchen run into the ground. I set up my picket fence, put the skirts back on the sides and we were back in business. The landlady didn't live close enough to know if the baby cried or not.

There were other families with small children in the park so I began to have a wider opportunity to meet people. There were also some older children who lived in the cottages. They would come over to the big field behind the trailer and we would often join them to play football, baseball or fly kites.

The trailer next door was owned by a member of the Coast Guard stationed at Curtis Bay, not far from our park. One day we had a brush fire behind the field and his wife had called him

227

because it was scary. He brought home a big fire extinguisher, but we didn't need it as the fire had been brought under control when it got to the mowed grass.

However, it turned out to be a good thing that he had it. The next day, a new rig had been delivered and a new family moved in and hooked up. Eli was outside when he saw yellow smoke coming from the new trailer. The owners were relaxing outside. He dashed over to tell them their place was on fire but they thought it was just smoke coming from the new stove. Eli went in and opened the closet door and flames shot out at him. He closed the door quickly and ran out. By now the wall of the trailer was showing a brown spot where the closet was.

I jumped in the car and raced down to the fire station about half a mile away. I yelled to them that there was a trailer on fire. They blew the whistle, but before the volunteers were assembled and on the site, the Coast Guard guy had punched the cone of his big extinguisher through the brown spot and smothered the fire with CO_2. When the firemen arrived they were surprised. It was unusual, as most trailer that had a fire were totaled in minutes. However, the people lost all their clothing which they said included a fur coat.

Television was just starting to be available in Baltimore in 1947. John Fishpaw had a set. It was as big as a bread box but the picture was about three inches square. To get reception, a large antennae was required and they were expensive. There was a single man at the park who had a small travel trailer. I guess he could afford a TV because he didn't have the expense of a wife.

After dark he would put his set outside and the neighbors would bring their chairs and sit around and watch. He had a big lens that he set in front of the picture to enlarge it. Boxing and wrestling were the favorite programs. I got a big kick out of watching the lady wrestlers.

One day, I read in the paper that the American Legion was forming an all women's post. I made the necessary inquiries and joined them. I think I was probably a charter member. It included a wide variety of women, from all the various services, but no nurses. I was even elected Adjutant. We had meetings, etc., but never really accomplished much. We did have a crab feast, another first for me. It was held in a park. They had a whole barrel of steamed crabs and beer by the keg. It was a money raiser and in that respect it was a success. Baltimorians sure like their crabs.

We even went to the state convention at the 5th Regiment armory in downtown Baltimore. I had the feeling that the men wished we weren't there. All we wanted was the authority to wear a Legion uniform modified for women. We had a big floor fight and were booed out of the hall.

Eli:

My sister, June, was the office manager for the Quaker City Life Insurance Company. It sold industrial insurance which isn't at all what it sounds like. They sold small ordinary life insurance and also health and accident polices in and area known as a debit. The duties of the agents included selling and collecting weekly from many families. I agreed to take the job so we could get on with our life. My debit was southeast Baltimore and included Dundalk, Holibird, and Sparrows' Point.

My supervisor was a man named Gundina who was being promoted and I was to take over his debit. He introduced me to his area and showed me how to sell a policy and the administrative procedure of processing the policies. When the policy was written I would hand deliver it to the customers.

I was also given the privilege of settling both death and sick and accidents cases. Not many of the agents had this privilege but it was nice because I made sure my people were taken care of. It helped me get new business because my competitors from big insurance companies usually had to wait a month or two before their benefits were paid.

Every morning I had a card listing the places that I was to collect from. I would makes the collections, which were usually rather small. Sometimes I would collect five cents on eight or ten different polices as most of the families had a policy on each of their kids. In some families, that could afford it, they had sick and accident insurance on the father as well. A good day's work would bring in about $150. I was paid a commission on new sales of 70% for the first nine months and 10% on collections thereafter. With the money in my pocket, I would go home and turned over the task of recording all the collections from the card to the debit book to Bernice. There was only a small box for each entry and she was a better hand printer than I was.

The insurance man was well respected in his own debit area. Most of my families would identify their insurance company as Mr. Fishpaw's insurance company. I had the feeling that all those people were looking out for me and that they made sure that nobody robbed me or bothered me in any way. I felt safer with all that cash in my pocket and everybody knowing it, than I would walking through down town with nothing in my pocket.

One day, after I had finished my collections and was on my way home, I decided to stop and have a beer at Baltimore St. near Pine. While I was drinking my beer, a young couple who were sitting beside me said they needed a ride to North Charles St. because their car had broken down. I told them that when I finished my beer I would run them up there. When we arrived we stopped at a beer joint in the middle of the block.

They got out and invited me in. I refused to go because I had to get home. They offered to bring me a beer that I could drink in the car and I agreed. That was about six o'clock. I remember that they brought me the bottle of beer and stood outside the car talking to me.

I took about two sips and woke up about two hours later with my left hip pocket cut open and my wallet that I would have been sitting on, laying in my lap. I knew that some thing was really wrong. The money was taken but all the checks were still there. That was good, because the amount that they stole was probably around $22. I figured that I was lucky to be alive after such a stupid mistake. When I got home, even later than usual, and told Bernice what had happened she told me, "It serves you right."

One day I was in the Hollings Market having a beer in one of the beer joints when I ran into one of those horse's butts that was being obnoxious. Many of the people left the place in disgust. As people left, he worked his way down the bar to where I was. I was determined that I was not going to take any crap off this guy. When he sat down beside me I told him that I didn't like his conduct and that I didn't intend to take any of it from him. He turned and looked at the front door and said, "You think you're tough but my friend is tougher than you and here he comes." When I looked up, I recognized one of the guys from my section in the old battery 'A' of the 110th FA, 29th Division, named Gephardt.

As Gephardt came over to where we were, he recognized his old sergeant and was all smiles when he came over to greet me. I told him to, "Shut up and don't say a word. Just sit down and buy that beer that you owe me." When he sat down and ordered the beer the trouble maker ran right out the swinging doors. While we drank our beer I told him about another one of my friends name Tuffy Spietel who ran a neighborhood bar on Lombard at Fulton Ave.

Tuffy had been the heavy weight champion of the Pacific Fleet. He and his whole family were great athletes around southwest Baltimore. Tuffy had an offer out that if anybody could beat him at arm wrestling, he would buy the whole bar a drink. Gephardt was a stevedore and was one of the strongest men I had ever seen anywhere. He had muscles that looked like cement bags that had been left out in the rain.

I told him about Tuffy's offer and we headed for Spietel's bar. In a few minutes we entered the bar and I introduced Gephardt as one of my old friends from the army. I said we wanted to take him up on his offer to buy a round. Tuffy put his arm on the bar and Gephardt took his hand.

Tuffy started to push as hard as he could and Gephardt never moved a muscle. He said, "Tell me when Sarge." I let Tuffy strain for a few seconds. When I said, "Now" old Tuffy's hand landed so hard on the bar that it sounded like a bass drum. Everyone in the place got a free beer.

Gephardt had been in the battle of Normandy. Shortly after 'D'day his battery had been hit by an incendiary bomb by the Germans and the ammunition was burning. The executive officer had ordered everyone to get out of the area. Gephardt ignored the order and took a shovel and proceeded to cover the burning ammunition with dirt until the fires were out. For this, he was awarded the Silver Star.

Another time I met a seaman from England at the market. While we were talking, he told me that he was the champion wrestler of the British Fleet. I told him about Tuffy and he agreed to go with me to accept the challenge to wrestle. I brought him into the bar and introduced him to Tuffy who agreed to wrestle the little guy. They cleared away all the tables in front of the bar to have a place for the match. Tuffy had just bought a brand new big screen TV. It was the size of a window and was up high where no one could hit it.

The rules were explained and they squared off in the middle of the floor. One of the bar customers was the referee and gave them the go sign. That little guy, in about ten seconds, threw Tuffy up in the air, feet first and he came down with his feet in the new TV. Glass flew all over the place and the match was over. Again the whole bar had a free beer. He told me that his place was off limits to any of my friends who wanted to challenge him.

It was football season again. The Miami team had failed and the franchise was being moved to Baltimore. They held a contest to name the new team. The prize was two lifetime tickets to all the home games. Bernice entered the name BANNERS because THE STAR SPANGLED BANNER had been written in Baltimore harbor. It didn't win. They chose the name "Colts".

When the new team opened for business, Tuffy bought a section of season tickets behind the goal post in the north end of the stadium. For the home games he would rent a bus, supply it with beer, sodas, chili and hot dogs. Then he would sell the outing to his customers as a whole package for $5.00.

We got a baby sitter at the park and would drive to Tuffy's, park the car and take the bus to the games. Tuffy had strict rules about people who bought his tickets. No body was allowed to get out of line. He asked three or four big guys from the group to patrol the perimeter of the section to see that our people behaved and that nobody else bother us. I was assigned to the back row.

On one occasion there was a fight above our section that spilled over to where we were. A bunch of older men were fighting with two young teenagers. The youngsters ran down behind our section to get away from the men who were after them. We let them get through before we stopped the older guys and told them to get to hell back where they belonged and not to bother the kids again.

We put the kids in the middle of our section to protect them. The police came and Tuffy explained what happened. He described the men as a bunch of communist and said that if they ever bothered us again they wouldn't be able to walk away. The police assured us it wouldn't happen again and went up and talked to the trouble makers.

One of my closest boyhood friends was Barney Goldberg. We had learned to play basketball in the alley with a peach basket nailed to a wall. With the Bach brothers, he had played organized basketball at Calvert Hall, a Catholic High School and had gone on to Loyola University where they had been on the varsity basketball team who had won the Catholic championship of the country. They had defeated Loyola of Chicago in the championship game.

The war was over, and in 1946 the National Basketball Association was being organized. Baltimore had a team that was called the Bullets and Barney and the Bach brothers tried out and became starters. Buddy Gennett was the player coach. They played their games in a small gym over some stores on Monroe street at North Ave. We liked to go watch my old buddies play the game we had enjoyed as boys in the back alley. We knew they were getting paid real money for playing and probably more than I was making selling insurance, but certainly nothing like NBA players get today. One thing is for sure though, they really loved the game.

When I was a kid, I had belonged to the Knot Hole Gang. That was a program that made it possible for young boys to attend the games of the Baltimore Oriole Baseball team in the International League. I belonged to a group from Carroll Park. For a dime we got a bus ride to the stadium and admission to the bleachers at the old Oriole Park.

In 1947 the St. Louis Browns moved their franchise to Baltimore and took over the name of Orioles. They played at the old Municipal Stadium. It was really a football facility. Left field was only about 200 feet from the plate to the seats but the right field went on forever. Later, the city built a new stadium for both the Colts and the Orioles. We enjoyed going to the baseball game. It was always fun to watch the games whether they were in the afternoon or under the lights at night.

After work, a couple days a week, I would stop by a small tavern in Brooklyn on my way home after work. The bar tender told many great stories about the fish he caught on his week ends off. I told him that I had been fishing the same week end that he claimed to have caught so many fish and I hadn't caught a thing. He said, "Next week, why don't you come fishing with me?" I took him up on the offer and picked him up about three o'clock in the morning at his apartment just down the street from the tavern.

The first thing he wanted to do was to stop by an all night tavern on the way and get a double shot of whiskey. I had a cup of coffee. After that we went down toward the Severn River just short of Annapolis. We pulled down a side road which lead into some residential home on the river. He told me to stop behind one of the houses. He would check with a friend to see how the fish were biting. He banged on the back door and his friend looked out the upstairs window and said, "We got plenty of them today."

The next thing I knew, we were out on a pier where there were several live boxes in the water that were full of live fish. It was obvious that they had been caught with nets. My bar friend took one look and said, "We'll take a bushel." They dipped out a bushel of live rock fish. He paid the man and I thought that he was crazy. "We really got them just like I told you." I put the basket in the trunk of the car and headed back to Brooklyn. On the way back, we stopped at every filling station along the way where he would brag about how we really got the fish fast this morning. He would give all of his friends a half dozen or so of the still jumping fish.

When we got back to his apartment he took about half of the fish that were left and gave a dozen to me in the basket to take home. All the time he kept saying, "We really got them, didn't we?"

I went straight home to the trailer. When I walked in the door Bernice said, "You sure got home early." I gave her the fish to clean while I read the newspaper. After she looked at one or two of them she said, "How come they don't have any holes in their lips." I started laughing. I hadn't intended to tell her this dumb story that dapper Dan the bar tender had pulled.

The following day, Monday after work, I stopped by the tavern on the way home which was loaded with customers. Dapper Dan announced as I walked through the door that if anyone didn't believe his story, they could just ask Eli. "Eli, tell them how many we got." I said, "One bushel". He kept right on bragging and I was embarrassed but I didn't give away his secret.

Bernice:

Winter was coming on and Ginny and I were not able to spend as much time outside. The inside seemed to be shrinking too. I got the mumps and really felt terrible. I was not very active. I lay on the bed and Ginny sat beside me, petting me like a kitten. She didn't understand the problem.

Eli was doing fairly well selling and collecting insurance. One of the elements of industrial insurance was the large amount of record keeping involved. This involved a book with little tiny spaces to enter the collections for each policy. Many of these policies paid 5 or 10 cents a week and many families had eight or ten kids, each with their own policy. While Eli's hand writing was legible, it was very heavy and almost impossible for him to fill in the tiny squares. Thus it fell to me to make the entries, using the card where he recorded the collections as he made them. Since it was often late when he got home, I was not fond of the job.

I felt that it was about time for us to start looking for a bigger place to live. There was a great deal of building going on. There were even whole cities being built. One was not far from us called HARUNDALE VILLAGE. They were mass producing houses and they all looked alike. Eli heard about a place near Jessup where a man was building houses. We drove out there to check it out. It was just off US 1. There were a couple houses built and they looked very nice. We selected a lot which was way in the back of his sub-division and decided to buy it and have him build us a house. We borrowed $2,000 from my parents and made a down payment.

The winter didn't seem quite so long or the space so cramped, knowing that we would soon have our own house. But it started to drag when we would drive out to our site and not see any building going on. It turned out that our builder was in jail for some problems paying his bills. They let him out to finish some of the houses he had started, but he could not start any new building.

By spring it became clear that we were not going to get our house, so we went to Ellicott City which was the county seat of Howard County where the lot was located. We engaged a lawyer to try to get our down payment back.

Eli:

When I was discharged in December 1946 I had been assigned to the US Army reserve. I had not been assigned to any specific unit at first but in late 1947 a missile battalion was formed in Annapolis to which I was assigned as a battery commander. I reported to an historic cafe across the street from the Naval Academy one night a month. We served on a volunteer basis and were not paid. Mostly, we listened to speakers who were officers on active duty. They were all excited about what a great thing we were doing and about the potential they envisioned for this new type of artillery.

~ 18 ~

Old Ally, New Enemy

Germany had been divided into four zones after the defeat. The United States, Briton, France and the Soviet Union each had an area for which they were responsible. It was known as occupation. Berlin, which had been the capital of the Third Reich, was also divided into four sectors. The city itself was situated inside the Soviet Zone. To reach Berlin by land it was necessary to go through the Soviet Zone by train or the super highway known as the autobahn.

The post war recovery was doing much better in the western zones than in the area controlled by the communist. The Soviets had suffered enormous damage at the hands of the Nazi. They were depleted of resources and were not eager to forgive and go on.

When it became apparent that the western areas were recovering, the Soviets, under their dictator Stalin, built an actual fence between their territory and the rest of the country. This was to prevent the people in their zone from migrating to the west where life was a great deal better. Briton's war time prime minister, Winston Churchill, named this the iron curtain.

On June 24th of 1948 the Soviet government set up a blockade of the highways, waterways and railroads into and out of the city of Berlin. The Templehauf airport was in the British zone so the Soviets had no control over it. All the supplies for three fourths of the city therefor had to be brought in by air. This was known as the Berlin Blockade. The international situation was extremely tense. The Soviet Union were as intent upon spreading their doctrine of communism upon the rest of the world as the Nazis had been in their efforts to rule the world.

The United States was providing most of the airplanes for what became known as the Berlin Airlift. The army's function up to this point had been to help the Germans restore government and to act as a police force. The troops were known as the Constabulary. With the onset of the blockade, the mission changed from a police force to halting, what appeared to be a drive of the Soviets to take over western Europe.

Discipline among the troops had slipped. There was an active black market which, unfortunately, was being exploited by many of the Americans. It, therefore, was necessary for the US Army to beef up the Constabulary as the mission swung back to a more military nature of defending the borders.

Eli:

An invitation went out to the reserves for volunteers to return to active duty. The emphasis was on experienced company grade officers with outstanding records during World War II.

Our housing plans were a shamble. Bernice was not happy with the endless chore of the insurance book and felt cooped up in the trailer. When the invitation came in late summer, it didn't take a lot of discussion for us to decide to return to the army, even as a temporary thing.

As soon as the decision was made, we had a lot to do. Families were permitted to go to Germany. The government even provided living quarters. We sold the trailer for $1300 and Bernice applied for a passport. Active duty people did not require a passport. Ginny and Bernice would move back to the farm until I had gone to Europe and obtained a place to live. We had just bought a new red Ford four door sedan. She would keep it in Wisconsin.

As soon as they were settled in Wisconsin, I reported to Fort Kilmer in New Jersey for active duty. I would retain my rank of Captain. I had only been there a day when I learned that if my family could be in New Jersey in three days with the car, they could go with me.

Bernice:

Ginny was two and a half and a good kid, but my mother thought that it would be stretching reason for me to drive alone

Ginny in her life vest aboard the USS Muir and the way to Germany. September, 1948.

with a small child for such a long distance. By now my dad had turned over the responsibility of the farm and the confining duty of a dairy herd to my brother. It was quickly decided that I would drive my car, and my mother and Ginny would ride with me. My dad would follow in their new DeSoto.

This worked out well and we met Eli in New Jersey early on the third day. From there Eli took over the driving and my folks turned into tourists, seeing New York for the first time, then heading south to visit the Fishpaws in Baltimore and to see Washington, DC.

Our ship was the USS Muir. It was a liberty ship, fitted out as a troop transport. Because he was traveling with his family, Eli was told that he would not have any duties except to take care of his family. We were assigned a small cabin on the port side of 'A' deck. There were three narrow bunks. Ginny had long been accustomed to sleeping without any side protection. There were not very many officers or dependents on this voyage. We ate in the officers' mess which was quite small. Although it was not elaborate, they did have table cloths on the table.

The first day out there was a life boat drill. We all put on our life jackets and went to our boat station. They had miniature life jackets for small children. Ginny looked as wide as she was high in her jacket.

Although the sea was rather rough, none of the Fishpaws became seasick. I remember going to the mess hall one morning where I discovered a practical use for the table cloths. There were little side rails on the tables and the table cloth was wet to prevent the dishes from slipping and sliding with the pitching of the ship.

Eli:

While at breakfast, I was told to report to the Troop Commander's headquarters. The sea was getting rougher and rougher. He told me that I had just been appointed as the police and sanitation officer. A large part of the military personnel aboard were seasick. He said, "Lets go down to the lounge and the theater and I will show you what I mean." When we arrived at the lounge all I could see was GIs laying everywhere, all looking like they were sleeping. The waste cans were all running over with puke. It was a sad looking mess.

He wanted to know what I intended to do about it. I said, "Do you mind if I show you?" "Go ahead". He had assigned two real big sergeants to assist me. When I tried to get the troops attention, not a muscle moved. When I made an announcement in my most commanding voice to the effect that all men were to go to the open deck, except the last twenty who would stay and clean up the place, there was a mad rush by everyone to get onto the stairwell and to the open deck. The major was caught in the stampede and he ended up two decks above before he could get out of the mob. The sergeants closed the door on the last twenty or so. It was a sorry looking bunch who had the onerous job of cleaning up the mess.

Then we repeated the exercise at the theater, but this time the major got out of the way. The next morning I went down to the lounge and the theater to meet with my sergeants. When the men saw me coming they cleared out. There wasn't a live soldier in either place. They were all up on the open decks. I went to groups of them, mainly the ones who were playing cards where there was money on the deck and instructed them to turn in their mess passes. Without it they couldn't eat.

When each Sergeant had twenty men, they were told to report to the lounge and theater to clean them up before they would get their mess card back. You would be surprised how fast they got those places cleaned up. For the rest of the trip we rotated the assignment of clean up detail to each of the troop compartments.

Before long I received a complaint that there were too many men on the open decks and that the deck detail was unable to wash them down. I went to the speaker system on the bridge and announced that everybody was to return to their compartment for about twenty minutes while the decks were being hosed down.

About two hundred of them refused to clear the decks so I made another announcement. They had one minute before the hoses would be turned on. No one moved until the water started flowing. There was another stampede when that happened. After that there were no more problems. All these soldier were what the army refers to as casual replacements and had no clear identification with any organized unit. Somehow they felt that everything was somebody else's job.

Bernice:

After two weeks at sea, we landed at Bremerhaven, West Germany, a port city on the North Sea. Eli got his orders to report to the 27th Constabulary, Field Artillery Bn. in the Bavarian city of Landshut. While he took the train to Landshut to arrange for housing, Ginny and I were on the train to a place called Bad Mergentheim.

Bad is German for bath and Bad Mergentheim was a city located near some hot springs. There were several large buildings which had been sanitariums before the war. They all sported huge white circles on the roof with big red crosses and had been used for hospitals so they were in good shape. The US Army had confiscated them and they were being used as a temporary housing center for dependents.

While on the ship, I had broken one of the lens in my glasses. The first thing that I wanted to do was to get this fixed. I went to the army dispensary and was told that they didn't have the facilities to help me. The doctor suggested that if I would take a package of cigarettes and go into the town I could probably get them fixed.

This was my first lesson in German. Cigarettes were a dollar a carton and were available to Americans in the tiny PX (Post Exchange) at the center. They were cheap because there was no tax. I had not gotten the cigarette habit but bought a carton anyway and Ginny and I headed for the village. We hadn't gone very far when I saw a small store with a a big pair of spectacle frames hanging over the doorway. This must be an optical shop.

I went in and a well dressed man was there. At this point I probably didn't know three words in German, but I held out my broken glasses and a package of cigarettes. I was rewarded with the biggest smile you will ever see. The man eagerly seized the glasses and the cigarettes and disappeared into a back room. I had no idea if I would ever see my glasses again. In about ten minutes he returned with the lens replaced.

The Reich Mark of the old regime was worthless. Germans were not allowed to use American money and new German currency had not become available. The whole economy was operating on barter and tobacco products were the most coveted, and therefor the most valuable. I have no idea what my little dime package of butts was worth, but that night there was one happy optician. Either he had a good smoke or maybe he was able to buy some much needed commodity. While it was only a dime to me, I had paid him a fortune on the black market.

If I were asked to relate my first impression of Germany, I guess I would have to say that it was looking out the window and seeing a woman, who was obviously a farmer, walking along the cobble stone street driving a wagon full of some sort of root crop, being pulled by an emaciated cow and a thin and tired looking horse.

It was Halloween night when we arrived in Landshut a few days later. It was just turning dark. I noticed that the men were wearing clothing that all looked alike. Their jackets were about the same color as the OD (olive drab) winter uniform of the US Army. They all had green lapels and pockets that were edged with green piping with an oak leaf design at the corner. I thought that they were probably wearing their army uniforms. It was some time later before I learned that this was the traditional clothing of Bavaria.

Our first apartment was upstairs at 22 Swimschule Strasse (Swimming School Street). The United States had taken over enough homes and apartment buildings to accommodate the families of the officers and non-comms (Non Commissioned

Officers). To assure that these buildings were properly kept, they also provided a maid for each household and a house man who was responsible for several units. Of course, this was also a way of providing much needed employment for this country trying to recover from the war.

My first maid was a young girl named Irmgard. She spoke some English and was helpful as I started to learn German. The Sears catalog became my dictionary. The house man was named Richard. He also spoke some English. He was from Berlin and considered himself above the Bavarians. His primary duty was to take care of the outside and the stove. This was a tile box between the living room and the dining room. The tiles were very decorative and their shape helped to radiate heat into the room. It was tended from the hall. The gas cook stove provided some heat for the kitchen and the bed rooms got heat only from the rest of the house. Coal was the fuel.

The apartment was completely furnished but was somewhat spartan. The first problem turned out to be the toilet. It was so high that poor little Ginny, who by now was well toilet trained, could not reach the seat. I picked up an orange crate at the commissary and prepared to create a foot stool to help her reach. The problem was, I had neither a saw nor a hammer. With the help of some elaborate pantomime, I explained to Richard and Irmgard what I needed and indeed, they complied. The saw was a buck saw, the kind used for cutting fire wood. Although awkward, I made do. I used the nails pulled from the crate and created a very serviceable stool.

Eli:

My first assignment was Liaison officer. That meant that I was given all kinds of miscellaneous assignments. The commanding officer was Lt. Colonel Hector. He told me that they were all set for battalion tests. When they went off to Grafenwohr, where there was an artillery range, to take their tests, I was left in charge of the rear and the responsibility for the Kasern (German military barracks) and the dependent community.

One of my responsibilities was battalion safety officer. On the very first day after the battalion left, I received a call from 7th Army Headquarters wanting to know why I hadn't submitted a full report on an accident involving a motorcycle and three men on July Fourth, of that year. I told them that I would sure get the report to them as soon as possible.

The officer kept implying that I was delinquent for not getting the report in on time. I finally had to tell him that I had only been in town two days and at the time of the accident I had been in Baltimore selling insurance as a civilian. I think he might have been embarrassed because after that he talked nice to me for the rest of the time. In two days, he got his report on the three dead motorcycle riders. They had all been riding on the same machine which was a no-no.

When the battalion returned, the Colonel took me on a trip around our area of the kasern, along with the Bn. Executive Officer. We paid a visit to the consolidated mess, mainly to get a cup of coffee. I spotted the cooks at the work table with five or six flip top bottles of German beer, taking a sip every now and then while preparing the meal. As they were not my men, I made no comment in front of them but later told the colonel and the major over our coffee that I wouldn't put up with that in my battery for five minutes. I was informed by the colonel to, "Take it easy, Fishpaw, you'll get used to it." I said, "I'll never get used to it."

After we finished our coffee, I excused myself and went back to the kitchen for a closer look. I checked the menu for the next meal which they were preparing. It called for a ten oz. steak. All I could see on the table was everybody chopping meat up in little pieces, making stew. When I asked the mess sergeant why he wasn't following the menu he stated that they had not gotten enough meat so they were mixing it with potatoes to stretch it. I checked the invoice of the delivery of the food which clearly stated that they had been delivered more than enough for every man to have a descent steak.

On the 15th of December, the battalion was re-designated as the 74th FA Battalion, EUCOM (European Command). We were a separate battalion in the Seventh Army.

During the time I was the liaison officer, I was sent on TDY (temporary duty) to a school for company grade officers which dealt mainly with administration. Administration was not my favorite activity but it did help me later when I had the opportunity to take a test which would qualify me for Warrant Officer in the Regular Army.

Shortly after coming back from the school, Colonel Hector made me the Bn. Adjutant. Oh how I hated paper work. I had been doing the work of the adjutant all along but he finally made it official. I served there until the first of June, 1949 when I was made Battery Commander of 'C' Btry. I was to relieve Capt.

Donald Thomson who was rotating back to the states. This assignment would also include being in charge of the consolidated mess, which included two other batteries besides my own.

I had been alerted to a problem a few days before I took command by one of my new Btry's officers, Lt. Robinson. He said, "Can I ask you a question?" "Sure, any time you ask me a question I will try to give you an answer." He told me of the conditions in the mess hall and that the former Battery Commander had told him to keep his mouth shut. Stealing from the mess hall had been going on for a long time. It even involved the Bn. executive officer. The men in those three batteries were not getting adequate food at their meals because of it. This was probably going on in the other mess too.

I told Lt. Robinson that he was now the mess officer and that when he got the evidence, we would court martial the whole bunch. Within four days after I took over the battery we were preparing the charge sheets against the personnel for running an organized conspiracy to steal food from the army to support a high priced blond who lived in one of the finer apartments in Landshut.

I was aware that there were at least two officers involved and we tried to get some of the accused enlisted men to witness against them, but they refused. I was even told by one the men that he had so much money in the bank in the states, he was afraid that if he said anything against the officers, they would have the army check his bank account and it might be impounded. He ended up being given six months in the stockade for illegally selling sulfa drugs in cahoots with the medics. He was also involved in an illegal loan business.

After a couple weeks, I went to the stockade to again try to get him to at least give me the name of the ranking people involved and I would have him released. He still refused to talk. I felt that the big shots were using him so I let him out with time served.

Battalion had him transferred to Headquarters Btry. We also court martialed another sergeant and at least one of the chief cooks. They got busted all the way but still refused to talk.

The battalion executive officer was president of the court and did a good job covering up for his co-conspirators. The Major was challenged by the prosecutor for being too close to the accused, but he refused to step down.

It didn't appear that the Colonel was involved with any of this but he sure didn't put forth any effort to know what was going on in his outfit. In a short while, most of these people were rotated back to the states.

We were allowed to also rotate twenty five men from each battery ahead of their rotation schedule if they didn't meet the standard of their new battery commanders. The new commanders were all recently called up as I had been. The old timers referred to us as retreads, but we sure did a better job than they had of making soldiers that we could be proud of. Those of us that had been recalled knew the reason. Discipline was terrible.

Col. Hector was one of those who went back to the states and Lt. Col. Gildart replaced him as the battalion commander.

Bernice:

The house on Swimschule St. only had one other American neighbor and was not as modern as some of the other houses. As soon as one of the better units became available in the center of the American area, we arranged to move. I was even able to take Richard and Irmgard with me. Our new apartment was at 9 Clemons Brentano Strasse. It had hard wood floors and a balcony. Balconies are very popular in Germany. Our apartment was on the second floor. It also had an apartment in the attic for the maid and Irmgard moved into it.

In the new apartment, the toilet was a separate room from the bath. It was a small, closet like space with a high window and was at the end of the hall. The door had an old fashion lock with a key hole that took a key from either inside or out. One day Ginny had locked the door to the toilet and had some how gotten the key out of the key hole. There was a problem. She didn't know how to put it back in the hole and get herself out. The window was too high for her to throw it out.

Richard and Irmgard were having a heated debate in German. Finally Richard said that he had something that could unlock the door but that it was illegal. I must not let anyone know that he had it. It was a simple little key like piece of metal which anyone could create from a small rod and was used to pick locks. I appreciated his volunteering to help and certainly never turned him in. Needless to say, I lost a little of my feeling of security, knowing how easy it was for anyone to pick the locks.

All our needs were available from the commissary and the PX. Because the German economy was trying to recover, we were

Our house at #9, Clemens Brentano Strasse, Landshut, Bavaria. Our apartment was on the second floor.

not encouraged to buy necessities from their stores. American money was not used. In its place, we received script. It was printed on regular paper and was different colors and sizes. It came in denominations of five cents to twenty dollars. There may have been hundred dollar script but, I don't recall ever seeing any. We had a fairly large portion of Eli's pay allotted to buying government bonds, which were held for us at the Federal Reserve Bank in Chicago. American Express operated a bank on the post.

Commissary meat came from Argentina. Eggs, milk and other dairy products came from Denmark. Fresh fruit and vegetables were available locally, both from the commissary and the weekly market in the center of Landshut. We were told to always soak any raw produce in water treated with halozone tablets because of the wide spread use of fecal waste for fertilizer. This did not alarm me as it did some of the other women. We had always used organic fertilizer on the farm.

On the outskirts of all the smaller cities there were large tracts devoted to vegetable gardens. Many of them had small sheds. These were the main source of food for many of the city families. People would walk out to tend their gardens. People walked everywhere. There were also a large number of bicycles but most of them were quite old. There were very few automobiles for the average Germans.

Cigarettes were so valuable that the maids took the butts home. It was not unusual for Americans to have their car windows broken by people to get the butts in the ash trays. It therefor was standard practice not to lock the car doors.

Landshut was a city of about twenty thousand people and was 60 kilometers (40 miles) north of Munich. It had not been heavily damaged by the war except around the railroad yard. It is located on the Isar river which rises in the Bavarian Alps in the south and runs north about 30 Ks west of the border with Czechoslovakia which was in the Soviet Zone of Occupation and was marked by a high wire fence. That was enemy territory.

There were two distinguishing land marks in Landshut. One was St. Martin's church and the other was the Berg Trausnitz (castle). Middle age custom called for the cross on the church to be the highest point in the community. St. Martin's was on the flat near the river. The castle was on the top of the hill. To overcome this problem the church, which was built in the early 1400s, had a very, very tall steeple. To support such a tall structure required a very broad base. It was built before structural supports were available. It was brick on brick. It was reputed to be the second tallest unsupported structure in the world.

There was a sundial on the south face of the steeple. In this face there was a clearly visible cannon ball that was said to have been put there by Napolean's army. There was also a large chunk of very new looking bricks where American artillery had nibbled off one corner. Church steeples are often targets during any war because they provided a clear view for observation of important military activities.

One of the early surprises was seeing a large group of huge, well nourished and powerful horses that were kept at the castle. Every day we could see them being exercised on the streets near the top of the hill. They were such a contrast to the horse and the cow that I had seen pulling the wagon at Bad Mergentheim.

There were two bridges in Landshut. One of them was intact and had not been damaged but the other one was gone and had been replaced by what was known as a Bailey bridge. This was an American contraption used by the Army Engineers to put up tactical bridges. It was like a big erector set. It was only one lane wide so we had to be extra careful not to enter the bridge until there was no traffic coming from the other side.

Since not many Germans had cars, traffic was not a problem. It was only a few blocks from our house and was the one we used most of the time. The ancient city wall with a picturesque city gate was just after we crossed the bridge.

I immediately got a bicycle to use when Eli had the car. I installed two wooden bars behind the seat for a hand hold and a foot rest for Ginny, who sat on a pillow on the rack over the rear wheel. It was great and I was free to explore or visit other Americans.

Most of the American housing was on one side of the river and the Kasern was on the other side. The Landshut Sub-post was in the Pinder Kasern which the 27th shared with a battalion of the 6th Cavalry Regiment. No horses. By 1948 light tanks had replaced the horses but they were still designated as cavalry.

All the social life of the Americans revolved around the battalion. We had a sub-post wives club, and a battalion wives club. We were all a long way from home and it was the battery that became the surrogate family and the BCs wife became the big sister.

The men were gone about half of the time, either training or off on patrols as a part of their mission. This called upon the families to be pretty self sufficient. Because we all had maids to baby sit, we were at some liberty to spend time together in each others homes. Bridge was one of the popular activities. When the men were gone we would sometimes play bridge into the wee hours of the morning.

There was a bowling alley on the post and we had a bowling league. I was a lot better bowler than I was bridge player. We even had a traveling team and went to tournaments at other posts. This was fun. Because I had a new red sedan, I was the one who usually drove. Germany was well known for their famous high speed highways called autobahns. Most of the bridges on the autobahn had been destroyed during the war but the roads were great. I loved to get out and drive fast. There wasn't much traffic.

Each battalion was commanded by a Lt. Colonel. Our first commander was Lt. Col. Hector and of course Mrs. Hector was automatically the unofficial leader and a surrogate mother so to speak. She was a very elegant person. I remember that she had half caret diamond ear studs and an emerald cut diamond ring which was at least a full carat.

The Colonel's house was larger and was located on the top of the hill. There were five or six other American homes up there. A great deal of the battalion social activity took place at their house.

Eli:

Colonel Gildart was a West Pointer and a strict disciplinarian. The battalion starting to perform like a field artillery battalion should. The new colonel with his strict standards of conduct and military bearing improved us further.

After a short while we went for several weeks service practice in the French Zone to a military reservation near Munsingen. We were down there over the Fourth of July. For the holiday each battery was allowed to give passes to fifteen men for the holiday. After the 4th, we were to practice direct fire. With the open date and most of my men still in camp with no special activities planned, as battery commander, I decided we would go out and set up our direct fire range. This included moving some old trucks around the area to use as targets.

We had a formation at 0900. At roll call I discovered over and above the people we had given passes to, we had seventeen unaccounted for enlisted men. They had gone back to Landshut on their own without any authority. My immediate reaction was that they were still trying to do whatever they wanted and whenever they wanted. We had to put a stop to it right quick.

We prepared charge sheets, charging them all with 'Absent Without Leave'. Their ranks ran from Sergeant down to Private. At reveille the next morning when everyone had returned, we handed out a copy of a charge sheet to each individual who had been AWOL and referred him to a Summary Court Officer for trial. To say the least, they were shocked.

When the copies of the charge sheets hit the new Ole Man's desk at battalion, I received an immediate call to report to him. His first reaction was that he didn't want to court martial so many men in one day. I said that I did not want to either but I knew that with new commanding officers, they would try us out and do the same things they had been doing when it was still a route order outfit. The Colonel said, "There must be some other solution."

I told him there was. "By this time, most all of them have already been court martialed. They have all pleaded guilty and have received a reduction of one grade". The heaviest fine that could be placed was $55 for a Sergeant and a private $15.

I suggested to the Colonel that as the reviewing officer, he could leave them all keep their rank but could leave the fines stay. He reluctantly agreed to do that. The outcome of that one incident was that we only had one court martial for rest of the year and a half that I was the battery commander.

I had some very good officers in that battery. The battery exec. was Lt. Wilke from Texas. He was also one of the recalled reserve officers. He shaped up the firing battery in a very short time. By the time we finished the service practice in the French Zone, our firing battery looked as good as any firing battery that I had ever seen.

Lt. James Robinson was a recent West Point graduate where he had been one of the top ten in his class. He was the Reconnaissance Officer who was in charge of communications, survey, and the forward observers. He was an outstanding officer and an expert at military justice.

He was frequently called upon to be defense council for soldiers from other batteries at special courts. He usually won the case. He enjoyed the legal work and later, after doing an exemplary job as an artilleryman, he transferred to the Judge Advocate General's branch of the army.

A few years later, as a Major, he successfully defended the soldier and won his acquittal in the world wide, highly publicized case of the death of a brass picker in Japan. The soldier's orders had been to guard the rifle range where local people were illegally scavenging brass shell casings at night.

He was ordered to shoot if the trespasser ignored the challenge. It was in the dark when he did this and he hit a Japanese woman. With the publicity all over the world, Americans were being portrayed as heartless predators. Because of Robbie's brilliant defense, the criticism went away and our credibility was restored. The defense was that the man was doing his duty by carrying out orders.

Lt. Dwayne "Whitey" Emerson was another West Pointer. He was close to the bottom of the class, just ahead of Glenn Davis, the hot shot running back for Army. Since they would never flunk their star football player, the grade cut off was always just below Davis. What Whitey lacked in scholastic achievement he made up for in leadership.

When he bitched about the food, I made him the mess officer. He told every body that I had made him mess officer because he missed church. He sure straighten out the problems that the consolidated mess had been experiencing though.

Lt. Nordeen was the motor officer and did an excellent job. The battalion was given a quota of two lieutenants to be RIFed (reduction in forces) and he was one of them.

Lt. Waddell and Lt. Campbell were assigned to the battery right out of college. They lacked officer experience but had at least a couple years each of enlisted experience during World War II. They did any number of miscellaneous duties in the battery and did them well.

This battery ended up being declared the best company sized unit in the Seventh Army several times and the best unit in the battalion due to the good performance of our officers, the NCOs and the men. Morale was very high.

Robby once told Bernice that if I told somebody to march off a bridge into the river they would do it. One time we were at Vilsec (part of the range at Graf) and were going to walk about a mile to a demonstration that was going on. We were looking for a short cut and were walking beside a muddy tank trail, looking for a place to cross. I told Emerson to go first and see how deep the mud was. He wadded in until it was above his ankles. When he looked back to see if we were coming we told him no, we were going to walk the long way around. Whitey told that story over and over, each time the mud got deeper until he was up to his neck.

Bernice:

When Col. Gildart arrived, Mrs. Gildart was quite different from Lea Hector. We loved both of them and enjoyed their rich friendships. Ginger Gildart had a vision problem and could not see out the center of her eyes. She always sat at the bridge table with her head turned. It was somewhat disconcerting at first to see this good looking woman driving down the street appearing to be looking out the side window.

Our next door neighbor was Chief Warrant Officer Moreau, the personnel officer of the battalion. He had four children. The youngest, Midgie, was the same age as Ginny and they played together. Ginny had gotten an annoying little habit of biting people and although I had tried to show her that this did not feel good, I guess I was too timid to deliver the message. One day, I was on the balcony and I saw Midgie and Ginny standing on top of the Moreau's car. They were biting each other, hard, and they didn't seem to know how to get down so they just kept on biting. By the time I had rescued them, neither of them ever bit anyone again.

There were probably about twelve or fifteen dependent children of school age. There was a one room school at the post for them. It was decided that the five girls who were about eight to thirteen should have a Girl Scout troop. Carolyn Waddell had been a Girl Scout and volunteered to be the leader. I volunteered to be her assistant. I was unfamiliar with the scouting program but we got a hand book, registered as a lone troop and got busy. There was no council or supervision so we were pretty much on our own.

Of Course, to have a troop, you need a meeting place. No problem. The sub-post commander, Col. Piper's daughter, Barbara, who was thirteen was in the group. Their house was the highest of all the houses on the hill and was quite large. It also had a good sized room in a turret about four stories up. It looked out in all directions and gave a beautiful view. On clear days we could see the tops of the Alps south of Munich. It was ideal for a scout room. It involved climbing a lot of steps but we were young and didn't mind a bit. We were also allowed to used the rod and gun club which was great for outdoor activities. With only five girls, transportation was never a problem.

Living in a foreign country has marvelous program opportunities. We contacted the orphanage and arranged to have five girls about the same age as our girls come to some of our meetings and be our guests. We had a cook out at the rod and gun club and had wieners. Our guests were greatly amused when we translated hot dog to heise hund. When it came Christmas time, they invited us to their Christmas party. We learned that there would be about twenty girls at the party, so we made Christmas stockings for all of them. They were filled with candy and trinkets which were still very scare in Bavaria.

At the party we were the honored guests. St. Nickolaus came and distributed the gifts, including the ones that we had brought. Our girls were so disappointed when one rather sad little waif did not get a gift. Instead she was handed some sticks and a lump of coal. This was the indication that she was a schlect madchen (bad girl). There was definitely a cultural gap but I think our girls had learned a good lesson.

The Christmas tree was originally a German tradition and Christmas ornaments were available in the stores. There were two styles that were different from any that I had ever seen before or since. One style as shaped like silver pine cones and another style was shaped like red mushrooms with white spots.

Toys had always been a major product of Germany and I found some very nice ones. I got a real rocking horse and some nice Bavarian dolls. I also made a rocking cradle for the baby doll and a small shronk (ward robe closet) for Ginny. I even made tiny coat hangers of wire for doll dresses. I was hoping to impart a message about hanging up clothes.

But the real prize was the electric trains. When Eli was in Bobingen after the war they had helped put the Marklin toy train factory back in production. All the Americans were their first customers and sent train sets home. By 1948, the production and variety of trains had increased dramatically.

I bought Eli a whole bunch of track and extra engines and cars to go with the starter set he had sent home in 1945. They were typical of the European style freight and passenger cars. Freight cars seemed very small compared to American box cars. They were four wheeled vehicles not much bigger than a farm wagon and were hitched together with a large three link chain. The toy trains were much smaller than the American style Lionel trains and ran on a narrower track. We put the track around the Christmas tree.

Early in January we were visited by several groups of German children. They were always in a group of three and wore a costume that included a crown. Richard explained that these were the three kings looking for the Christ Child. Somehow, I got the feeling that we were supposed to give them a treat, which of course we did. This probably represented a gift for the Baby Jesus but I suspect that the kings ended up eating them.

Eli:

On the fall maneuver we were supposed to be pulling back to the west side of the Rhein. We had gotten as far as the Neckar river west of Heilbronn when we were starting to get low on gasoline. Col. Gildart issued an order that all the vehicles except the trucks with the howitzers should go into a defensive position. We were to drain the gasoline from all the other vehicles to put in the prime movers to get them across the river. Battalion headquarters, 'A' and 'B' battery's guns had gotten across before the enemy force took all the highway bridges which were marked with black flags.

'C' Btry was the last in line. I did not want to leave any of my unit behind, least of all the kitchen. I had been in this area during the war and knew that there was a wooden bridge that had been built during the war for heavy vehicles. I checked it out and found that it was still there but was inside a wire fence in an industrial area with a watchman on duty.

Since none of the maneuvering troops or umpires knew about it, it was not marked. It was being used as a foot bridge. I explained to the watchman that we had built the bridge during the war and had used it to move heavy tanks. I knew that it could hold our trucks. It was the middle of the night, so he opened the gates and pulled up the footbridge signs in the middle of the road way to the bridge and let us through. For his co-operation I left him a carton of cigarettes and some candy.

Just as we were getting ready to move, service battery trucks with gasoline showed up. They were lost and couldn't find the other units. I had them fuel up all our vehicles and then had them fall in line behind us to cross over the wooden bridge. When we got across I tried to raise Bn. Headquarters but got no answer. We had been directed to turn south and proceed parallel to the river, which we did.

About dawn I got headquarters on the radio and Col. Gildart came on. He was real grumpy and wanted to know where the hell I was. When I told him I had the battery and the gasoline trucks on his side of the river, he felt a little better but wanted me to report to him immediately.

I asked if he minded if I finished breakfast first. That was when he discovered that I had disobeyed his order to leave half the battery behind. He said, "What do you mean? How come you're eating breakfast? We haven't had anything to eat but apples for a whole day." They were holed up in an apple orchard. I had the cook send a truck with some coffee and hot food over to their position. They were sure glad to get it and afterward he said that I had no idea how mad he was at me until he got that food.

He had to report to Seventh Army as to how many vehicles had gotten across the river. With all of my battery along with the gasoline trucks, the battalion looked real good.

On that same maneuver the driver of the supply truck for the kitchen went to sleep on a mountain road and ran off. The truck was tumbling down the mountain but didn't go far when it was stopped by a tree. The assistant driver was supposed to be in the cab with the driver to keep him awake but he had gotten sleepy and crawled in the back, on top of the cargo and had gone sleep.

When we started looking for him he couldn't be found until someone discovered him running down the road screaming. He thought that the top of his head had been knocked off because when he put his hand up there all he could feel was something squishy. A jar of mayonnaise had broken and that was what he was feeling but he thought it was his brain.

Bernice:

For some time, Irmgard had become increasingly arrogant and when I found that she had been entertaining her SS (German storm troopers) boy friend in OUR apartment, I decided it was time to let her go. In her place, I hired Katie. Katie was a little older, probably in her thirties. She was much more stable. She had a daughter about five years old. Sometimes she would bring her madchen to work and she would play with Ginny. There was never any reference to a father so I assumed that he was a casualty of the war.

Richard's wife, Annie, worked for the family downstairs. When Irmgard left, Richard asked if he an Annie could have the attic apartment. This was, of course, agreeable.

Housing was critical everywhere. Even in cities like Landshut that had not suffered pattern bombing like Munich and Frankfurt, every square inch of living space was utilized. That was because Bavaria had received a large number of displaced people from Czechoslovakia.

Back in 1938, Hitler and his party had declared that because there were a large number of ethnic Germans living in the area called the Sudatin Lands, that this territory should be German. The British Prime Minister, Neville Chamberlain, had even bargained the territory away in exchange for what he hoped would be peace. It was called 'The Appeasement'.

When the war was over and the Nazis had lost, the Czechs wanted all the Germans out. They were all rounded up and put on trains to Bavaria with only what they could wear or carry on their person. They put on as many clothes as they could and every one in the family carried the tools of the father's craft. The Bavarians had to make room for the Sudatins. Thus every attic in the province housed a family.

These industrious people set up little factories in the cellars and started turning out merchandise. The most popular items were oil paintings, cut crystal and porcelain figurines. The father would create these and the mother would go to the American homes to peddle what they made. The most popular tender was cigarettes. I was not actually legal, but it was helping this war torn country to recover. I got a whole set of China for ten cartons of cigarettes. I was glad that I had never taken up smoking.

One day a strange little man showed up at the door wanting to make our picture with charcoal. Ginny and I both sat for him to do our portrait. He beautifully captured Ginny who had been a very animated subject. My picture wasn't fit for an outhouse wall. It cost me a pound of coffee. Another lady took a photo of the farm in Wisconsin and her husband created an oil painting of it.

Beautiful cut crystal was also popular. I bought a set of twelve water glasses and a pitcher. The cuts were very deep and reflected light exquisitely. One evening I was entertaining the battery officers and their wives. I was using my new crystal. It was a real shock when our prissiest guest took a drink and water ran all down her chin and into her plate. How embarrassing.

One of the cuts was so deep that it broke through from the pressure of the water. When the vender showed up later to sell more crystal, she graciously took that glass back and replaced it. They even designed a set of sherbet glasses especially for me to match my china.

When spring came, the Isar flooded and our cellar was full of water as was our entire front yard which was below street level. We had enough water that the neighbor boys were riding around our yard in a make shift boat. It never got deep enough to evacuate and after a few days, it went away.

There was one problem that we had not anticipated. We had a sand box in the front yard where the kids played a lot. After the flood was gone and the sand dried up, we let them go back to playing there, never realizing how contaminated the sand was. Before long Ginny developed a skin rash on her legs. The Sub-post doctor didn't seem to know how to treat it and I finally had to take her to the American 98th General Hospital in Munich when it started spread to her arms and neck. I bought a large wash tub and soaked her in potassium permanganate twice a day. It stained her brown but the rash went away.

Eli:

While in Landshut, hunting deer was very popular amongst the military people who were stationed there. I went out hunting a couple times with the local Jaegermeister who co-ordinated the hunt. We were told not to shoot the young, well developed deer but were allowed to shoot the older deer and the deer that were known to be dangerous. They would have sharp, straight antlers that they would use to fight the healthy bucks. The deer we hunted in our area were called Raebuck. They were a small deer that when matured weighed about 55 to 60 pounds.

Because of my interest in hunting, I joined the Landshut Rod and Gun Club. This was an American organization. An official of the club told us of a school run by the Germans that would qualify the graduates to receive a certificate which made them qualified Jaegermeisters. I thought this was great, so I took the course and earned my certificate. It was a very difficult course and strict. Many of the people in the class failed to graduate. At the graduation ceremony, prior to getting the certificate, we had to go through an initiation conducted by the German Jaegermeisters. For the final phase, as they pronounced us an official Jaegermeister, one of the instructors would bring a big sword down on your right and then the left shoulder. Since it was laid flat it did not hurt but having that sharp blade so close to your neck, and in the hands of a not too long ago enemy, required an act of faith in the holder.

As the result of this school, later, when I was on the fish and game commission at Ft. Benning, I introduced the German procedure of controlling the hunting on the reservation.

While I was at intelligence school at Oberamergau, a lieutenant gave me an old rusty looking World War I German sniper's rifle known as an 8mm Mauser. It had been found in the bottom of a fishing creek. The barrel had been filled with heavy grease as well as all the working parts. I took it to a German gunsmith.

He cleaned it up and told me that it was worth restoring. He measured me up so he would know how big a stock to make to replace the original. After the rust on the outside was removed and the weapon was blued, it really looked a sharp. I had him add a telescopic sight.

With my fresh knowledge and my new rifle, I was able to hit a small deer with great accuracy at 400 to 600 meters. The meat was very good. The Jaegermeister would clean the kill in the woods and leave the cleanings for the fox. His compensation was the tongue, the heart and the liver.

With the more stable Katie, we felt comfortable leaving Ginny with her and her daughter while we did some traveling.

The Army had established recreation centers in the Alps. Our first excursion was to Berchtesgaden which had been one of Herr Hitler's retreats. His actual home had been destroyed because there was some concern that if allowed to stand, fanatic followers would make a shrine of it.

Two or three hotels had been confiscated for use by the Americans. One was the ski lodge, high above the city. It was a beautiful locations and oozed character. It was reached by a twisting road. At the time we visited it, it was winter. We were winding our way up the narrow access road which was dry when we started up with our car. However, as we reached a higher elevation, there were patches of ice in a shaded areas. On one especially steep stretch, to our alarm, we were not able to go up and instead were sliding back.

We discover that there was no hint of side rails or other barriers to prevent a car from going off the road and down the side of the mountain. To make matters worse, if any traffic should be coming down, they would not be able to see us because of the curve. Bernice told me that if I wanted to keep grinding away as the car inched closer to the drop off, OK, but she was going to walk around the corner so she wouldn't have to watch our new car disappear down the mountain.

Everything works out though. There was a three quarter ton truck coming down from the lodge with several soldiers aboard. She flagged them down and explained the problem. It was a big relief to see these husky guys put their shoulders to our red car and push it up the mountain to the dry road above.

Neither of us knew anything about skiing but we enjoyed the scenery and the atmosphere. We had a room with a balcony and could see the log rafters on the underside of the roof. It was not real warm, but once we were under the feather comforters we were cozy as could be. Even though it was well below freezing, we could eat lunch in luxury on the patio, protected from the wind and warmed by the sun.

Naturally, we had to try skiing. We paid for an hour of instruction and rented boots and ski gear. Everything was going nicely as we were taught how to use the poles and how to do a herring bone and how to turn around. Then the instructor told us to go down this gentle slope. Bernice was well on her way down when she realized she didn't know how to stop or turn and there was a utility pole right in front of her. Rather than hit the pole she fell down and twisted both knees.

It seemed like the natural thing to do, since I was in Europe to go back to the place where we had fought some of our roughest battles. We decided to combine a trip to Paris with a stop over in Rohrbach and Binning which was right on our way.

We crossed the Rhein at Strasburg. The bridge was still a wooden one that had been built by our Corp of Engineers. The concrete bunkers of the Maginot line were still there and had been closed and secured as if they planned to use them again. There was even a hole in the wall of one of the buildings where the driver had backed into it the day Capt. Henson had blown his hand off.

Bernice:

As we drove through the country side of France, we needed to have a meal. We stopped at a restaurant and went in. We were in the middle of France and the people did not seem to understand English or German and neither of us could speak French. After much confusion, the lady finally took Eli out into the kitchen and opened the refrigerator for him and so he could point out what he wanted. He came back with two of the best ham sandwiches I have ever eaten. They were on crusty fresh french bread with spicy french mustard. This was the first time I had tasted Dijon mustard and I was hooked for life.

In Paris we took a room in what sounded like a classy Hotel called the Champs Elysees on a street by the same name. It looked quaint from the outside and was just as quaint on the inside. It was a real dump. The next night we moved to a much better place on the Rue De La Paix called the Le Grand Hotel. We were right under the roof but the bed was comfortable and we had a magnificent view of the city of Paris.

We did all the tourist stuff. The Paris Metro (subway) was very modern and a good way to get around. We went to the Eifel tower. My lasting impression was of the latrine at the top which was like a hole in the floor with two indentations for the feet. I think it was intended for men only. There were similar accommodations on all the streets of Paris. They had metal privacy shields around them but the users were clearing visible for passengers on the busses.

We visited Notre Dame and the Louvre. We also went to Pigalle. I was fascinated to see prostitutes working their trade in the niches between the buildings. I hung onto Eli for dear life as the pimps were over zealous. On the street were hustlers trying to get us into the night clubs. We had been told that such clubs were a rip off. The word was, that if you sat down a bottle of champaign would be instantly opened and then you were charged about a hundred dollars.

We did get tickets and went to the Follies Bergere. This is really a very elegant burlesque show. Even though the comedian spoke French, he threw in enough English that Eli anyway understood the jokes. But then, he had been to burlesque shows in Baltimore. The dancing and the costumes were outstanding. I got used to the exposed breast by the third number. I think my favorite number was Adam and Eve being tempted by the serpent and the dramatic effect of the scenery of the garden suddenly obscured when Adam tasted the forbidden fruit and gates of paradise slammed shut.

Another fascinating depiction was of Queen Elizabeth visiting Mary, Queen of Scots in the dungeon and ordering her beheaded. The headline entertainers were three rather large American women of color called the Peters Sisters. They sang and also cracked jokes in English which I found amusing. Instead of popcorn, elaborate alcoholic drinks were sold at the concession stand.

We took a tour to Versailles and saw the hall of mirrors where the Peace Treaty that ended World War I had been signed. We also saw the thatched roof cottage, called the Trianon, where Marie Antonette was supposed to have gone when she wanted to escape the rigors of court. I thought it was interesting that one of her favorite activities was baking bread. Another sight was the Aragon, which was the cottage where one of the Kings Louis kept his concubine named Madame Pompador.

We were adapting well to army life. We enjoyed the security of an assured income and Eli was doing what he did best: leading soldiers. We both knew that as a reserve officer, he served at the pleasure of the army and that any time he could be relieved of active duty.

In the summer of 1949 the army was giving tests to active duty personnel offering them an opportunity to become warrant officers in the Regular Army. There were several types of duties for warrant officers that Eli was qualified to do. We also reasoned that being in the Regular Army, we would enjoy the security of life time health care and a retirement income. He decided to go for it. We said that if he passed, we would get Ginny a dog, he could have a good German camera and I could have a baby. Of the three, my reward has lasted the longest.

The dog was a beagle named Tippy. He was a nice little dog but unfortunately, he was hit by a car and had to be put down. The camera was a Retina. I had to wait almost a year before Mary Jane joined the family.

Maneuvers are a constant in the army. On one occasion, they were to play the part of an aggressor army. They were even issued different uniforms which were used wool ODs dyed dark green.

They were to be gone two or three months. After Eli left, I discovered that he had taken both sets of car keys. This was critical. Fortunately, the car doors weren't locked. Richard helped me push the car out of the garage and we were standing around agonizing over my problem.

Richard, Katie and the Moreau's maid were jabbering in German that the Hauptman (Captain) was in big trouble while I got under the dash board and jumped the starter with a hair pin. Were they ever surprised! I drove the car to a garage and had a real mechanic install a by pass switch to use until the keys came home.

There were two American Military Hospitals in our area of Germany. The 98th General was in Munich and the Tenth Field Hospital was in Regensberg. Both were about the same distance from Landshut. I decided that I preferred the one in Regensberg which was smaller and easier to reach, even though the autobahn was available for part of the trip to Munich.

A few times, when a husband was away, as they so often were, I had accompanied other military wives on the trips to the hospital to have their babies. Because I was a nurse, presumably I would know what to do if the baby came during the long trip. I even had a kit, just in case, but never had to use it. It included a clean, white shoe string, a pair of scissors, a blanket for the baby and a basin for the placenta.

I knew that I was pregnant when I again started experiencing morning sickness. This problem was to plague me for the entire nine months. The doctor even prescribed phenobarbital for this but it didn't seem to help much so I didn't take a whole lot of it.

The hospital in Regensberg may have sounded primitive from the name, but it was actually in a building that had formerly been a sanitarium and was very well appointed. There were all private rooms for obstetric patients and each room had a balcony. This faced the Danube River and was very pleasant in June. Rather than waiting for the mothers from the outlying areas to go into labor, they had developed a system where, if she wished, she could be admitted a week or so before the due date. With the uncertainty of the availability of a husband, many of us took advantage of this program. The cost was $1.25 a day to cover the cost of the food we would eat.

It was a pleasant experience. There must have been six or eight officers' wives there when I was. One of them was Virginia McWillie, the wife of the CO of the other battalion in Landshut. We got to be good friends. A lot of bridge was played. No money was wagered on the games, which was good, as I was not an especially good bridge player.

I went into labor first and Virginia stayed with me during the early stage because Eli was not available. Mary Jane arrived about 0200 on the twelfth of June. I was 29. I do not remember the delivery as I was anesthetized. It had been four and a half years since Ginny was born and things had changed a lot. Now, we were gotten out of the bed and expected to ambulate as soon as the anesthesia permitted us to safely do so. It surely made for a faster recovery.

Ginny was so excited when I arrived home with her new sister. She came running down the walk to meet us. The quartermaster had issued me a real Bavarian cradle with rockers. It was painted blue and had flowers painted on it. My mother had sent me a refill kit for a bathinett and I bought the necessary wood to make the legs. I believe it may have been the first one in Landshut.

Although bottles and nipples were available in the Px, I chose to nurse my new daughter. Everything was going nicely for about two weeks when we got word that communist North Korea had invaded South Korea and that President Truman had sent American troops from Japan to reinforce the small garrisons that were stationed in South Korea. The entire Seventh Army was put on alert. There was some concern that this could be the beginning of a communist drive to add additional territory to their control and Bavaria seemed like a prime target.

We all tried to be nonchalant about the situation but my milk factory shut down completely. I had a hungry kid. I went to the little dispensary at the kasern and asked the doctor to give me a formula. The doctor was a displaced person from Hungary.

Although he spoke and understood English, he was completely confused by my request. He then told me what the women in Hungary did to supplement breast milk. He said to take oats, the kind you feed to horses, and to boil them in water until they became slimy. Then mix half milk and half slim. I had no idea where to get oats and the whole idea did not appeal to me. I went to the PX and bought a Dr. Spock. From this I created a formula of evaporated milk, Karo syrup and water.

Mary Jane's birth certificate was written in German. To assure her American citizenship, I went to the consulate in Munich and had her registered. I also had a picture made and added her to my passport.

Shortly after I came home from the hospital with Mary Jane, the city of Landshut renewed a festival that they had held before the war. It was to commemorate an event from centuries before when the Duke of Landshut had married the Princess of Poland and brought her home to Landshut.

It was quite spectacular and could be described as a tourist event. They had a parade, recreating the arrival of the princess and her party, complete with knights wearing armor and riding on huge horses. Now I knew the purpose of these beautiful animals. They were necessary to carry the men in the heavy armor. After the parade, they even had jousting on the green. I can't imagine how they could do anything wearing heavy armor, but I guess they did. I didn't get to see it.

I really wanted to see all the festivities but didn't feel up to standing on the side walk, watching the parade. However, the Drexel Mar Hotel was also the BOQ (Bachelor officers' Quarters) and one of the Captains who had a room facing the Ault Strasse (old street) offered to let us watch the parade from his window. When the parade was over, I went home but Eli and Ginny stayed to continue the celebration.

Since I had taken the car, they had to walk home. It wasn't very far but they were very late coming home. Eli was enjoying the beer at a gasthaus (beer hall) where a Bavarian band was playing and Ginny had joined in the dancing to everyone's delight. When they finally got home, she even had the bouquet that the princess had given her. I was annoyed.

We were feeling very rich and full of ourselves now. Not only did we get the Retina but we also bought a movie camera. It was called a Nixo. It took 8 mm pictures and had a wide angle and a telephoto lens. It was powered by a spring that had to be wound every two or three minutes. It even had a right angle view finder which allowed you to aim the camera side ways so that people would not know that they were having their picture taken.

The concept of pre-school education was originated by the Germans. The word kindergarten actually means children's garden. Ginny had learned German from the maids at the same time she was learning English so understood it and spoke it much better than I did. Eli had little need to use German so his vocabulary was much more limited. When she was about four, I had an opportunity to enroll her in one of the German Kindergartens. It was on the hill. She says that some of her earliest memories are of that experience.

There were two things that impressed me. One was the custom of having house shoes at the school. When the children arrived in the morning they removed their street shoes and put on their house shoes. It made a much quieter class and cleaner too.

They also had pallets on the floor for the after lunch nap. The younger children napped on the pallets but the older ones were allowed to sit with their heads on the tables. Ginny was really miffed that she had to use the pallet but did not have enough command of the language to explain to the teachers that she was old enough to sit up and did not want this indignity.

Our community of Americans was filling up with more and more reserve officers who had young children. It was decided that it would be nice to have our own preschool. The War Department provided for those of school age but did not have such a program for pre-school. A group of mothers got together and we organized our own kindergarten. The army provided us with space and a small bus to pick up the kids. We hired a sergeant's wife who was a trained kindergarten teacher. We each contributed a fixed amount to pay her.

The first space we used was in one of the smaller apartments on Clemons Brentano Strasse. All Ginny had to do was walk across the street. Later, the class got so big that we needed a bigger space. A second small hotel had been rented to provide more BOQ rooms. Since the Officers' Club, where meals were served was at the Drexel Mar, the dining room of this hotel was not being used. It became the new kindergarten.

We even had a graduation ceremony. The students put on a program and were awarded Certificates of Completion. Ginny was the 'ME' of Bobby Shafto's gone to sea. Her act was to wave good bye to Tommie May. The poems says, 'someday he'll come back and marry me', but he never did. Since I was the president of this mothers group, I got to award the certificates while Eli operated the movie camera.

Katie had an opportunity to get a better job so of course I was glad for her. In her place I hired a young Sudatin girl named Margit. Margit was so different from Irmgard, although they were about the same age. She did not show any bitterness about the hand that fate had dealt her. Her family were together when they came out of Czechoslovakia and had settled on a farm east of Landshut.

Her father was a furniture maker. On several occasions we would drive out to see her parents who had built a nice new house. Virginia remembers that Margit's mother would have fresh baked black bread that she would spread with lard and sprinkle with salt. That may not sound very appetizing but it sure was good.

In 1950 the city of Oberammergau, south of Munich near where the Alps begin, was able to resume the presentation of the Passion Play which had been a tradition since middle ages when they had made a covenant that if God would save them from the plague, they would re-enact the passion every ten years. It had been suspended during the war.

Eli was not especially interested in going but I felt that this would be a once in a lifetime experience. My next door neighbor, Marge Moreau and I decided to go together. She drove. We were behind a large truck about 6 Ks north of Munich when a man on a bicycle suddenly landed on our hood and hit our windshield.

I was in the passenger seat and was covered with glass. He had been sucked into our path by the truck. We stopped and he was alive when I reached him and was soon conscious. However, he did not seem to understand German, even when the German people, who had gathered around us, tried to talk to him.

We did the only thing we could think of to do. We put him in the back seat with his bicycle. Someone had removed the front wheel so that we could get it in. We didn't know where any of the emergency facilities were except the American 98th General Hospital, so we took him there.

At the hospital they said they could not admit him as they were limited to Americans. We did find out that he was a Lithuanian displaced person, which was the reason he didn't understand German. The hospital personnel called someone to come get him. We unloaded the bike and left it with him. He was so pleased that he still had his bike as it was brand new. When we went back to the car, we found his cap full of vomit. As scared as he must have been, he had carefully avoided soiling our car. I set it out on the parking lot.

We went to the Military Police station in Munich to report the accident but they didn't want to hear about it and refused to take the report. We went on to Obergammergau, a bit shaken to say the least.

The play lasted for eight hours. It was all in German but we had purchased booklets with the text in English, which, with our limited knowledge of German and basic knowledge of the story, we were able to follow without difficulty.

Besides the Passion Play, Obergammerau is famous for its wood carvings and religious furniture. I picked up a plaque carved in walnut of the praying hands.

Eli:

In late September of 1950 Lt. Wilke took command of the battery. I was assigned to Intelligence School in Oberammergau in October. The Intelligence School was an outstanding organization, only the best and most experienced intelligence officers were the instructors. It was also the army's foreign language school.

One of the most interesting things that happened was the training that they gave us on the use of infra red equipment for the purpose of locating man made objects at night. At this time this was new technology. Most of it consisted of telescopes on the rifle which magnified whatever it showed. It would not pick up anything natural but would pick up such things as trucks, rifles, tanks, etc.

Our first problem was to locate and gather information about a platoon of infantry, dug in along side of a mountain stream, without being apprehended. They did not have the infra-red equipment that our platoon was equipped with. We started at one end and slowly tramped through snow up to three feet deep on both sides of the creek, until our lead people reported seeing what appeared to be people.

We slowly worked our way around the simulated enemy and proceeded to count the number of troops and any special equipment they had, without them catching us. The snow was an asset because we could move without making any noise. We reported twenty three men, two machine guns and three bazookas. The instructor said that was very good. We missed the man count by two and the machine guns were correct but we had an extra bazooka. We had not been detected. It was a good exercise but I kinda think our enemy was helping us so they could get it over with and get out of the cold and back to the barracks.

The school was mostly class room lessons, with the instructor reading out different situations and we would be called on to tell what was going on. We also had written exams on all types of intelligence subjects. Military Intelligence means information on the enemy and all phases of his combat ability, plus re-supply and support.

When I returned to Landshut on December 22 of 1950 I was assigned to be the S-2. I was responsible for all the intelligence information and the security of all classified documents. One of the first things I discovered in my new role was that food was disappearing again from the mess hall. We were tipped off that a German employee was slipping it out through the garbage cans and later carry it out in his backpack.

We staked out the front gate and checked every knapsack and other bundles the German civilians might be carrying. While we were looking primarily for food, we got a bonus when we discovered copies of all our personnel rosters and morning reports. Even though this was not considered secret, it could be very useful to an enemy when he would be setting up his order of battle. It would also be helpful for their agents to use in making contact with our personnel. We turned this person over to the CIC (counter intelligence corp) as a possible enemy agent.

Shortly after that, at about 1600, I received a call from the front gate guard. There was a man who claimed to have special information and he wanted to talk to an officer, so they called me. I went down and talked to the man with an interpreter, even though he spoke pretty good English. He explained to me that he was a double agent. That is, an agent for the Soviets as well as the Americans. After questioning him, I telephoned the CIC who had a small detachment in Landshut. I gave them the preliminary information on what we had and they said, "Hold him until we get there, We've been looking for him".

We treated him with a fine supper in the mess hall and he was glad that we had contacted the CIC. About the time he was through eating, the agents came by and took him away with all the documents that we found on him. It was a friendly sort of thing. These people would play both sides. Both sides thought they got more information this way but, in fact the Soviets could get more out of our daily newspapers than anything these agents carried.

Colonel Gildart had done an excellent job as commander of the 74th FA Bn. The new Seventh Army Artillery Officer had been highly impressed with how our battalion had performed on field problems and service practice. He wanted Gildart for his assistant.

Our new CO was Lt. Col. Canty. He came down from corp artillery. He had spent the previous year running battalion tests for all the separated artillery battalions in the corp. We were all very familiar with him and he was familiar with us. There were times we thought he was great and other times when we hated his guts. Now he was with us full time. He knew every officer and what we did and how well we did it.

One cold and windy night, just after Col. Canty's arrival, we were taking battalion tests. Most of the officers had gathered in my S-2 leanto, next to the operations van when they came in from the field. Early that night the weather turned bad. There were strong winds and heavy rain. Things were pretty miserable. We had moved the colonel's cot out of his tent and into the leanto to use as a place to sit. We had a little stove in there that helped too.

During the howl of the wind he asked me to look out and see how his little tent was holding up. I told him that his tent looked useless and was flipping around up in the air with only a rope holding it to the ground. I suggested that he spend the night with us in the leanto which was secured to the van and a two and half ton trucks. The Colonel conducted a briefing on the test and laid out the next days plans.

After the meeting, when most of the officers had left, the Colonel turned to me and said, "We are wasting your talent as the S-2. I've watched you when you commanded a firing battery and you are one of the better battery commanders. I am going to make you the Headquarters Battery Commander."

About this time Lt. Emerson who had been on the OP came in. I told him that I had been made the new Headquarters Battery commander. Whitey just about broke up laughing. When he asked who my officers would be I said "You are now my Battalion Communications Officer and my Battery Exec." This put a

268

new take on the situation and he started to groan. Then I told him that the old man said that after I had him trained, I would turn over the battery to him and go back to S-2.

At the time, Headquarters was in a shamble. Half of the tents had blown down, most of the officers and men were soaking wet, the switch board was flooded and the mess tent was just hanging on. I asked if we could delay the change of command until we were back in the garrison, which would just be a few days delay. Then we could check the property in an orderly manner. To this he agreed.

When I looked around my new battery, I determined that the chain of command was not being properly utilized. Each staff officer was giving orders to his section but was neglecting to inform the First Sergeant or the Battery Commander. I called a meeting of all my new NCOs and the staff officers. I informed them that they were not properly using the chain of command.

I told them that there was only one Battery Commander and one First Sergeant. That all requests for materiel and personnel should go through us as well as a copy to the chief of the staff section involved. I informed them that I was the commander and staff officers must work through me to use the men and equipment. Although many doubted that this would work, within a week, we had a much improved outfit and excellent co-ordination with the staff. From then on, the men would take their orders from the First Sergeant, who would pass them on to the lower elements so that everybody knew what was to be done.

The men had been doing a lot of bitching and grumbling about the staff officers and their battery officers too. I had heard it openly expressed on all field problems by enlisted men of different ranks. I made it clear that from now on, all complaints would be passed up to me through the chain of command.

The rest of my tour with the battery was rewarding because of the lack of major problems. It was only a short while before I turned it over to Lt. Emerson. Because of his leadership and the success of the battery, he had earned the position as the battery commander. I was transferred back to the job of the battalion S-2 which I held until it was time for us to return to the states.

Bernice:

There was a nice two story single family house at number 3 Clemons Brentano which was occupied by a Captain who was rotating home. It was much nicer than number 9. It had steam heat. By now, Eli was one of the more senior Captains so we were able to move to this place. It provided a separate room for Mary Jane who by now had outgrown the cradle and was in a crib.

It did not have a garage but it had a place to grow a garden. Eli and the Colonel even had a contest to see who could grow the largest tomato.

Because of Eli's interest in hunting, we acquired an English setter and I built a house for him out back. Because 'Sad Sack' was supposed to be a retriever, we were told not to let him taste raw meat. I bought horse meat from the local metzger (butcher) and cooked it for the dog. One day I had a real nice piece in the refrigerator.

Eli came home and, as usual, checked the fridge. He saw this nice looking piece of meat so he cut off a couple slices, made a sandwich and ate it. When I came in, he complimented me on how good the roast was. I couldn't resist telling him what it was. Actually, it was very good, but I never made a habit of buying horse meat for the table.

Eli:

As S-2, one of my duties was to have a class for all the personnel in the battalion who were cleared for secret. The subject was intelligence and how easy it was for sensitive information about our own unit to get in the hands of enemy agents at no cost to them. Getting the same type of information about them was costing us millions of dollars through our agents.

I had the class scheduled in the theater on Friday. On Thursday night before the class, I was in the officers club, just listening, when I heard a senior officer tell a group of people that we would soon be changing to the 74th 'Armored' Field Artillery Bn. and our first two guns would be M-10/105mm self propelled Howitzers that would be arriving the next week. This was all classified secret and should not have been discussed with anyone except those cleared for secret with a need to know and certainly not in the club. I used this as one example of a careless 'slip of the lip'.

During this same period we received a new batch of recruits. Twenty five percent of them were fresh emigrant to the US from eastern European countries. By serving in our military, it was easier for them to become United States citizens. Most of these people did a fine job. But we had one in the battalion who told his buddies that he didn't like this soldiering business and at the first chance he got, he was going to defect to Czechoslovakia.

He even told them that he intended to do it over the following week end in Munich where he would make his contact. This information was passed up through channels to my section by a private. We immediately notified the CID (criminal investigation division) and the CIC (Counter intelligence Corp). We even knew that he was going to contact the Czech agents around the Munich Bahnhof (railroad station). They picked him up about 2000 at the bahnhof as he tried to walk off with what appeared to be civilians. They were all arrested. I used this as an example of how just one man could help to keep the turncoats out of the ranks. After the class, the CO, who had attended the class, came to me and said that I was taking my job too seriously.

We had a Hungarian doctor who was a 1st. Lieutenant. He too was a displaced person. He had married an Italian. It came out some time later that she was a member of the Italian Communist Party. They both attended underground meetings in northern Italy and were also doing a lot of activity on week ends amongst the DPs in Munich. Every one of these actions was recorded in what is known as a field file. That is a file that is kept on any suspected enemy agents or sympathizer. A copy is kept up to date by the Bn. S-2. When I left they were still keeping a file on him.

Bernice:

As noted before, the men were frequently away for extended periods of time and this often made family planning a bit unreliable. I was no exception.

When September came, it was time for school to start. Ginny would be six on December 29th. The cut off was December 31. I hesitated to start her, knowing that we would likely be returning to the states before the school year was over, but her friends would be in first grade so she was enrolled too.

I thought that I was due in late March. This pregnancy was no different than the others. I experienced morning sickness from the very beginning. However, life goes on, so I would lay in bed and stuff enough crackers down to have something to throw up and get the day off to a reasonable start. I was tired of bridge, so this made a perfect excuse to give it up.

271

Eli:

A normal overseas tour was supposed to be three years. However, because of the war in Korea, many of us had been extended. In December, I was already three months over my normal date for rotation. Col. Canty asked me to extend another six months, until he had completed his tour with the battalion.

Bernice was due to deliver in late March and would not be allowed to travel if she waited any longer and I just felt it was time to move on.

Bernice:

The year was 1951. It was decided that the American community should give the children of Landshut a Christmas party. I was made co-chairman of the committee to produce this affair with another Captain's wife from the 6th Cav. We sent word back to our friends in the states that we needed toys and money and it was forthcoming. All the women pitched in to wrap and label gifts according to age and gender.

The party was held at the Rathaus (city hall). We had one party in the morning for the girls and one in the afternoon for the boys. Some soldiers out at the kasern had adopted a fawn and it was very tame. The fawn came along with St. Nickolaus and was the hit of the party. There were over a thousand kinder.

Each American family was also assigned a displaced family to sponsor for Christmas. I took Margit with me to visit our family, who were on a farm. It was not unusual for the living quarters of Bavarian farmers to be located at one end of the barn. Even though most of the indigenous farmers by now had separate houses to live in, many of these barn/homes were occupied by the Sudetins. This was where our family lived.

I had a cold the day we called on them. Although my nose was completely stopped up, when I enter their living area, the stench of ammonia cleared my head immediately. This sounds grotesque, but I had only been there a few minutes when I realized it was really quite invigorating. It also struck me that if Jesus was born in the stable, it was probably healthier than if they had been in a drafty inn full of drunken travelers.

I wanted to get my family a goose which is the delicacy of the Bavarians for Christmas, but Margit told me that they didn't want a goose and would prefer swinefliesch (pork). Of course that was what we took them. They also had six small children. Since we would soon be leaving, I took them several items that we had acquired that were distinctly German, such as the children's sled. The last thing I saw as we drove away after delivering our contribution to international friendship was a small boy sitting on Ginny's sled.

Sad Sack had gotten to be such a big dog that he was knocking the kids around. Eli had not had time to train him to hunt so we gave him to the Jaeger.

Eli:

After Christmas, I took the car to Bremerhaven to ship it back to the states. I wanted to be sure it was in New York when we arrived in January.

While we were in Bremerhaven, a Red Cross man hunted me down with the news that my mother had died. Our hold baggage was already on the boat and our car was on the way to New York. They volunteered to take me off the passenger list for the ship and fly me back to the states. However, they told me that the weather was very bad over the Atlantic and they could not

Eli, Virginia, Mary Jane and Bernice in Landshut. 1952.

273

promise me how long we would need to wait to fly out. I decided the best thing to do was just go ahead and get on the ship. We probably would have missed the funeral anyway.

Bernice:

After all our belongings had been packed, we moved to the Drexel Mar. They had provided us with a crib for the baby. However, the first night she refused to sleep in it. She screamed until we took her out. I tried putting her in bed between us but she still would not settle down. It must have been one or two in the morning before she finally fell asleep, right in front of the door. I covered her up with a blanket and we finally got some sleep.

Since she had never refused to go to sleep before, we thought that she sensed this situation called for extreme measures to be sure that she didn't get left behind. The next night we spent on the train. We had a sleeping compartment and she again would only sleep in front of the door. The pattern continued after we got to Bremerhaven, where we were billeted in a BOQ.

When we boarded the USS Washington, there was a band on the wharf playing Auf Wiedersehen. An American flag was unfurled and we were on our way home. There was a crib in our cabin, which Mary Jane again rejected, but she did accept one of the regular bunks. She knew we couldn't leave her now.

~ 19 ~

Schooling the Infantry

Eli:

Our ship was the USS Washington, operated by the United States Line. It was not the Washington that I had sailed on in October of 1944 when the 100th Division had gone to Europe. This ship was scheduled for retirement and this was said to be her last crossing. It was to be replaced by the new USS United States.

Everything went well the first day out. We were in the North Sea and the weather was beginning to get rough. When we entered the English Channel it was getting worse by the hour. Bernice and Mary Jane both became quite seasick. Mary Jane had thrown up in her bed. Bernice tried to clean up, but got sick and ran to the head and asked Ginny to clean it up. In a matter of seconds, Ginny got sick and ran to the head. That left only me to get the job done. I only lasted for a few minutes when I had to join them. That was the only time that I was ever sea sick.

Mary Jane was quite sick so I took her to sick bay which was way down in the hold below the water line. They gave her an antibiotic. Although the ship continued to rock and roll we made it back to our cabin and before long we were able to survive in relative comfort.

As always, after we were out to sea, I was given the detail of police and sanitation officer.

As we were traveling along the coast of England, the storm kept getting worse and worse. A freighter named the Enterprise broke in half at the same time that we were only a few miles away. Our Captain offered assistance but the Enterprise Captain from the front half of his ship said that everything was under control. He was going to hold out until salvage vessels could reach him.

The rule of the sea is that a deserted ship is the property of who ever reaches it. By staying with his ship, he saved his company millions of dollars. He wasn't as crazy as he seemed. We just plowed on toward the United States.

We landed at Brooklyn Army Base and spent the first night at Fort Hamilton. I reclaimed the car, which had been shipped ahead of time and we headed for Baltimore on the New Jersey turnpike.

Bernice:

Because I was pregnant, the medics said I should take the new nausea pill, dramamine. That was a mistake. The first tablet got no farther than my throat when I started to gag. By the time we had reached the English channel I was non-functional. We were unaware of it, but there was a shipwreck in progress off the English coast at Lands End at that same time.

Ginny and Eli seemed to adapt well to the heaving ship but Mary Jane was as sick as I was. At least, she wasn't hard to keep track of as she had no interest in wandering. Eli had reluctantly been assigned to troop duty. Ginny remembers the best part of the trip was when she was taken to the mess hall. Her dad was called away and she was turned over to the mess steward. Not many people had shown up to eat because of the weather, so the steward kept her entertained by feeding her all the unclaimed desserts.

As we were headed toward Baltimore, Mary Jane threw up all over me. Being on the turnpike, it was quite a distance before we could get off to clean up the mess. When I did get to a rest room, I had another problem. I had only one maternity dress. Thankfully, it was a brown jersey, so I took it off, washed it in the basin and put it back on, wet, even though it was January. Thus, I arrived in Baltimore.

The first stop was Lane Bryant for two new dresses. Carrie and June had moved out of the house on Ramsey Street and were living in an apartment on Old Frederick Rd. Ginny was fascinated by their radio with the pictures. After a short visit, Eli went on to Fort Benning to his new assignment and I headed for Wisconsin on Pennsylvania Airline.

We were scheduled to fly to Janesville by way of Cleveland and Chicago, but when we were in Cleveland we were re-routed to Detroit on Eastern because of engine trouble. No problem I thought. I was wrong. Because it was a tight connection in Detroit and because I was awkwardly pregnant with a six year old and an eighteen month toddler, the airline had a porter meet me and deliver me to the plane for Milwaukee. It was on the extreme other end of the airport. With the porter carrying Mary Jane and poor Ginny running to keep up, we made the plane and took off immediately for Milwaukee, 15 minutes behind schedule.

Just as we were arriving over Milwaukee, Mary Jane became sick again. There was a snow storm in progress and the plane was unable to land. My dad and mother with Aunt Cora (Uncle Charles had died while we were in Europe) had come to Milwaukee to pick me up. I had called them from Cleveland about the change in destination. Dad said that the plane actually touched the runway but accelerated immediately and took off again. I wouldn't know, I was too busy with my own problems. Mary Jane was sick again. The stewardess washed the soiled dress and she made the rest of the flight in her underwear.

We went back to Detroit. There I was, alone, pregnant with two small children and four suitcases at 11:00 PM in an enormous shed that had once been a bomber factory. The airline announced that we would be bussed to the railroad station in Ypsilanti (a small town south of Detroit) where the Motor City Special would have a sleeping car added for us. It would make an unscheduled stop to pick up the stranded airline passengers and take us to Chicago. In the confusion, one of my suitcases fell apart. A kind porter tied it together with a piece of rope.

The ticket agent came down to the train station and opened the window to sell us our tickets but there was no porter or other signs of help. I called home but got no reply. Kenneth was out and my folks were in Milwaukee. They had decided that it would be unwise to try to drive back home in the blizzard. My army friend, Genivieve Middleton, offered them a place to stay at her house in Milwaukee. My mother had called her when she learned I was to land there, so she had been at the airport to see me.

Desperate, I called my old high school friend, Doris Anderson Bowen, in Milton Junction. They had just gotten home from a political rally, so I didn't get them out of bed. She was happy to make the necessary calls to my brother about the time of my train's arrival in Janesville.

But how was I to get my two kids, my four bags and myself from a ground level platform of a dark railroad station onto a train making an unscheduled stop? I needn't have worried. I put Ginny in charge of Mary, who was sleeping on the bench and picked up a suitcase and headed for the platform. It was snowing in Detroit too. The other passengers were mostly men who appeared to be business types as they all had brief cases and small over night bags. They could not miss my condition nor my problem. Several of them picked up my four suitcases, and my two kids. They even gave me a boost as the train made its brief stop.

I was so glad to be safely aboard and in my lower berth bed that all I did was take off our shoes and coats. Mary was already undressed as her clothing was in an airline barf bag. I didn't even get a chance to thank them. I have always remembered their good deed on a dark, snowy night in Michigan. When ever I have an opportunity to give someone a hand in a difficult situation, I feel it helps to repay some very thoughtful people.

In the mean time, Eli had gone on to Columbus to his new assignment and had rented a house. It was just off the Fort Benning post on Torch Hill Road and was completely furnished. As soon as he could, he drove to Wisconsin and we drove back to our new home. By now I was eight months along and had managed to gain more weight than most doctors approve of.

Eli:

I was assigned to the 41st Field Artillery. The mission of the artillery battalions at Fort Benning, where the Infantry School is located, was to support the school with all types of artillery demonstrations. It included service practice for Infantry Officers and NCOs to teach them how to use artillery and how to adjust fire. We also taught them the proper use of radar for picking up enemy mortar positions.

My first assignment was battery commander of 'C' Battery. The battery discipline had broken down because the previous commander wanted to be a good guy and had let the troops get away with anything short of murder.

General Palmer, an artillery officer, and a rough disciplinarian from Third Army, was inspecting the battalion and observed that the men were wearing a hodge podge of uniforms and seemed to be disorganized. He gave the battalion commander

278

some strong advice to take immediate action. That was how I got to be a battery commander for the fifth time.

The battalion commander had the habit of getting the troops up at 0300 to go out and be ready to fire by 0900. Only a short while after this, we got a new battalion commander, Lt. Col. Egan. To correct the problem of men standing around for hours with nothing to do, which is a morale buster, I suggested at BC call that the instructions be changed to "Be ready to fire by 0900." Immediately the units started getting up at the usual time and would leave the battalion about 0745 which was plenty of time to be ready to fire at the designated time.

When my men finished firing for the day and came back and had cleaned up the guns and trucks, they were given the rest of the day off. With these two practices and stronger discipline in both the field and the garrison, the battalion took off to be one of the best units in the Third Army.

With the new and better appearance and eye wash of 'C' battery we were now the honor battery of all the artillery units. I had introduced the use of Bulldog Stove Black on the tires. It became our assignment to fire artillery salutes whenever dignitaries visited Fort Benning. This included such highly placed individuals as Kings and Prime Ministers, and high ranking government officials of other country. It even included some high ranking Soviets.

One day, after inspecting the troops, they stood with the Commanding General of the Third Army where at least a division passed in reviewed. After the ceremony for the Soviets, one of my men said, "Instead of honoring those commies, I felt that I should have been hitting them over the head with the trail hand spike." I told him that I agreed with him but it was better that we lay off that kind of talk.

About this time, the order was sent out that the armed forces were to be integrated. Up to this time there had been many colored units in the army, especially in the service outfits. The entire 92nd Infantry division was completely colored. I received the first two black soldiers in 'C' Btry. One was a corporal and the other a private.

While I was interviewing the private, he told me that he could not wear boots because of an accident he had in Alaska. After the interview, I checked his military record. His feet had been burned while saving four white soldiers from a helicopter crash. He had been awarded the Soldier's Medal for his heroic action.

I called him back in and told him that he was excused from wearing boots. The following Saturday we were having a mounted parade in downtown Columbus, the home city of Fort Benning. Despite me putting out that he was excused from any duty that required boots, in the center three quarter ton truck I noticed the corporal and this private, in position with the mounted machine gun.

When I looked in the vehicle I could see that he was wearing boots. I asked him how come he had on his boots. He said, "Captain, I wanted to be a part of the first integrated parade in the south and I talked the sergeant into letting me wear my boots." The corporal verified the story and I commended him for his Esprit de Corp.

Within a few days he was wearing his boots whenever they were required. They ended up being two of my better soldiers. I made him PFC and before long he was a machine gun corporal.

Col. Egan was pleased with my performance as a battery commander and had appreciated the advice that I had imparted as an experience troop commander. Most of his duty to this point had been as a staff officer. When a vacancy came up for an S-3 he gave me that job.

In July, we received a commitment to send a battery to Birmingham to fire the salute. With the third Infantry Battalion of the 29th Infantry Brigade under Major Bud Bolling, whose dad was the Commanding General of the Third Army, we were to be in the Fourth Of July parade through down town Birmingham.

I flew down in one of our light airplanes to observe. When I got there, the salute battery was in position in the city square in the center of town. I told the battery commander that if he fired those guns right where they were, he would blow out most of the plate glass windows in the area. He had already talked about this very problem with the Chamber of Commerce chairman who was in charge of the parade. It seems that the insurance companies had agreed that they would replace any damage without any expense to the city or the Army. This was all verbal. In those days, you could make verbal agreements and they would be honored.

When the first round went off, six or eight store windows cracked and fell into their display areas in big pieces. Nobody was injured because the glass had been blown in by the concussion and the police had kept people away from the windows as this had been anticipated. Everything just went ahead as planned and was a big success.

By this time, we had a few more blacks and the Infantry battalion must have had at least 25. The Chamber of Commerce had arranged a dinner and party for all the troops. They held a black party and a white party. Attendance at the party was voluntary. The blacks went almost a hundred percent to the black party and about three quarters of the white men went to the white party.

When I interviewed the men about how the parties went, the black party was declared to have been the best, and they had the most fun. They had nothing but praise for the people of Birmingham and for how they had been treated. The white people had enjoyed their party too, but they didn't seem to appreciate it as much as the black men. This was the first time that integrated troops had marched in Birmingham.

I flew back in the L-20 army airplane with my young pilot. It was getting dark and I was trying to follow on the map where we were flying. I told him that I thought he was too far north of the route we had came on. He laughed. He said everybody has a problem following a map when they are flying. As we approached the Chattahoochee River, which has as many curves as a snake, he checked in for permission to land.

I look out and saw what looked like a runway just like the one at Lawson Field at Benning. As we made our approach and were, at the level of the light poles, he realized that it was the main street of a town named West Point which was twenty five miles upstream from Columbus.

He gunned his motor and got back up where he checked in with Lawson to tell them that he would be a few minutes late. We followed the river south and landed with no problems. He said that he needed to have his radio checked out as he had been following a radio beam that had taken him to the wrong place. I never told anybody about getting lost so as not to embarrass the young pilot.

I was only the S-3 for about two months when I was made the battalion executive officer. Lt. Col. Neale was now the commanding officer. He was a West Pointer and thought he was a pretty good golfer. He asked me to pick the best golfer in the battalion. He wanted to go out and play golf the first day he was on duty. I found a young Lieutenant who was a College All American golfer from Yale University. I asked the battery commander to excuse him so that he could play golf with the new Ole Man. There is no better place for a new commander than on the golf course to get him out of the way.

Bernice:

The first order of business was to get Ginny into school. Since we were off post she would go to public school in Columbus. The Baker Village School, which was nearest to our house and the post, was full so she was assigned to an older school downtown called the Eleventh Street School. She rode the school bus which stopped at the foot of the hill.

There was a beautiful Methodist church next to Eleventh Street School. I reasoned that if Ginny went to school there, then the children who went to that school would go to that church. How wrong I was. Down town Columbus was no longer a residential area. All the members had moved to better areas and the school was used for overflow from the military families out by the post.

I had only been to church once when Ginny's Church School teacher, Eugenia Bradford, came to call on us and invited me to be one of her assistants. I was delighted, as this would give me a great opportunity to get involved and to make friends in the community, something that had been lacking in Germany. St. Luke's was a big congregation.

43 Torch Hill Rd. was a nice house and had a fine chain link fence around the back yard. I thought that would be so nice because Mary Jane could play in the back yard, safe from traffic. What a surprise I got when the first day she was out there I saw her using the fence for a ladder. Her feet fitted perfectly between the wires. It was better to just leave the gate open and reinforce the idea that she should not go near the street.

The baby's arrival was early on the morning of the 23rd of April at the station hospital at Fort Benning. He was almost three weeks over what we thought was the due day. He weighed eight pounds, twelve and a half ounces. We named him Billy Eli. Eli had left the girls asleep while he took me to the hospital at Fort Benning and went straight home. Once again he had escaped the father in the waiting room routine.

I don't remember too much about the delivery although I believe that I was awake for most of it. I do remember that as they wheeled me past the nursing station, they helped me make a phone call to let daddy know that we had a boy and we were both OK. Our neighbors, the Rattans, phone rang whenever our phone rang. It was a two party line, our phone rang once, theirs rang twice. On that phone call Jane Rattan, half asleep, also answered, thinking she had heard two rings I suppose. When she heard me say we had a boy, she said, "Bernice, that's wonderful."

In 1952, most of the post, including the hospital, still had many wooden buildings. Labor and delivery was a separate building from the post partum ward. Because Eli was a Captain, I had a private room. It wouldn't have mattered, I only stayed there three days. I went through the motions of nursing but started supplemental feedings from the beginning.

One day, Eli and I were lounging on the bed and Mary Jane was quietly playing between us when I mentioned that I thought I had heard her say shoe. To our surprise, she spoke up and said, "I say shoe." She was making a sentence with her first word.

Most of our neighbors were military families. However, the lady next door up the hill was a widow of an officer who had been killed in Korea. She had two children, the girl, Leslie, was Ginny's age and the boy Reece, a little older. Our bedroom window was next to their kitchen door.

One night we heard a noise outside the window and when we looked out there was a man trying to get in our neighbors house. Eli hollered at him and told him to freeze while pointing his finger like a gun. The guy froze, but when I turned on the light to look up the number of the police, he saw it was only a guy in his pajamas pointing his finger and proceeded to smash the glass in the door and enter. When the police came, it turned out to be one of Mrs. Cody's numerous boy friends and she refused to charge him.

Down the hill lived the Rattan family. Captain Rattan was a West Pointer and was on crutches when we moved in. He had broken a leg refereeing football. They had two girls, Jeannie and Nancy. Ginny especially enjoyed playing with Jeannie. They even continued to be friends after the Rattans moved to on-post housing. We got our first cat from them. Ginny named him Black Prince. We later got a female that she named Grey Pearl. Grey Pearl could jump straight up in the air about three feet.

There were enough small children around us that we had a birthday party when Mary Jane turned two. We had them on the porch and she crawled right up on the table to get at her cake. Ginny was more excited than Mary Jane and opened all her presents for her as I ran the movie camera.

Torch Hill Rd. was just being developed at the time by a man named Hamilton. He had built the house we were renting. It seemed to be fairly well built so we decided that we would use

126 Torch Hill Road, Columbus, Georgia. 1953.

our GI Bill of Rights benefit to have one built just down the hill. It was exciting to watch our own house come to life. We paid twelve thousand dollars for it.

Of course, there was no landscaping. A man came around and sold us a whole variety of shrubbery and we added others. Camellias are a favorite in Columbus and I had some very pretty one. We also had rose bushes and a hedge of sassanquas. For a lawn, one of Mr. Hamilton's neighbors let us pull bermuda roots from their shrubbery to sprig our lawn. We were really naive. Bermuda is a real weed when it gets in the shrubbery. We had weeded his shrubs. But it did grow fast and we soon had a thick lawn. Our first lawn mower was the kind you push and the wheels turned a reel.

One day I learned about someone who was moving that had a swing set to sell. It had been constructed from regular two inch water pipe and was larger and heavier than the swing sets that were sold in the stores. Eli wanted to be sure it wouldn't tip over, so we set it in holes two feet deep with concrete. It was solid alright. The last time anyone in our family has seen that house, the posts were still there.

The galvanized tub that I had bought in Germany to soak Ginny in when she had her rash made a great vessel for mixing concrete. We mixed up several batches of cement which we colored

284

different colors. We poured them in twelve inch square molds and made a dandy colorful patio in the back. There were some left over red bricks and I made a real neat barbecue to complete the project.

Even though we had abandoned the fence idea up the hill we still went ahead and had a chain link fence installed in the new back yard. Billy would be learning to walk and I thought I would feel more secure if he was behind a fence.

There was quite a gully at the back of our lot that eroded noticeably every time it rained. We bought a load of cement and lined this. That stopped the erosion.

One of the fun things about the new house was buying all new furniture. Eli had received some money from his mother's estate and we had some war bonds that we cashed, as well as getting time payments from Sears. One thing that I wanted most was a rocking chair. The one I bought was a platform rocker.

One day I got a phone call and a lady asked me who was buried in Grant's Tomb. I thought that was a pretty silly question so I gave a silly answer, "Robert E. Lee." "Congratulations, you have just won a free portrait at such and such photo studio." Never one to let something free get away I took her up on the deal. The gimmick had worked.

We didn't really have any professional pictures of the kids so I had all three of them done. Ginny was animated and a very good subject. Bill was too young to have any opinion. He couldn't even sit up unassisted so I held him while I was concealed behind a drape. But Mary Jane chose not to co-operative. I finally had to give up and take her back another time.

Again I acquired a used crib and bought a new mattress. This time there was no messing around with a bathinett. Bill got his bath in the kitchen sink.

It was while we were at Fort Benning that we discovered Florida. The Infantry School had a camp with several cottages on Choctowatchee Bay near Destin in the Florida pan handle. They could be rented for next to nothing (I think it was $30 a week). Our first trip to Destin was while Bill was still play pen size. After Eli came home from Korea we went again a couple times. We even took Black Prince once. The mosquitoes were sometimes excessive, but the cottage had good screens and we just didn't go out after dark.

Eli had a lot of fun catching crabs. The water in the bay was clear enough that he could wade in waist deep water and see the crabs on the bottom and dip them out. Sometimes he had to run them down. He floated a tub with some water in it where he deposited his catch. For that week we gorged on crabs.

The Gulf of Mexico at Destin has the whitest sand and the clearest water that I have ever seen. To reach it, we had to drive a couple miles from the Infantry Rest Center. The place we found to park was near a real shanty called The Back Porch. It was a little hot dog and cold beer stand between the road and the beach that was run by a retired sergeant and his German wife. When we went back to Destin after Korea, the packing box style had been replaced by an 'A' frame, but the food was still the same and good. The last time we were in Destin, the whole area had gone commercial and the road had been re-routed. The Back Porch was a large and expensive restaurant. It just didn't seem the same.

We had only been in Columbus about a year when Eli got orders to Korea. We decided that because we were buying the house and because we had so many advantages of the post such as the commissary, hospital etc. that I would stay put.

~ 20 ~

Advising the R.O.K.s

Eli:

After saying good bye to the family, I boarded a plane and eventually landed in San Francisco. I had one day to kill before I was to reported to the Port of Embarkation. I had learned that my old friend, Whitey Emerson from Landshut was at the nuclear school at the Presidio. I gave him a call and he said that Captain Marsh, another officer from the 74th was in town on his way to Korea too. We decided to meet downtown in the lounge at the hotel where I was staying.

We had a couple drinks at the bar and decided to go to Chinatown to eat. Whitey was with a good looking blond girl friend who had a bright yellow convertible. She drove us to the restaurant where we had supper. We talked a lot about our service together in Landshut. The girl friend took me back to my hotel and they delivered Marsh to his billet. That was a very pleasant first day on my way to Korea.

The next day I reported for duty and was immediately informed that I was on a priority list of officers to be flown to Korea, by way of Hawaii. We were on a propeller driven Flying Tiger Airline airplane. We landed in Honolulu for breakfast and fuel. They had some sort of trouble so we had to stay there about four hours longer than planned. That was fine with us, we would have gladly stayed there for the duration of the war.

About 1300, we took off for Midway Island. We landed there almost at dawn and had breakfast again. It was a very small island. It seemed almost too small to land a plane on. It was being converted to a civilian airport, mainly for the purpose of refueling commercial planes flying to Asia. It was very hot, about

104 degrees at dawn, and we were glad to leave there before it got really hot.

We flew into Tokyo and took a train to the Replacement Depot. From there I received my orders to Sasebo which was in southern Japan and took a ferry to Pusan, Korea right on the southern tip of the Korean peninsula. It was here that I discovered that I was assigned to be an artillery advisor to the 9th Division of the Republic of Korea, called ROK for short.

Of the ninety some officers on the plane who were supposed to be high priority replacements needed right away, only two, including me, actually ever got to the front line. All the rest were picked off by higher headquarter in Japan and Eighth Army in Seoul.

We went to Seoul where we were told that we were to deliver about thirty jeeps to Taegu. A Colonel and I would be responsible to deliver them to KMAG (Korean Military Assistance Group) headquarters. We had about thirty men counting the Colonel and me, with one man per jeep. We were briefed that bandits often attacked these convoys and would pick off the last vehicle in the column, shoot the man and take the jeep.

The Colonel announced that it was every man for himself in case of attack. I told him that was a hell of a way to run a convoy and that I would take the rear vehicle and that if anyone was attacked that I would be right there with him. The only event that happened on the trip was that the jeep just in front of me got a flat tire. While I stood by with a carbine loaded and ready, he quickly put the spare on and we were back on the road in five minutes.

When the convoy realized that the last two jeeps were missing, they speeded up and we never did catch them until they got to Taegu and had reported us as missing.

Taegu was KMAG headquarters. We dropped our baggage off and reported in. Upon reporting in, they informed me that at 0900 the next morning I was to fly out in a C-47 that would drop me out near Kumhwa. I was also told that a man would meet me at the airfield and take me to the 9th ROK Infantry Division, KMAG section.

I was assigned to the ROK 30th Field Artillery Bn. as the artillery advisor. The battalion was 105mm towed howitzers. I had been an artillery mechanic when the very first 105s had been delivered to the army in 1941 at Fort Meade, Maryland in the 29th Infantry Division, 110th Field Artillery Battalion. I had commanded five batteries of this weapon including my combat during World War II and knew it well.

Kumhwa was thirty five miles north of the 38th parallel in North Korea. It was a major invasion route for centuries between the Chinese and the Koreans and later, the Japanese coming from the South.

Korea is very mountainous, with lots of little streams that turn into raging rivers during the spring monsoons. It was beautiful, but showed many scars of war in the towns and forests. The mountains were covered with lavender azaleas. Especially where the forests had been cleared out by artillery fire. The nitrogen and iron in the shells was ideal fertilizer for azaleas. The Koreans said they were more brilliant than ever.

So much for smelling the flowers, I had to get ready to go to work. The shelling around the area was going both ways. I was told by the Captain that I was relieving that everything was going to be peaceful as they would soon be signing a peace treaty. The very first night, before I had even met my commanding officer, the shells and the firing went on throughout the night.

The next morning I reported to the Division KMAG Chief, Colonel Spicer. He referred me to a Lt. Col. Osborn, the artillery advisor for the Division who would be my boss. I met with him and another Artillery Lt. Colonel in their bunker for about an hour. They seemed more interesting in their soon to be rotation back to the states.

I felt that I was on my own and that my knowledge of artillery far exceeded theirs. I started out by inspecting my new battalion. Especially the materiel and equipment. Their howitzers were American but the trucks were Japanese similar to our old Dodge truck of pre World War II.

The whole time I was traveling to my new assignment, everyone was telling me how dumb the Koreans were and how they knew nothing about mechanics. When I inspected their motor pool with an interpreter, I asked them a lot of questions about these old trucks. I could tell they were very proud of them. I asked them to start them up and those old things purred like kittens. I was impressed by the way they solved the many problems of repairing these trucks that Americans would never dream of.

One day I saw a Korean truck out in the boondocks that had a broken fuel line. The driver went over in the field, cut a hollow reed and fitted it on the broken line and tied it in place with a tough weed like a piece of string. It made the truck run. Not many Americans would do that.

Then I inspected the firing batteries, mainly the maintenance of the Howitzers and storage and care of the ammunition. Again,

I was impressed by the cannoneers' knowledge of their weapons, ammunition, and gun drill.

I made up my mind right then, that the Korean people were some of the smartest people that I had ever ran into. The men for the artillery units were all taken out of college to form the artillery battalions. They had quickly adapted to the military equipment and procedures with great enthusiasm. I knew then that my job was not going to be hard, even though they had never been trained during peace. Their training had come in actual combat, shooting at the enemy. They did all the little things that make a good outfit.

I reported to the 9th ROK Divarty Commander Colonel, Kang Mim Kwan. We took a trip to visit all the artillery battalions of the division and some of the OPs. We talked to the forward observers and the infantry that we were supporting. I saw many of the mountains that I had read about in the newspapers. The one on the right was Sniper's Ridge. Then there was Jane Russell hill toward the center. The left end of sector was on what was called Boomerang Hill. The biggest mountain in the area was Papa San. It stood just north of Kumhwa in enemy area.

The Division was known as the White Horse Division. It had gotten that name by defending the mountain just to our left known as White Horse. They were credited with wiping out an entire corp (three divisions) of Chinese. They were also known as the only Korean Division that gave no ground to the enemy. All the other Korean Divisions were inspired by the Ninth ROK and fought like hell after that. They were defending their own country.

While I was still nominally advising the 30th Bn., I was in fact advising Col. Kang for all the artillery, including the division fire support co-ordination center. On the first of May I was named assistant Divarty advisor.

On the first of June, I was promoted to Major. I didn't actually have the orders in my hand on that day. I first learned about it when Bernice wrote that she had seen my name of the list in the Army times. When Col. Osborne heard through the grape vine that I had been promoted, he came right over and pinned a set of gold leaves on me.

This was contrary to Army etiquette as the that honor is reserved for the Commanding Officer. Col. Spicer was actually my CO. When I walked in the mess hall, the Ole Man saw me wearing the leaves and was upset. He called Corp Headquarters, and they confirmed it. He congratulated me and apologized for not pining on my leaves himself.

Shortly after I was promoted to Major I had to go to KMAG headquarters in Taegu on business. I had been there only once before, when I had arrived in Korea, and had remembered the mess set up. There was a regular officers' mess hall for Captains and lower and there was a dining room labeled Field Grade Officers, Majors and above. I could look through the door of this mess hall and see the tablecloths and Korean waitresses serving the big brass. Now I was a field grade officer and I could eat in that dining room. The road was sixty miles of bumps and pot-holes. When I arrived and went to eat, the signs on the first room had been changed and now read "Majors and Below". My mother would have said, "It serves you right."

The main road from Seoul, the capital of the south to P'yongyang the capital of the north run through Kumhwa which was the central area of the division. It was no autobahn. It was more of a muddy trail although the American Engineers had put down a crushed rock surface. This was called route 3. The route was as ancient as Asia itself. There was also a newer road going east to west, also made of crushed rock called route 6.

One day, as my jeep approached this intersection, the driver hit the gas and went roaring through about 60 miles an hour. I was sure surprised. When I asked him why, he said, "MPs have-a-no." To him, that meant that the enemy was shelling the inter-sections and the MPs were in their holes. He was right because sure enough, within seconds, two or three enemy rounds hit right where we had been.

Kumhwa was well known in the area as the place where the rich came to hunt the Asiatic tiger. We never saw any tigers but one morning we saw tiger tracks in the snow at one of our out-posts and the men who had been there were missing.

There was a domestic cat who had gone wild that had found a place in the walls and ceiling of our little officers' sleeping bun-ker to have her kittens. One night about 0200 we heard a lot of noise in our walls. It was the kittens crawling around between the plywood interior and the sand bags. They were making a lot of noise trying to get back in the ceiling.

We caught the kittens but we had to build a special trap to catch the mother cat. They were all as wild as they could be. Finally we caught her and put her in a bag. We had the bag in a jeep and were going to take her out in the country to let her out when we met a jeep with some French officers and stopped to talk. They saw the bag move and wanted to know what we had. When we told them it was a cat and that we were going to turn her loose. They asked if they could have her. We were happy to give her to them. She was destined to become a gourmet dinner.

A lot of the Americans looked down on the Koreans and called them the little brown brothers but I thought they were pretty smart. A lot of their equipment such as their trucks were left over from the Japanese army. Even though they were worn out, the Koreans had repaired them getting the parts from other broken down trucks.

Another time I was out in an isolated area when I had a flat tire. When I got out the lug wrench to fix it, I discovered that the wrench was too big for the nut and just went round and round. An old Papa San was standing beside the road and when he saw my problem he came over and motioned for me to give him the wrench. He laid it on a rock and with another rock hit the business end a few times which bent it in. When we tried it, it fit perfectly.

The 187th airborne Infantry brigade were to replace the 30th Infantry regiment of the Ninth ROK, which was the left side of our Division. It was an area which was very quiet. We never had more than a platoon attack for over 3 months. I was assisting changing the 30th ROK FA Bn. position to make way for the American 678th Airborne Field Artillery Bn. I personally posted all their forward observers and liaison officers on the OPs and gave them our Korean maps. That relieved the Koreans of the responsibility for that sector.

The new artillery had no problems occupying a prepared position. They were motorized and we ran them right into their new positions. On the top of the hill beside the headquarters position there was a bunker made of heavy timber. The Koreans had been using it for observation and protection for their head-quarter's battery. The 678th FA said they didn't want the bunker and that the Koreans could take the timbers with them.

While I was talking to their staff one of the ROK trucks, carrying the timbers, was coasting down the side of the mountain in neutral to save gas. It got to going too fast to be able to shift into second gear. We could hear the gears grinding as the truck picked up speed. One Korean was killed.

The 678th had a brand new mess tent. It was really nice, the first one I had seen of a new design. The truck went right through that new mess tent and it wrapped around the truck. All that was left was two stoves and the Mess Sergeant. When truck finally stopped, they rescued their tent which was not too badly damaged. The enlisted men said it was a shame that the ROKs didn't get the mess Sergeant. The officers agreed. They invited me to stay for supper. When I saw what they were cooking it looked like 'C' rations so I thanked them very much but went back to our own mess.

I had taken some of my Korean officers up to watch how an American outfit operated. I was really embarrassed by how disorganized they were, especially the infantry. I told the Koreans to return to their units before it got dark.

Most of the confusion was caused by the fact that they were all told to dismount about ten miles behind the line and had to walk in with their heavy packs on their backs, all uphill. There, in the confusion, two of their own companies got in a fire fight and ended up shooting at each other because it was dark by the time they arrived. A first sergeant had accidently discharged his 45 which started the fighting that lasted forty five minutes before they could figure out what was happening and get it stopped.

We could have brought them in by truck to within a hundred yards of their new positions and there was no reason to make them walk all that way with those heavy packs and try to occupy their position in the dark.

It was their commanding General's idea to not allow any supply convoys to move through his area during daylight because he thought they would attract enemy fire. The road that ran behind his area was route 6 and the Main supply line for the entire front. The responsibility for keeping it open rested on the 9th ROK division. The Americans had control of the air so the enemy could not have air observation and it was certainly better to move the trucks when the drivers could see what they were doing.

I found out about this when I went by the intersection and the MPs told me that the road was closed during daylight hours. I asked the Sergeant if I could make a call to his headquarters. I got the MP switchboard who put me through to Brigade Hqts. The Chief of Staff and I discussed the problem. He talked to somebody else and said they would open it up. The problem had been solved.

One night the Chinese destroyed the gasoline dump at Inchon which supplied the entire front. They had come down the valley in an L-5 and threw two hand grenades which hit a gasoline tank. This had set the whole dump on fire. Our jets couldn't maneuver in the valleys because they were too fast, and we couldn't attack them with ground fire as we would hit our own troops on the other side of the valley. They had been running up and down the valley for a couple weeks and we had sorta laughed at them. Now it was not nearly as funny. They were finally brought down with an old propellor type trainer equipped with a machine gun that could get them from above.

Even though the war was still going on, Vice President Nixon came to Korea and the United Nations held a review. There was a massing of the colors of elements of all the units on the plain south of Kumhwa and a little to the west. It was well within artillery range of the Chinese. The 9th ROK were represented and were given the honor of firing the salute.

A full Colonel from 8th Army was in charge of organizing the review. He wanted the salute battery to be about a half a mile away from the formation. I told him that it would not be effective at that distance and that they should be a part of the formation and fire the salute from the ready line. He told me that it was going to be fired just like they did at Fort Benning.

I had spent more than a year as the commander of the Infantry School Artillery unit which had fired all the salutes for Ft. Benning and the Infantry Center. When I told him this he said that I could put them where I thought they should be. They were deployed on the line with the rest of the troops. During the VIP ride by, the salute battery was part of the troops being reviewed.

Besides the VP and his wife, the entourage included the President of South Korea, Sigmund Rhee and his wife, General Maxwell Taylor, 8th Army Commander and representatives from all the units that were participating in that war including the Greeks, the French, the Aussies and the British. Even the Philippines had a Battalion in Korea.

It was a very impressive formation, the ready line was at least a half mile long so that you could actually see the curvature of the earth from one end of the line to the other. The colors were all massed in the center, in front of the reviewing officers. They moved out to troop the line with two three quarter ton command cars.

When they returned to the reviewing area the command was given to pass in review. It was one of the most impressive military parades that I had ever been a part of. It was further enhanced by sound of the artillery firing on the actual front line near by. Fortunately it was friendly artillery firing at the enemy to keep them from getting on their guns and raining fire on our parade.

One day General Maxwell Taylor, the theater commander came up to see how we were doing. We were on one of the observation points and he said he would select a target and wanted to see how long it would take us to adjust and fire a time on target barrage by all the artillery in the corp that could reach it. Our men were so good at reading co-ordinates and adjusting fire. I was so confident of the ability of my observer to locate the target, using only the co-ordinates, that when the first round was so accurate, I ordered "time on target, all units, two minutes".

All rounds landed at the same time exactly as they were supposed to. It was very impressive except that a single round which landed at least a thousand yards away from the target. I know the General was impressed but couldn't resist pointing to that one round and said, "What happened there?"

There was activity on the front almost every night. The enemy would attack in small units at different times from a platoon up to a battalion. Most of the time they would partially penetrate our line and the ROKs would beat them back by dawn.

One night we set up a plan to let the Chinese over run one of our infantry companies. We had been there for three or four months now and we had permanent bunkers dug into the mountains with heavy wooden doors made of 2×8s over the entrance.

The plan was for the infantry to button up behind they doors and when the Chinese came we would open fire with VT fuses right over our own position. The VT fuse is a variable time fuse that puts out a radio beam in front of it and the shells explode thirty to forty yards in the air automatically. That would rain down shrapnel on the troops.

If everything went right the Chinese would be caught in the open with out any shelter. This would work because the Chinese would have already used up their grenades and would be armed only with their riffles.

That night, when the attack came, our infantry was already in the bunker. As soon as the FO determined that the enemy was in our position, he called for immediate fire using the VT fuse. This was our first experiment with this type of fire and was very successful. We caught the Chinese by complete surprise. Just when they thought they had won another prize, it had suddenly become a disaster for them. Most of their men were dead or wounded in less than fifteen minutes.

To our knowledge this was the first time that this plan was ever tried. General Maxwell Taylor, came up from Seoul to be briefed by the ninth ROK commander, Maj. Gen. Lee Han Lim. He also interview the company commander and others who had been part of the operation. He was an old artilleryman and was highly impressed.

Not long after this a plan came out of Eighth Army for us to prepare to go on the offense. I had noticed that the Chinese would fight real hard for two days, then they would run out of ammunition. That would be the time for us to jump off. That was part of the plan.

After moving our artillery up close to the front line, in offensive posture, the ROK Capital Division (the historical first unit in the South Korean army that could do no wrong) came under attack by a strong Chinese force. The division as a whole were pretty nearly wiped out.

During this battle, I called the artillery advisor who was with the Cap ROK and told him that his entire front line had collapsed. I advised him that I had many battalions of artillery available to help him and just let us know where to direct it. In the confusion of the battle, the higher commanders refused our offer of eight battalions of artillery that were attached to the 9th ROK.

He answered that his front line had not collapsed and they didn't need any help. The next day Col. Kang and I spent all morning rounding up elements of one of his battalions. We put it back together and equipped it with excess equipment that we had around and attached it to the 9th ROK until further orders. Only one regiment had held out. The KMAG advisor had been killed before they collapsed. He had stuck by his regiment and kept them fighting until he was killed. After his fall, they fell apart and ran too.

The next day we were given orders to prepare for defense which to the 9th ROK meant taking our artillery back where we had been. With the collapse of the Cap ROK, our right flank was completely exposed. During this battle the American 555 FA Bn. known as the 'Triple Nickel' of the 7th US Infantry Division was attached to the 9th Corp and were in support of the Cap ROK.

They reported that they had been over ran and that they were evacuating their position. We had put the our 30th BN across the

296

road from them in preparation for the planned offensive. At dawn Col. Kang and I proceeded with our two jeeps up the mule trail to check our battalion and to move them if necessary.

We were continuously running into an armored company from the third US Division coming at us in retreat. When they finally got out of our way, we reached the 30th FA position. The Bn commander met us and wondered why we were all the way up there. We told him that we couldn't reach them on the radio and that the battalion next to them, across the road had been run over so we had come to see for ourselves.

He said he had no problems and had only received some small arms fire during the night. Several shells had hit in the area and had damaged two trucks but there were no casualties. He even requested to stay there because he liked being up front ready to support his infantry.

I looked across the road at the Triple Nickel's position. As far as I could see, the howitzers were sitting in position and there were no personnel anywhere around. I picked up, four soldiers walking down the road from their battery. We put two of them in the Colonel's jeep and two of them in mine. They told me that the they had been told it was every man for himself as they were being run over.

I asked them where their carbine and their field equipment was. They said they had thrown it all away. Col. Kang and I decided that our 30th was now the front line. We thought it would be best to move them back into the previous position. The two trucks had been hit with fragments and were leaking gasoline. I advised them to burn them up to keep them from the enemy. Later that day I went by the battalion in the new position and saw those two trucks in Service battery to be repaired.

The Bn. commander said he had left a few men to guard them and he had borrowed an extra wrecker and towed them back. Nobody had bothered them. I commended him for a good job.

About 0900 I went by KMAG CP. On the hot line from Corp Artillery to the Advisors, I heard General O'Mera talking to the battalion commander of the Triple Nickel. He gave him a direct order to round up all of his men that he could find and to retake his battalion. The Bn. commander questioned if the guns were still there. He was told that the 9th ROK had reported that the guns were still there. The Bn. Commander's exact words were, "I'll try." I never knew how it came out.

We went through several more nights of small unit fighting and some shelling by both sides. On the 14th of July the ROKs came up with a new battle plan. It seems that the light aircraft was seeing a lot of movement from deep back in North Korea, towards the front of our division. Most of it was out of artillery range at this time. We laid on several air strikes and also at night we sent the B-26s using radar guidance to bomb these targets.

On the night of the 15th we put an entire infantry regiment on the outpost line. The purpose of this was to make the Chinese think that we had moved the main line of resistance about 2000 yards north of where it actually was. This unusual move make the Chinese army deploy their units and stack them up. After engaging them for about an hour, the 30th ROK Regiment would quickly drop back behind the line and go into reserve. Then we would increased our artillery fire to 17 battalions on the now densely populated north Korean and Chinese armies. We also brought in air strikes by the B-26 bombers on their rear areas.

It was Sunday afternoon and the advisors were playing soft ball against the Koreans. In the middle of the ball game, it was reported by a runner from the radio section that the North Koreans were marching four abreast down the railroad track toward Kumhwa, but were out of artillery range. They had never done anything like that in daylight before. This broke up the ball game and we all went back to work. We knew what was coming.

I immediately had the forward air controller contact all available flights. We opened up with the long range artillery that we had, which made it to the front of their advancing column. We swept the railroad track with artillery causing their troops to get in the ditches beside the railroad track.

We were lucky to pick up two flights of airplanes who were already in the air and carrying napalm. They were diverted to our sector When they were two minutes out, we fired some red white and blue smoke rounds to mark the target and the whole flight came right in two abreast, one up the right ditch and the other up the left ditch and wiped out everybody that was in the ditches.

Later more air strikes with napalm were brought in. We were hitting supply lines and assembly areas. Our light aircraft were doing one hell of a job spotting targets. We knew that this was the big one we had been expecting.

About 2000, when it got dark, the Chinese launched a full scale attack against our outpost line. About 2100 the outpost regiment quickly withdrew back through our line and returned to their mission of reserve. The Chinese had stacked as many troops and equipment as they could (well over a division) when they first hit our outpost line. It was the biggest concentration of the enemy recorded during the war. We immediately opened fire, using seventeen battalions of field artillery and one company of 4.2 mm mortars.

Forward air controllers called for night missions of B-26s. They bombed all supply points leading to the Kumhwa valley. I was on duty in the 9th ROK Fire Support Co-ordination Center. We proceeded to fire all battalions at their maximum rate. After two hours, I received a phone call from the 9th Corp Commander, General Jenkins himself, telling me, to "Make the valley a living hell." The reason I seemed to be in charge of everything was because I was the senior American in the Center at the time. I was the Assistant Artillery advisor to the 9th ROK Infantry Division Commander General Lee, who was in charge.

During the time leading up to this battle, there had been a drive to save ammunition. When I heard that General wanted to speak to me, I thought that I was going to catch hell for firing too much ammunition. It had been two hours before he called and we had already fired the maximum. I thanked the General for his call and told him that we were putting out everything we had. His statement relieved me of the responsibility of firing over the allotted amount. We continued to fire heavy artillery concentrations of both Korean and American Artillery battalions until around 0200 of the 16th. At that time the enemy activity had slowed down and they were no longer pushing forward. They never did engage our main line of resistance.

It had been raining cats and dogs all night. Little green tree frogs had invaded the FSCC. This was my first experience with those little frogs as they climbed up the wall and stuck on the ceiling. It was kinda entertaining to the personnel. It sorta relieved the pressure of the situation. The FSCC was well placed behind a mountain and never received any enemy rounds. When he wasn't watching, I slipped some of the little frogs in the air force Captains bedroll.

The next day we were notified that the North Koreans were willing to sign the truce but the South Koreans would not commit to signing it. As it turned out, the artillery concentrations supported by the Air Force B-26s was the last big battle of the war.

I talked with my Koreans about their refusal to accept the truce and their stock answer was, "Major Fishpaw, do you trust the communist?" Of course I said, "No". That was the same way the South Koreans felt. To this day the truce has never been settled and still for that very reason.

Near the end of the war, we were aware that the ROKs were building up enough supplies and equipment to outfit two more divisions. The plan was to continue fighting in the event they found the truce un-acceptable, even if the Americans pulled out. I was given orders to report to the American Third Infantry Division if this had happened.

On the 26 of July, 1953 it was announced that the truce would be signed and would take effect on Sunday, the 27th of July at 2200 Korean time. Up until that time the war would go on, all units would hold their position and not come out of their fox holes. The advisors would check all ammunition and be sure that it was all in the boxes, except for the rounds that would be needed until that time. The ROKs used that time to continue our usual routine of firing artillery and small unit engagements until 2200.

At about 2000, a battalion of a US airborne brigade marched out of the area that was going to be used as the DMZ (demilitarized zone) even though the army policy had been clearly disseminated to every officer and man. This battalion was hit by a Chinese artillery barrage while they were marching down the road toward their new position. Many men were unnecessarily killed, caused by their leaving two hours ahead of the designated time.

Starting on the 28th of July, the 9th ROK moved their line south about 3000 yards. North Koreans and Chinese also withdrew the same distance to the north. Within a few hours the demilitarize zone was established.

Now that the cease fire was in effect, we started a training program for all our artillery battalions. The infantry were doing the same thing. About this time, the 105 shells were arriving with a new explosive in them and I had heard on the grapevine that once in a while, they would go off about three seconds after leaving the gun. This was called composition 'B', which was like small corn flakes, packed in the shell. If there was any airspace left in the packing, the flakes would cause friction and ignite. When I was observing one of our units firing. I saw that their fire directions was in front of our guns. It was a good place to have it

300

when the Chinese were shooting at us and it was not unusual during combat to have the FDC in front of our own guns.

However, I told Kang that now we need to think more about safety. I suggested that we cease fire and move the personnel before we fired any more shells. He told the unit commander that the problem of possible premature bursts had increased and to move fire direction back behind the guns. In a few minutes they were set up to continue firing. They had left the camouflage net and some tables in the position that had been in front of the battery and would pick them up later. The very first round fired after the move exploded right over the FDC which by now had no personnel in it. Shell fragments tore the net down and busted up the two field tables that had been left there.

Col. Kang turned to me and said, "The reason I like you as an advisor is because you tell me about problems before things happen instead of after they happen."

Because many of our men had come right out of college and were put directly into combat with no training to speak of, Colonel Kong ordered the battalions to start unit training in preparation to take battalion tests by the United States umpire team from higher headquarters.

The first week we had battery training every day leaving just one battery in position, just in case something happened by the enemy. The second week, all four battalions started their training for the battalion tests. By my observation of the training, it was outstanding. I stopped worrying about their passing the tests. That is until I heard that the Chief Umpire was going to be Colonel Donald Thomson, the Captain whose battery I had taken over back in Landshut in 1949.

At that time he had come up short of about $300 worth of ski socks. I had made up a report of survey to write them off and asked him to give me a statement and his exact words were, "To hell with them, they will just have to catch up with me." I submitted the survey including his statement to me.

When he arrived to brief us on the tests he said that they had caught up with him and he had been made to pay for the shortages, as well as interest. But he didn't seem to be bitter about it. I was happy that he could laugh about it.

He started the tests, one battalion at a time and each battalion took three tests, one was a normal battalion operation, one was a problem occupying a position at night with survey and metro data and communications.

Major General Lee Ham Lin introduces Eli to Sigmond Rhea, president of the Republic of Korea. 1954.

The third test was rapid occupation of position from the road. The object of all the tests were to hit the target. The firing range was parallel of the DMZ firing east along highway 6. They finished testing in about two weeks and wrote up the report and held the critique with all the officers. Our battalions average score was in the mid nineties out of a possible one hundred. This was the highest score that I had ever heard of in Korea or any where else.

Because of the record that the 9th ROK had established, they were later chosen to represent South Korea in Viet Nam.

On the other hand, my opinion of the Chinese Army was that they weren't worth a damn. They had no concern for their troops and they would usually charge in mass. Only the lead platoon would be completely equipped with rifles. The second platoon might have a few rifles but the third, fourth, and fifth platoon had none. They were expected to pick up the weapons dropped by the leading platoons. The mass tactic of the Chinese made them easy targets for artillery, machine guns and the tactical air force. They would usually run out of ammunition after about two days of fighting. On the other hand, the North Koreans like the South Koreans make great soldiers.

It was time to start rebuilding the villages that had been destroyed by the war. United Nations were supposed to be providing building supplies to be delivered to each village by the army. Every unit was expected to provide the labor for the project. The biggest problem was that none of the material had arrived at our area and we needed to get started because winter was coming on. Our Division Artillery were assigned to rebuild thirteen villages.

Colonel Kang wondered how we could do this without the material. I said, "How did they build them before the war?" He said that they used natural materials that were available in the area. I suggested that we couldn't wait for supplies to be brought in. Why not do it the old fashioned way?

He thought that was a great idea. The men went into the forest and cut small trees for the framework of the building and they used clay for the floors. They made tunnels under the clay floor where a fire would be built at one end of a tunnel and the smoke would go out the other end. This would keep the clay floor warm all night. We would call that radiant heat. They had used this method for centuries. They could heat the whole house with a hand full of weeds.

The frame was made from three to four inch thick logs. Then they would gather vines from the woods and wrap them between the log frames to make the base for the walls. The clay was mixed with grass while it was wet. Two or three bare foot soldiers would tramp in this to mix it before it was plastered into the thatched vines. When they were finished it was as smooth as any plaster job in the states.

The roofs were thatched from straw. The Korean army engineers had already laid out and graded the streets. When it was finished, they had a very neat looking village which was much nicer than the ones that the war had knocked down.

The people who had been evacuated from there during the war would all be returning along with their mayor, their leaders and the Papa San. Every village had a Papa San. He was the elder of the village. Asiatics revere age. Papa San wore a black pointed hat woven from hair which had holes in it so that his wisdom could get out and be caught by all the people in the village.

Each family was put in a home almost exactly where their house had been before the war. We had to have a ceremony on a cold day to open the new village. To my surprise a little girl presented a bouquet of flowers to Colonel Kang and one to me. The division band played and it was a happy occasion.

In about a week after we finished the project, the UN supplies arrived. When we divided up what came in, there was about three 2×4s, a few boards, a roll of roofing felt, and one bag of concrete for each house. This was probably less than 5% of what was supposed to come in to rebuild these homes.

We delivered these items to each house and the Korean civilians put down the side walks with the cement. But they were mixed with so much sand that before a week had gone by, they were all cracked.

The new occupants took the two by fours and made lean-tos on the side of the houses with the black roofing felt. In a couple of weeks the place looked like shanty town. They would have been better off without any of the supplies, except for the school house and the city hall.

We probably had 80% of the material for them. The reason for that was because the size of the timbers made it hard to steal and sell on the black market. Most of the material had disappeared before it was put into the army's hands. The State Department representatives supervised the control until it was issued to the army at the port.

The United Nations also sent food for the Korean civilians. They delivered polished rice from the US which no oriental wanted to eat. They would trade a one hundred pound bag of American rice for a ten pound bag of unpolished rice. At first I was upset that they were dealing in the black market. The Korean officers explained that when the rice was polished, most of the beneficial parts were washed away. Because rice was their main food, it was very important that they use the unpolished rice because it was the most nutritious by far. Today, we use the powder washed off the rice in a popular dietary supplement called Q-10.

One day my Korean driver told me that one of the batteries in the 51st ROK Artillery Bn. was not feeding the men properly. I took a ride over and talked to some of the men who revealed nothing. I asked if I could touch their arm. When I pushed my thumb into their arm, the shape of my thumb would stay. This alerted me to the fact that they were undernourished.

I went to Col. Kang and alerted him to this fact and we went to the battery at lunch time. As the soldiers brought out their rice bowl after being served they looked to be heaped up. The Col. took one and with his fist, came down as if it were a catcher's mitt. His fist hit the bottom of the bowl.

The mess man had made it look as though the bowl was full by putting his fingers in the bowl as he was filling it. He would pull his fingers out and it looked like a heaping bowl of rice but the bowl was probably three quarters empty.

Kang relieved the battery commander on the spot. They had been selling the rations intended for the men on the black market. Korean military justice was swift and sure. I never saw that Captain again. Cheating the men of food was not a common practice.

The ROKs were renting out trucks to supplement their unit fund to increase the regular rations. It too was being stolen so they were not even getting their supplemental rations such as fish and kimshea. The Americans didn't like to see the military vehicles used as transportation for civilians between the villages but it was set up that way.

In the spring the Korean soldiers and the Korean Service Corp planted truck farms in the open fields in the area that they could cultivate. They grew mainly carrots, turnips, and cabbage. From these crops they made a concoction known as kimshea. It was their favorite food. The chopped up the vegetables were put in crocks where it was allowed to ferment for about six months. The 9th ROK had a kimshea factory in Seoul to process it for their division.

It smelled terrible. When we had a briefing, kimshea was served and the room smelled so bad, I could hardly stand it. Although some of our advisors really enjoyed it, I never got enough nerve to try any. All the oriental people love kimshea.

Poppies were another popular crop with the Koreans. They even grew them right behind the howitzers and the poppies were as well guard as the ammunition or the guns. They would bloom in early spring. I was invited by the battery officers to come around when they would be ready, to have a party with them.

I told them that I couldn't do that while I was on duty. Of course, I was always on duty. I did observe one of the battery opium parties. Because they knew how to use this drug, it never seemed to effect them in such a ways as to make them unable to do their job.

On a very cold day, when the temperature was below zero, two of my former Lieutenants from Landshut, had heard that I was near Kumhwa. They flew over to visit me in an L-19. They were with the US 3rd. Infantry Division. Campbell was the pilot and Waddell was with him.

When they landed, the spring that held the rear wheel broke in half, probably caused by the cold weather which made the steel brittle. He controlled the plane and came to a safe stop. The 9th ROK mechanics came out and looked over the problem. They gave them a jeep and offered to repair the spring before they came back from visiting me. Nobody spoke the others language. The average American who was not associated with the Korean people did not like them and did not trust them.

When the jeep arrived at the KMAG command post a few miles down the road, they told me what happened when they came in. Although they were doubtful of the ability of the ROK mechanic to fix their plane, I assured them that it was probably already fixed. I repeated that these were some of the smartest people that I had ever had the privilege of working with.

The Koreans immediately discovered that the strut holding the wheel could not be repaired so they called around to the other ROK airfields and found a brand new strut in the parts department. They took one of their own aircraft, flew over and picked up the new part and returned. The plane was repaired by the time we returned to the airfield. When we approached the field we could see the plane on ready line and in good shape. They both went over and carefully inspected the repairs and were amazed that they had been so well done. The plane had even been refueled and was ready for them to take off.

There were twenty six ROK airplanes on the field and the worst looking, maintenance wise, was the one that Capt. Campbell had just flown in. I told him that his plane needed a good washing and looked so bad, it was a bad example for my Koreans. He said, "This plane has been in continuous use during the war." I asked him what he thought we had been doing with our planes.

They hopped in the plane and got ready to start it up. It wouldn't start. A little Korean mechanic finally stood up on one of the wheels and looked in to see what Campbell was doing.

We assigned one of our mechanics to try to get it started by turning the propellor by hand. After we wore out about two mechanics, the little guy on the wheel gestured to the pilot for permission to make some adjustments of the controls in the cockpit. This took about thirty seconds. Then he signaled for the mechanics to turn the prop again. The plane quickly started and was purring like a kitten immediately.

I got to laughing so hard that despite the cold weather and a strong wind blowing down from Siberia, tears of laughter were rolling down my face and freezing on my parka. I watched them take off, back to the 3rd. US Division.

Colonel Kang, who had been my closest and most trusted associate in the 9th ROK, was getting married. The wedding was to be in the Catholic Church in Seoul. The Church had brick walls and a clay floor. The pews were made similar to pews in almost all the catholic churches that I had been in. The Commanding General Lee Ham Lin was to perform the ceremony.

The General and I were the honored guests at the wedding. I found out later that I was to brief the bride and groom about the important task that they were about to undertake and warn them of all the pit falls that they could encounter. I told them that I would rather not be trying to give him advice on marriage because I had probably already given him more advice than he wanted to hear. So the General selected another VIP to take my place.

The ceremony went off perfectly, each VIP was giving them all the gloomy news of what terrible things could happen to them. Then the General stood behind the pulpit and administered the rites of marriage. After the ceremony, most of the honored guests got in our jeeps, many were decorated with bunting and flowers and small flags. We paraded through town and up to a castle way up on a hill overlooking the city. We drove the jeeps right up to the main entrance of the building on the brick walkway. We got out and looked at the scenery. The Koreans pointed out the important landmarks of their history.

The purpose of this little trip was to give them time to set up a banquet in the largest restaurant in Seoul. When I stepped into the banquet room there were six or seven hundred soldiers in uniform setting at the tables. My table was right up front. I had a ROK 1st. Lieutenant with me as an interpreter. The 9th ROK Division band furnished the music. At that time I learned another small detail that I was expected to carry out. I was expected to sing at least one American Song and the band would accompany me.

I figured, what the hell, they wouldn't understand any of the words anyway, so I got up there and started to sing. My first song was the 'Beer Barrel Polka'. To my surprise, I hadn't sang three words when the band picked up the melody and played it perfectly, including the verse and the chorus. I got a standing ovation and they wouldn't stop cheering until I sang another song. I had already been served some kind of wine. I sang 'Stout

Hearted Men'. Again the band accompanied me without a flaw. Again I was applauded but I refused to sing anymore.

After that, many of the guests sang their favorite Korean songs. Short speeches by many VIPs were completed before they served the meal which was kimshea. They asked me what I wanted to eat and I told them steak and french fries which I was served. It was the only time I had steak while I was in Korea.

I had earned some R and R. to Japan. I elected to go to the southern Island of Kyushu to the resort city of Beppu. The town was very similar to Florida. It also featured hot springs and hot baths. There was plenty of fishing and swimming. It was a nice place to spend a restful week. The Japanese were very courteous and seemed happy to see us.

After the seven days, I boarded the train that took us back to the airport near Tokyo to fly back to Seoul airport K-2 where my driver picked me up with my jeep.

With the war over, the USO booked Marilyn Monroe and her husband, Joe DiMaggio with other dancer, singers and comedians to entertain the troops. Johnnie Cash and his future wife, June Carter were billeted in the KMAG Commander's quarters and three of the dancing girls were in my bunker. We moved out and slept in the BOQ. They gave a show for the troops, including the Koreans, in our area around Kumhwa. It was put on in the Arrowhead Bowl which was the named for the US Second Infantry Division, who had created it in a natural setting between the mountains.

There must have been twenty thousand troops there. I was so far from the stage that about all I could see was a purple dot singing, 'Diamonds are a Girl's Best Friend'. This was a very democratic theater and it was first come, first serve. There were no chairs or seats. You could pick a good hard rock or sit on the ground. No problem, we were used to it. Both the Americans and the Koreans appreciated the efforts of the entertainers. The Americans all felt it was a touch of home and the Koreans were eager to hear the American music.

In our post war CP, the Koreans quickly built a small house as quarters for the KMAG detachment commander who was now Col. Radcliff. About a day after his quarters were completed a brand new Jamesway hut was delivered in a big box for the CO. He asked any of the field grade advisors if they wanted it. None of the others did, so I accepted it.

Major Eli Fishpaw and Colonel Kang Min Kwan ROK. Eli received two citations from the Korean government and the 9th Republic of Korea Division. Also a mother of pearl inlaid name plaque and a pair of Korean shoes. 1954.

The 9th ROK engineers graded a spot for it and put it up for me. The box it came in became the floor for the quonset style hut. The outer surface was all one piece of OD plastic and the inside was white. Between the plastic sheets was about two inches of insulation. The front and back both had doors in the plywood. It was put together like an erector set. The Koreans made a patio in front of my hut with a stone border all around and a barbecue pit. They even created an underground ice box made from sawdust and ammunition boxes for me to have a place to keep my beer cold. We got our ice from the Quartermaster who would put out an extra piece for my box when they delivered the food.

They also made me some really nice outdoor furnitures from empty ammunition boxes. The Colonel liked it so much when it was finished that he wanted to let me have his cottage and he would move into my hut.

In about two days, Lt. Col. Stevens was transferred in from the US 955 FA Bn. It was a 155mm howitzer outfit where he had been the battalion commander. He was to spend a couple weeks with me getting oriented to take over my job because I was due to rotate back to the USA.

Col. Stevens had been a West Point football player and later coached the plebe team and recruited players for the great Earl Blake during the glory years of Army football. He had been sent to Korea about the time the truce went into effect and had taken over a battalion.

As it came near the time for me to rotate, my job was suddenly a choice assignment and many of the West Point types were eager to get it. After taking him around to meet the unit commanders, he started to make rounds on his own. I began to sense that he didn't really like the assignment.

In July of 1954, word came that the army was looking for two Lt. Colonels with Military Academy credentials to go to South Vietnam as observers. They would wear civilian clothing and display no weapons. They were to report directly to the Pentagon on the situation in that country. The French were still there but were on their way out.

Col. Stevens immediately volunteered and got the job. We had a lot of discussion about the assignment. I said that it seemed to me that we were about to get into another useless war that would be worse than Korea. He said that the Chinese were about to take it over. My answer was, "We should give it to them and it would serve them right."

The French found out that although they had made a lot of improvements there during the time that it was one of their colonies, it was still an unappreciated liability to them.

A few days before Col. Stevens was to take my job, an Australian Colonel from Eighth Army had been to the 9th ROK making an ammunition inspection. He said that our ammunition was in good condition. He didn't dream that we were not all screwed up. That was the way everybody who did not know the Koreans thought.

While we were eating supper, he told me that he knew where we were going to fight the next war. He observed that the Americans always fought where the beautiful women were and that the women in Saigon were more beautiful than those in Paris, London or Rome. He'd been in all of them. When he went back to Headquarters he gave us a superior report.

With Stevens leaving for Vietnam my departure was delayed until I could train a new replacement. A major came in a few days later. He had experience in all phases of artillery so that, other than introducing him around, he was ready to take over. I so informed Col. Ratcliff and received my orders the next day to report to Inchon Port of Embarkation as a casual officer to return to the USA.

I was told that I would be the detail officer, but there was no need for me to be in the advanced detail and to just go aboard in the normal troop loading procedure. As I waited to be called, I heard them call Fishpan. I was in no mood to correct them. I just answered, "Eli I." and went on up the gangplank.

Half way up, the adjutant was leaning over the rail of the main deck and hollered at me to hurry up and get aboard, and report to the Troop Commander as soon as possible. "We need You." I hadn't been that important yesterday. I took my time getting my gear in my stateroom before I finally reported.

When I talked to the troop commander, he said that his biggest mistake was thinking that I wasn't needed in the advance party. He said, "The detail officer is responsible for loading the troops." The Colonel told me that everything was screwed up because the men who would carry out the various duties for the voyage, such as mess personnel, security, police and sanitation details to clean the public areas including the heads were all over the ship. Nobody knew where anybody was. They hadn't eaten since they got on the ship because none of the mess people had shown up when they had been ordered to report to the galley on the public address system. The entire boat load of soldiers were casuals. They were mostly combat veteran and their only interest was to get home. Working was not on their mind. He said, "That is the situation, What are you going to do about it?"

I already knew the problem from past experience and immediately told him that we would just have to unload the ship and reload it. He ran to the port hole and looked out. "We're already twenty miles out to sea."

I explained that we would instruct the troops to take all their gear and go up on the open deck. I told the adjutant to make up a complete new set of mess passes with different colors from the ones that they had originally been issued. When the men were all on the deck at about 1000 I got on the horn and announced that all cooks and KPs were to report to boat station 'A'. There we had three mess Sergeants take the old boarding passes and give each man a new pass that was a different color. We broke them down into three shifts and each Sergeant took his group to a compartment near the galley. The MPs were treated the same way as were soldiers who were designated for the cleaning of the various public areas. Every man aboard had some detail but none of them were expected to work more than two days during the 12 day voyage.

The old man thought that I was crazy. By 1115 everybody was in their proper place and the situation was under control. I announced on the public address system that if anybody failed to report for their duty, disciplinary action would be taken. I told them, "The fastest way to get back to the States is for everybody to do their assigned share of the work."

The very first day, three men were missing from the mess detail. I took a couple MPs and a mess Sergeant and went up on deck looking for them. We found them in a short while playing cards on the open deck. I told the MPs to place them under arrest and put them in the brig, and we would determine what action we would need to take.

When I went to the Ole Man and told him that three people had failed to show, I recommended that he should give them Troop Commanders punishment. The maximum punishment was confinement in the brig for 7 days on bread and water. He was very reluctant to give them that punishment, but I insisted that if he didn't take strong action, right then, we would end up with a route order boat load of soldiers.

Reluctantly, with tears in his eyes, he agreed to do it but he didn't like it. The men were brought in and allowed to tell their story. In general they had no real excuse. The sentence was given and they were taken to the brig immediately.

The brig was in the most uncomfortable part of the ship, right over the screws. We immediately hit a large storm and it was a rough place to be. Then I went to the Colonel after three days and told him that it would be a good idea to release them and let them tell the other troops about what had happened to them. It also made him look like a good guy. My part was to be the bad guy.

With the problem solved, the rest of the trip I spent playing cribbage with the Colonel. When the voyage was over he gave me a hand shake and a "Well done." Every officer and man on the ship appreciated what I had done.

When we arrived in Seattle the mayor and a full band was out to greet us. It turned out that we were the first ship to arrived after their reception center had been re-opened. After checking in I was told that I had the rest of the day off. I called a cab and told him that I wanted to get some hard crabs and some good cold beer. He knew just the place and took me to Seattles Fisherman's Wharf to a restaurant right over where they unloaded the fish and crabs. I ordered a dozen crabs and a bottle of beer.

The waitress asked me if I was sure that I wanted a whole dozen. She asked if she could bring them one at a time and I said yes. While I was looking out the window at the scenery, she returned with an a Alaskan King Crab on a big meat platter and it hung four or five inches over both ends. It was the biggest crab I had ever seen. It was not like the Atlantic blue crabs that I was used to. I could not even finish eating that first one.

21

On My Own

Bernice:

Neither one of us wanted to feel sorry for ourselves but we both felt sorry for the other one. Neither of us mentioned it until Eli was almost ready to go.

He had his foot locker out in the back yard and was packing it with clothing and stuff when Mary Jane, who was about three, got in the locker and announced that she was going to Korea with daddy. Eli laughs about that to this day. She would have had a long stay in the dark as he didn't see it again until he arrived in Seattle when he had returned to the states.

We decided that it would be easier for all of us, if I just took him to the airport and left. I didn't want to stand around waiting for the plane to take off. Bill was too young to understand the situation but Ginny summed it up the best when she kissed her daddy and gave him a direct order, "Daddy, don't get killed". Mary Jane's reaction was a little different. We had just gotten home and she threw up on the kitchen floor. I was on my own.

Every time the Army Times arrived, I would check the promotion list which they always carried. That was how I learned that Eli had been promoted to Major. That was 1 June, 1953. Don Rattan, our former neighbor, had been promoted to Major on the very same list. Being a West Pointer he eventually got to be a Major General.

As soon as school was out, I decided to visit the folks in Wisconsin. I loaded up the family and headed up the road. Bill wasn't able to walk yet so he rode in the little chair that I had tied to the passenger seat in the front. It was before safety chairs for kids had been designed.

Mary Jane was still bothered with motion sickness. I crossed the Chattahoochee river and had just barely passed a big, slow moving truck on the two lane road when I had to stop to take care of some problem. Problem solved, the truck went on by and no sooner had I passed him again on the curving road than I had to make another stop. I have no idea how many times I stopped, but I must have passed that truck a dozen time before I got to Birmingham.

By the time I got to Tupelo, Mississippi it was about three in the afternoon. It was not nearly as far as I had planned or hoped to go that day, but I was so tired that I had almost crept into town. I felt that if I needed to make a quick stop, I wouldn't know how. I got a motel and as soon as the kids were settled with books and crayons, I collapsed on the bed. Motels had not yet installed TVs in their rooms. The next day I was recovered and made better time. In all, it took three days to get to Wisconsin.

Kenneth's kids, Dan and Sue, were about Ginny's age and they played to-gether nicely. Sometimes they included Mary Jane and some times they made a game of excluding her. My mother and dad had moved into their new house, but there was still a pile of cement block in the back yard that the kids could climb. Dan was an acting enthusiast and they created elaborate plays. Sometimes the cement blocks were the stage and sometimes the back porch of grandpa's house was.

I was able to help out with some of the many projects such as painting the new house, installing tile on the cellar steps and chopping up old boards for heating fuel.

I guess I had been there about three weeks when the war in Korea was in its last stage. One day I read in the paper that there had been a major battle at Kumhwa. This was where Eli was. He was the senior and only artillery advisor to the 9th ROK Division at the time. The report was that one Korean division had been destroyed and one American Major, an advisor, was missing. No name, no division number. That sounded very much like our man. I decided that since my address of record was Columbus, it was time to go home. When I got there, I found a letter from Eli describing that night.

It had, indeed been wild, but his division had held and their artillery had actually prevented the Chinese from breaking through until the line could be restored. Soon after that, the cease fire went into effect. He stayed in Korea for almost a year after the cease fire.

It was while Eli was in Korea that Ginny decided that she wanted to join the church. It was the custom to hold preparatory classes for fourth graders, prior to joining the church, but she made the decision on her own and was very sincere so I followed up on her decision.

The pastor at the time was a retired bishop named Cushman. He had come to us because the newly assigned pastor had dies shortly after his arrival and the conference felt it necessary for a church of such stature to have a pastor of equal stature. All the good ones had just been assigned, so they dragged the Bishop out of retirement.

Bishop Cushman was a good one. He had about two good sermons and he delivered them often. He wrote poetry and recited some of his favorites from the pulpit. He claimed that he had met God face to face and was very convincing. After hearing his sermons one Sunday, she just said she was going to join the church the next Sunday and she did. She just walked up to the front of the church with all those other new members and joined. I walked up and stood with her. I don't know what she was thinking but I cried.

I joined a bowling league in Columbus. I felt that it was best if I could have some time away from the kids so I arranged for a lady to come in one night a week while I went bowling. One night she didn't show up, so against my better judgement, I left Ginny in charge and went anyway. When I got home Billy had defied his big sister by cutting up the favorite Child Craft book.

As a bowler I did fairly well. At that time, most of the south preferred the smaller duck pins, but ten pins were just becoming popular. While I was in Columbus, the state of Georgia organized a Georgia Women's Bowling Association and held their first state wide tournament in Marietta. Our local league sent a team of five. I was on the team and we won all the prizes.

The organization held an emergency meeting and voted that no team could win both scratch and handicap so we took the scratch trophy which is more prestigious. I can say that I was a member of the first Georgia Women's Bowling Association championship team. I have the trophy to prove it.

That summer they were widening Benning Road just down the hill from us. To do this they had to break up several cement drive ways. I arranged for the trucks that were hauling away the broken chunks to dump them in my drive way. I spent the whole summer laying cement chunks against the bank between our house and the one up the hill which was eroding. I didn't use any mortar but when I was finished I planted English Ivy between the blocks. It proved to be very hard on my back, which has given me problems ever since.

The builder had put down a low wall of eight inch concrete blocks along the drive way to channel off the water coming down the hill. Ginny, Mary Jane and their friends used to sit on that wall and break little stones they found, which were often transparent. They said they were making diamonds.

I had discovered that there was no good place to store cleaning supplies and other bulky equipment that every house hold needs. With Eli gone, Ginny in school and Billy and Mary close enough to play together, as well as with several other neighborhood children their age, I had time to pursue any number of projects. My first one was to create a broom closet. It went from floor to ceiling and had two doors and two compartments, one over the other.

One of our neighbors was the Purvis family. They were the only family that didn't have army connections. He was a manager for Royal Crown Cola. They had two children, Laurie and Timmy who were about the same ages as Mary Jane and Billy. He also had a band saw and a table saw with a set of shapers, that could be put on instead of the blade. Best of all, he didn't seem to mind if I used any of his toys.

I was in heaven. I made a rocking horse and a toy stove big enough to stand up to. It had an oven that you could open and close and control knobs made with thread spools. I even made cowboy suits for Billy and Mary Jane. I painted the horse with aluminum paint and we called him Silver.

When Ginny was ready to start the third grade, Muscogee county had built a new elementary school about three quarters of a mile from the house and they were organizing a PTA. Most of the families were associated with Fort Benning and with my inability to keep my mouth shut, I ended up as the first president.

I remember the first real meeting we had. I had arranged for the County Superintendent of Schools, William Henry Shaw, to be our speaker. I had met him at St. Luke's church where he taught an adult Sunday School class. Well, we had over a hundred people show up for the meeting and no Mr. Shaw. I was frantic. What a downer that would have been. I called him at his home and although he had not gotten the message for some reason, he came right over. The organization was off to a flying start.

Some of my other officers were from civilian families who were a little less likely to move away than the military variety. At the time, I had acquired an old walnut table that Uncle Charles had found in an old house they had rented. It wasn't worth anything except for the wood. It had turned legs so I cut off about three inches of a leg. The man who lived behind me turned a handle and I had a gavel for the new PTA. The civilian ladies thought that was the greatest. They bragged to their Columbus friends that their Yankee president used "YANKEE" ingenuity.

On another occasion I demonstrated Yankee ingenuity for our Sunday School class. We were studying about American Indians and had the project of making sock dolls. The problem was, we couldn't find the right color socks. I remembered all too well how the red Georgia mud made the kids underwear impossible to keep white. So we bought several pairs of white socks and I buried them in the ditch beside the drive way. By the end of the week they were the exact color we wanted.

I remember one project of PTA to raise some money was to have all the various classes collect used coat hangers to sell to the dry cleaner. The prize was to be a party. The kids were enthusiastic and we had literally thousands of wire hangers. That was the biggest mess. I eventually sorted them all into bundles of 25 and we realized a nice profit.

Another activity that I became involved with was the Girl Scouts. I had been an assistant leader in Landshut with Caroline Waddell, whose husband was in Eli's 'C' Btry. At South Columbus, another experienced leader, in the person of Helen Reigle, came forward to take a troop and I became her assistant. We became close friends.

She did not have any children, but she had two beautiful cocker spaniels. They also had an MG sports car. Ginny was in a different troop. We did many fun things with the girls. Helen was a specialist in crafts. She had a loom in her family room and did weaving and things of that nature.

For Halloween one year we had a carnival at the school and there was a prize for the best costume. I did Ginny up as a witch. I had some old, high button shoes and a black shawl. I made a pointed hat from a soap powder box and I made some green grease paint for her face with noxema and food coloring. Because I had lived in Germany, I had seen the brooms the Germans made of twigs, so I made a real witch's broom. The supreme touch was Black Prince. She held him in her arms. He wasn't at all happy about the whole affair and I got him back into the car as soon as I could after the judging. She won first prize. It was a large bag of bubble gum. I had always had an aversion to all chewing gum so it was an act of courage and restraint for me to put up with the prize. I encouraged her to be very generous with her friends.

The house was heated with a gas floor furnace that was located in a small hall in the center of the house. To function properly it was necessary to leave the doors to the three bed-rooms, the bath room and the living room open, especially the living room as that was where the thermostat was located. One cold day, I was out in the back yard hanging out clothes when I heard Mary Jane screaming. When I rushed in, I discovered that Billy had fallen on the floor furnace and burned his hands.

They had discovered that it was fun to close all the doors in the hall and then jump on the register over the furnace in the dark. This made a grand noise that echoed like being inside a drum. Of course, they didn't realize that with the doors closed, the furnace would go on and since the heat did not reach the thermostat, it would not go off. The register had become extremely hot. When Billy fell he naturally tried to get up which pressed his hands even deeper into the hot metal.

After I had stopped the burning with cold water, I took him out to the post hospital and they applied a burn ointment and bandaged both hands. Because the burns were third degree, there didn't seem to be a lot of pain. But I had one very bewildered two year old boy who couldn't find his hands. Up to that point he had been a thumb sucker. That is such a harsh way to be cured.

Mary says that is one of her earliest memories. It seems I blamed her for the incident and of course, Bill bears the scars to this day. I am sure she was not old enough to realize the danger involved, and I was wrong to scold her. I'm sorry Mary. I wish your earliest memory could have been a more pleasant one. After that incident, I bought a guard to set over the register to prevent any more accidents. Eventually, the floor furnaces were aban-doned for less dangerous heating systems.

That same little hallway also had a drop down attic door with a ladder in it. I stored stuff in the attic. One day I was in the attic throwing down some things that I thought I might use I found a German celluloid doll that went down and landed on the furnace. When the furnace came on a few minutes later, the heat ignited the doll and I had a full blown fire in my hall. I came out of the attic without using the ladder. I filled the waste basket in the bathroom with water from the faucet in the tub and doused the fire. No great harm was done, but I was one very scared mother with one very smelly house. I took my two kids and went to the neighbors while my house aired out.

Columbus, Georgia was one of the hottest places I had ever been. When they were building the house, we had bought a 36" attic fan and had it installed. It helped some. The windows on the shady side of the house were left open about two inches so that, with the fan, the air was at least always in motion. The summer before Eli came home from Korea, the furniture was paid for, so I went all out and bought a room air conditioner which was installed in the dining/living room window.

That summer I also bought our first TV set. The combination was a great temptation for kids to stay inside. The favorite kid shows were Howdie Doodie, Pinkie Lee, and the Mickey Mouse Club. We also enjoyed I Love Lucy, Lawrence Welk, and the Honeymooners.

Ginny had a strong desire to be a dancer. She had a dress with a flared skirt and she would twirl around in the back yard to make her skirt stand out like a ballet dancer. There was a dance school at the post so I enrolled both Ginny and Mary Jane. I don't believe either one of them were very good, but they went through the motions. They were even in a dance recital. Each of them did one ballet number and one tap number.

The school had many more students than those on post and the recital was in an auditorium down town. It was quite elaborate and costumes I thought were too expensive. It was for two nights. Half of the mothers were to be back stage one night to help dress the kids, while the other half watched the show. Then they traded around. My night to watch, I took movies, but the light was not good enough and about all I got was a picture of the silver and glitter star that Ginny held in her ballet number.

For Christmas of 1953 my mother and dad drove to Georgia to spend the holiday with us. By then Billy was walking and the girls were the right age to really get excited about Christmas. My mother was in her glory, making Christmas cookies with the help of her granddaughters.

Mom had often welcomed people at the church in Milton who would occasionally drop in for Sunday service as they were traveling. She planned that sometime, when she was traveling, they would do that. When they left Columbus to return to Wisconsin, they left on Sunday morning. They had gone as far as Selma, Alabama, where they attended the Methodist church service. She was so thrilled, because everyone had been so friendly. Several years later, when there was a civil rights flare up in Selma, she was so disappointed that such a friendly city could be a part of that unhappy problem.

∼ 22 ∼

Back Home at Benning

Eli:

I had requested to return to Fort Benning and that request had been granted. When I left Seattle by plane I had my orders in my pocket to report to the 41st Field Artillery with fifteen days delay in route. I was going to be the S-3.

Bernice met me at the Columbus airport with the whole family. It was great to see them. The first impression was how much they had grown. The girls who were now three and eight. They both recognized me immediately. Billy who was only a year old when I left was now over two but probably did not remember me. However, when he saw me kissing his mother and his sis-

Left to right: Mary Jane, Bernice, Eli, Billy and Virginia. Columbus, 1954.

ters, he was standing there with his arms out, waiting his turn. My first assignment from Bernice was to teach him how a man goes to the bathroom.

I called the battalion to tell them that I was in town and would be reporting on the 15th of August 1954. When the commander heard that I was in town, he had the adjutant call back and ask me to come in and see him.

This was what I was hoping to avoid during my delay in route. I reluctantly agreed to meet him in the mess hall for coffee around 0900. This was the battalion that I had been in before I went to Korea and felt that I was well acquainted with their mission, which hadn't changed.

When I went out, he and the adjutant were at the mess hall drinking coffee when I joined them. Right beside the Colonel was some sort of a book that was twice as thick as the Sears catalogue. I knew then that he was up to something. After a short greeting and a sip of coffee he said, "I have something here for you to study before you sign in." He passed it over to me. I could see that it said, STANDARD OPERATING PROCEDURE FOR TRAINING, 41 FA Bn.

I just glanced at it and said, "It looks like it is in great detail. I'll study it when I report in," and pushed it back to him. He pushed it back and said he thought I should study it before I reported in. To tell the truth, his SOP was, like we say in the army, "Cover your butt with paper." Several times during the conversation, that big SOP was pushed back and forth. Later the adjutant was telling the rest of the officers that it looked like a tennis game with the Ole Man's SOP moving back and forth between the Colonel and the Major. "When they both left it was still on the table, so I took it back to headquarters."

It wasn't long after that when I learned that he had, personally, made a major mistake. He had been in the fire direction center and had made them change to his data. But he had failed to account for the difference of the elevation of the target. They were firing timed fuse to break forty yards in the air over some tanks. Because of his error, rounds hit the ground amongst the tanks and caused a lot of noise which was hard on the tankers' ears. Several tanks were damaged and many antennas were blown off. The next day, he had made all the personnel in the battalion fire direction ride in the tanks as punishment for the error that he had made. They made sure the data was prepared correctly and went out and got in the tanks. The tanks attacked the same hill again and the rounds broke in the air just as they were supposed to and hardly scratched the tanks.

On the 2 December, 1954 the 41st FA was re-designated the 23rd Field Artillery Bn., 23rd. Infantry Division. Nothing was changed except the numbers and the colors, history and arm patches which was now a blue patch with the four stars of the Southern Cross. It had been the Americal Division in the Pacific during WWII.

I was the S-3 from August, 1954 to May of 1955 when I became the executive officer for a couple months. When the Colonel was transferred to the Artillery Committee of the Infantry School, I was appointed the battalion Commander of the 23rd Field Artillery Bn. on 5 August, 1955.

Late one night, there was an incident in the motor pool involving security. The guard on post yelled for the Corporal of the Guard. When the Corporal and the OD went immediately to where the call had come from, there was an officer, caught in the barb wire on the top of the eight foot high chain link fence. The guard had slammed a round in the chamber of his carbine and ordered the intruder to stay right where he was.

When the OD and the Corporal arrived, they helped the man down from the top of the fence. He identified himself as Major John Eisenhauer, Fort Benning staff duty officer. He said that he was out checking security of the motor pools. After checking his identification he was released. He questioned the fact that the guard had live ammunition. He was told that in this battalion nobody goes on guard with an empty gun. He was very lucky that he had not tried to move from the top of the fence. Case closed.

One of our biggest missions was giving demonstrations to the Infantry schools on how to use artillery to the best advantage. If properly utilized the artillery could and did save many lives in combat.

We would go out on the range and set up on Monday and fire a few practice missions. We also practiced co-ordinating fire power with the Air Force for putting in bombing stricts, including napalm. The planes came from Texas. We would practice again on Tuesday and the Artillery Committee would observe and make corrections or add to previous demonstrations. On Wednesday we would run a complete dress rehearsal which many of the classes at the Infantry School and sometimes the dependents of the Army personnel would be invited to attend and watch from bleachers.

On Thursday, the problem known as 2660 also called 'Types of Artillery Fire', took the center of the stage. Many Congressmen and industrialist would be invited guests, along with lots of high ranking military personnel from Washington and the Military Schools all over the country.

The civilian VIPs would be invited to have their lunch with the troops and eat out of a mess kit. Some of them were even allowed to fire a round and then keep the brass casing. One day General Jimmy Doolittle, the hero who lead the bombing of Tokyo, was attending our demonstration. He made the remark that while they were eating, we should turn those guns around and hit all the no good politicians. Of course we ignored that comment.

New permanent barracks had been completed and we had been assigned a new area in the new buildings. We had been living in old WWII wooden barracks. The unit morale was very high and the men had just finished painting all the buildings. The grass was looking good. Every battery had two whole barracks with their own mess hall, orderly room, day room, and supply room.

No one really wanted to move to the new facilities. The consolidation of a whole battalion in only part of a large building with a consolidate mess and other activities would break down completely the unit integrity that our five batteries had worked so hard to achieve. I was stonewalling and did not schedule any time for the move.

Right in the middle of a 2660 demonstration, when I returned to the battalion about 1700, I had orders to report to my commanding Officer, Col. Sutton. He immediately asked what steps had been taken to make the move. I answered that the phone system had been installed. I said that I was hoping he would forget about moving us and let us stay where we were.

He informed me that he had no plan to forget it and gave me a direct order to move immediately. "How long will it be before you will be operational in the new area?" My answer was that we would have supper in the old area and by 2000 we would be operational in the new area and have breakfast there tomorrow morning.

He said, "That's kinda fast isn't it?" I told him, "Morale is high. I will give them the order as soon as I leave your office and our telephones will be operating by 1800. The unit move will be completed by 2000." I saluted and went out the door as fast as I could.

I held a battery commanders meeting. They were all at my headquarters waiting for me. I told them that we had been given an order to move as soon as possible and to start moving right now. The move should be completed by 2000. The only question they asked was if they could use the civilian truck that the men owned, because there were not enough military vehicles.

I gave my permission and you should have seen the mass movement to the new barrack which was not more than half a mile. All the traffic stopped and moved off the road to watch the action. We did get a squad of MPs to assist in traffic control for safety reasons.

Before 2000 all the units had reported that they were completely in the new area and the mess personnel had reported to the consolidated mess. The whole battalion had to be at the range at 0900 the following day to begin the VIP phase of 2660. The problem went off without a hitch.

Whoever designed the motor pool at the new area did a stupid thing. They put the gas pump just to the side of the drive way and behind the wash rack. When the drivers would wash their vehicles and back off the wash rack, once or twice a week someone would get careless. They would cut their wheels too soon and run over the pump. This was dangerous and a nuisance to say the least. Whenever this happened, the damage was just put on survey and there was no cost to anyone in the unit. It was really unnecessary and it didn't take long for me to put a stop to it. I had a sign put up in front of the wash rack saying, "Back straight back. Any driver hitting the gas pump will pay for the damage." Only one man paid the cost to replace it. After that no one ever hit another pump.

My S-3 was Captain Millard Allen. He had been captured in North Korea and had spent many months of the war in a North Korean POW stockade. He told me that he had received notice that he was to be brought before a board of officers to see why he should not be eliminated from the service due to his conduct in the prison camp.

He explained to me exactly what had happened. He had taken over feeding the other prisoners. He told about how the Chinese would just put the food in the gate and it was every man for himself. The food would be gone before the sick and the wounded were fed. He went to the highest ranking prisoner, a Lt. Colonel who was sick and asked to be put in charge of the food. He got the job. Then he went to the Chinese and informed them that he was in charge of the food and asked for it to be given directly to him instead of just pushing it through the gate. They agreed that they would handle it that way.

He established a system where the sick and wounded were fed first. What was left was divided with the rest of the camp. He also would go around the camp and find prisoners who had nothing wrong with them but had just given up. They would just lay there and wait to die. He would get them on their feet and make them walk around.

He even made furniture out of the trees that grew in the compound. He had taken the steel arch out of his boot and sharpened it on a stone to make a knife. Most of the prisoners were Air Force officers.

Not long after I heard his story, I received a call that there were only three officers on the post that were qualified to be on this board of investigation. To be qualified, the officer was required to have served in combat in Korea as a commander, you needed to have top secret clearance and a clean record of service. The board was made up of three officers. I tried to challenge myself off the detail because he was one of my better officers, they refused to allow me to be excused.

In about two days the board convened in the Infantry Center to determine if he should be discharged from the service. Captain Allen discovered that there were many of the officers at Eglin Air Force Base in Florida who had been in that camp at the same time that he was. He called a senior officer at Eglin and told him of the situation. He volunteered to bring a whole plane load of officers who had also been in the same camp with him to testify on his behalf.

When the board met they went through the formal ritual requesting that any objection to the make up of the board be stated. I objected because I was Captain Allen's CO and also a close friend. They still refused to excuse me and board proceeded.

The evidence was introduced by the CIC investigators who had interview all returning prisoners. Many of them complained about a Captain Allen who had been a turn coat and spoke on the radio for the enemy. He even had a fancy apartment in town. Many of the statements made to the CIC in Korea had been made by officers who had come from Eglin to speak for Captain Allen. There must have been about thirty five of them.

After the CIC had made their opening statements, and read a few of the statements of the other prisoners, they called the first person present who had made a statement against Captain Allen. He explained to the board that there were two Captain Allens in that prison camp. During the interview, there was no mention of first names. He said that the Captain Allen he was making the statement about was a negro and he was a turncoat. He thought that they were making a mistake and that Captain Millard Allen had probably saved his life as well as that of many others.

After listening to several more of the Air Force officers present, it was obvious that the investigators had the wrong Captain Allen. Witnesses were asked if anyone knew if the other Captain Allen, whose name was Clifford, was still in the service. It turned out that he had been promoted to Major and was stationed at the Presidio in California. Because of the pending meeting of this board, Captain Millard Allen had been passed over for his promotion to Major. The board recessed and re-convened the following morning at 0900. Prior to opening again, contact was made with the Presidio and it was confirmed that there was a Major Clifford Allen and he was there and in good health. He was invited to testify before our board but refused.

The finding of the board was that Millard Allen was

(1) completely innocent of all charges and on further review, should have been award a metal for his conduct. That he should be promoted, retro active, to the time that he had been passed over.

(2) All records of the proceeding including all statements from witnesses, be forwarded to the Army headquarters in California for the purpose of determining the fitness of Major Clifford Allen to remain in the service and the possibility of Court Martial.

The board thanked all the witnesses including those who did not have an opportunity to testify for their co-operation.

Bernice:

When Eli came home, we paved the driveway with concrete. We did a section about eight feet wide by ten feet long at a time. When the driver of the cement truck saw what we were doing he offered to bring us the bottom of his barrel each day after work which he would normally have to waste. We paid him for it but not nearly as much as we would have paid for a fresh load. It did come at an inconvenient time and had to be worked quickly before it set up.

Torch Hill Road was not paved when we first moved there and that was sometimes a problem, especially when it was dry. The dust would really fly. It was such a nuisance because the windows were always open in the summer. I learned that if the homeowners would buy the material, the county would pave our street.

I opened an account and set out to collect from the owners. Most of the owners were military people like ourselves who lived on the street and wanted the problem solved as much as I did. The owners of the rented homes were not nearly as eager but I finally got the money and one day they paved the street. The method used was to spray the clay with hot tar and then throw a mixture of sand and small pebbles on top of the tar.

Black Prince got caught on the other side of the street when they spread the tar. When he came home, he got it all over himself. I had to take him to the vet and have him anesthetized so we could clean him up.

I had become quite the civic activist. The house numbers on Torch Hill Drive were duplicated on both sides of Benning Drive. I got up a petition to the post office to have them add a one on our side to avoid all the confusion. They agreed.

While he was in Korea, Eli read the Army Times, a weekly newspaper that carried ads for real estate in Florida. He decided it would be nice to retire in Florida and proceeded to make down payments on several parcels of real estate. Then he sent the contracts to me to make the payments. I cancelled some of them, but we ended up making payments and eventually owning three parcels. One was in Escambia County near Pensacola, one in Bellevue near Ocala and one in Lake County near DeLand. We did eventual visit these sites and they seemed OK. We later sold all of them. We may have broken even.

It was about this time that our older daughter decided that she no longer wanted to be called Ginny because it was too baby-ish. She would hence forth be known as Virginia.

After Eli was home from Korea about a year he got order to report to Meridian, Mississippi to be the senior advisor to the reserve component. They wanted him there last week but we did manage to get a delay long enough to sell the house and to find a nice place to rent in Meridian.

329

~ 23 ~

Artillery, Laundry and Moonshine

Bernice:

We hardly knew what to expect as we headed west out of Columbus. In 1956 there was a great deal of information that was less than flattering about Mississippi. Common belief was that their schools were the worst, they hated Yankees and mistreated negroes shamefully. We were determined to keep an open mind.

We went on a reconnaissance to find a place to rent and to get a handle on our new assignment. We found the downtown was very modern looking. The traffic was not bad at all. We stayed at the Lamar Hotel which was at least eight stories tall and there were other tall buildings, too. The general impression was that of a thriving urban city.

There didn't seem to be very many houses for rent but we found one on the west side of the city in the area known as Oakland Heights. It was fairly new and clean. There were three bed rooms, and one bath. It was on a dirt street and not too far from the reserve center where Eli would be working. It belonged to a fundamentalist preacher who had moved to Philadelphia, Mississippi. His name was Rudolph Cooksey. The rent was $75.00 a month, which was a little less than our housing allowance at the time.

Eli:

The reserve center was located at Key Field, an old Air Force base which also housed the Air National Guard and the city airport. The center consisted of two wooden barracks, a supply room, a warehouse and another wooden building that was used as a headquarters. There was sufficient room for a motor pool. It was all enclosed with a six foot chain link fence. Our class rooms were in the barracks. There was one small room which the unit that was drilling on any given night used as an orderly room. All in all, it was a very good set up. It was approximately six acres.

The reserve units that I was to be the advisor to were the 205th Artillery Group and the 302 Quartermaster laundry company. I was also responsible for any problems concerning the army in a six county area. Mississippi Senator, John Stennis, the chairman of the US Senate Armed Forces Committee lived in Scooba, a small town in Kemper County, about twenty miles north of Meridian. He took a personal interest in reserve matters and in Meridian.

My commanding officer was stationed at the Mississippi US Army Reserve Headquarters in Jackson, which is the capital of the state. As soon as we were settled, I drove to headquarters and signed in. I talked with the officers in Jackson and learned that Meridian was scheduled to have a new training center built, but they had been unable to find a suitable site. By the end of the fiscal year in July the money would revert back to the Army unless we had a site and had broken ground. They told me it was probably too late to salvage the project. If that happened it would take another year to re-submit the request and get it back in the budget.

I signed in at the detachment headquarters in Meridian. It was 1 April, 1956. I talked to Master Sergeant Murphy who was the NCO in Charge. There were two other sergeants, a motor sergeant and a personnel sergeant. After discussing the efforts that had been made to get a site for the new center with Sgt. Murphy, I realized that the attitude of the community was very negative. They did not want any more Federal activity in the area. If they had their way, they would probably move the Post Office outside of town.

After spending a few days looking for sites and talking to the mayor, the county engineer and others, I got the feeling that they would support the program. In the past, nobody had ever bothered to consult the community leaders and explain what we were trying to accomplish. The mayor really wanted to be cooperative and before I left his office he had offered us ten acres in the city park.

We found out from the city attorney that the land had been donated to the city for a park and any other use would cause it to revert to the estate of the donor. The heirs were scattered all over the world and getting all of them to sign off would have been a long and useless exercise.

Now that the local attitude was changing, they became eager to help find a suitable site. They gave me two suggestions to start with. I contacted both these owners who happened to be veterans and they were willing to sell their property for our use. One night while I was in my back yard, I told Bernice our problem was finding a place on a main highway. She pointed to some rough looking vacant land just a few hundred yards from our house. I said, "It's not on a main highway, but I'll look it over in the morning."

When I looked at the parcel in the morning, to my surprise I discovered it was actually on old US 80, only a few hundred yards from State Road 19. I checked with the county engineer and the mayor to determine if it was feasible to pursue doing the paper work and have the army engineers inspect the site. The only obstacle that I didn't clear was that old US 80 was now designated as a secondary road by the Department of Transportation. But the traffic count exceeded the volume of the count on the new US 80.

After gathering up all the information, site sketch, zoning, etc. and a canvas of the near-by residents, I submitted the site to my headquarters for approval before it went to the army engineers in Mobile. By the end of my first week the site had been approved.

Army engineers needed to do their site survey and inspection which they told me they couldn't get to for at least two months. When I gave this information to Col. Brackman the reserve commander he said, "Let us take care of it." The next morning at 0800 the army engineers were on the site getting their survey done. The Colonel and one of his officers, Judge Billy Nevill, had called Senator Stennis who got on Department of Army and the engineers. The complete plans were made up by the engineers and in about ten days the contracts were available for bids on the entire project. In another ten days the contract was let and we broke ground officially, only a few days before the fiscal year ended.

We needed a name for our new center and I turned the selection process over to the Chamber of Commerce. They came up with the names of two men from the community who had been killed in World War II. We decided that we would name it after both of them and it became known as the HARRIS-LOCKHART ARMY RESERVE CENTER.

The primary unit in Meridian was the 205th Artillery Group. It was commanded by a full Colonel, Oliver Brackman, and included many prominent citizens of the area. The first Sergeant was Cecil Germany, the director of the local television station, channel 11. Judge Billy Nevill was the S-3. Col. Brackman was the forester for Flintcote, who manufactured composition siding and pressed wood flooring.

There were around a hundred and twenty members of the outfit. About two thirds of them were WWII and Korean veterans. They were fulfilling their balance of obligation of military service. By joining the reserve a young man could meet his obligation which would exempt him from the draft. They would take six months of active duty and after that they would serve five years in the reserve.

Every unit in the reserve had a specific mission come M-day (mobilization day) and could be called to active duty. These were a high caliber of people and we were often envied by some of the regular army outfits.

We drilled once a week, usually in the evening. Every summer we went on active duty for two to three weeks. If we drilled for a whole weekend, we could miss two of the weekly drills.

Another unit that I advised was the 302nd Quartermaster Laundry Co. under the command of Captain Scarborough. Even though the army had been integrated by this time, this organization was primarily composed of black soldiers. The closest we came to being integrated was the officers who were white as were the First Sergeant and the company clerk who was a WAC. These were basically civilians and it was my opinion that we should stay within the customs of our community. This unit was good and always received a superior rating every year when they were at camp.

Their mission was to operate a mobile laundry unit which was extremely useful in all sorts of situations. At least once a month they would all bring in bags of dirty laundry from their community. They would wash, dry and fold it, all as a part of the training. On several occasions we used them during emergencies in the local area.

Once there had been a fire in an apartment building near the airport and all the clothing in about twenty five apartments was full of smoke and needed to be cleaned. We called in one section.

They tapped into the fire plug on the property and did the job. By the end of the day, all the clothing and bedding had been washed and returned to the apartments that were occupied. The whole operation was treated as a drill day and they were paid as such.

When we went to summer camp, they took over the laundry detail for the camp. Each day they would do the laundry for different units so that by the end of the week, all troops in the area had clean cloths at no expense to them. All that was needed was a source of water. It could even be a pond or a creek. They even made their own soap from the grease traps with old fashioned lye. At first, I had my doubts about this, but was amazed at how clean it made the laundry.

During the time I was there, the 320th CID (Criminal Investigation Detachment) was organized in Meridian. This was primarily a group of policemen from the area and the Federal Alcohol and Tobacco people plus detectives from Meridian Police Department and deputies from the Lauderdale County Sheriffs department.

We were issued the complete set of photography equipment normally issued to criminal investigating units. It included a whole array of cameras, and a complete dark room with enlargers and all. We set up a dark room and I took a course in photography from the Meridian Junior College.

As part of our weekend drill, I had gotten an underground report that someone was stealing chickens and utensils from the 205th kitchen while the rest of the unit was at chapel. We set up a surveillance movie camera in the day room and with a telephoto lens, focused it directly on the kitchen. Only the mess sergeant was in the kitchen. About the time the chapel service was singing the first hymn, the camera took a picture of the mess sergeant putting frozen chickens, utensils and a gallon of anti-freeze in the trunk of his civilian car. I got the battery commander and the first sergeant out of church and told them that it was the mess sergeant who was stealing the stuff.

They said that was absolutely not possible. We stepped over to where the mess sergeant was and I invited him to open his trunk, which he did reluctantly, as I took movies. They included the inside of the trunk and the loot. I questioned the sergeant, if he had taken anything else from the unit over the past few weeks. He said no. When I asked him if he would mind letting us check his house, he also agreed. I called the local police and two detective were waiting for me when we arrived at his house. I gave them my story and told them that he had given me written permission to inspect his home. I wanted them to be witnesses of the facts.

As I entered the house he immediately told me that he had a sick aunt in one of the bedrooms and to please not bother her. When we went to the kitchen, his wife was cutting up chicken with a big butcher knife clearly marked US Army. I picked up several other army items in the drawers. I told the sergeant that I would not have him arrested for stealing government property and the chickens that were still in the car. "The charges will be prepared by your battery commander for Special Court." He was reduced to the grade of private and discharged from the service.

Just up the street from the center was an old Air Force warehouse. The sign on the outside said, "PECAN SHELLING". The outside of the building was littered with thousands of pecan shells. They were pulling a big old eighteen wheel truck with Illinois tags into this building about every three days. I talked to my CID men and they agreed that this was awfully suspicious. At night, I noticed that there was a lot of coming and going of vans. Most of the activity took place on Tuesday nights which was when the CID was having drill.

For a couple days, other than drill night, a CID member who worked for the Alcohol and Tobacco people, was stationed on the second floor of our barrack observing the activity. They made up a plan. They would get reservist from the 205th to drive the CID's civilian cars and park them in front of the center. That way the people in the pecan place would think that the CID was in the center drilling. After one or two of the vans went out, they closed in and raided the joint.

They had warrants and seized the equipment and arrested the operators. They found not only the eighteen wheeler but hundreds of pounds of sugar, hundreds of empty Coca Cola gallon jugs from Cairo, Illinois and all the materials needed to make moon shine. The place had been a supply operation for all of east Mississippi and west Alabama for moonshiners and bootleggers. This could be best described as on the job training.

Bernice:

Virginia was in fifth grade and Mary Jane had been in kindergarten at South Columbus, but there was no kindergarten here. I didn't really feel that this was a serious problem because she had been in a class of seventy three and I had often wondered if that was even worth the effort. The Oakland Heights school was very new and modern and the principle was widely recognized for her innovative programs.

Of direct interest to us was the fifth grade teacher who was Mrs. Florence Shakelford. With only two months left of fifth grade, I was concerned that Virginia might loss some valuable learning because of the move. The fear was unfounded. She was able to fit right in without as much as a ripple. Mrs. Shakelford made sure that she became a part of the class. 'Southern hospitality' starts young in Mississippi.

The first task we had after we moved in was to do something about the back yard. It was an absolute thicket, with all kinds of tangled wild grape vines, blackberry bushes and what have you. We had just gotten an electric lawn mower called a Huffy. It cut off if the mowing got too hard. To our utter amazement, that Huffy mower cut right through all that brush with comparative ease. All Eli had to do was go slow in the heavy areas. In a couple days we had a usable back yard. It sloped off to the back and a part time creek ran across one corner. There was a wooded vacant lot next to us and the entire set up was just what we needed.

Our neighbors included the French family who lived directly across the street. His name was Cooper and he was a carpenter. His wife was Sue. They had two sons, Mike who was a year older than Mary Jane, and Rodney who was Bill's age. Bill and Rodney were good friends all the time that we lived there. They also had a little girl named Chris. The French family was very religious.

Next to the French family were the Parkers. They had two children, a boy, Murry, who was Bill's age, and Belinda who was a year older than Mary Jane. Belinda and Mary Jane were good friends, also.

One day, I noticed that Mary Jane and Belinda had taken an unusual interest in my nursing books. Curiosity got the best of me and I had to see what they were so interested in. It turned out that they had found my obstetrics book. Well, at least the information they were getting was correct.

Mary Jane started first grade at Oakland Heights the first fall that we were in Meridian. Her first teacher was Mrs. Pitman. I thought she was an outstanding teacher. Not at all the illiterate teacher that we had been lead to believe staffed the Mississippi schools. Mary Jane was in the bluebird reading group. Even though the groupings were disguised by different names, everyone knew that the bluebirds were the smartest.

When Billy started first grade, he had Mrs. Pitman too. Billy was not a bluebird. In fact, he was very slow learning to read. I even took him to the eye doctor who prescribed glasses before he started second grade. For some reason the boys in the neighborhood had a big attraction to the garbage man. I discovered he had a comic book exchange going. That seemed to be the factor that motivated Bill to learn to read.

One of the major events of the Oakland Heights school year was a pageant at Christmas time. Mary Jane's class had a north pole scene and she had a speaking role. She was the ice fairy with a crown, a wand and a white dress with glitter.

I had felt so warm and comfortable with the downtown Methodist Church in Columbus that we joined the downtown Central Methodist Church in Meridian. However, I didn't get involved with Sunday School teaching. Eli and I attended an adult class. They were all very friendly, but we never did make any close friends.

When our furniture had arrived from Columbus, one of the legs of the sofa was broken and we had set a beer can under that corner until we could get it fixed. One day the minister came to call on the new members and we sat there hoping he didn't notice the beer can.

Without a PX, I had to find someone do my hair. I met a lady at church who had a downtown shop with her mother, so I made and appointment. I had only been there a time or two when I heard the two of them talking in the most unkind manner about one of the ladies who was under the dryer. It upset me so badly that when my hair was set, I paid for the bobby pins and left with a wet head. I never went back. I found a neighborhood shop only a few blocks from the house with only one chair.

Eli:

The new training center was well on its way. It was being built only a few hundred yards from my house. The site was badly eroded and full of gullies because it had been used as a source of clay for building roads. That required it to be filled, graded and packed to make a suitable area for the building and grounds.

The contractor was a Meridian car dealer, as well as the owner of the concrete plant. The Army engineers from Mobile were working on the Meridian Air Port and were in charge of our project at the same time. It was their duty to inspect and pass on each phase of the construction.

When we were well along, the engineers started to be real strict on some of the contractor's work. I thought they were too strict, and I suspected that there was something going on. When we got above the floor and were putting in the main hallway from one end of the building to the other, approximately a hundred and thirty feet, the inspector measured both ends of the walls and they were a quarter inch off. The walls were rejected and they had to tear them out and rebuild them. I thought that was a crime. They tore them out on Saturday and rebuilt them on Sunday in order to stay on schedule.

The motor pool hardstand called for three or four inches of black top over a suitable sub surface. When it was ready to be put down, tests were made and turned down because they could not get the compaction in clay needed to hold the asphalt. As a way out, the contractor offered to give them six inches of reinforced concrete. The engineer rejected this on the spot. They said that they could not change the specifications. Because we had heavy self propelled artillery, the concrete was almost essential.

I put in a call myself to Colonel Love, who was in charge of the Mobile headquarters of the engineers. I explained to him what I thought was a big injustice to the contractor who was offering a product that was even better than that of the specification. He said, "What you say makes good sense." He got some other high ranking people on the line and they had a conference. When I hung up the phone, the concrete motor pool had been approved and the plans would be in Meridian the next day.

One of the men in the conference said that they had just completed a new black top motor pool in Enterprise, Alabama and it was working ok. I was sure surprised that he thought that was ok. I had been to Enterprise just a couple days before and seen that even the two and a halfs had already torn it up. When the Colonel heard that, he ordered the inspector to get over to Enterprise and give him a report.

A couple days later, an FBI man stopped by my office. He told me that all the inspectors at the airfield project were involved in bribing the contractors. The contractor's company had given the inspectors credit cards, whiskey and other favors.

These were the same people who were inspecting the training center. I asked our contractor if the inspectors had ever asked for any special favors. He said that they had wanted him to sell them new cars under cost. He had told them, "HELL NO!". That had taken place just before the inspectors had gotten so super picky. The investigator said he was glad that our contractor had not submitted to them. As a result of that investigation, all the inspectors were fired except the Chief.

One day, I needed to talk to the inspector who was on the roof where the men were working. There was a ladder rated for one person at a time leading to the roof. I was on the ladder when, just as I reached the top, someone got on it at the ground and was coming up. It started shaking and so I quickly jumped onto what I thought was solid plywood. Before I knew it, I had gone through what was actually a soft composition insulation board to be covered with light weight concrete. As I went through, I hit one of the steel rafter with my head. It was fourteen feet to the concrete floor in classroom number one. I put out my left hand to break my fall and as a result, broke my left wrist.

I was taken to Rush hospital which had an excellent reputation for orthopedics. They gave me an anesthesia and operated on the wrist. Dr. Leslie Rush had invented what was known as the Rush Rod, which he used to repair my wrist. All that I could see when I woke up was a bandaid. I later learned that it had a hook on the end and ran through the bone marrow for about six inches and held the bottom end of the radius, that had been broken off, to the rest of the bone. As soon as I woke up I called Bernice.

The doctor explained what he had done and insisted that I start using my hand and wrist immediately. My arm hurt clean to my shoulder. He asked me to bend my hand forward and backward. When he told me that I hadn't bent it enough, he took it in his hand and bent it backwards and my feet went right up in the air. Then he bent it forward and I almost did a somersault.

I said, "Doc, you're rougher than an Army Doctor". He said, "I am an Army Doctor, in the reserve." I was put in the hospital for the rest of the day for observation. During the day a therapist came in and bent that wrist every hour or so. It hurt like hell. They brought me a shot for the pain but I refused to take it. I didn't want to be a drug addict. By morning, I was hurting real bad. A new nurse came on shift and said, "How come you didn't get your pain shot." I told her that I had refused it. She told me that I was getting a shot, whether I wanted it or not and she hit me in the butt with that baby so hard it felt like a sledge hammer. Within minutes, the pain was gone.

The Harris-Lockhart Army Reserve Center, Meridian, Mississippi. It was the temporary home of the new Oakland Heights Methodist Church. 1959.

The sad thing about it was that I had a brand new class 'A' uniform on and it sure got dirty awful quick. Bernice picked me up at 0700 and I was back at work at the center by 0800. I had kept my record of never missing a day of duty for sickness or injury as I had not been out twenty four hours. I started driving that day and continued to move the wrist, even though the first few days it wasn't easy.

When the center was finished we had a dedication and invited the public, the reservists, the mayor and local dignitaries including our local congressman Winstead. He was the chairman of the Armed Forces Committee of the House of Representatives in Washington and was the main speaker. Everybody was fed lunch in the big drill hall by the 205th field kitchen.

We got word from the military district that we could activate one eight inch artillery battery in Newton about twenty miles west of our center. About that time, an artillery lieutenant had reported in. We took five or six NCOs with artillery experience, who lived in Newton county, and opened a recruiting drive over there.

I contracted with a doctor to do our physicals. I was the contracting and purchasing officer for the army for six counties. The doctor ran a privately owned clinic. I stopped by to get a bid on the cost of having him do complete physical on the reserve members of this new outfit. We started negotiating. I offered to make the contract for this service at $9.50 per man. He asked for $13.00. He said, "Major, did you see all those people sitting in that waiting room?"

When I complemented him on his good business he said, "Eighty percent of those people will never pay me a cent. I have to charge a little extra to compensate for those that don't pay." I took a good look at the bunch and offered him $12.50. He said he'd take that. The national average for the same service was $25.00. I rented a car dealer's empty building to be the training center.

We almost immediately filled the unit with personnel. Many of them were recent high school graduates, willing to take six months of basic training and assume the obligation that went with being in the reserve.

The 205th Artillery group were issued an eight inch self propelled howitzer, it arrived in Meridian aboard a flat car. It was sure a big thing. The tracks must have stuck out over the edge of the flat car about a foot on each side. To unload it they backed the flat car up to a dead head. That is where the rails ends. There was a big mound of dirt there and we just drove that thing off the flat car and down the mound of dirt. This was out at the airport and there was quite a bit of space to maneuver.

Before we went down to claim our gun, we got out the training manual to study up on how to operate it. Our full time mechanic had operated a tank on active duty and he was the first one to drive it. It was the simplest thing to drive. There was a stick that swiveled and all you had to do was push the stick in the direction you wanted to go. Several of the reservist took turns driving it around before we took it on the road.

When it was time to take it to the training center, we called the city police who provided us with an escort. Those two motorcycles looked awfully small in front of that big gun. We later took it to Newton county where the battery trained with it. We never took it to summer camp as it would be too expensive to ship it. Instead we used a gun that was already at Ft. Benning when we fired service practice.

Bernice:

Virginia was in an intermediate Girl Scout troop when we left Columbus, so I wanted to get her in a troop in Meridian. There was a troop in Oakland Heights and the leader was Annie Edney. My offer to assist was greatly appreciated.

The Girl Scout council was called the Meridale Council for Meridian and Lauderdale County. The director was Betty Hanby, a divorcee with two teen age children. The council had a camp south of town called Camp Meridale. When the director learned that I was a nurse, she asked me if I could fill in as the camp nurse for a week during summer camp.

Because I had two small children, who were not old enough to be in the regular session, they arranged for me to have a small cabin separate from the staff cabin. It was really primitive, just a roof with screens on the four sides and three metal cots. Even though she was not a regular camper, Mary Jane took part in most of the activity including riding the horses. My duties were mostly to hold sick call after each meal. I had a supply cupboard in the big lodge building. Cuts, scratches, blisters, splinters and mosquito bites were about as complicated as it got.

Bill and I were free to roam the camp as we wished. The part that I enjoyed the most was the singing. After every meal, while we were still at the table, we sang scout songs, folk songs and the like with Mrs. Hanby leading. On Sunday, after the first week, we had visitors day when all the parents came. I was told that this was usually the most difficult time, and that they would usually lose some of the girls who would want to go home with their parents. We didn't lose a one that year. Just before it was time for the parents to leave, Betty gathered the campers in a circle and we started singing. That reinforced the feeling of companionship that had been developed and every one of the girls stayed.

It was at Meridale that I really became a dedicated scout adult. They put me on the camp committee and I used to enjoy going out to camp, even when there were no campers. I just puttered around on little maintenance projects. There was a wooden foot bridge that led to the artesian well. The decking had become rotten but the stringers were in good shape. The council bummed the planking which they had cut at the lumberyard and I hauled it out to the camp and rebuilt the bridge. Bill wasn't in school yet and he helped me by bringing the planks as I nailed them down.

They also had regular pit latrines which many of the girls were uncomfortable with. I got the idea that maybe if we put regular toilet seats with lids over the holes, it would be more like home. I got a bunch of old seats from the junk yard, painted them, and nailed them down.

The bakery owned a farm on the road out to Meridale where they raised pigs and fed them the bread that was returned from the stores. It smelled very hog like. One day, as we were driving past it, the pigs were close to the road and Bill exclaimed, "Look at all those big banks."

When Mary Jane was old enough to be a Brownie, I felt that I had been an assistant long enough, so I volunteered to organize a Brownie troop. We met at the Oakland Heights Baptist Church. Since we had a shady back yard, we often met there too. That was my most fun troop. Brownies don't mind letting you know they like you and are having fun. We didn't have badges to work on, or specific skills to learn, so we just did anything that was fun. Although Bill was not a Brownie, he entered into all the activity and we gave him a Brownie 'friendship pin'.

We learned to weave baskets and we had lots of sessions molding clay. One of my assistant's husband worked at a tile factory and she could get all the clay we wanted. The girls molded all sorts of objects. These went over to the tile factory and were put into the kiln with the tile and came back all nicely glazed and permanent. We wove sit-upons from folded newspaper, and we learned to cut letters from construction paper and make signs.

One project that I was especially proud of was the scrap books that the brownies made. They brought magazines to troop meetings where they cut out and mounted pictures that they liked. When they were finished, we hiked to the Mattie Hersey Hospital, which was only about four blocks from our house. We gave the scrap books to the head nurse, for the children in the hospital. She was very gracious and told us of some children who had been burned in a house fire who would enjoy the books.

She also said that they needed hard candy because they had to drink so much water. Bless my girls, they went straight from the hospital to a convenience store next door and all of them gave their allowance to buy candy for their unknown friends. Every mother should have a chance to be a Brownie leader with a daughter.

At the same time, I also had an intermediate troop. Virginia's group had gone on to Junior High downtown and Annie had opened a restaurant out at the airfield. Most of the girls had dropped out. Virginia had joined a troop of girls her age who were at Kate Griffin Jr. High. Even though they were still called intermediate scouts, they wore a uniform with a green skirt and white blouse and did more advanced activities. I wanted to continue as an intermediate leader and nobody objected.

The troop was mostly younger girls who had moved up from Brownies. They enjoyed camping. On more than one occasion we took them out to Meridale troop camping. One time we were to be there during the weekend. It was decided that we would take our dress uniforms and attend the church that was next to the camp. That was quite an experience. It was Baptist and it was my first experience with the 'Shouting Baptist'. The minister paced all over the church, gestured wildly, thumping his bible and calling the 'Wrath of God' on all sinners. Some of the girls were familiar with this style, but most of them were as fascinated by it as I was.

One year the council asked me to take charge of the cookie sale. I discovered that cookies were big business. We had a very successful sale. Each troop kept some of the profit for their own projects and much of the money went for improvements at the camp.

The ultimate award for Girl Scouts at that time was the 'Curved Bar'. It was thought of as the equivalent of the Eagle rank in Boy Scouting. Virginia chose to pursue the curved bar and achieved it in her troop. When it was awarded to her, she was honored to have it presented by Betty Long, a local woman who was a representative in the Mississippi state legislature. Women in elective politics were unusual in the fifties, especially in the deep south.

Eli:

One day Colonel Brackman and I were going duck hunting at one of the lakes on the property that was owned by Flintcote. We were driving out there in one of Flintcote's jeeps and got stuck in the red clay. The lake was in sight and we could see ducks all around. We started out on foot to where the ducks were. They saw us coming and moved just out of range. No matter where we went, they were just out of range.

When we tried to get the jeep out of the mud with the winch, the winch broke. Finally we had to walk out to get help. The mud was so sticky that with every step we took, it built up on our boots. Every ten or fifteen feet we had to stop and knock it off with a stick. You could look back at the road and every ten of fifteen feet there would be four clumps of mud.

The nearest phone was at a country store about three miles away. It was a real old fashioned store with the pot bellied stove in the middle. Brackman called one of his foremen who came out and rescued us with a winch that didn't break.

The foreman was a total abstainer from alcohol. Brackman told me a story of how one time the man was a heavy user of moonshine and always carried a gallon jug of it around in his jeep. The reason the jug was in the jeep was to keep it where his wife wouldn't see it and throw it out. One day he went out to his jeep in the back yard to get a drink. He reached for the jug and took two or three deep swigs without looking. He had gotten the wrong jug and had swallowed a stump killer that was a strong poison. He almost died. After that he never took another drink. That was a good example of why is a bad idea to try to keep something from your wife.

One day I got word from the local barber that the Secretary of the Army, Wilbur Brucker, was coming to Meridian to visit his brother. I notified the military district in Jackson that he would be arriving and they notified the Third Army. I began to lay on plans to meet his plane and to make my army sedan available. There was an investigator from third army working in the area at the time and we borrowed his car too.

The secretary's official reason for being in Meridian was to visit the new Reserve Training Center and be briefed on the reserve activities in the area. When the plane landed, I met him and drove him to the reserve center. The second sedan took the plane crew into Meridian to Weidman's restaurant.

After the briefing, we took him to his brother's place. His main interest was to see how the brother was living and see if he had any problems. He lived in a rooming house, not in a great part of town. On previous visits, the barber and the mayor, who were both good friends of the family, would find the brother and stay with him for three or four hours to be sure that he was sober before the secretary arrived.

I met them at the rooming house with the secretary. The brother came to the front door and said, "Come on in Wilbur." I told the secretary that I would wait outside and asked when he needed to take off. His aide and I sat on the front steps. About thirty minutes before time for the plane to take off, I told him that it was time to leave in a few minutes. He asked a lot of questions about the town, so we rode around some of the different areas where major projects were being built before we arrived at the airport. That was the first of several visits from the Secretary of the Army.

We were the half way point for the 82nd. Airborne Division traveling in convoy from Ft. Bragg to Texas, on their way to Ft. Hood for maneuvers. Their overnight stay was at the Meridian stadium where showers and latrines were available. It was necessary for all the vehicles to be refueled. As the contract officer, I called around to the oil company distributors to get bids on the per gallon cost for approximately 25,000 gallons.

Two companies came out tied for the low bid. One of these companies had a former West Pointer in charge of sales. He had played football for Earl Blake. When I explained my ideas to facilitate gasing such a large number of vehicles, he could relate to the problem well. We determined that two tankers with six hoses on each side could fill up a company size unit in about five minutes.

The convoy was set up to arrived at seven minute intervals. The tanker trucks were in the center of the dirt road leading to the stadium grounds. As the vehicles pulled in, the column split into two columns with vehicles on each side of the tank trucks. They would all stop at one time and the hoses went into their tanks. They would be on the way in a matter of minutes. It was the most efficient gasing of a convoy that I had seen.

Bernice:

When Virginia was in sixth grade, they encouraged the students to learn to play musical instruments. Since I had a trumpet, Virginia chose to learn to play it. She was not that eager to play trumpet but she wanted very much to be a majorette, and all majorettes had to come from the ranks of the band.

She worked very hard to learn to twirl. I thought she did rather well, but she was never quite good enough to win a place on the team when try outs were held. One year, she even went to a one week baton camp at Mississippi Southern College in Hattiesburg. All the time she was getting much better at playing the trumpet. She was far better than I had ever been. They had band practice every day, where our school only had practice one hour a week. She also went to summer band. The Meridian High School Band even won state and national honors but we left before she reached the ninth grade.

The year we took Virginia to twirling school, we continued on to the Gulf Coast. We had seen an advertisement in the newspaper for a cottage east of Mobile, Alabama called REX. As we approached our destination there were a lot of signs along the road advertising REX. We expected something fairly nice. It turned out to be a real shanty. It looked like it had been made of packing boxes. But it was on the beach. It had the necessities and we had paid our money.

One day, Eli had taken the garbage out the back door to the black spot in the sand where garbage was obviously supposed to be burned. While the fire was going nicely, a wind came up and blew some embers into the palmetto bushes. They were so green that we never dreamed how volatile they were. We were both bare foot and we had to douse the fire before it reached the building. I was filling two waste cans with water from the shower and running it out for Eli to throw on the fire. We stopped it, but had a new respect of palmettos.

On our way home from that trip, our brand new Pontiac broke down. It was Sunday afternoon in a town called Wiggins. The universal joint bearing had fallen out. We made a call to the Pontiac dealer in Wiggins and a man came out and replaced the joint, right beside the road. That was the way people worked in Mississippi.

Fifty Sixth Avenue in front of our house was unpaved when we lived there. I discovered that we could get used motor oil sprayed on the street to help keep the dust down. It was like being back in Columbus.

During our stay in Meridian, we bought a food freezer and filled it with a side of beef. Everything was fine until one time when we were away for several days, the freezer went bad. When we got home all our meat had thawed out. It was still good but was a horrible mess. We put it in some bushel baskets and carried it to a commercial freezer place where we they rented lockers. They froze it for us right in the baskets. The baskets were too big to fit in the locker and just stayed in the far corner of the freezer room. After that, every week or so I would go to the freezer to get meat. It was all one solid block of ice and I had to pry the packages apart with a crow bar and a hammer.

When we tried to get our money back for the freezer, the dealer was not at all co-operative. Eli asked one of the reservist who was a lawyer to write the dealer a letter. It wasn't long after that when we got our refund in full.

I was having some gynecology problems and the doctor in Meridian said I needed a hysterectomy. Even then, surgery was somewhat expensive in the civilian facilities and CHAMPUS had not been passed. We tried to get an appointment at the Biloxi Air Force Base but they encouraged me to go to Ft. McClelland, Alabama. We arranged for Bill to stay with Rodney. Mary Jane stayed with Belinda and Virginia was to stay with her scout leader's family. The Browns had several girls around her age. That left Eli free to go with me to Anniston where the fort was.

The doctor at McClelland was a woman who said the Meridian doctor had incorrectly diagnosed my problem, but she sent me to Fort Benning for a second opinion. By now, Fort Benning had a new modern hospital. They said I didn't need a hysterectomy but that I should have a perineal repair. So I stayed at Benning for the surgery and Eli went home and reclaimed his family.

Eli:

Mr. French was going to build a garage in their back yard. He had his forms in place and had ordered seven yards of cement for the floor and the drive way. He had arranged for some friends from his church to help him, but they had not showed up. About 0600, I heard the noise outside the window and looked out to see what was going on. I knew that he was in a jam because no one man could work that much concrete by himself. I put on my boots and working clothes and went across the street to give him a hand.

His wife also pitched in and the three of us finished the double garage first. By the time we got to the driveway, Sue had to go. The two of us could work it by then. Every time we got a load smoothed out, another load would arrive. I was one tired neighbor when we were finished. Sue insisted that I have lunch with them. She had prepared what was more like a dinner. It was a delicious meal. It was most appreciated as Bernice was at Ft. Benning in the hospital.

One night the phone rang and Sue French was on the line. Cooper was away and there was an awful racket in the chicken house in the back yard. I picked up a ball bat and went across the street. She was standing at the back door with a candle as there were no lights in the hen house. It was a windy night and the candle kept blowing out. She had tried to get the dog to go with us but the dog was scared to death.

348

When I opened the door, the chickens were all making a big fuss. I saw something in the middle of the floor not moving a muscle. I couldn't see it well enough to know what it was. I took the ball bat and touched it. It started to move so I hit it hard. That was the end of the life of a possum.

Bernice:

When Mary Jane was in second grade her teacher was Mrs. Iola Thompson. Her husband was a disabled veteran named James Thompson. One day I had a phone call from Mrs. Thompson inviting us to her house one evening. Since Mary Jane was no longer in her class, I thought that was a bit unusual. When we arrived at their home, we found a good sized group of people. Some of them were people we knew and many we did not.

Although there were several Methodist churches in Meridian there was none in Oakland Heights and not a single one had an elevator. All of them had many steps to reach the sanctuary. The previous Sunday, James had been unable to reach the sanctuary at the Fifth Avenue church where they attended. Iola thought it was time for Oakland Heights to have their own Methodist Church, one without steps.

Everyone there agreed. Eli offered the new Reserve Center for their use until they could get organized and build their own facility. This type of activity was encouraged by the army to foster civilian-military co-operation.

Eli:

One day after work, I was on our front porch drinking a beer when the District Superintendent, the pastor of the 5th Street Methodist Church and district lay leader, Brogan Price, drove in my driveway. I put the beer down beside my chair and went to greet them. I brought some chairs and we sat down. They had had a meeting about the organization of the new church and had come to ask me to be the chairman of the Official Board.

We had a discussion and I explained that I did not know enough of the people who would be involved in the new church. They said that was the reason they thought I would be the best person for the job. I would be a neutral person. It seemed that there were three different congregations in the community. I said that if I were doing it, I would pick people from each congregation to be on

349

each of the committees. There were three bankers. It just happened that there was one from each group, so I would make them the finance committee.

I also told them that I would be going overseas in about six months. They still wanted me to do the job, so I agreed. It would certainly be a new experience for me. I thought that I would enjoy it.

They talked about renting a place or even buying a place to hold their meetings. I again offered them the use of the training center. I explained that once they got in a substandard facility, they would be stuck there. Also our facility was all on one level and would be readily accessible to handicapped people.

The Fifth street pastor filled in and held services at our place while his church was having Sunday School. We had our Sunday School after the church service. I put Bernice in charge of Sunday School and there were enough Sunday School teachers who lived in Oakland Height with teaching experience in the other three main Methodist Churches to have a very reliable organization.

The first Sunday morning that we held a service, we had a hundred and thirty people show up. We put up a big sign out front with the words OAKLAND HEIGHTS METHODIST CHURCH and the hours of the service. The service was held in the big class room that I had fallen into during construction. It was almost full.

The church was to pay the janitor of the reserve center for the work he did for them on Sunday. I told him to only set up about fifty chairs. I had no idea how many people would show up and I sure didn't want the place to look empty. It was a nice surprise to see so many people interested and to see them all pitch in to set up the extra chairs.

After the service we served cake and coffee out in the drill hall. The soft drink machine was popular with the kids. Our eight inch self propelled howitzer, capable of firing nuclear shells, stood not too far from the cookie table. It made me think of that WWII song, 'Praise the Lord and Pass the Ammunition.' Much of the success of the our new church was the twenty minutes of fellowship between the services when all the people got to know each other. The drill hall was big enough for the kids to run and play while the parents got acquainted.

Bernice cut a cross out of shelf paper and put it on the front of our olive drab painted podium for a pulpit. We brought the benches from the locker room for a communion rail and folded army blankets for kneelers. Two wooden salad bowls were used to take up the collection.

I received my orders to go to Europe as expected in July. Before we left, the church had picked a site and made plans to build a new church across the street from the Training Center. It was to be financed with a bond issue.

One Sunday morning, many years later, when we were traveling through Mississippi, we stopped at our church. It was now a fine red brick building that was a combination education building and sanctuary. Many of the charter members recognized us and made us welcome. As they passed the gold plated collection plates, they were engraved with the words, "Donated in honor of the Fishpaw Family."

~ 24 ~

Back To My Roots

Since we did not own the house in Meridian, and since we were informed that it took at least a year to get housing in Germany, I decided that I would prefer to spend that year in Wisconsin. I could be near my folks and our children could get to know their grandparents. My dad knew of a vacant farm house about three miles from the farm which he thought was in good shape and would be available for us to rent. It was owned by a family named Sturdevant.

We put Blackie, the cat, in a cage and shipped him to the farm while we drove. We felt it would be a hassle for him, and us too, if he rode in the car. The furniture went by moving van.

Our first inspection of the house was one of mixed emotion. Eli's reaction was immediately negative, and Mary Jane was completely turned off. I was the only one that thought it would be a good place to live. It was a two story farm house, the sort that I was familiar with. It was August and there was a swarm of honey bees keeping house in the walls near the front door. There were some trays of rat poison setting around. This upset Mary Jane.

To its advantage, it was close to home and was on the school bus route to the consolidated Johnstown township school and the Whitewater City High School. There was indoor plumbing, electricity and a good coal fired furnace. It was a typical farm setting with barns and out buildings. I felt it would give my children an idea of the ambiance of rural Wisconsin. Also, the rent was cheap.

We killed the bees and moved in. The parlor in the corner became the girl's bedroom. Bill's and my beds went in the downstairs bedroom which was next to the bathroom. The bathroom also connected with the kitchen. There was lots of nice cupboard space and a place for the washing machine and dishwasher in the kitchen. All our furniture found a place. We left the upstairs alone as we had no need for it. Blackie came over from the folk's place where he had been unhappily housed in the cellar. He was instantly happy and felt immediately at home with his people and his furniture.

Eli was taking the Pontiac station wagon with him to Germany so we bought a used $200 Dodge sedan for me to use. Eli left late in August for Germany and we were on our own, again.

Bill was put into a mixed class of first and second graders. With his new glasses, he settled in reasonably well. Mary Jane decided that she wanted us to call her Mary and drop the use of the Jane. She was in fourth grade and I can't remember anything special that year as far as school was concerned.

Virginia was accepted into the band but did not make the majorette corp which had already been selected. In the rural schools, the ninth grade is always like an ingathering of many smaller schools, so aside from what Wisconsin people thought was a southern accent, she was just another new freshman. Ignorance, fostered by stereotypical thinking that Mississippi schools were somehow inferior, was soon overcome by her own academic competence.

Grandma was so pleased that the trumpet she had bought for me was back in use. The first public appearance of the band was at a football game. I took my mother to the game to see the half time show. They played in the Whitewater University stadium which was little more than permanent bleachers, so there was lots of room. We found good seats where I could explain the game without annoying anyone else. It was the first time Mom had ever seen a football game. It wasn't long before she understood what was going on. I think that she actually enjoyed the game as well as the half time show.

Autumn in Wisconsin was a new experience for the Fishpaw family. There was an apple tree in the pasture with some very good apples on it. Bill, Mary and I rescued two or three bushels which I stored in the enclosed porch off the kitchen where they would be cool. That was a mistake. The first night that the temperature went below 32, all my apples froze.

There was also a hickory nut tree on that farm. We gathered and hulled several bags of nuts. It is best to let fresh hickory nuts dry out so I spread them on the floor in one of the upstairs rooms to dry. A month or two later, when I went upstairs to retrieve some nuts, all that was left were shells. The squirrels had helped themselves. Actually, they were theirs in the first place, I suppose. So much for the bountiful harvest.

In the same pasture was a mare and a foal. They tolerated us, but we made no lasting friendship. One Sunday morning I discovered that the foal was out of the pasture, roaming around the dooryard. I thought I should call Mr. Sturdevant but reasoned that would be unnecessary, even silly. After all, I was a farm girl and should be able to go out there, open the gate and chase the colt back where he belonged.

I had failed to reason with the mare. The instant I took the gate down, instead of the colt going into the pasture, the mare came out, and both of them headed down the road going west at a full gallop. I was in a mess. I jumped in my car and went after them, not sure what I would do if I caught them. I had managed to get past them where I left my car and was heading them back to where they belonged when, lucky for me, one of the neighbors came by going east. He had instantly figured out my problem and stopped at my driveway and was able to head them back into the pasture and close the gate. The gate closed, all that I had to do was walk a half mile back to get my car. I thought that was a good example of how rural people help each other. The kids were still in bed.

Country Halloween does not lend itself to "Trick or Treat" but Grandma thought it would be nice to have a costume party for her grandchildren. We created costumes, as did Dan and Sue. Grandma planned games and refreshments. That was the year that I made a Superman costume for Bill out of his blue pajamas and my nursing cape, worn with the red side out. He liked it so much he often wore it around the house, even when there was no party.

Winter set in quickly. We had our first snow in October. I ordered a ton of coal. The furnace worked seemingly well. We all learned how to shovel fuel and how to bank the fire for overnight. There was a thermostat to regulate the draft. It was Bill's duty to get up first, go to the cellar and shake out the ashes, replenish the raw coal on the remain red coals and turn up the thermostat so the house would be warm for the rest of us when we got up.

The term warm would have to be used relatively. I soon discovered, that although it seemed like a tight house, the Wisconsin wind was very efficient at finding its way in. I put transparent plastic over all the windows and laid folded towels under all the outside doors. We were able to stay comfortable but were far from cozy.

That was one of those winters when there was a great deal of snow. This was the first time Bill and Mary had ever had a prolonged experience with snow, but they accepted it with good grace. I think they must have liked it, because in later years as adults, they have both chosen to live where it can be found in abundance.

The first vehicle through ever morning was the milk truck. It never failed to get through to pick up the milk from the farm just east of us. The school buses were not always so punctual. Every morning, after there was a new snow, we listened to the local radio for the long list of which schools would be open and the ones that would be closed. There were several times that one or both of our schools were closed.

Quite often, after the buses had gone and I knew the road was open, I would catch my morning soap opera and then head for the home place. That was why I was there. I helped with many of my mother's chores, had long conversations with my dad and generally enjoyed my parents more than I ever had before.

For a long time, I had wanted to make a personal desk for myself. Uncle Charles had made one from an old table when he was a manual arts student in California and I wanted to try it. When I asked my dad for some of the old furniture stored in the tenant house, he had taken me out to the tool shed where there was a stack of rough cut walnut boards. They came from a walnut tree in the yard that had died. He had them put through the saw mill at the time they sawed the oak and cherry for their new house.

We brushed off the chicken manure and the rat nests, trucked them to the Lima Center millworks where we had them put through the planer, making boards up to nine inches wide and a little less than an inch thick. I spent a lot of time over the winter in the basement of the new house, using my dad's tools, designing and making my walnut desk. It was very special for me as it was one of the tree I had rested and day dreamed under when I was a child.

We started to go to the Methodist Church in Milton where I had gone as a child. It was still the same building with the same windows but it had been renovated, turned around and added onto. Most of the members were people I had grown up with.

Right away, they put me to work, teaching a Sunday School class of fourth graders, which included Mary. I don't think I was very effective. Some of the boys were less than attentive, but I tried.

At Christmas, as usual, the Sunday School produced the annual Christmas program. As a teacher, I helped with the planning and preparation. This involved night meetings. One night, when I was driving home, it was bitter cold and extremely clear. In the north I saw a shimmering blue glow in the sky. That was the last time that I have experienced the Aurora (northern lights). It is a genuine experience that one never forgets.

Bill and I set up the German trains in front of the double windows in the dining room. He and the Gregg Toten from down the road, who was his age, enjoyed playing with them. There were young boys right across the road from us, living in the old converted Sturdevant School, but they did not go to the Johnstown school. There were three of them and they did not come around.

I often talked with my high school friend Doris, who lived in Janesville. The Richmond phone exchange, which served us, had toll free connection with both Janesville and Whitewater, but not with Milton which served the home place. One of her group invited me to a Christmas party. This was very nice. It gave me a chance to interact with adults my age. They sang Christmas Carols and played adult games such as charades, which I enjoyed. It reminded me of my mother's club in my childhood. No alcohol was served.

That year we had the family Christmas at my place. Bill was seven, going on eight, and too big to embrace the stereotypical Santa myth, but I wanted him to have that special feeling that Santa and Christmas is supposed to foster. He was, therefore, designated to be the family Santa. With his red flannel pajama pants, tucked into his black four buckle overshoes and wearing Mary's red jacket with the red hood, he made a very presentable Mr. Claus. It was his job to distribute the gifts. Aunt Cora was with us as well as the grandparents. Eli had sent wrist watches to all of us. For my mother, he had selected a dainty model and for Mary he had sent a sturdier model. Mary thought Grandma's was much nicer than hers and Grandma liked Mary's because it was easier to read, so they traded.

I also received a rose colored table cloth with twelve matching napkins. I stretched my table, used the new table cloth and we all enjoyed Christmas 1958.

By Easter, I was getting a bit tired of snow, but Wisconsin weather was not concerned about my feelings. It snowed anyway. Again we had the family to our house for dinner. That year the grandparents gave their last grandchild a bible. Billy seemed to appreciate it. My mother had a bad case of laryngitis but they enjoyed being with us as it was getting near to the time that we would be leaving for Germany.

One morning, Blackie was having a fit in front of the cellar door. This was his normal route to the outdoors through the cellar, but he was much too nervous to just want to go out. When I opened the door, a mouse ran right between his legs and across the dining room into the cold air register, with Blackie and me in hot pursuit. Neither one of us caught it.

During the winter, we had carried out the ashes from the furnace and put them in the deep frozen ruts in the driveway. When spring arrived, we got another big surprise. At least a hundred grass snakes had come out of the stone foundation of the house, where they had hibernated for the winter, and found the soft ashes for their nests. Each adult must have delivered at least a hundred babies. My entire yard was one crawling mass of tiny snakes.

Even Blackie viewed this development with alarm as he would pick his way across the yard with caution to avoid stepping on a snake. Because of Mary's often finicky tendencies, I took one look and figured she would be a basket case. I surely would have to take her to her grandparent's until the snakes dispersed to do snake thing. I was pleasantly surprised when she went right out the door and shoved them away with her foot like the rest of us.

Blackie had other things on his mind. The neighbors across the street had a female cat. They had been tolerant during the winter. She had even found the passage into our cellar that Blackie used for coming and going. I suspect that the always warm furnace was just right for winter cat comfort. With spring, friendship blossomed into romance, and the cat we called Yellow delivered four kittens on the elevated base of our furnace.

To my surprise, Blackie did not take offense to the kittens as I had known other tomcats to do. He actually acted very fatherly, even assisting with the grooming detail. It was many years later that I learned from a National Geographic episode on TV that the first thing a new dominant male in the large cat families did was to destroy all the male cubs. Then I understood Blackie. These were HIS off spring. That was certain as, with my children, we had witnessed a lesson in procreation from his activity. He also acquired a disagreeable habit of spraying urine on my furniture.

The Whitewater High School Marching Whippets (band) were invited to Chicago for an Armed Forces Parade. They were issued brand new gray uniforms and every uniform fit. Virginia was excited because they had been near the Miss America float. Miss America was Linda Lee Mead that year. She had been Miss Mississippi, and had been a teaching intern in Virginia's English class in Meridian.

With the advent of summer, we were anxious to get to Germany and reunite the family. The housing was available and the application for our transportation had been made. We had given notice to the Sturdevants. The furniture had been put in storage and the household good was on the way. We moved into the house with my parents for what we expected to be only a few days. But the port call did not show up. I had a real challenge now. I needed to keep my active children from overstressing their grandparents. We took day long tourist excursions. We went to picnics everywhere I could think of that would hold their attention. I bought and read many of the classic book of childhood. Mostly to Bill and Mary. They included Little Men, Little women, Tom Sawyer, Huckleberry Finn, and Moby Dick to name a few. With Sue and Dan next door, entertaining Virginia was no problem.

Blackie was back in the cellar which he hated. I figured that since we were in the house too, it would be OK to let him out. He immediately disappeared. Billy and I went straight back to the Sturdevant house and found him. The family across the street had claimed their kittens and he went back to be with them. We tried once more to take him with us but he escaped again. We didn't insist.

Time really dragged. In fact, I became so impatient that I finally decided to take the train to Chicago. Fort Sheridan was headquarters of the Sixth Army Service Corp where such matters were supposed to be handled for Wisconsin. While I was in the Janesville station, waiting for the train, my dad showed up with the message that Eli had called and that our port call was eminent.

Chief Warrant Officer Moreau, our next door neighbor from Landshut was personnel officer at Supreme Headquarters in Heidleberg. When Eli contacted him, he was able to run down the problem of the delay. Our passport had been misplaced and the port call was contingent upon the passport.

Instead of going to Chicago, I drove to the junk yard and sold the car.

25

Hanau
(The Final Tour)

Eli:

Once more I kissed the family good-bye and rode off on a new adventure. I was on my way to Germany. This time, I took the car, a '57 Pontiac station wagon. It was 21 August, 1959 when I arrived at the New York Port of Embarkation at Fort Kilmer. The first thing I did was take my car to the Brooklyn Army Base for shipment to Bremerhaven. When I returned to Kilmer, my orders were waiting for me. I was to fly out of McGuire Air Force Base. We arrived at the Rhein-Main Air Force Base at Frankfurt after stops at Gander, Newfoundland and Shannon, Ireland for refueling.

My new unit picked me up at Rhein-Main and we went by sedan to Hanau, which was only thirty minutes away. When I arrived there I went by the 212th Artillery Group and signed in. After a short chat with the commander, Col. Serdic, I reported to the 4th Battalion of the 18th Field Artillery. This was a battalion of 155mm self propelled howitzers. At my interview with the commanding officer, he told me that the battalion was about ready to go to Vilseck (where the firing range was) to take battalion tests. He informed me that he did not want to break up his team.

When I went to the billeting office to get a room in the BOQ, they didn't have any field grade facilities available, but they had an apartment in the Old Argonner Dependent housing area. Two captains were quartered there and the third bedroom was available if I wanted it. That was ok with me so I moved in. My fellow officers were Captain Torraco and Captain Snyder. They were both in the battalion that I had been assigned to.

The battalion had been notified that Corp Artillery in Darmstadt was looking for an S-3. They submitted my name as a candidate and I was sent down to be interviewed by Brigadier General William Harris, Corp Artillery Commander. As I was getting out of the jeep, I ran into one of the lieutenants that I had known in Landshut. He was now a Captain and was the Headquarters Battery Commander of Corp Artillery. The first thing he said after he recognized me was, "Are you looking for the S-3 job. You don't want it. The last guy that had that job had an heart attack." I assured him that I wasn't all that eager to get the job, but I had been sent down.

When I reported to the General in his office. He was very cordial. We had a long discussion on what he was looking for in an S-3. He could tell right away that I was not very enthusiastic about the job. Finally he came right out and said, "You don't want this job, do you?" I told him that was correct. We shook hands, I saluted and returned to Hanau.

I felt that I wasn't really wanted in this outfit and they kept giving me all sorts of little details, even though I had been made the battalion exec in October. Early in November, when they were scheduled to go to Vilseck to retake the battalion tests it was decided that the best place for me would be in Hanau in charge of the rear. They did me a real favor.

The tracked vehicles were shipped by rail while the wheeled vehicles traveled by convoy. When they pulled out for Vilseck I went out early in the morning around 0600 to watch them depart. The first problem I ran into was the ammunition trucks of Service Battery wouldn't start. A couple had even torn up their clutches. I ended up with seven trucks, loaded with the basic load that was required to be in the battalion at all times, that wouldn't run.

I called the CO of the ordinance, Major Callahan, and told him I had seven trucks that wouldn't start because the unit had failed to use the required additive for gasoline to prevent the fuel from freezing. Two trucks had ruined the clutches. It was a priority for us to get them back in operation. Since most of our mechanics were already on the road, could he give us some help?

He sent a crew over to work on the gas problem which was soon solved and those five trucks were on the way by 1100. They towed the trucks with the damaged clutches to their shops and had them repaired and ready to roll by 1300. They had to do the work outside in the cold, because the trucks were loaded with ammunition. Needless to say, the battalion completely flunked their tests.

After the outfit returned, I was sent on TDY (temporary duty) to Operation Winter Shield as the Chief Umpire for the anti-aircraft defense. It is the duty of the umpire detail to see when anti aircraft have gotten off simulated fire that would have hit the target. We had enough enlisted men as umpires to have one with each section. It was their job to observe the simulation and report by radio to the Chief Umpire. He would be on a high hill near the center of the exercise area. That section would then compile the data and radio other umpires near the target who would then mark where the simulated round would have landed.

One good example of how this worked was when about 30 L-19 helicopters were carrying infantry north up the Rhein River. They flew low near the river to avoid anti-aircraft fire. They flew right between elements of an automatic weapons battery that were high on the hill, over looking the river. In a real situation, all they would have needed to do was lower their weapons and fire as the flight went by. I ruled that all the choppers had been shot down. I was actually watching as this action took place. When it came up at the critique that the infantry company and the helicopters had been lost, a lot of high ranking officers rebutted it. I told them they would have been dead ducks from just small arms fire. There is no way you can fly helicopters that low over enemy territory.

In February, the battalion was sent back to Vilseck to retrain and take the battery test that they had failed back in November. As the exec, I was appointed the chief umpire for practice tests. Group Artillery furnished umpires for the actual tests. Major Allen Dingwall who had been my battery exec back at Ft. Campbell was now the battalion S-3. We set up a tough training schedule with one battery taking a practice test as another battery would be practicing on their own and the third battery was doing maintenance.

Each day, for about nine or ten days, every battery was getting good training, much that they should have been doing in the gun park back in Hanau. The first day of this routine, at the critique, I said they looked like the 'Keystone Kops'. By the time we were ready to actually take the tests, I was able to tell them that I thought they had improved enough that they could pass the tests with a little luck.

The next three days, each battery went out and Group gave the test for the record. Early reports from the group umpire was that he was highly impressed with the improvement of the batteries. As soon as the tests were over, the CO had gone back to Hanau to take care of something or other. I advised him that he should stay for the critique, but he ignored my advice. General Harris, Corp Artillery Commander had gotten word from the Chief umpire, telling him of the great improvements that had been made, so he came down to Vilseck to be at the critique.

When Col. Serdic came through the door where the critique was to be held, he immediately wanted to know where the battalion commander was. I told him that he had gone back to Hanau. He told me to get on the phone and call him up. I was to tell him that he had a direct order from the CO to report to him as soon as possible. When I reached him at home, he had just walked in the front door. I gave him the message and he said he was on the way. He arrived about 0200 in the morning. We had received word from Col. Serdic for the CO to be standing in front of him at 0600.

From what I was told, all that Serdic said was, "You are relieved as the battalion commander. Major Fishpaw is now in command of the battalion."

I didn't get the word that I was the new CO until I arrived back in Hanau. Mr. Faupel, the personnel officer, met me at the gate with the order in his hand, for me to take command of the battalion. All I had to do was sign it, but I refused. I felt that I had worked like hell for the battalion commander to get the battalion up to the now superior level, and that when he was relieved, it reflected on me. Of course it was his arrogance that had gotten him relieved. He had insulted the General by leaving for Hanau. He had told me, "I know the battalion did a good job and I am not going to hang around for the critique. I've got business to do in Hanau."

We held a command and staff meeting for which we made our plans for pay day that was coming up. The Chaplain asked if we would support a campaign to raise money to buy stained glass windows for the Chapel. When we paid the troops the next day, they voluntarily donated twice what we needed for the new windows. That was an indication to me that morale was high.

The following morning, I got a call from Col. Serdic saying that he had not received the signed order that I had assumed the command of the battalion. I explained to him how I felt. That made him angry. He said, "I'm giving you a direct order to have that paper signed and on my desk in twenty minutes." "Yes Sir." It took twenty minutes to drive from the Francois Kasern where the 4th of the 18th was to the Fliegerhorst Kasern where the 212th Headquarters was.

I took it over myself and put it right in the middle of his desk. His adjutant was with me. I tried to escape before he came in, but he caught me at the door. He congratulated me for doing a good job on the battalion tests. He said that he knew I would be a dependable battalion commander.

He mentioned that the relieved commander would be brought before a board to see if he should be eliminated from the service. He mentioned that several of the officers had made statements concerning different things that had happened in the past year. They had volunteered to appear at the board to testify against their commander.

I returned to the battalion and immediately called a meeting of all the officers. I told them that I strongly disapproved of any officer who would make a statement against his commander before a board. If they testified, I would do my all in my power to see that they would be eliminated too. I told them that loyalty runs two ways. It is impossible to run a unit when the officers are disloyal to the commander.

Within twenty four hours, they had all withdrawn their statements and announced that they would not testify. All the efforts of the group headquarters to find out why were futile. When the board met, the former commander was put on six months probation with Third Armored Division Artillery. After he had completed his probation he was retained in the service and rotated to the states. He was a West Point graduate.

Probably this was to be one of the most important jobs that I had held during my army career. Our battalion had been assigned a contingency plan to support an armored infantry battalion in the event the Soviets decided to re-establish the blockade. That included the autobahn, the railroad or a downed US plane in the Soviet zone.

In the Soviet zone of Germany, they had twenty six divisions that could get involved at any time or place and we were designate to force our way through. This was cosmic clearance which is above top secret, and was strictly need to know. Only four people in the battalion were aware of this plan.

I did inform the battalion that we had a highly important and classified mission that would make Custer's last stand look like a

Sunday School picnic. The difference was, that we would be trained well enough to live through it. When the average soldier does not have a clear purpose for doing something, they are inclined to loaf. They had to know that it might be necessary to fight their way out the front gate. I didn't want to see any more machine guns without firing pins and to be told that they were on requisition. You can't shoot requisitions. We had the highest priority in Europe on all parts or anything else the was essential to our being able to function. Anything that was not available in Europe would be delivered from the USA immediately on the next plane.

One night, I was at the club and the First of the 75th were having a party. They were all sitting around with their ladies talking. They asked me to join them. Col. Arnold was complaining that General Harris at Corp Artillery had shortstopped a couple of new West Point officers who had been assigned to his battalion.

The 75th had just flunked an IG inspection. He said the reason was because he never got any good officers. That seemed like a pretty dumb thing to say in front of his own officers. I knew that his officers and NCOs were just as good as mine and I told him so. I even said that I thought their wives were even better looking. (I could say that since none of my battalion were there). I made him an offer. I said that we would go to the 'Ole Man' and ask him if we could switch battalions.

Since it was their party, I went back to the bar for the rest of the evening. One by one, many of his officers came to me and begged me to go through with the swap idea. Of course we never did. However, Colonel Serdic did ask me to send over some junior officers and extra mechanics to work with the 75th to get their vehicles and records up to date.

They did pass their second inspection and Col. Arnold wrote letter of commendation to the officers and men who had helped them accomplish the good outcome of the inspection.

At this time, the troops stationed at Fliegerhorst were having a great deal of racial problems. They had a demonstration at the gate because they thought the gate guard had mistreated them. One night two or three of the men had tried to take their girl friends through the gate to the cab stand a few hundred yards up the road. They did not have passes, so were not allowed through the gate. After scuffling with the guard, the Corporal of the Guard was summoned to bring re-inforcements.

A crowd formed and was estimated at over a hundred, mostly black GIs. The Special Police, who were on duty at the gate, withdrew into the guard house that overlooked the gate. One man reached in through the window and grabbed the barrel of a carbine that a policeman had pointed out the window. When the man pulled on the barrel, it went off because the guard had his finger on the trigger. He had shot himself in the stomach and died immediately.

The complete Military Police Detachment of the Hanau Post were called. The executive officer of group tried to calm the mob and was struck in the face by one of them and knocked down. It was then when the Special Police and the Military Police got tough. Using their riot clubs, they ran most of the demonstrators back to their barracks.

A few of the leaders were detained in the guard house. The following day, a couple of my men, who were on temporary duty in the Group band, which was at Fliegerhorst, came to Francoise Kasern to collect money for the family of the man who had been killed. I had put out an order allowing nobody from Fliegerhorst to enter our Kasern. I sent word to the men in the band that as long as they were on TDY to the band, they had better stay there.

Brigadier General Hill, Third Armored Division Artillery Commander, who was the senior officer on the Hanau Post, sent out a letter to be read to all troops on the Post. In general, it said that the army was a pioneer in the integration program and that these racial riots were a disgrace to all soldiers. He asked them to take another look at the situation and to stop the activity that was causing the problems. At the bottom there was a note that nothing was to be added or left out of the statement when it was read to the troops.

After I finished reading the letter at the Friday afternoon formation, I put his letter in my pocket and made my own statement. The first thing I said was that I was fed up with the riots and that the people who started them should be charged with mutiny. "I have heard from the grapevine that another riot is to be held in Hanau this Saturday night, so I'm inviting them to have it here on Lamboy Strasse, so we wouldn't have to go very far to break it up. Right now, I'm ordering all battery commanders to cancel Saturday morning inspection and train in riot gear. That includes our armored personnel carriers. When they get here, I will personally tell them to disperse and give them two minutes to leave. If they fail to do so, we will go in first on foot and if there is resistance we will make a fly wedge of armored personnel carriers. We will lock up everybody we can and shoot them if necessary. We will charge everyone of them with mutiny".

On Saturday morning there was some outstanding riot control training at our Kasern. Everyone had live ammunition in their weapon, but of course, did not fire. They also had tear gas grenades in their pockets. Machine guns were mounted with live ammunition on the armored personnel carriers.

Even the German civilians came and watched through the fence. They were impressed and appreciated the fact that steps were being taken to prevent real problems that could affect them. As a result of my statement, and our training on crowd control, the racial riots stopped instantly. That little display of how we would do it was highly impressive. Word spread through out the theater that the Army was bearing down.

I might mention that we had not had many racial problems in the 4th of the 18th, even though 22% of our people were black. I had a black Captain who was commander of 'C' battery. A dark skinned Puerto Rican commanded 'A' battery. When two black soldiers complained to me that the Puerto Rican was prejudiced against them, I had them transferred to 'C' battery. Captain Williams wouldn't put up with any crap from anyone and they wished they had kept their mouths shut.

During the time that I commander the battalion, some of my best NCOs were black and Captain Williams was one of my best BCs. They were more anxious to put a stop to the racial problems than anyone else in the Army.

Colonel Serdic had gone out on a limb when he made me the battalion commander and he was always pleased when our outfit did something that drew positive attention. He was rotated home in August and Colonel Roger Lilly became the new 212th Group Commander.

Bernice:

The blue lights that marked the runway at O'Hare moved by the window of our jet faster than anything I had ever experienced before. This was my first ride in a jet. It was still possible to take a commercial flight from Janesville in 1960. We had left Wisconsin early in the afternoon and within the hour were at Midway Airport on the south side of Chicago, on the first leg of our journey to Hanau, West Germany. Our schedule called for us to take the limousine from Midway to O'Hare on the north side. The limo was nothing more than an ordinary bus. It took a full two hours to get across town. We were in time for our flight but there was no time to spare.

It was dark as the big bird rose and headed east over Lake Michigan. It is very dramatic at night to look down and see a great city of lights, suddenly go stark black where the shore of the lake begins. We were in Baltimore in less time than it had taken to change airports in Chicago.

Eli's brother, John and his wife Catherine, met us at the gate. The jetways had not been developed then and people meeting passengers were allowed on the tarmac, close to where passengers came off the planes. The kids were fascinated by the resemblance of John to their dad. In fact, from a distance, they thought their dad had come to meet us in Baltimore.

We spent a couple nights in a cottage on the Magothy river that Eli's sister, Annie and her husband, Johnnie Downey, had rented. It was a good break in the trip. Our Bill and his cousin, John were close to the same age and got along well. I enjoyed visiting with Johnnie's mother who I had gotten to know as a good friend the year and a half that I spent in Baltimore. She was getting quite feeble and it was the last time that I saw her.

We flew from Baltimore to New York, landing at LaGuardia. Our seats were in the back. Just as we landed, Mary got sick. It was a DC 6 and the exit was made from a set of steps that dropped down from the rear of the plane. Because I was busy helping Mary, we did not deplane until everyone else was off and gone.

As we were gathering our belongings, an elderly lady came from the first class section. She looked somewhat annoyed at seeing other passengers still on the plane and we heard her say to herself, "I suppose when you have little ones it is easier to wait", and went on her way. The only reason I mention this is because she looked exactly like Eleanor Roosevelt. Since the Democratic convention in Baltimore had just concluded, it could have been.

Our next stop was Fort Hamilton, which is in Brooklyn. It hadn't changed much since the last time we had seen it. It is an older post made up of red brick buildings with a beautiful green parade grounds right in front of the buildings where families bound for Europe are billeted and processed. They played bugle calls for everything. One day I saw two small boys about four or five years old, standing at attention, right hand at the forehead in perfect 'present arms', as the bugle sounded 'Mess Call'. We were told that the parade grounds was soon to be used as the approach for a new bridge to be built across the entrance to New York Harbor.

While in New York, we had time to do a little sight seeing. The subway was entirely safe in those days and we took it to Manhattan. We saw the Rockettes at Rockefeller Center and took the ferry to the Statue of Liberty. We started to go up the inside of the statue. It was very hot. Then we were told that there was a fire near the top and that we should leave. I can't imagine what there was to burn, but I was getting tired anyway and did not feel at all gypped. The kids had a chance to experience the inside and to get a feel for the nature of the structure.

On the day of departure, a bus delivered us, with our baggage, back to LaGuardia where we were scheduled to fly to Frankfurt on 'Overseas Airlines'. I had never heard of this airline as it was a charter outfit. The plane was a four engine propeller driven style. Our seats were in the last two rows, right against the bulkhead by the latrines. Across the aisle was a sergeant and his wife with two good sized children. I think that we must have had the only five kids aboard that were not in diapers. Mary made the trip without any problems.

Next to the latrines in the rear is not where you want to be on a long bumpy ride, but I surely preferred it to being farther forward with all the crying babies. We stopped at Newfoundland and Ireland before we arrived at Frankfurt. Eli was there to meet us. He had rented rooms at the guest house at Rhein Main Air Base for the first night. It was afternoon when we arrived and we were all ready to get some sleep. The kids dropped off immediately. I had to wait a while.

Our new home in Hanau was a two story duplex in the New Argonner Kasern. The duplexes were for field grade officers. There were a dozen or so three story apartment buildings for company grade officers. We had four bedrooms and two bathrooms upstairs. It was the best place we had ever lived in. The elementary school was about a half mile away in the area known as Old Argonner. Virginia, who was a tenth grader in High School, took an army school bus to Frankfurt about 20 miles away.

Things were different from our first tour in Bavaria. We were not furnished with household help, and just about every German we met, spoke English. The rubble was gone and everything was booming. The stores were full of merchandise and we used real American money in most of them, as well as in the American clubs, commissaries and PX. Another sign of prosperity was that while in the 40s and 50s there was not litter on the streets and roads, now there was litter. There were also advertising bill boards and everybody and his sister had a car. The Marshall plan, the American program to restore West Germany, had worked well. We were no longer conquering enemies. We were there to prevent the incursion of communism into Western Europe.

Our very first official duty was to attend a briefing on the evacuation plan for dependents in case of enemy hostility. We were to take our private vehicle to a designated collection point. We were required to be ready at all times with a supply of food and beverage, to last several days. Part of the plan called for each of the new arriving families to make a test run of the designated route. It certainly got our attention that this was not the USA.

We were driving a white and green 1957 Pontiac station wagon at the time. Eli had taken it with him when he went to Germany in 1959. I was glad he had, because he had transmission problems and I didn't have to deal with them. It had another strange quirk. The gas tank was empty when the needle was on one quarter full. I had forgotten about this. Before long, I ran out of gas. One of Murphy's laws says that when you run out of gas, it will always be in the worst place. In this case, it was right in the middle of the main gate at the Post Headquarters. Even worse, it was just after retreat and everybody was going home, but there was a station wagon blocking the gate. It didn't take long for a bunch of GIs to come to my rescue. A couple of them stopped traffic on the busy street while three or four pushed me across to the Quartermaster gas station.

Gasoline was plentiful and inexpensive. The USA had an agreement with the host countries that Americans stationed in Europe did not have to pay any gas tax, which was considerable. The mechanism by which this was handled was by using coupons. We bought them at the PX for which ever country where we planned to travel. There were two types of tickets. Regular gas was available at Quartermaster stations and high test was available at Exxon stations, using Exxon coupons which cost more.

I arranged for a German lady to come by a couple days a week and I paid her. Her name was Marguerita Rosenlotcheur.

She said we should just call her Frau Rose. Although she spoke fairly good English, she hadn't quite mastered the American culture. One day, when I arrived home, after the kids had come in from school, Mary was most annoyed. Frau Rose wouldn't allow her to get a drink of water. The good lady did not realize that the American housing was on a separate water system. Germans, for centuries, had avoided drinking water because it caused disease. They had never needed to purify it to the level that Americans insist upon to make it safe to drink.

The original Passion Play was first produced in a town in Bavaria called Oberammergau. The people of the village reenacted the passion of Christ every ten years. I had seen it in 1950. It was held again in 1960. When we arrived in the late summer, Virginia expressed an interest in seeing it. The rest of the family had no interest. Virginia and I were privileged to take it in. The weather was not very good. The stage was in the open but the auditorium had a roof for the audience. I noticed that Christ wore a white body suit in the crucifixion scene. I didn't blame him, but thought it had been more effective in 1950 when he wore only the loin cloth.

It doesn't take long for new families to become part of a military community. We had arrived in time for all three kids to start school at the beginning of the school term. Bill was a third grader. He liked his new teacher, Ms. Zimmerman, and he did better than any of the previous years. Mary was a fifth grader and made many friends and did well also.

Bicycles were still a major form of transportation. There were well kept bike paths on all the major streets. It wasn't long before Mary had a bike which I used while she was at school. It lived in our front hall, just inside the front door. Virginia had never quite got the knack of riding a bike.

At last Virginia had her chance to be a majorette. The biggest problem was that practice would be after school, and the bus left for Hanau as soon as classes were over. Since public transportation in Hesse was plentiful and reliable, we decided that she could take the train home on days that she had activity after school. One day, I took the train to Frankfurt and met her at school to work out the details of such a trip. We took the strassen bahn (street car) to the hauptbahnhof (main railroad station) and bought tickets for Wolfgang, a small station near our house.

When we arrived at the platform where the trains departed, they had just called the train that we were to take. Just as Virginia got aboard, they blew the whistle and the train started to roll. I had one foot on the train but the conductor shoved me off, back onto the platform and the train left with Virginia but not me. The only thing to do was wait for the next train.

When I arrived a half an hour later I encountered a tearful Virginia. In Germany, the tickets were collected at the arrival stations, before the passengers are allowed to leave the platform. She had detrained OK but because she had been sold the wrong ticket, which was for a different destination, she had not been allowed to leave the platform. She was unable to understand a word they said and they were unable to understand her. It must have been the only place in all Hanau where nobody spoke English. When I arrived, I was able to straighten out the mess with my limited German and we went home. Later, she became quite adept at the language, and the trek, so she used the trains often.

The hub of social life on overseas tours, revolve around the various military clubs, and the individual and collective units. As wife of the 'Ole Man' (commanding officer), I was expected to act as the stand-in mother or big sister, depending on the age, of the other military officers' wives in our unit. There were wives clubs for the battalion and for the 212th group which was the next higher headquarters for the 4th of the 18th as well as for the Hanau post which included all the units.

Protocol was very important. We would have coffee in the morning and teas in the afternoon. We would put out our finest china and linen. It was an honor to pour at tea. The first time I was asked to 'pour' I was being so proper and careful to ask if the guest wanted sugar or lemon and to carry on light conversation. I was doing just great until the Colonel's wife arrived at my side. I got so involved in doing it just right that I forgot to put the cup on the saucer and poured her a saucer full of tea. What can you do? I couldn't help but laugh. She laughed with me and we became close friends.

The men were gone a great deal of the time on service practice where they fired the guns on the range at a place called Vilseck. There were also maneuvers and exercises a great deal of the time. When the battalion was out, we would meet at each others homes several evenings a week. These meetings were much more informal than the day time stuff. We might have light refreshments. We often played games like charades and other parlor style activities. I enjoyed these meetings.

Bridge was also popular, but I had sworn off bridge years before and refused to get trapped in that web again. However,

371

they often played far into the night. On one occasion, one of the captain's wives sorted her hand and being first to bid said, "Eenie, meanie, minie, moe." She did not realize what she had said until one of the ladies, who was black, took strong exception. That broke up the bridge game and there was real hard feelings. I heard about it early the next morning. It was one of those happenings where the news, often distorted, had spread like a fire in the wind. It had even reached the men in Vilseck.

I had to do something and do it fast. First, I called on the girl who had made the Faux Paux. She was beside herself with remorse and told me she had never given the least thought to the complexion of her bridge partner. Next I called on the lady who was so upset. I explained that had there been any real malice intended, the expression would never had been used. She accepted that with good grace. The two apologized to each other and everything was OK. I was sure glad to be able to report this to the 'Ole Man' when I got his call.

We had monthly luncheons at the officers' club where different units rotated being hostess. We got all dressed up and wore hats and gloves and were very proper. The V Corp in Frankfurt also had periodic luncheons, which field grade wives were expected to attend. One, I vividly recall. That day the ambassador's wife, Mrs. Dowling, was the speaker.

Being twenty miles away, several of us car pooled. On this day, I was supposed to bowl in our league in Hanau at 2:30 PM. I thought I would have plenty of time to get home and change. However, the rest of the ladies in the car wanted to go to the big PX in Frankfurt after lunch. I still thought I could get back in time, but knew I couldn't go home to change. I bought a shirt and slacks, so I could change at the bowling alley. I did make it but discovered that my new slacks were so small that I had to remove my underpants to get them closed.

I have no idea how it happened, but that day I bowled better than I had ever bowled before. I even had a 200+ game. That is the thing that superstitions are made of. After that I always bowled without my underpants and it worked. That is, it did until one day as I delivered the ball, the seam in the front of my slacks split wide open. What a problem. The way such things happen, it was just at the time about 200 GIs were on break from their training and had come into the building behind the lanes, having a coke while they watched the ladies bowl. I had to bowl four frames, backing off the approach, before they went back to work and I could go to the rest room to pin up. That superstition was no longer operable.

Perhaps the most unique features of Hanau am Main (on the Main river) is that it was the birth place and home of the Brothers Grimm. Americans always think of the Grimm Brothers for their fairy tales, but actually, they were most notable for being the first to bring order to the German language and to set forth the rules of German grammar. The fairy tales were just recreation. They would do what Germans have done for centuries on Sunday. They would walk in the country side. In their travels they talked to the old wives and story tellers of the region. From those visits they compiled their collection of stories.

In the center of Hanau, like every other European city, there was a Marc Platz (market place) where the farmers and other trades people brought their produce and wares on market day. In the middle of the Platz was a large bronze statue of the Brothers Grimm. One was sitting and one was standing. The local people told their kinder that every year on New Year's eve the brothers would trade places.

There was a chapel on the Francoise Kasern which had been the stable when Napoleon had occupied that area. We attended Chapel where our troops were. The battalion Chaplain was Chaplain Maas. He thought it would be nice to have a children's choir and recruited one of the lieutenant's wives, Nancy McClurg, who was a music major, to organize it. Both Bill and Mary were in the choir. That did present a problem to Nancy, who thought that Bill was not a very good singer. But how could she ask 'Ole Man's' kid to drop out? She solved the problem by asking Bill not to let the sound come out of his mouth. I didn't think he sounded all that bad. I even bought him a guitar.

The army, in cooperation with the Red Cross, decided that every adult dependent should be trained in first aid. To do this, they selected a small group of volunteers to be trained as first aid instructors. I was one of them. During our two years in Hanau, I gave a great many first aid classes. When I ran out of adults, I was even invited by many of the teachers at the elementary schools to have classes. This was one of my favorite activities. I enjoyed having the kids ask questions and being able to answer them. Sometimes we got way beyond the Red Cross outline.

One of these classes was Mary's sixth grade room taught by Mrs. Snow. I became so much a part of the class that when they had a field trip to Frankfurt, I was one of their chaperones. It was a wonderful day. We visited a prestigious art gallery in the morning, and saw the original paintings of many of the great renaissance artists.

In the afternoon, we went to the museum of natural history. The skeleton of a large dinosaur dominated the first room. In another room a stuffed anaconda snake with the full grown pig in its mouth demonstrated how large the snake's mouth could stretch. Very impressive. There were lots of interesting displays. The kids seemed to be enjoying the experiences as they roamed the exhibits.

They were well behaved but certainly not quiet. Therefore, it seemed rather strange when suddenly a hush fell over the whole group. I hurried to see what had captured their attention. It was a display of many bottles, each containing a human fetus in formalin. The display started with an embryo, no bigger than a pea and progressed up to what looked to be about five months. There was no giggling. They demonstrated a sort of reverence for what they were seeing. Even I was impressed by the clear progress of the creation of the human being.

It was not long after that when Mary and her friend Pam came to me one evening and informed me that they knew that babies came out of their mother's belly but they didn't understand how they got in there. Just then Eli arrived home and I had to get supper. I told Pam to go home and ask her mother. That evening Mary and I, just the two of us, had a long talk in her room.

Eli had told different people that I was a Girl Scout leader and they wasted no time getting me involved. I'm not sure what my first job was, but before long I was not only a troop leader of Mary's intermediate troop, but also had a cub den for boys Bill's age and was the Hanau neighborhood chairman. Getting leaders was not much of a problem and we had many good troops. However, there was only one senior troop as there were not as many teen age girls still interested in scouting or mothers who wanted to lead them.

A Captain's wife with no children in Europe was their leader. As neighborhood chairman, it was brought to my attention that she had been conspicuously under the influence at one of the meetings. It was my job to visit her at her quarters and ask her to give up the troop. It was the hardest thing I had to do. That left a void which I then filled, by also becoming the senior troop leader.

The Scouts had an overseas council known as NAGS (North Atlantic Girl Scouts). They quickly recruited me to help plan a council wide event for Senior scouts. One of the events that I coordinated was a conference in Heidelberg called "Honor the Past-Serve the Future". I don't remember a whole lot about it except that I was criticized for doing too much of the work. In theory, the girls were supposed to do.

The next year, the senior event became a February week end camp in the Taunus Mountains. We were at an army rest camp north of Frankfurt. Our Hanau troop was responsible for developing and running a wide game. This is an activity where a story is developed, having the different patrols follow clues and instructions from one place to another. At each station they would perform tasks using scouting skills such as fire building, lashing, compass reading and the like on which they are graded in competition.

We used the 'Wizard of Oz' as our story line. The participants demonstrated exercising to limber up the tin man and feats of courage (nothing too dangerous) to inspire the cowardly lion, etc. It was a lot of fun and took most of the day.

We camped in pup tents in the snow. Some of the girls from other troops refused to sleep out and stayed in the lodge. All of my troop used their camping skills to be snug and warm in the snow. I wouldn't think of using the lodge and slept out too. The only real challenge was forcing myself to get out of my bed roll to go to the latrine. But of course, I was an army veteran. My greatest discovery was that by putting a pair of wool socks over my sneakers before putting on my rain boots, my feet were completely comfortable for the whole weekend.

Another adventure with the troop was the trip to England. There is a World Center for Scouts and Guides in England called 'The Ark'. The girls wanted to visit it. They raised the money for the trip. We planned to travel by train but very late in the planning, that fell through. We chartered a German bus with a German driver. We left from our quarters about nine o'clock at night. I had two of the scout's mothers as chaperones and about three other young wives who went along to fill up the bus and help pay the bus bill. They did not stay at the Ark.

The very first glitch developed right in front of my house. After everyone was aboard and the bags all stowed in the luggage compartment, I was checking off and asked each passenger to hold up her passport. Of course, one girl had put hers in her suitcase. Since we would be crossing the border into Belgium during the night, we had to unload all the luggage until we found her bag and of course hers was in the very rear. Eli was so amused, I wanted to kill him.

It was like a slumber party to the girls. They all had to put rollers in their hair before they went to sleep. In the process one girl stood up just as one of the chaperones was getting something from the overhead rack and scratched the lady's eye. I had a full first aid kit but no eye drops.

By the time we got to Brussels, she was in great pain and I had to do something. It was early in the morning and I saw a milk store open. Since French is the language of Belgium, one of the girls, who took French in high school, accompanied me into the milk store to explain that we needed to talk to the American Express. The number was dialed and I talked to a representative in English. He offered to call an eye doctor and would tell the bus driver how to find him.

This all took time and after getting lost a few times, we saw the doctor. It could only be described as a comedy of language errors, with my German bus driver in a French speaking country. We had to be in Osteen by ten AM in order to board the ferry for Dover, and it was getting late. We did get there on time and we got the troop aboard. The bus sat on the dock as I watched a hundred cars loaded. Then, to my horror, the boat started to move and my bus was still on the dock. Sometimes, not being able to communicate has its reward. I discovered, by watching, that the bus was too long to clear the top of the entrance to the auto deck. They had to move the boat a few meters, to reduce the angle of the gangway. What a relief to see my bus drive aboard.

It was night when we arrived in London. I had a map of London and instructions on how to reach the Ark. It was now necessary to drive on the left side of the road which was unfamiliar to my driver. However, he was aware of this and did very well. It was raining and being rush hour did not make it any easier. One of the girls was old enough to drive, so was able to help me read the road signs and the map. Between the two of us, and another scout who attended a German boarding school and was fluent in German, we guided a frustrated driver across the Thames and eventually to the Ark. The poor man was so glad to deliver his cargo that he left his bus in front of the Ark and found a nearby pub with rooming facilities, not too different from a German gasthaus. I presume he spent a happy three days doing his own thing without a bunch of noisy American women giving him orders.

There was no planned program at the Ark except that breakfast and supper were included in the package and I insisted that the girls be present for these meals. Some of the girls also enjoyed taking 'tea' at the house. Tea is actually a late afternoon ritual involving not only tea but bread and butter as well as scones (cookies) and other tid-bits. For breakfast the first morning we had canned beans. I couldn't help but think of that old children's song, "Beans for breakfast, beans for supper, great big beans for tea."

The very first thing we did, we did as a group. We took the underground to Buckingham Palace to watch the changing of the guard. We were somewhat disappointed to learn that during the winter, the ceremony took place at Clarence house, a few blocks away. We quickly hiked over there and were just in time to see the military band lead the new guard around the corner and turn into the court yard of this palace. There was quite a bit of marching up and down, while the band played a short concert before the guard being relieved marched off around the corner. Instead of the red coats that we had expected, they all wore blue overcoats. From there, having mastered the underground, we broke up into interest groups.

The girls did not mind the lack of program. They went every which way on excursions of interest to each group. Only one girl went alone. I discovered that this was a mistake. She was the last one to get back that night. I sat up worrying about her. She had some strange story about witnessing a murder in the subway. In later years, it was a hard and fast rule that, whenever I was responsible for an organized group, we would always use the buddy system.

The group that I was with went to the wax museum and some of the art galleries. Virginia and I, just the two of us, enjoyed some activities together. One of them was a visit to Herrods, a high class department store just off Piccadilli Circus. We bought her a very nice green and white tweed suit. We also had tea at a pub across from the Tower of London. To my disappointment, we had arrived there only minutes after the doors to the crown jewel exhibit had closed. Seeing the crown jewels was one of my main interests.

There were other Girl Guides from many other countries staying at the Ark. Most of them were older than our group and were using the Ark as temporary residence while in London, many of them as students. I enjoyed talking with them as did some of the girls. We were the only real group.

On Sunday morning we all decided to go to Westminster Abbey. The service was Church of England which we know as Episcopal. We sat in one of the transepts. Of great interest to all of us was the long row of marble boxes along the side of the chairs which contained the bodies of long dead English heroes.

When we left England and were once more on the continent, I heard the audible sigh of relief from my driver as he pulled away from the pier saying to himself, "Rex Fahrn" (drive on the right).

It was decided that instead of going to a restaurant in Belgium for supper, that we would have a picnic on the bus. We had bought bread, meat, cheese, chips, etc. in London with this in mind. When it came supper time, the girls started to unpack their groceries to start eating. The driver became very upset. He had a brand new bus on its first trip and he was not about to let a bunch of crazy Americans mess it up. I didn't really blame him but we needed a place to eat.

With much bilingual discussion, he finally agreed to get us to a place where we could have our picnic. I was expecting him to stop at a park or even beside the road in a grassy place so it was a surprise when he stopped at a Bistro (a Belgium beer joint and restaurant). I couldn't imagine the owner, who was in business to sell food, allowing someone to use his tables for their own groceries. I was pleasantly surprised when he not only permitted us to spread out but actually seemed to welcome us. Even the other customers were enjoying the action. I bought beverages all around and before long the girls and the local people were chatting in a fractured, multilingual way, part American, part French, part German and mostly pantomime. Everyone seemed to be having a great time.

The Cub den was entirely different from the girls, although I used a lot of the material I had learned as a girls scout leader when planning programs for the boys. I had about ten third graders in my den. I had a nice room in the cellar that was ideal for a meeting place. Instead of having the boys come in the front door and through the house to get to the cellar stairs, we used the outside cellar window. It was located under the outside kitchen door that opened out. There was a steel grate over the window well. The cubs would pull the grate up and lean it over the kitchen door, them jump down into the well and through the window that I would have open for them. They thought this was really great.

While girls are not exactly quiet, boys can be unbelievably noisy. One day I decided that we would have a contest to see who could yell the loudest. I never did that again.

It never occurred to me that anyone might be watching this unorthodox entry until one morning when I opened the kitchen door. I heard the grate crash back into place. I thought that the guys must have forgotten to put it back after they left. Later, when I went to the cellar, I found all of our coats on the cellar steps. I still was confused and thought that Bill had gotten angry with his sisters and me and thrown our coats into the cellar. He denied it. Later inspection disclosed that the cellar window had been forced and left open. Someone had been in our house, but must have been scared away and left his intended loot of our coats. The most mysterious part of the episode was that my bowling ball was out in the back yard without the bag. Several days later one of my neighbors called and told me that she had seen her small children playing with the bag.

Eli:

When Colonel Roger Lilly became the new 212th Group Commander, He had hardly found the PX when we had a murder on our hands. Under the previous battalion commander there was a soldier in 'B' Battery, who had cut another soldier on the arm with a switch blade while we were at Vilseck. After I took over the battalion he had been court martialed. He had been given six months confinement at hard labor and fined two thirds of his pay.

I received a call from the Corp JAG officer saying that he had reviewed the case. The soldier had been examined by a psychiatrist. The Psychiatrist said that the man's commander was picking on him and that he should be released. I was given an order from Corp to get him out.

Not long after that, one Sunday morning while I was at Chapel, the Chaplain was praying about the problem on Lamboy Strasse last night. When the service was over, I went straight to Battalion Headquarters to see what had happened last night. I was told by the OD that a man had been all cut up across the street from our front gate. He had been cut from his throat to his crotch and the genitals had been cut off. He was dead.

Reliable witnesses had reported that the assailant had ran into our Kasern. Right away, I told them to call 'B' Btry and asked them if Benny Williams had a pass last night. They said that he had been on pass and had come in just after curfew at 2300. I called the MPs and told them that I had a prime suspect for that murder. I gave the OD instruction that Benny Williams should be released anytime the MPs came for him.

By the time we got home, I had a call that Pvt. Williams and two others had been picked up and were being held in the Hanau MP station for questioning. About 1300 I got a call from the Chief of Staff of the V Corp. He told me that he was in my office and wanted to know if I knew what was going on in my battalion. I briefed him on the action so far and told him that I would be right out. He told me not to come.

I immediately put on my uniform and headed for the Kasern. As it turned out, the two extra men who had been taken in, were with Benny Williams just before the time of the incident and had tried to get him to go back to the barracks. He told them that he was going to go across the street and cut up that guy.

They had tried to restrain him, but he threatened to cut them up if they tried to stop him. He ran across the street and had done exactly what he had said he was going to do. They had seen the man fall in the gutter in a pool of blood and they knew that he was dead.

Later, Benny William showed up in the room where they pretended to be sleeping. They saw the bloody knife and were too scared to move. He was gone for a few minutes and returned without the knife and he had washed his hands. An intense search for the weapon took place and it was finally found on Tuesday under a roof tile in the attic of the barracks.

My office was over run by investigators, the CIC and the CID and several other big shots were there. They thought that there must be something subversive going on. They suggested this to me and I told them that the only thing subversive that was going on was the JAG officer and the policy of Corp Headquarters that ties the hands of the junior commanders to administer justice in their units because they wouldn't let us put people in the stockade. I told them that the soldier had been released from confinement by their orders and that it would never have happened if he had been kept where he belonged.

A major, who was still wearing his golfing clothes, pointed out that he was writing this all down. He wanted to know if I really wanted the Corp commander to be told everything I had said. I said, "I sure do. I want him to hear every word of it. We need to do something to get these bad apples out of the service. I would like to see Corp change their policy on military justice and give the authority back to the junior commanders where it belongs."

By 2000 Sunday evening the Corp Commander, General Adams was briefed on the whole affair and on my comments. He made no comment except that he wanted to see every General officer in the Corp in his office at 0600 Monday morning.

When that meeting took place, we learned that all he had said was, "My corp policies have been hurting our unit commanders. I want all of you to go back to your units and let them know that they have the full support of the chain of command and to get tough and eliminate the bad apples."

They held a general Court Martial for Private Williams in Frankfurt at V Corp Headquarters. The trial only lasted a few days. The evidence was so complete that there was no doubt that Benny Williams had committed the murder. The defense was that the prisoner was crazy and couldn't tell right from wrong. When I heard this, I sent them the psychiatrist original report that had been sent to me which had kept me from boarding the man out of the service. It had given such a glowing report on the man that if he was that good, he should be sent to OCS.

When that was presented to the court, they immediately adjourned until they could recall the psychiatrist. He was conveniently in the United States where he had accompanied a group of patients. He was brought back to testified. He had no idea that he had ever seen the prisoner before. They found the prisoner guilty and sentenced him to twenty years at Levenworth and a dishonorable discharge.

In December of 1961 I was promoted to Lieutenant Colonel. Colonel Lilly, the 212 Artillery Group Commander, who was my commanding officer, came to my office where he and Bernice pinned on my silver leaves. We had a party at the officers' club at Old Argonner to wet my new leaves. Every officer and his wife in Hanau must have been there.

Shortly after I was promoted, a master sergeant was assigned to our battalion. His name was Bill Craig. He stated that he was going to put in for retirement in a short while. He was disgusted with things that happened in a signal battalion in Mannheim where he had just been assigned. The unit had been deactivated and that made him excess.

Colonel Roger Lilly is all smiles as he pins silver leaves on the new Lt. Colonel Eli. Bernice is pretty happy about it too.

I asked him to wait. I needed a Sergeant Major at the time and he looked like a good prospect for that job. He said he'd give it a go. It was one of the best moves that I made. After two weeks, he was operating at his job which was to work with the first sergeants by daily contact. Everything really brightened up around headquarters with him there. The first time I saw him, his appearance reminded me of the much respected English Sergeant Majors. After a couple weeks, he decided to stay in the army until it was time to retire.

I appreciated how he kept in touch with what was going on in the battalion at all times. Every morning when I arrived, he would brief me of what was going on and if and where there were any problems.

He went on to be the Command Sergeant Major in many prestigious units, including the Army that was in Vietnam. He missed being appointed Command Sergeant Major of the whole Army by one person. At one time he was the Command Sergeant Major of the Third Army in the southeast US.

While I was still the battalion commander of the 4th of the 18th I was appointed by Colonel Lilly to be on the Hanau Post Dependent School Committee. My job was to be in charge of discipline referred to the committee which the school principles had found they were not able to handle. There were three elementary schools and a junior high in Hanau. The high school students were bussed to Frankfurt.

About the first problem that I encountered was confusion at the school bus stops at Fliegerhorst. There were at least ten or twelve buses that picked up students along the curb near the dependent housing area, to take them into Hanau. There was lots of confusion when they were loading in the morning and some student were getting into fights.

I went out to see what the problem was and discovered that there was no specific place for each bus to stop. They just parked where ever there was a place. The kids never knew where their bus would stop. When the buses came in, there was a lot of running around and bumping into each other as the kids tried to find the right bus.

I told the Sergeant Major at that Kasern to extend the area designated for the school busses and to mark the curb with a number for each bus. We had signs made and put in the busses that everyone could read, with the number of the bus and the school that they would be going to. That way all the kids would know where to wait as each bus would stop at its designated spot.

There were reports that there was fighting on some of the junior high buses. There was a German driver for each bus. He was in charge. Some of the kids took advantage of the fact that he was German, which added to the problem. Some of the parents wanted an MP on the buses. I was opposed to that. I had a better idea. We gave the driver the authority, when he had a disturbance, to pull right into the MP portico. The MP would come on and remove the trouble makers. They would hold then until the sponsor came and got them.

The first day, the kids on one of the junior high buses didn't take it serious. The driver drove into the MP station and dumped half the bus in the station. After their fathers had been required to get the kids out of detention, the problem disappeared. If any body didn't like it, they could see me. End of problem.

Someone had been throwing stones off the railroad bridge near the Pioneer Kasern and had been hitting some of the trains. The MPs staked it out and after about a week, they caught the star quarterback for the Frankfurt American high school who lived in Hanau. His father was an NCO in another outfit.

It was decided immediately between the father's commanding officer and the senior commander, that the family would be returned to the United States as soon as possible. This created quite an uproar. The football fans of the school didn't want to see their star leave, but to no avail. He was gone.

During the year and a quarter that I was the commander of the Fourth battalion of the Eighteenth Field Artillery, we had lots of training including field exercises and unit tests. We were rated superior in most of the things that we did. The battalion ran with a minimum of problems.

Bernice:

Each of the apartment houses had three floors for apartments and on the fourth floor there was a very nice activity room. The army was always supportive of youth activities and assigned several of these rooms in the various housing kaserns to the Girl Scouts for weekly meeting places. They even put tables and chairs in them, but there was no running water. As neighborhood chairman, I spent a great deal of energy pulling strings to get sinks in all the rooms.

Scouting occupied a major part of my activity in those days. I took a course in day camp directing offered by NAGS at Rhein-Main Air Base. It was a good course but the building we were using was directly under the approach to the busiest airport in Europe. We were frequently interrupted by loud aircraft noises.

I learned a lot and was able to direct the Hanau day camp in 1961. The army made a good sized tract of land at Fliegerhorst available. They put up some kitchen flies and some pyramidal tents. They even erected a flag pole so that we could have flag ceremonies. The 212th Group assigned a private and a sergeant to assist us with many details. They seemed to enjoy teaching the girls such things as proper flag protocol and handling.

It was a good camp and well attended. We had four patrols, one for every group including brownies, intermediates, Jr. high and seniors.

By now, Bill was too old to be expected to take part in girls' activity. Because all the females in the house were going to be occupied for two weeks with camp, he and Eli decided to take a trip on their own. They set the station wagon up to use as a camper. I think probably this was mostly to make me believe that they were being super thrifty. They actually stayed in gasthauses and castle type tourist accommodations as they moved around southern Germany. Even though they had some car trouble, they both enjoyed the opportunity to be together and away from me and the girls. The girls rode the bus that the army provided to pick up the campers and I rode the bike.

That summer, someone got the idea that it would be fun to have a soft ball game between the officers' wives and the NCOs' wives. One of the captains held practice on the playground at New Argonner. I joined in and found out I could still hit and throw a ball fairly well. I borrowed Bill's glove and Eli and I spent our evenings in the back yard playing catch. I had been a pitcher back in Johnstown, so I brushed up and got fairly good at it.

I also liked to run bases. Before long, I got the job as the starting pitcher and the lead off batter. I certainly was not invincible, but when the day of the game came, I did fairly well. I soon discovered that the opponents were not expecting me to steal bases, so I ran every time I got on base which was every time I came to bat. I even hit a home run and got the game ball.

One of the bonuses of being on foreign assignment in Europe is that there were great opportunities to travel. The Defense Department had several recreation areas for the use of the troops and we had many opportunities to use them. Our favorite was at Berchtesgaden. Eli and I had been there in 1949 and 50. Now we could visit there as a family.

Berchtesgaden is in southern Bavaria and is dominated by twin mountains called the Watzmann. There are two large peaks with several smaller peaks between them. They are supposed to represent the father, the mother and the kids. At the foot of the Watzmann there is a beautiful clear deep lake called the Konigssee (king's lake).

One year during spring vacation from school, we went to Berchtesgaden. Poor Virginia had a paper due at school so she stayed at the hotel one day while Eli and I took Bill and Mary on a boat ride on the Konigssee. Because the lake is located between mountains, one of the features of the boat ride is when the guide plays the bugle and the sound comes ringing back in the echos.

The high light of that day was discovering another, even more beautiful lake above the Konigssee called the Obersee (high lake). Centuries ago there had been an avalanche that had created a natural dam. This lake was fifteen or twenty feet higher. It could only be reached by hiking from the boat landing about a mile. The view was certainly worth the effort.

Berchtesgaden is only a few miles from Austria. A favorite attraction near Saltzburg (salt city) is a tour of the salt mine. Everyone has to visit the salt mine. We were given miners' clothing to put on and ride through the mine on a personnel train that you straddle. Salt is mined by flooding cavities in the mountain with water. That dissolves the salt which is then pumped out and evaporated. The pipes are made of hollow logs which centuries exposure to salt have preserved.

In Bavaria, most of the men wear a green felt hat. Many of the American boys enjoyed this particular style of head gear. Every village and hamlet had a crest which they made available to tourists in the form of small pins. The boys would purchase these pins every where they went and put them on their Bavarian hat. The more pins on the hat the greater their status as a traveler. Bill's hat was almost covered with pins. It actually became quite heavy.

When we went to the mountains, a walking stick was also a popular accessory. These were canes with a sharp pointed tip. Crests and symbols of each locality were available to be nailed to your cane. Bill's cane was covered with these shields. I only put one on my cane because I thought that having so many was poor taste. The cane was certainly a useful items as we hiked the sometimes slippery mountain trails. We had given Bill a box camera and he took great delight in snapping our picture if we took a tumble in the snow.

Another favorite recreation area was Garmisch. This area was developed for the 1936 winter Olympics. It is located at the foot of the Zugspitz (train of peaks) which are the tallest Alps in Germany. To get to the Zugspitz, it is necessary to ride on the cog railroad. This is a very popular European skiing area.

We rode up there but didn't try to do any skiing. On one visit, when it was winter, the Special Service were using the golf course at Garmisch for a beginners ski school. I had had all the skiing I could handle twelve years before, but the kids all wanted to try it. We rented clothing, boots and equipment and they lined up with other beginners' for a class in skiing. Bill and Mary were doing OK but it wasn't long until Virginia fell down. The ski instructor ignored her, so Mary came to her rescue and helped her back to the lodge. This caused both of them to lose out on the lesson.

The Olympic ice arena built for the 1936 Winter Olympics had been made into a night club and they had ice shows every

The Fishpaw family enjoy an evening at the Casa Carioca ice show in Garmish. From the left, Bernice, Virginia, Mary, Eli and Bill.

evening. This was another family fun event. It was called the Casa Carioca.

Eli:

The colonel had been pleased with my handling of the battalion. When he needed a new executive officer, he wanted someone with experience as a battalion commander. Although I was the junior Lt. Colonel in the group he selected me.

My replacement at the 4th of the 18th was Lt. Colonel Woodward. He had lead the artillery testing team for the V Corp for a couple years.

The 212th Artillery group Headquarters was at the Fliegerhorst Kasern. It had been a large air base for the Germans. The group consisted of eight battalions, seven which were nuclear capable. The weapons ranged from the 155mm self propelled howitzers to the Corporal, an intermediate range missile capable of firing 300 miles. We were directly under the control of V Corp Artillery in Darmstadt.

387

The mission of the group was to supervisor the training of the Artillery battalions in the command and to see that they were combat ready at all times. We were not actually in a shooting war, but our presence was a major factor in the so called 'Cold War' to prevent the Soviets from taking over Western Europe. Our nuclear strength was a very big factor in preventing any mass attacks.

Colonel Lilly's year as Group Commander had been very successful because he, like Serdic before him, was a good commander. He went to Seventh army, where General Harris had recently been assigned as their Army Artillery Officer.

In his place, Colonel Roderick Wetherell, a West Point officer, took over the group. His wife's name was Jo. She was the daughter of General Bolling. When Col. Wetherell reported in, we had a long talk about what he expected. I was highly impressed with the statement that he made. "I'm going to depend on you to help the battalion commanders in any problem that may come up. Only bring the serious problems or those of a personal nature, to me."

Most of battalion commanders found this acceptable except one who insisted in always talking directly with the commander because he outranked me by about two years. That was ok by me.

About the first thing after Wetherell arrived, he was sent to language school at Oberamergau. That left me in charge of the group. The senior Lt. Colonel, who commanded the Corporal battalion, was the nominal acting commander and signed any paper that were required, and was briefed on major problems. Actually, he left the day to day operation of the group to me.

During this period, we were on a Seventh Army CPX (Command Post Exercise) This is mainly a test of communications and tactics and does not involve large movement of actual troops. Major Paul Willis was the group S-3. He kept a beautiful situation map in the operations van with the location of every unit involved with the exercise. It was very impressive.

Not long after we had gone out, General Kerwin paid us a visit. He was the Division Artillery Commander of the Third Armored Division. It turned out that the real purpose of his visit was to find the location of all his battalions and to communicate with them. He had lost contact because his radio did not have enough range to reach them. With his big map, Willis was able to brief him on all the locations and then handed him the microphone on our radio so that he could contact each of his unit commanders.

When the problem was over, we attended a critique put on by the umpires from the Seventh Army. One of the first officers to give the critique had been assigned to evaluate the 212th Artillery Group. He stated that he was highly impressed with the efficient operation of the group during the three day exercise. The group's eight battalions made up the largest group in the entire US Army. He said that he was surprised to find out that the junior Lieutenant Colonel in the group was in charge.

General Kerwin stood up and told about the help that he had received from the 212th. "They not only knew everything about the locations of all the units, but they actually put me in radio contact with all of my battalions. I want to thank them."

Fliegerhorst was a large Kasern, just outside Hanau that housed many units, including many of the units of the 212th. The 212th was in charge of the kasern because they were the senior headquarters located there.

One night, at about 2000, a report came in to headquarters that there was about to be a riot on the drill field in the center of the kasern. There were around 2000 troops, half black and half white, divided by a narrow stripe of grass about 40 feet wide.

Captain Bailey, a young black officer, was the staff duty officer when the report was received. He quickly put on his steel helmet and rode out to the field in his jeep. Sure enough, It was just as it had been described. He drove right up the gap in the middle of the field and with the bull horn. He gave them two minutes to return to the barracks that were all around the field.

Most of the troops, both black and white obeyed the order. About 50 or 60 black soldiers refused to move. Again The captain gave them 30 seconds to dispersed. When they refused, he pull out his 45 and emptied the clip at their feet. They were all in their barracks in less than half a minute. He set there a few minutes and when nobody else appeared, he went back to headquarters.

Bailey's comment on the duty officers book showed a small disturbance on the drill field. "The men obeyed my order and returned to the barracks." Everyone on the post knew what happened before the first cup of coffee had been finished. What could have been a nasty incident had been prevented by the courage and decisiveness of one officer. He was the assistant adjutant and the athletic officer.

Bernice:

One of our more ambitious trips was the summer of 1961 when we drove to Italy. Driving south we went by way of Austria and through the Brenner Pass. It was of some interest and concern that the Italians and the Austrians were having a minor border war. It didn't seem to have interfered with the use of the pass by the tourists. We did notice an unusually large number of soldiers hanging around, not doing much of anything. At first it was Austrian soldiers and later Italian soldiers.

The situation was of no consequence to us until we got ready to stop for the night. There were no vacant rooms anywhere. We were on the east side of Lake Guarda. We later learned that because of this minor war, the Europeans, who usually vacationed on the west side, were on the east side this year. At first Eli, speaking English, tried several places with no success. Finally, I said I would try, using my somewhat limited German. I actually succeeded in getting us five beds in an Inn Keeper's store room. My family never let me forget about that.

We visited Verona first, then headed for Venice. Venice, being surrounded by water, does not allow cars. Everyone we tried to get information from told us to go to Chioggia. This was a fishing village on the mainland south of Venice. There we stayed at the Grand Hotel. That sounded very grand. It was not bad but certainly not opulent. At a grand hotel, one expects grand food. My family are not as adventurous about food as I am. While they ate beef, I had squid. The location was good, as it was only a few miles from one of Europe's more famous beaches. The Lido is on the Adriatic Sea and its reputation is well earned.

It was decided that Eli would take Bill and Mary to the beach and Virginia and I would take a ferry across the bay to Venice. We did all the tourist things like a ride on a gondola. I was disappointed that our gondolier did not sing to us but he took us to all the most popular attractions of the city. We fed the pigeons in St. Mark's square and bought glass souvenirs at a glass factory where we watched the glass blowers making ornate objects.

Rome was another adventure. We had no sooner entered the city than a young man on a motor scooter offered to help us find a place to stay. After our earlier experience with housing, this sounded like a great idea. We followed him to the Pension Gallia. Pensions are hotels that provide breakfast and supper. Pension Gallia was on one of the squares which are so prevalent in Rome.

It had a rickety elevator which only worked part of the time, seldom when we were going up. Our rooms were on the third floor. It was right across the street from the Church of the Madonna.

Eli informed us that he would see Rome by walking and using the guide book. I always suspected that he toured some of the bars as well. The kids and I decided to take advantage of the guided tours. We visited the forum where we saw a heated discussion between a policeman and a taxi driver. This was, of course, the seat of democracy and they were exercising free speech. Virginia bought a booklet that had photos of the remains of the many structures of the forum with transparent overlays with artist renditions of how it must have looked when it was the center of western civilization. Her favorite was the Hall of the Vestal Virgins. The Coliseum looked more like a pile of ruble than a stadium.

I liked the Pantheon, which is a gem of antiquity, hidden away amongst the buildings of modern Rome. When we visited the Fountain, each of us threw in our two coins. That is to assure that you will return to Rome. So far, Mary and Virginia have had the opportunity to return. I doubt if I ever will and don't expect Bill will either, as his interests are in other areas. I suppose that two out of four is not bad.

The tour took us to a church where we saw Michelangelo's famous statue of Moses. The guide also pointed out a very nasty looking chip on Moses' left knee where the sculptor had become so enraged because the life like statue would not speak to him that he had thrown his hammer. It was in this church where we were told that a fragment of wood in a glass box by the alter was a part of the original cross of Jesus.

Rome is full of Catholic churches. The one I liked the best was called St. Paul's outside the wall. This was where we were told that St. Paul was supposed to have been crucified, upside down, at his request. It was a beautiful church with windows of yellow alabaster instead of glass.

One of the more interesting observations about Rome was what seemed like a large number of whole blocks where buildings were missing, probably a hold over from the war. The ruble was cleared away and the sidewalks would surround the block about ten feet higher than the ground. In these holes there would be dozens of cats.

No visit to Rome could be complete without a visit to the Vatican. The great alter by Bernini at the Basilica of St. Peter was magnificent. I was most fascinated by Michelangelo's Pieta (the dead Christ on the lap of his mother, Mary). The Christ was a graphic portrayal of a mature man who looked very dead, but the mother looked like a teenager. Our guide told us that Michelangelo's mother had died when the artist was very young so he had portrayed his own mother as he had remembered her.

I was somewhat surprised by the Apian Way. It was supposed to be the original of all paved military roads and still in its original condition. We did see a small portion of the original. It was about six feet wide and made of stone about 18 by 24 inches on the surface. It was probably great when it was built and kept the war chariots from bogging down in the soft ground but in 1961 it was no autostrada.

When we got to Pizza, we were beginning to get a little low on cash. It cost a few lire to climb the leaning tower so we gave the kids a choice, they could climb the tower or have an ice cream cone. Mary took the ice cream and Bill and Virginia climbed the tower. There are several walkways about two feet wide around the outside of the tower, but there are no hand rails.

At about the second level, Bill walked right up to the edge of the ledge on the low side to look over. Poor Virginia thought he was going to fall off, but was too timid to try to pull him back. She was having a fit when an Italian soldier told him to get back. I have to admit, I was standing on the ground feeling a little nervous too.

As we headed back to Germany, our finances were now beginning to dwindle seriously. As we traveled north along the Mediterranean sea, it was night about the time we arrived at the Italian Riviera. We stopped at a hotel called Rex. The price was about fifty dollars. This was a very posh resort. Since we only had twenty three dollars left, Eli walked out. The inn keeper ran after him and they had a heated discussion before it was decided that we could stay for $18 including supper and breakfast. Wine was extra but we didn't need it anyway.

We even got to take a dip in the Mediterranean, which was as clear as the Gulf of Mexico. The bottom was covered with small rocks. I even wore my sneakers in the water.

Our return trip through Switzerland took us over the St. Gothard Pass. This is a very high and twisty road. However we discovered that there was a train with flat cars where private autos, for a small price, could be ferried through a tunnel in the mountain. We took advantage of this and saved quite a bit of time and gasoline.

In Switzerland we needed one more meal. We still had some Swiss Francs, which I used at a grocery store where I bought bread, cheese and bottled water. We stopped along the side of the road to fix our picnic, using a cord of wood as a table. That seemed to be just the right height. Someone dropped my scout knife between the logs and we were unable to retrieve it. We have often wondered if anyone ever found it and what they might have thought.

Gasoline was now becoming critical. We had used up all the coupons we had bought for Italy. We had no Swiss coupons so would have to pay the full price, and we were out of money. By some strange quirk of Geography, we crossed from Switzerland into Germany where there was an Exxon station. We still had a few coupons for German Exxon. It was the only gas station on what turned out to be less than ten kilometer of road, before we again crossed into Switzerland, but it provided enough to get us back to Germany and a Quartermaster station where we had enough coupons to get us home.

While we were in Italy, all hell had broken loose in Germany but we knew nothing about it because we had not seen an English language paper or heard an American radio. East Germany had built a wall right through the city of Berlin. American troops had not been mobilized but had been on alert.

Eli:

In 1961, a new missile battalion was attached to the 212th Group. The Weapon was known as the LaCross. It was a short range weapon that looked like a small jet airplane with about the same range and capability of a 155mm howitzer. The difference was that while it was in flight, it could be picked up by a guidance central on the observation post that would guide it to the target. It was nuclear capable and the unit had nuclear war heads available.

It had been developed by Glen L. Martin in Baltimore, MD for the navy, who wanted it for the use of the Marine Corp. It had cost $42 billion.

The first thing we noticed about this weapon was that about every fourth round that it fired would turn around and come back toward where it came from. I called it a homing pigeon.

We were ordered to run a complete field test and report to the Pentagon. It was late in November or early December when we alerted the unit at 0300. It was eight below zero. We gave them the necessary orders to move out of the barracks to the assembly area. The missiles were stored in the basement of the barracks where the temperature was around 68 to 70 degrees.

When the missiles were carried out of their storage area and put on the sidewalk, two civilian technician from Martin checked them and the guidance equipment. Right away, they told us that the instruments had all frozen up. That was before transistors and the glass vacuum tubes were cooled by small electric fans. The fans would not operate and the whole system was immediately useless. We still went through the motions of the day long test but it was a complete failure because of the equipment.

When we critiqued the problem, the factory reps told us that through out the design phase, they had never tested the weapon in cold weather. I gave them a completely unsatisfactory rating because of equipment design. The men and officers of the unit were well trained and had done their job well, but were victims of the failure of the designers. In two weeks, the battalion was deactivate as was the other LaCross battalion at Ft. Sill.

When Col. Wetherell joined the unit, I told him that he should wait to arrive at headquarters each morning until I had a chance to check in and find out what was going on around the group. Then he could get in his chopper and go visit the units. One might have done something good and they would appreciate the commander showing up to commend them. If there was a problem, he could show up and assess the problem.

One morning, we learned that there was a 175mm gun in Darmstadt, with the tub on the ground. It was an order that any of the nuclear weapons that were deadlined, for any reason, must be reported to the Pentagon immediately. The old man got in the chopper and the pilot put him down right next to where the thing laid. They were sure surprised. To add insult to injury, the helicopter had just missed an unauthorized wire that could have crashed them.

Another time, I decided to make an unscheduled visit to the 3rd. of the 18th to check training. It was a rainy day. When I checked with the battalion S-3 he gave me a copy of the training schedule and told me that they were down by the Rhein River practicing occupying position. The battalion commander asked to go with me.

We got in the sedan and went to the training area. It was about a quarter of a mile. We ran up and down the river three or four times and could not find any signs of activity or even the battalion. We returned to their headquarters and confronted the S-3. He said he had made a mistake, that they had changed the schedule and were training right across the street.

After getting a couple hundred yards off the road, I saw one of the batteries. It was an eight inch towed howitzer battalion. I stopped one of the trucks that was returning to the Kasern. The battery commander said that they had finished the training and were on their way in.

When I looked at the guns, I saw that they were clean, not a drop of mud on them. When I looked in the cab, the driver and the chief of section were completely dry. In the back where the cannoneers were, they were all soaking wet. They had just been out in the assembly area doing nothing.

I informed the battalion that their training was completely unsatisfactory and not controlled by battalion headquarters. After the group commander received the report he relieved the battalion commander and I recommended that they also relieve the exec and the three who had all been a part of lying and trying to cover up their lack of interest.

Just prior to this, the same battalion had fired an eight inch shell into a squad tent at Grafenwohr and had killed or wounded twenty six soldiers. They were not in our group at the time but had been transferred to the 212th right after that.

One Saturday morning, the Colonel came in and had to attend a meeting at corp around 1000. I noticed that his pants needed to be dusted off and pressed before seeing the General. He said there wasn't time to take them to the cleaner. I told him that if he would take off his pants, the driver could brush them and press them and have them back in ten minutes. He could just set behind his desk and nobody would know the difference. "But what if the building should catch on fire?" I told him, "This building has been here for thirty years and hasn't been on fire yet." He reluctantly agreed and the driver went out the door with his pants.

About the time the driver got into the room where the ironing board was kept and had started the job, the fire alarm went off. I couldn't believe it. I headed up the steps to see where the fire was. It was in the day room on the third floor. That was next door to where the driver was ironing the pants. The wall of the day room was on fire. A soldier was doing some painting and had thinned the paint with gasoline. When he lit a cigarette the whole wall caught on fire. That set off the fire alarm. It was brought under control by soldiers in the building before the fire truck arrived. In the meantime, the driver had ran down to the Colonel's office with his pants half pressed. About that time, the all clear was giving and he took them back to finish the job.

That fall, 212th Group were assigned the V Corp football team. We were to house the players, who would be on TDY to our headquarters and provide the home field and training facilities. I was assigned to be the manager. I appointed our Athletic and Recreation officer, Captain Bailey, who was also the adjutant, to create a field, erect stands and put up a workable electric score board. He took over a field that had been used by the Germans for soccer. He found an old scoreboard that had been used by the Frankfurt American High School but it wasn't working. He put the communications section to work on it and they made it work just fine. Our engineers were available to survey and lay out the field and to put up the bleachers.

We had three professional football player who had been drafted into the army. They were not allowed to play service football because they were under contract to the NFL. We made them our coaches. The players were all ranks. They came from all the non-divisional units in the Corp. Many of them had played in college, some had even been on professional teams. Our team was called the 'V' Corp Guardians.

In preparation for the first game, I mentioned to the Colonel that there would be Generals at every game we played at Fliegerhorst and it would be nice if he had a pre-game cocktail party at his house, which was on the Kasern. He said, "Hell no, I'm not going to wine and dine the brass every week end." Since I was president of the Hanau Officers Club, I arranged to use the Fliegerhorst branch, and set up VIP pre-game parties. I also told him that in his position, it was very important to keep the really high brass happy. He reluctant agreed and I assessed the cost to the public relations fund.

The team was adequate and actually defeated some of the better teams. The Seventh Army, each of the Divisions and the other Corp had teams. The Guardians didn't always win and the championship of the theater went to another team. Because there were so many units billeted at the Fliegerhorst Kasern, the GI and the dependents, turned out and supported the team in numbers. It turned out to be one of the more popular activities that fall. All the clubs at Fliegerhorst, including the private's club had their most business on the weekends of the games.

Seventh Army was given the assignment of putting on a demonstration on the capability of our nuclear weapons and how to best use them for The North Atlantic Treaty Organization (NATO). Army bucked the detail to the V Corp who had most of the nuclear weapons and they sent it to the 212th Artillery Group to put on. All the top ranking military of NATO were invited.

I advised Colonel Wetherell that he would make a good master of ceremonies at the demonstration because it would be conducted in both German and English. He had just finished German Language School. After he stopped yelling, I told him that this was his best chance to impress the brass he'd ever have and he agreed. We also had a Captain who was fluent in all the languages as the back up.

A few days before the first demonstration, we got a call from the German police, warning us that there would be a big demonstration at Fliegerhorst. He said they would be putting on extra patrols outside the Kasern. I suggested that maybe what he was hearing about was actually our NATO demonstration. He agreed that this might be the case, but said they would be on the alert anyway. I thanked him very much.

We rehearsed for about two days in a row with a full rehearsal on Thursday. Our rehearsal audience included the lower ranking NATO people and the military dependents. It was impressive. It gave the families a chance to see and better understand just what it was that their sponsors were doing.

The display included all the weapons that were capable of delivering nuclear war heads upon an enemy, if that was ever needed. We invited the US president to speak to the group by satellite but he declined. He did send his greetings, which were read at the start of the big demonstration.

It was a great success and the V Corp commander was so impressed that shortly after that he made Colonel Wetherell his Chief of Staff.

We had a big farewell parade at Fliegerhorst. All the battalion of the 212th group, except one, participated. The line ran all the way from one end of the Fleigherhorst runway to the other and was very impressive. This parade was repeated later for President Kennedy, who visited the troops later that year. The reason Fliegerhorst was selected for the president was because it was considered the most secure post in the command. The Fishpaws were no longer there when this took place but the event of his visit went off without a hitch.

Bernice:

It is a German custom to celebrate Fasching, which is something like Martigras, just prior to the onset of Lent. They do it up in grand style. By now, Virginia was happily a member of the majorette corp for the Frankfurt American High School band. Their band was invited to be in the parade in a city south of Frankfurt call Russelsheim. She went on the school bus with the band but Eli and I, with several others from Hanau, drove down to see the kids in the parade. It was bitter cold, but the girls bravely marched about five miles in their abbreviated black and gold majorette outfits. I had to admire their courage. The band wore black wool uniforms which were created from second hand OD military uniforms, dyed black. They were much warmer.

One evening, when we were at the officers' club, there was a furrier exhibiting stoles and coats for the ladies. While Eli was at the bar, some of the officers were nervous about having their wives exposed to such tempting merchandise. Eli was foolishly bragging that he didn't need to worry as his wife was too stingy to be interested in such finery. I was totally unaware of his boast when I walked into the bar wearing a really great looking $300 sable dyed muskrat stole. Did he every get the raspberries. However, he sheepishly agreed to buy it for me. I wore it for a good many years and always felt quite elegant when I did.

In February of 1962, the Girl Scouts were observing their 50th anniversary. This was a very special occasion so NAGS held a retreat at Berchtesgaden for the leaders from the entire European Command. It was held at the American operated General Walker hotel. It was fairly high up on the mountain, in an exquisite locations. We got to mingle with American leaders from other commands and other countries as well as with a number of Girl Guide leaders from our host countries. There was no rank among scout leaders and the generals' and master sergeants' wives were only distinguished from the those of the younger officers and NCOs by their more mature age. Most of the wife of higher ranking officers served on various committees. I don't recall that any of them actually lead troops. Looking back from my now advanced years, we were ALL, even the general's wives, so young and eager.

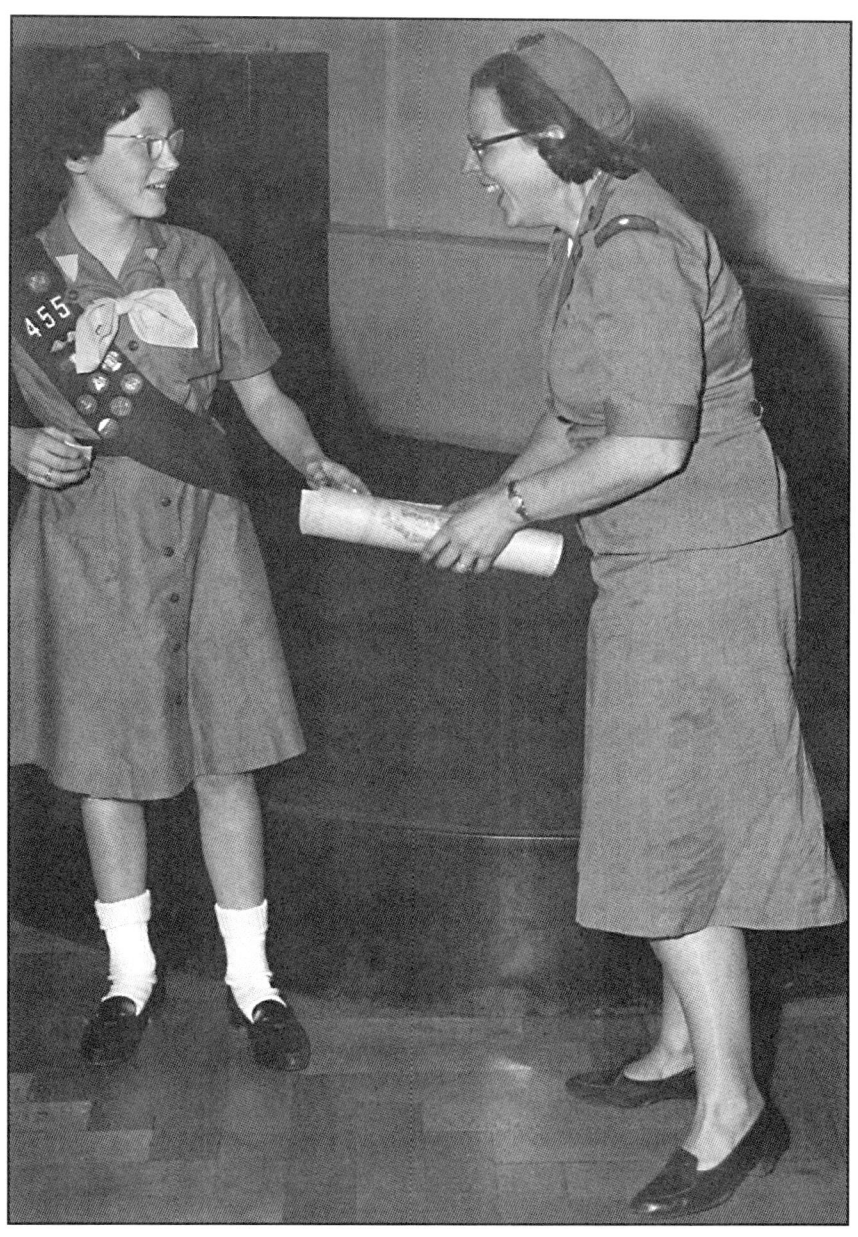

Girl Scout, Cindy Paul, Troop 455 dubs Mrs. Bernice Fishpaw, Hanau Neighborhood Chairman 'First Knight of the Order of the Sink'. 13 March, 1962.

The Hanau neighborhood had made yellow roses of crepe paper and we gave one to each of the ladies there. It was an extremely exhilarating experience. In the large ball room there was a huge window from floor to ceiling that overlooked the city and framed the Watzmann beyond. As the meeting got underway, snow began to fall. With each inspirational ceremony and speaker the snow fell a little thicker, gradually shutting out the rest of the world. By evening we were in our own world of friendship and service. We sang scout songs, played scout games and folk danced into the night. Two days later, when we were ready to leave, the snow had stopped and the roads had been plowed out so we could return home, renewed of spirit and resolve.

Every spring, our neighborhood held a family event for the scouts, their parents and their leaders. It was always well attended and would include different awards and recognitions. That year I was completely surprised when one of the younger girls presented me, on behalf of the girls, a scroll proclaiming me a knight in the "Order of the Sink" in recognition of my efforts to have that amenity installed in all the scout rooms. Stars & Stripes was there and took my picture as I received a very handsome document on high grade, imitation parchment, all hand done and embellished with gold lettering.

However, after the photographer had taken his camera and left, one of the highly respected Colonel's wife, who was on the Girl Scout Committee, presented me with something even more meaningful. I was awarded the Girl Scout 'Thank You Badge', by NAGS for my service to scouting. This is a gold pin, seldom and carefully given to individuals who have donated exceptional time and talent to the organization. I was truly humble to receive it.

Because our senior scouts, for logistic reasons, would not be able to attend the big US summer scouting event planned for Denver that year, NAGS decided that we would have a mini jamboree in England. By now, many of my girls who had been to England were gone. There is a high attrition as military families come and go. Planning the event included the custom of exchanging small gifts, usually little, hand made symbols to be worn on camp hats or jackets. Because Hanau was the home of the Brothers Grimm, our girls decided to make tiny dolls from wooden bead heads and pipe cleaner bodies of Little Red Riding Hood. She was dressed in red felt with a small safety pin so she could be attached to the recipient' cap. They were quite attractive.

Because we would be going back to the states before the event took place, Virginia and I were unable to make this one. We decided that instead, we would go to Paris. We signed up for a tour out of Frankfurt. It was a bus tour and took us one night on the road.

In Paris we had some activities planned by the tour company and some that we took by ourselves. We took the elevator to the Eiffel tower. It was of interest to me that the latrine with only a hole in the floor had been replaced with a modern toilet. We visited Versaille and the Louvre, where we saw the Mona Lisa and Venice De Milo as well as many other famous works of art.

The city of Paris was having its face washed. Centuries of smoke and grime were being scrubbed from the sand stone buildings. It was most dramatic where the work was in progress to see the golden stones emerge from the gray wall under the brushes of the workers. There were even a couple of men squirting each other with the hoses, high up on the scaffolding.

Sight seeing can be extremely tiring and I was totally exhausted by the end of the second day. There was one more thing that I still wanted to do and hadn't. That was to take a boat ride on the Seine river. It turned out to be the high point of the trip. Relaxing on the upper deck of the boat on reasonably comfortable benches and wrapped in blankets as it was chilly, we watched the city of Paris glide by. All the great monuments that make the city famous were illuminated against the dark sky, some in their new golden glory and others still waiting their turn to be scrubbed.

We were well on the way back to Germany when our bus burned out a rear wheel bearing and was disabled. We were still in France. Fortunately, it happened near a country bistro, so we could all get off the bus and have food and beverage. It is under adverse conditions that people are at their best. Before this, most of the passengers, who were all Americans, had little more than acknowledged each other. Now with time on our hands and nothing to do, we all got acquainted with each other.

The tour company sent a substitute bus out to pick us up and carry us to the border. It could not cross into Germany as it did not have an international license. It must have been a street bus because there was no place to put the luggage. We ended up with all the baggage stacked in the aisle. We sang and joked all the way to the border. The bus that met us had a trailer for the baggage. We finally arrived at Frankfurt, several hours later than scheduled. Since trains ran frequently in Europe, we took a train to Wolfgang, where we got Eli out of bed about 2 AM to pick us up.

Eli:

I was soon to have completed twenty years of active duty and because I was a reserve officer, I was either to retire or, if I chose, I could revert to Warrant Officer, the grade which I held in the Regular Army. The Seventh Army in Stuttgart wanted me to be their personnel officer. Bernice and I discussed this at length. I reasoned that I was only 42 and rather than continue another ten years to start over as a civilian, I would just as soon do it right then. I had always disliked paper work anyway.

At the same time, A new Group Commander was coming from the United States. At his request, I took the sedan and met him half way to Bremerhaven. He rode with me in the sedan and we took an extra driver to drive their private car with his wife. He wanted to know all about the units, their strength and their morale, etc.

His first day of duty, he called me into his office and said, "All the way from the Pentagon and every headquarters in between, everyone was telling me not to worry, just let Fishpaw run it. I want you to know that I'm the commander. You are just a staff officer and I run this outfit." I told him, "There is no question that you are the commander. I will be carrying out your orders and policies as your executive officer." He told me that this job was going to make him a general. This meeting made my retirement from the army look much better.

During the short time that I had left, we went on a CPX which was held right along the border with the Soviet Zone. Security was necessarily very tight. Relations with the Soviets was very tense at that time. One night, about midnight, he came to my tent and woke me up. He said he couldn't sleep and he had a great idea. He had a message on a piece of paper that he wanted to take up in a helicopter at dawn and read as all the battalion commanders listening on their radios.

I read his statement and was shocked. It was labeled at the top, "Exercise Only". The message was that we had been pushed back but this morning we were going to push the Russians back to Moscow. I told him that if he read that from a plane, so close to the Russian Zone that it could trigger another war. I told him that I could have the message copied and have the scouts deliver it to all the commanders to be read at the First Light formation. He reluctantly agreed to do this, but I could tell he wasn't convinced.

The group arranged to have a retirement ceremony for me at Fliegerhorst. I hadn't expected anything like we had for Wetherell, but couldn't believe the understated ceremony that was held across the street from headquarters. It was about one platoon of soldiers from each battalion. It was cold and raw and I wanted to get it over with as soon as we could. They played the music on the PA system. General Hill, who was now the Corp Artillery Commander, had come up from Darmstadt to attend the ceremony.

After the ceremony was over, and we were walking back toward headquarters, I was a little behind the Colonel and the General. I overheard the General ask the Colonel, "Why do you hate Fishpaw?" He said, "I don't hate him." The General then told him that the formation he had just witnessed, to honor a man with so much service, was a disgrace. He had probably just lost his star.

They did have a very nice farewell party at the Hanau Officer's club. Colonel Wetherell and his wife came from Frankfurt and most of the officers and their ladies from the 212th group and others from other units at the Hanau post were on hand and wished us success as civilians, where ever we went and whatever we did.

They presented me with a nice scrape book with photos of my tour with the 212th group. They gave me a German beer mug, engraved with the crest of the group and my name in gold. Instead of the insignia of the field artillery, there was a picture of the corporal in the center and two 175 millimeter guns arranged just like the insignia. The center piece was a picture of the Hanau Rathaus (city hall) which was the most picturesque building in the city.

Bernice:

Virginia was now a high school senior and was most reluctant to have to start over again, and at a civilian school at that. She had worked hard and was now the head majorette. She had

A Flying Tiger plane sits on the flight line at Rhein-Main Air Base in Frankfurt, West Germany to bring the Fishpaws home. October, 1962.

designed and I had made her a gold corduroy outfit with black satin box pleats. But we were going back to the states.

We cleared quarters and moved into the guest house at Rhein Main Air Base to await our departure. There was one last piece of business to be completed. We were to depart on Sunday morning but Saturday afternoon was the homecoming football game at Frankfurt American High. Virginia lead the band for the final time. She never strutted higher and when the band played in the stands during time out, she did aerials, the baton going higher than ever before. And she never dropped it, even once. After the game, our station wagon, long since gone to Bremerhaven for its return to the states, and Eli's military sedan no longer a perk, we boarded the strassenbahn for Rhein Main.

As a bus delivered us to the flight line, the plane we were to board bore the name 'Flying Tiger Line'. Flying Tigers had just lost a charter, flying military families, in the Atlantic the week before. It is a tribute to the discipline of the military that, even though they had ditched at sea, there had been no casualties. This bit of good news had no effect on Virginia. She was very reluctant to board. However, she had no choice. I laid my shoulder to her rear end and up the steps she went.

Crossing the Atlantic always seems longer going west than going east because you travel with the sun. We made one stop at Prestwick, Scotland and landed at McQuire Air Field in New Jersey about 2 AM. Clearing customs was fairly routine and we were transported to Fort Hamilton by bus.

I had never seen New York at this hour before. The song may call it a city that never sleeps but the streets looked pretty deserted to me. The most striking thing about that was the sheer volume of trash blowing around the empty streets.

While we had been in the air, the country had faced a major crisis. The Soviets had placed nuclear missiles in Cuba. The crisis had been averted, when the missiles were withdrawn before we landed and we had known nothing about it.

At Fort Hamilton, Eli was offered the privilege of taking part in a group retirement ceremony, but declined. He had already endured this event. He picked up the Pontiac at Brooklyn Army Base and we headed out of town as quickly as practical, on our way to Florida and civilian life. School was in session and we needed to enter our family as soon as possible.

The last thing we saw as we left the army was the massive forms and pilings of the new Verrazano bridge, growing across the parade grounds of Ft. Hamilton.

It was 28 October, 1962.